WARFARE
IN ANCIENT GREECE

Warfare in Ancient Greece assembles a wide range of source material and introduces the latest scholarship on the Greek experience of war. The author has carefully selected key texts, many of them not previously available in English, and provided them with comprehensive commentaries.

For the Greek *polis*, warfare was a more usual state of affairs than peace. The documents assembled here recreate the social and historical framework in which ancient Greek warfare took place – over a period of more than a thousand years from the Homeric Age to the first century BC. Special attention is paid to the attitudes and feelings of the Greeks towards defeated peoples and captured cities.

Complete with notes, index and bibliography, *Warfare in Ancient Greece* will provide students of ancient and military history with an unprecedented survey of relevant materials.

Michael M. Sage is Professor of Classics and Ancient History at the University of Cincinnati. He has published widely on Tacitus and aspects of ancient military history.

WARFARE IN ANCIENT GREECE

A Sourcebook

Michael M. Sage

London and New York

First published 1996
by Routledge
11 New Fetter Lane, London EC4P 4EE

Simultaneously published in the USA and Canada
by Routledge
29 West 35th Street, New York, NY 10001

© 1996 Michael M. Sage

Typeset in Garamond by Keystroke, Jacaranda Lodge, Wolverhampton
Printed and bound in Great Britain by TJ Press (Padstow) Ltd, Padstow, Cornwall

British Library Cataloguing in Publication Data
A catalogue record for this book is available from the British Library

Library of Congress Cataloging in Publication Data
Sage, Michael M.
Warfare in ancient Greece : a sourcebook / Michael M. Sage.
p.cm.
Includes bibliographical references and index.
1. Military art and science—Greece—History.
2. Military history, Ancient.
3. Greece—History, Military. I. Title.
U33.S24   1996
355'.00938—dc20   95–39155
CIP

ISBN 0–415–14354–3
0–415–14355–1 (pbk)

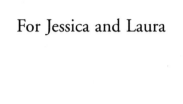

For Jessica and Laura

CONTENTS

ABBREVIATIONS

ABSA	*Annual of the British School at Athens*
AC	*L' Antiquité Classique*
ACD	*Acta Classica Universitatis Scientiarum Debreceniensis*
AHB	*Ancient History Bulletin*
AJA	*American Journal of Archaeology*
AJAH	*American Journal of Ancient History*
AncSoc	*Ancient Society*
AncW	*Ancient World*
BCH	*Bulletin de Correspondance Héllenistique*
CE	*Chronique d' Egypte*
ClasAnt	*Classical Antiquity*
CPh	*Classical Philology*
CQ	*Classical Quarterly*
CSCA	*California Studies in Classical Antiquity*
CW	*Classical World*
G&R	*Greece and Rome*
GRBS	*Greek, Roman and Byzantine Studies*
HSCP	*Harvard Studies in Classical Philology*
JHS	*Journal of Hellenic Studies*
P&P	*Past and Present*
PBA	*Proceedings of the British Academy*
PP	*La Parola del Passato*
RhM	*Rheinisches Museum*
SO	*Symbolae Osloenses*
ZPE	*Zeitschrift für Papyrologie und Epigraphik*

INTRODUCTION

The last quarter century has seen a renewed interest in the study of Greek and Roman warfare. This has developed as part of a more general revival of the place of war throughout the history of European society. An increasing number of books and journal articles bear witness to this trend. An important part of the revival has been a change of focus. Traditional military history has concentrated on strategy, tactics and the encounter of battle. A new perspective has emerged, however, that has led to a more comprehensive view of war as a social phenomenon whose outlines and substance are conditioned by the social and cultural system of those involved in making war. Studies have concentrated on the relationship between warfare and social solidarity and its links to sacral-religious views as well as on the ideology connected to fighting.

THE GREEK UNDERSTANDING OF WAR

This broadening of interest has led to the realization of the centrality of war-making to Greek civilization and the profound formative effect it had on it. Satisfactory definitions of war and war-making are difficult to provide. At its center is the potential or actual use of violence by organized and politically independent groups. No definite line can be drawn to separate it from raiding and other organized violent activities. The Greeks themselves conceived of it as marked off from other pursuits by formal declarations and various symbolic and religious acts. The elaborate codes and procedures such as the erection of trophies or the asking for the bodies of the dead back to signify the acceptance of defeat are manifestations of this mentality (146, 153). In part such limitations reflected a desire to keep the human losses and the economic costs of warfare within limits that did not destroy the groups or states that waged them. The so-called "heraldless war" in which states opened hostilities without observing the traditional preliminaries was evidence of an intention to wage a total war that would lead to the extinction or total submission of the losing side. This institution throws into relief the importance of the normal mechanisms in containing the destructive effects of conflicts (128, 129, 153), though they were not always successful (168).

Though such limitations and boundaries may have checked the most destructive effects of conflict, it did little to restrain the frequency of war among Greeks states in the fifth and fourth centuries BC and into the Hellenistic period. Athens, the state we know best, was at war two out of every three years down to 338. Though we have no comparable figures for other Greek states, and Athens' status as an imperial state for much of this period may have increased its involvement in war, the sources reveal that most states of any size were engaged in recurring conflicts with traditional or newly acquired enemies. The Greek view of relations between states reflected and justified this situation. Hostility was considered as the typical condition in Greek interstate relations and war and other forms of violence a normal expedient in political life (181). Further evidence for the normality of armed conflict is provided by the attempts of Greek intellectuals to analyze warfare. Though prone to generalization in other areas of political analysis, they offered no analysis of the causes of war. Rather they remained preoccupied with particular reasons for individual conflicts. It has been suggested, I think rightly, that the reason for such neglect was the view that war was simply a fact of human life and its ubiquity did not require explanation; only the specific reasons for a specific conflict warranted examination. Later periods of European history have also been marked by frequent war and violence but there were factors specific to Greek civilization that contributed to increase the frequency of armed conflict. The aristocratic ideology in the Homeric poems, which are among the earliest extant Greek literature, had as its center the idea of competition and struggle as the means to preeminence. Individual military success was the key area in which to achieve standing among a noble's peers and the most important measure of a man's worth (1–4). Developments in military tactics and equipment were to transmute and change the way this value system expressed itself but it remained intact and vital. In the Hellenistic period success in warfare was still the crucial element in legitimizing political power and remained the most important royal activity (271–275). The agonal conception that underlay Greek attitudes to war is perhaps most clearly expressed in the continuation of archaic, ritualized struggle between the Argives and the Spartans for the border territory of Cynouria extending from the sixth century on (129). Though specifying the exact effect of such ideology is difficult, the emphasis it placed on struggle and military success created a predisposition to resort to warfare to resolve conflicts.

Warfare served other important functions, such as the acquisition of wealth in the form of land, money and slaves. From the Homeric period on, military activity was accepted as a source of profits and was practised for that reason. In the *Iliad* Achilles boasts to Agamemnon of the success of his plundering expedition in the Troad, and Athenian soldiers and sailors setting out in the summer of 415 on the conquest of Syracuse and the rest of Sicily had dreams of the wealth that would result from the conquest (5, 180). Treaties and other diplomatic agreements carefully detailed the division of spoils in the event of victory (187–189). Mercenary service also acted as another avenue of wealth generated by warfare. In contrast to the great powers it was generally the marginal areas such as Arcadia and Achaea that were unable to provide a living for their populations and so exported them in the form of soldiers for hire.

On the other end of the scale warfare or the threat of it allowed the great powers like Sparta or Athens to increase their resources far beyond the level that they alone could sustain. Athens' empire acquired through war with Persia and eventually kept together by the threat of Athenian force provided wealth in the form of tribute and land for citizen colonists. The Spartans, after a vast increase in their land holdings as the result of warfare during the Archaic period, used their military strength to exercise hegemony over much of the Peloponnese through imposing military service on their allies (124). War seems to have been a more frequent activity for these large ruling states than for more typical Greek cities. The struggle for hegemony among them and the new great powers that emerged in the fourth century such as Thebes imposed greater burdens along with the rewards. Violence or the threat of violence could be used by the dominant imperial states to expand wealth and power. Athens was able to acquire land for its citizens in its overseas empire as well as a yearly income of tribute. The Spartans who had initially acquired rich and productive land in the western Peloponnese by warfare and conquest in the Archaic period were able to dominate the Peloponnese by using their military superiority to create a league that they directed and from which they could draw troops for service.

Perhaps the most basic function of military strength, especially from the fifth century on, was the maintenance of a state's political position or its very survival. Athens, defeated in the Peloponnesian War, was stripped of its empire and temporarily reduced to the status of a Spartan client (194), while Sparta herself in the wake of her loss of Messenia after 370 lost the resources necessary to remain a great power. Smaller cities could be extinguished as Plataea was by the Spartans and Thebans in 427 (163) or Scione in the Thraceward region of the Athenian empire in the summer of 421 (168). The importance of these various factors in initiating warfare changed over time, as did the scale of violence. Despite these changes the apparent overall level of military activity remained high until the Roman period.

THE SOURCES

Any attempt to trace the changes in the way war was made in Greece over the vast period between the Bronze Age through the end of the Hellenistic period is bound to encounter problems with the available evidence. For the period down to the end of the Dark Ages we are dependent upon two sources which do not always usefully supplement each other: the results of archaeology and the Homeric poems. Though some Linear B tablets have been discovered at Pylos and elsewhere that provide some information about military arrangements, the bulk of our information consists of remains of weapons and fortifications that require interpretation and can provide only the barest outline of how war was waged. The poems, especially the *Iliad*, are full of descriptions of fighting and equipment. The poems are the product of a long oral tradition extending over three quarters of a millennium and combine institutions, descriptions of weapons and narratives of battle into a picture of a world that never existed as the poet describes it. The style of warfare best suits the Dark Ages (1200–800) but there are weapons and equipment described that clearly date from the Bronze Age such as the boar's tusk helmet or the man-size rectangular shield (10–11). Added to these difficulties is the fact that these are poems and not descriptions of actual encounters. They contain exaggeration and probable inaccuracies that do no harm to the poems as literature but hinder any attempt to reconstruct the reality of the period.

Our picture of Dark Age warfare suffers from the same limitations as the Bronze Age. Homer remains our major source as well as archaeological finds, especially burial, that provide evidence of weapons. Towards the end of the period painted pottery illustrates weapon type and stylized encounters. There are also references in later writers but they must be used with caution and their interpretation is not always clear.

The second half of the eighth century began a period of unparalleled expansion and experimentation in which the main forms which Greek life was to take to the end of the fourth century were produced. Warfare too underwent a development that led to the evolution of a new style of fighting utilizing heavy infantry – the hoplite – that was to become the basic mode of Greek warfare until the conquest of the eastern Mediterranean by the Romans. The evidence for the period of transition to the new style of combat and its early development is fragmentary. It depends mainly on archaeological material. Especially important in marking the transition are finds of weapons and armor. These are found as dedications at shrines after 700 when for some unknown reason the Greeks stopped burying warriors with their weapons. Also important are representations of combat on Greek pottery, particularly from the city of Corinth. The other important source of information are the fragments of the lyric poets along with a scattering of references in later writers (33).

A qualitative difference appears from the middle of the fifth century with the development of Greek historical writing beginning with Herodotus and Thucydides. Important material is also contained in the great outpouring of Athenian literature from the same period such as the comedy of Aristophanes and the tragedians. This is a watershed in our knowledge of warfare: from the Persian Wars on it is possible to make attempts at reconstructing individual battles, Marathon being the earliest, and the course of at least some military campaigns. There is now evidence as well for other aspects, such as logistics and training, that can only be guessed at before (50–55, 93–100). The mid-fifth century marks the beginning of the so-called "epigraphic habit" especially at Athens but elsewhere in the Greek world as well. Though there are earlier inscriptions the volume of the inscription of public documents rises sharply. This allows us access to the texts of treaties, alliances, casualties and other important sources of military history that were not available earlier (49, 119, 143, 171).

This relative abundance of material has large lacunae. Logistics are rarely touched upon and difficult to reconstruct. The exact mechanisms for selecting individuals for service on a campaign are often obscure (**56, 57**). Even the exact way in which Greek hoplite battles were fought is far from clear and subject to continuing controversy (**130**). The geographic spread of our information is uneven. Most centers on the two great powers of the period, Athens and Sparta, and our evidence for other Greeks states tends to be sporadic and anecdotal.

The fourth century is relatively well documented in the same areas as the fifth. The quality of the military narratives available are inferior to those of the fifth century but the written material has a broader scope. There is the memoir of Xenophon, the *Anabasis*, detailing his adventures as a mercenary in Persian service at the very end of the previous century (**96**) and the first sizable fragment of a military textbook by Aeneas on siegecraft (**166**).

The rise of Macedonia is relatively poorly documented until the reign of Philip II (359–336). Philip's military campaigns are for the most part obscure: either there is little information or when we do have evidence it is often of a late or a biased source like the Athenian orator Demosthenes (**239, 252**). Archaeology and epigraphy continue to be of great importance. Particularly striking are the tomb paintings that have recently been uncovered in Macedonia that portray weapons and military dress. Another crucial archaeological find has been the royal tombs at Verghina. Whoever the occupants may have been, the finds, especially of weapons, have led to the solution of some long debated problems with Macedonian arms (**232, 233**).

The sources for the reign of Alexander the Great are numerous though of uneven quality. The best is the description of Alexander's campaigns by the second-century writer Arrian of Nicomedia. After his reign the sources for the Hellenistic period are more problematic. The only connected account for much of the Hellenistic era is Diodorus Siculus who is only as good as the source that he draws upon. But the rich harvest of documentary papyri in Egypt sheds light on conditions of service and the financial and social conditions of the military in the Ptolemaic kingdom. Some of the conclusions can be extended to other Hellenistic kingdoms and states, but Egypt is in many ways singular and analogies can be misleading. For the last two and half centuries we have access to the extant portion of Polybius of Megalopolis' history of Roman expansion in the eastern and western Mediterranean. He provides unparalleled insights into Hellenistic military institutions and methods of making war, but his text has only been fully preserved in part.

EARLY GREEK WARFARE THROUGH THE END OF THE DARK AGES

The topography and climate of Greek lands have for the most part dictated that land warfare would be conducted with infantry as its major striking force. Except for Thessaly, Macedonia and parts of Boeotia on the Greek mainland there was not in antiquity sufficient pasturage to raise large cavalry forces. Though after its advent around 600 true cavalry was used and would be important in various periods, generally it was relegated to a secondary role on the battlefield (56, 86–87, 89, 90). The other characteristic of Greek warfare which again was to remain for the most part constant was the primary role of the face-to-face encounter. Unlike large parts of the Near East such as Assyria and Iran where missile weapons played a predominant role in warfare, it was the javelin with its relatively limited range that was employed, even in periods when missile weapons were a crucial element of the battlefield.

The early forms of Greek warfare are poorly known due to the lack of documentation mention above. The most frequent archaeological weapon finds are spear points that belong to heavy thrusting spears. Finds and representations on sealstones and in other media also point to the importance of the sword. Linear B tablets at Pylos and Cnossus also record large numbers of chariots or chariot parts. The problem remains as to how to interpret this material. The only reasonable inference to draw from the archaeological material is that combat was mostly the close encounter of heavy infantry and that agrees with at least the picture presented in the Homeric poems (15, 16). More troublesome is the role of the chariot attested on grave stelai, in other media and in contemporary written sources. Greek terrain was not suited for the massed chariot tactics of contemporary Near Eastern powers like the Egyptians or Hittites. The most plausible use of these vehicles which were kept in large numbers by the palace centers would seem to be transport. There are contemporary Near Eastern examples as well as later instances in which they were used as transport, perhaps for élite units or commanders, and not directly employed on the battlefield (19, 20). Aside from a few titles known in the Linear B tablets nothing is known about the command structure of the armed forces of the palace-dominated small kingdoms that formed the political map of late Bronze Age Greece. The tablets themselves paint a picture of a highly organized, bureaucratic economy and administration in which minute care was exercised over the distribution and redistribution of goods. Since the military forces of the state would have been the greatest single expense there is every reason to believe that these heavy infantry forces were highly organized and probably fought in some sort of compact formation.

The highly organized and bureaucratic character assumed for the late Bronze Age raises the perennial problem of the picture of warfare presented in the Homeric poems. With due allowance for exaggeration and the fact that their long period of oral transmission has preserved the memory of late Bronze Age equipment and a memory of some of the modes of warfare of that period, the world and the fighting of the poems seem to best fit the world of the late Dark Ages (the ninth and eight centuries). Though there is a mixture of vague memories of earlier forms of warfare, what stands out most clearly are two facets of the fighting the poet portrays in the *Iliad*: the use of missile weapons and the importance of the individual noble hero on the battlefield (13, 17, 18). The importance of missile weapons is clear from the multiple spears found in warrior graves and in the late Geometric pottery from Attica. In this the period is exceptional in that weapons of close encounter do not predominate. This may be linked to the importance of the heroes as the decisive warriors in the poems. Except for a few magnificent burials dating from the end of this period, the picture of Dark Age Greece that archaeology presents is a land of small fragmented settlements often with little connection to the outside world. The economic picture found in the poems fits the results of archaeology. Despite exaggerations it is a world that is for the most part made up of small autonomous households that were the main units of production. The amount of surplus that such a society could devote to warfare was small and so a military structure such as that in the poems emerged, consisting of a mass of poorly armed and poorly protected fighters headed by well-equipped nobles who stood in the forefront of the ranks and displayed their prowess. Fighting was their most important activity both to protect their followers and to enhance their standing and as a source of wealth. The lack of protection and the means to enforce discipline and cohesion led to the necessity to fight in open order and so enhanced the importance of missile weapons which are suited to such tactics.

The period was not static. There were a number of technological innovations. The most important for warfare was the adoption of iron as the major metal used for weapons and tools. It may have been lack of access to supplies of tin and copper for bronze that determined the change rather than any initial advantage that iron conferred. It was not till after *c.* 1000 that tempering of the iron was employed routinely and iron enjoyed a decisive advantage over bronze in hardness and in its ability to be sharpened more finely.

THE OPENING OF GREECE AND THE DEVELOPMENT OF A NEW MILITARY PARADIGM

After 750, for not totally understood reasons, a period of greatly accelerated expansion and innovation began. Colonization on a large scale in the eastern and western Mediterranean greatly enlarged the scope of Greek settlement over its earlier spread to western Asia Minor. It brought the Greeks into contact and conflict with new opponents: Carthage and various Italic peoples in the west and different Near Eastern powers. It created frontiers and borders that had to be managed in different ways than had been true at home. At the same time there was an intensification of trade, an astonishing receptivity to foreign cultures and a marked ability to utilize and transform cultural imports. This dynamism was also visible in the development of internal political organization. In many areas of central and southern Greece new patterns of population settlement and political organization developed. The crucial novelty was the growth of the city-state. In practice, this new form of social and political organization is hard to describe but it might best be defined as a semi-urban or urban conglomeration with a dependent countryside consisting of rural areas, towns and villages. The city-state became the center of government for the area. That government took the form first of an aristocracy which gradually expanded the limits of citizenship to include other property owners as well. The proportion varied from place to place, but in all instances it involved the obligation of military service. This service was to take a new and enduring form that would determine the conditions on Greek battlefields for the next six centuries. A heavily armored infantryman called a hoplite became the mainstay of Greek city-state armies. His main offensive weapon was the heavy thrusting spear, with a slashing sword as secondary armament. He was encased in bronze that had now come back into use. He carried a round shield with a new holding mechanism that limited mobility but allowed the warrior a firm grip and lengthened the time the shield could be held in the ready position (35, 36). Armed in this fashion, the infantry was organized in rectangular phalanx formation that used its depth and weight to break opposing formations that were similarly structured. It may be that technological innovation and political change spurred these developments. It has been argued with some plausibility that the aristocracy were the innovators in extending and consolidating this new mode of fighting as a means of retaining their position. This receives some support from developments in ideology. Aristocratic warrior values were adapted to the new situation and subordinated to the needs of the community (47–49).

The cost of the equipment for the hoplite limited the segment of the population that could fight (37–43). This may have been at least in part purposeful. It was an excellent method of limiting participation without explicit rules for doing so. There was little use of native light-armed troops until the late fifth and early fourth century except in a supporting role, and this may have had a political as much as a technical purpose given the typical equation between full citizen and warrior. The military structure developed in Sparta by about 600 represented the logical outcome of this process (44–46, 59–60). Citizen and warrior became coterminous concepts. Access to a large semi-servile population allowed Spartan citizens to devote themselves to warfare as a full-time occupation. Inability to fulfill the social demands that accompanied warrior status meant the loss of citizenship. A further illustration of this link is the prohibition in all Greek states on military service for slaves. This rule could be breached in exceptional cases when demands on manpower made a levy of slaves a harsh necessity, but in general the exception was stringently enforced.

The other aspect of this approach to supply is that it allowed the governments of these city-states to remain relatively simple and unbureaucratized. On the battlefield this led to short sharp clashes that were the product of mutual agreement and had some aspects of an arranged contest. These sharp decisive engagements were a way of reducing the number of casualties and limiting the social and economic disruption that prolonged warfare would have entailed. This method of fighting also made relatively light demands on the individual in most Greek states. This also lessened the impact of war on the city's existence. Large areas of northern and central Greece did not experience urbanization and remained largely rural (69). They retained the older style of open fighting formations in which missile weapons formed the main offensive arms. They lacked the economic structure and political forms necessary to produce large bodies of heavy infantry capable of fighting in close order. They illustrate, as Thucydides realized, the close connection between the social systems of an earlier Greece and the style of fighting it employed.

Many questions about military institutions and practices from this period remain either unanswered or unanswerable. The sources contain little explicit information on training, enrollment, size or chain of command. Even what took place when two phalanxes encountered each other is far from clear. There has been dispute as to whether in essence what took place was a shoving match on a grand scale or if some form of mass dueling took place. We know little of the battles before the last third of the fifth century and even in this period there seem to have been few engagements of any scale besides the battle of Delium in 424 between the Boeotians and the Athenians, and that of First Mantinea between the Spartans and their allies and a coalition that included the Athenians and Argives among others (130). How typical they were of lesser contests is not clear.

True cavalry, that is cavalry that fought from horseback, seems to have developed out of mounted infantry. The most effective cavalry came from areas with sufficient pasture land that allowed them to develop a tradition of cavalry service (73). In the Classical period Boeotia and Thessaly (74, 75–76) were the preeminent areas for cavalry. In most Greek states it was drawn from the upper classes as only they had sufficient wealth and land to maintain cavalry. This is true of Athens about whose cavalry we know the most (81–85). The nexus of birth and wealth that it represented meant that it kept the aristocratic connections with the horse that had been traditional. But it was of limited effectiveness on the battlefield. The physical limitations of the Greek horse, the absence of saddles and stirrups meant that it could not develop into a shock cavalry. Its role on the battlefield was secondary. It major employment was in reconnaissance and especially in the pursuit of infantry whose phalanx had been broken (88). Occasionally it could inflict heavy casualties on infantry in open order, but it could not ride down infantry in formation.

Light-armed troops including javelin bearers, archers and slingers were for the most part relegated to a secondary position on Greek battlefields down to the end of the Peloponnesian War at the end of the fifth century. As in case of the cavalry they could not face disciplined heavy infantry while in formation. The disparity in protection and the relative ineffectiveness of their weapons on the compact mass of hoplites limited their role to serving as a screen, to harassing or to pursuit once the enemy had been routed. Their similarity in tactical roles to the cavalry was not matched on the social level. They represented the classes of low social status and were on the economical and political fringes in most states. Athens was an exception, at least in theory, as there they enjoyed full citizen rights. The failure to employ such troops effectively until the end of the fifth century has occasioned serious debate among scholars. The closing years of the fifth century and the fourth were to show how effective they could be when used in conjunction with other arms, and the broken terrain of much of Greece would seem to make such use obvious. It may be that the true explanation is social and that because they represented marginal elements in the social structure of most Greek city-states there may have been a disinclination to arm them and to allow them a role on the battlefield that would bring them prestige and confidence. It was the increasing use of foreigners in this role and the growth of professionalization that allowed the effective use of these forces. The last two trends may have increased the perceived social distance between them and the citizen body and so allowed their use without challenging traditional notions of what constituted a citizen.

THE PERSIAN WAR AND ITS EFFECT

If anything the small-scale Persian attack on Athens and Eretria that was turned back at Marathon in 490 and the massive expedition a decade later under the direct command of the Persian king Xerxes may have reinforced the tendency to exclude such troops from serious consideration. Persian strength lay primarily in the archery and cavalry (135–137). Their infantry was simply unable to match the superior armament and tactics employed by Greek forces. Persian recognition of this fact is clear from their increasing use of Greek mercenaries as the mainstay of their infantry forces. The closed spaces of Greece favored the compact hoplite formation and hindered the employment of the Persian cavalry in any effective way. Though at the culminating battle on the mainland at Plataea in 479 Persian and allied Greek cavalry as well as archers inflicted serious casualties on Greek forces caught in exposed positions they could not bring about a decisive result. They were a serious enough threat to promote the formation of permanent cavalry forces at Athens and perhaps elsewhere, but their role remained subordinate. The invasion fixed the tie between missile weapons and barbarians more firmly in Greek minds. Writing within ten years of the struggle at Plataea the tragedian Aeschylus could contrast the Greek spear with the Persian bow (135). The consequences of this identification were magnified by the tendency visible before to make a clear division between Greeks and foreigners with a decisive superiority assigned for different reasons in various authors to Greeks (131–132, 177–178).

THE CONSEQUENCES OF THE PELOPONNESIAN WAR: ALTERATIONS TO THE PARADIGM

The half century after the Persian Wars saw a change in the balance of power and political alignments in the Greek world. Athens emerged from the war as the strongest naval power in the Aegean and in the course of the following decades forged an empire with tributary territory in the Aegean, the mainland of Asia Minor and in Greece itself that made her one of the two great powers on the mainland. Her rival was Sparta, the preeminent Greek land power. The latter's strength lay in her own peculiar social system, in the military specialists she produced in a world of amateurs and in the Peloponnesian League whose military forces she controlled. By 431 the two rivals had clashed openly and in mobilizing their allies created a conflict on a scale that its historian Thucydides recognized dwarfed earlier wars between Greeks.

The prolonged and exhausting conflict, lasting with pauses from 431 to 404, was a watershed in Greek military, social and political history. The strength of the two protagonists and the length of the struggle transformed warfare from a seasonal activity to one in which at least low-scale conflict lasted throughout the traditionally inactive winter months. Low-level conflict was in fact characteristic of most of the war. Only two large hoplite battles were fought, Delium in 424 and First Mantinea in 418 during a formal lull in the war. There were also large-scale engagements by Athenian forces attacking Syracuse between 415 and 413 but for the most part the traditional decisive encounter did not take place. Much of the low-level activity on the Athenian side was in the nature of seaborne raids on the Peloponnese, and the war showed the limitations of traditional rules of conflict. Because of her dominance at sea and in fortifications Athens could allow enemy occupation of her land without abandoning her food supply, which could be transported from the Black Sea and other grain growing regions. The war also illustrated the limits of that seapower. It could be useful in stalemating an enemy overwhelmingly more powerful on land without being able to bring about a decisive result on its own.

Other developments that were to make changes in warfare in the fourth century were foreshadowed in this war. Mercenary troops had been employed before but for the first time they were used on a large scale throughout the war (207–208). They included not only Greeks, particularly Arcadians from one of the poorest regions of central Greece, but also foreign specialist troops, particularly Thracian light-armed infantry armed with javelins and known from their shields as peltasts. These troops were employed as supplements to regular hoplite forces and especially to counter enemy superiority in cavalry. The war revealed the possibilities of light-armed troops in encounters with hoplites. In 426 the Athenian general Demosthenes' hoplite forces were severely mauled by Aetolian light-armed troops armed with javelins (69). In the next year Demosthenes put his experience in Aetolia to use by employing a combined force of hoplites and light-armed men to defeat an isolated Spartan party of 440 hoplites on the island of Sphacteria in the Bay of Naverino (70). The effectiveness of light-armed troops in combination with other types of troops in circumstances where hoplites could be fixed in position or with their formations disrupted was appreciated, and the knowledge gained was applied with important results in the following century.

The most immediate political result of the war was the defeat of Athens. With her removal from the rank of great power the Spartans were for a time in an unchallengeable position of ascendancy. The natural result of this as well as Spartan policy blunders was to create a serious of coalitions involving the other major Greek states such as Athens and Thebes to counter Spartan hegemony. The period after 404 till the Macedonian conquest under Philip II was a kaleidoscope of shifting alliances to contain the various dominant powers as they emerged in the course of the fourth century. The other important result was the greater impact of direct Persian involvement in Greek affairs. Persian money had played a decisive role in allowing the Spartans to build a fleet that could match and finally defeat Athens' navy. Persian intentions were not only directed to recovering Greek cities in Asia Minor that had once been in their possession. They were also interested in preventing the rise of an unfriendly dominant power in Greece and in assuring a continuing supply of Greek mercenary hoplites. The inflow of Persian money helped make possible a greater use of mercenary troops whose availability was increasing due to the economic and social disruption that the Peloponnesian War had caused (210). The duration of the war had by itself turned what might have been a temporary opportunity to earn extra money as a mercenary into a professional career. The economic and social problems of Greece in the aftermath of this war provided a ready supply of men who might not have chosen such a path in the years before the war. A surely unintended but important result of the increased use of paid professional troops was to create a fissure in the old link between citizenship and the obligation of military service (214–217).

THE FOURTH CENTURY: INCREASING FLEXIBILITY AND INNOVATION

The fourth century witnessed important changes in the way warfare was conducted as a result of the developments mentioned above. Major battles such as Nemea and Coronea were still decided by the clash of hoplite armies, but tactics became more complicated then they had when battles were decided by the head-on crash of phalanxes. Already in the Peloponnesian War the Spartans had developed a tactic of using their superior skill to encircle the left of the enemy's phalanx and then to take it in the flank. At the battle of Leuctra in 371 the Theban commander Epaminondas, building on traditional elements in Theban hoplite tactics, devised a method to successfully counter the Spartan attempts to outflank his forces. He chose his left wing as the offensive wing of his phalanx and stationed his troops in an exceptionally deep formation at that point while refusing his center and right. The Theban commander successfully struck the Spartan line at the point where it was attempting to outflank his left (196–197). The result was a victory that prepared the final blows that were to end Sparta's long supremacy on Greek battlefields. Epaminondas had drawn on the inherent tendency of phalanx encounters to be decided not along the entire length of their fronts but at some decisive point and thereby made that formation a much more flexible and supple instrument. The use of reserves first recorded in connection with the Athenian expedition against Syracuse further expanded the possibilities open to commanders in disposing their forces for battle. The fourth century witnessed the creation of a more complicated battlefield than had existed earlier.

That complication was also evident in developments concerned with light-armed troops, particularly peltasts and cavalry. It was the growing differentiation of the roles of warrior and citizen that created the necessary conditions. The increasing use of mercenaries in place of citizen soldiers allowed the growth of specialization and a level of prolonged training not possible earlier. Unencumbered by the weight of a considerable amount of protective armor, peltasts could harass, demoralize and finally break hoplite formations. This approach was particularly effective against hoplites who had lost the support of other arms. The most famous incident of this type was the destruction of a unit of approximately 600 Spartan troops isolated at Lechaeum, Corinth's western port (201). The Athenian unit that inflicted the disaster was the very type of professionalized fighting force that was to help transform aspects of fourth-century warfare (202). The isolated Spartan unit was subject to a running barrage of javelins but, unable to catch their pursuers, retired to a nearby hill to make a stand and then disintegrated at the approach of a force of Athenian hoplites. Such developments affected hoplite equipment. The advantages in mobility enjoyed by peltasts were quickly perceived and there is a noticeable lightening of the protective armor worn by hoplites in the course of the century. Though never to play a central role such troops became increasingly important, as did the cavalry that often operated with them.

THE OUTCOME OF PROFESSIONALIZATION: THE RISE OF THE MERCENARY

The increased use of mercenaries meant that the finances of war had undergone a profound change. Before the Peloponnesian War, the fighting had been essentially self-financing. The citizens themselves supplied their equipment and must have met the expenses of training. At Athens and presumably elsewhere they were obliged to buy the initial supplies for the expedition and financed the rest of the campaign either from foraging in enemy territory or through supplies or money they themselves had brought. There were two major exceptions to this system. The Spartans, through the military obligations of members of the Peloponnesian League to supply and support troops called up by the Spartans, were able to substantially increase the numbers of soldiers at their disposal with no increase in cost. The other major exception was Athens. Her acquisition of an empire allowed her to draw upon subject states for contributions in the form of a yearly tribute. This enabled her perhaps as early as the 460s to compensate her citizens for military service and through confiscation from rebellious subjects and settlement of Athenians in the confiscated territories to increase the number of hoplites available to her.

The growing use of mercenaries and the development of semi-permanent commanders who served as their organizers and paymasters changed the rules of the game. A demand for ready money was created which most Greek states were unable to supply. That is why Persia loomed as a more significant force in Greek politics after the war. Her financial reserves were immense in comparison to those available to the Greeks. Her wealth could prove crucial, as it did in the closing phase of the Peloponnesian War. For those without access to Persian gold, financing war became a perennial difficulty. We know most about Athens in the fourth century and our sources, mostly contemporary political oratory, have strong biases that make an accurate estimate of the situation difficult. Allowing for these problems a picture of growing divorce between military service and citizen obligations appears to have made for a reluctance to adequately fund military operations (210, 214, 216). Increasing concentration of wealth may also have been a factor as well as the fact that many Athenian expeditions were ship-borne and so incurred even greater expense. Not only did financing become a problem for traditionally dominant states but also new opportunities were opened to previous unimportant areas. The seizure of the treasury of the temple of Apollo at Delphi by the Phoceans in 356 allowed them to become a major military force for a decade. This was a situation that had been previously unthinkable. The death of the aged Spartan king Agesilaus serving in Egypt to earn funds for his state epitomizes the new conditions of the fourth century.

THE RISE OF MACEDONIA: PHILIP II AND WARFARE ON A NEW SCALE

The constellation of political forces on the mainland was to be drastically changed by the rise and consolidation of a new power that was to overshadow the traditionally dominant states. The kingdom of Macedonia had played only a tangential role in Greek politics to the middle of the fourth century. A kingdom established in Aegae near the coastal area of the Thermaic Gulf had made attempts at integrating the whole of what was only a geographic and ethnic unit. Macedonia suffered from severe problems. It was composed of a number of autonomous kingdoms, tribes and Greek city-states that jealously guarded their independence. Its geographic position made it serve as an unwilling buffer for Thessaly and the other Greek states to the south. It was an especially difficult position as Macedonia was surrounded by various warlike and energetic opponents including the Illyrians and Thracians (227). The situation was further complicated by internal divisions within the royal house that was unable to establish a secure line of succession for much of the period due to a powerful nobility and internal dissension. These difficulties had been exploited by various Greek powers, especially Athens, that had tried to weaken the kingdom and any threat it presented to Athenian possessions in the area. Athens had also wanted access to Macedonian timber for her naval needs on the most favorable terms. For much of the fourth century the existence of the monarchy at Aegae was in jeopardy and Macedonia was too preoccupied with its local problems to be a serious participant in Greek politics (227).

The situation was altered dramatically by the accession first as regent and then as king in his own right of Philip II (226, 229). The previous king had just been killed in battle with the Illyrians and Macedonia was in a desperate position.

Within the year Philip had extinguished the Illyrian threat. The exact stages by which Philip revitalized Macedonia are unclear due to the poor state of our sources. One thing that does stand out is Philip's realization of the importance of the army to Macedonia's future. Philip's most pressing difficulty was to create an infantry that could compete with those of his enemies. In an amazingly short time he created a force that could more than hold its own and by the end of his reign was the superior of any competing infantry. First, he seems to have introduced a number of technical innovations. He continued the existing trend to lightening hoplite equipment by discarding the corselet and using a small shield suspended by a strap from the shoulder as protection for the upper body (234, 236). The suspension of the shield was made necessary by the other crucial innovation: the sarissa. This was an eighteen-foot pike wielded in both hands that enormously increased the number of lethal spearpoints that the phalanx could present as well as increasing the range of its killing zone. These technical innovations were accompanied by a close attention to drill and general discipline as well as measures to hold excess baggage to a minimum (230–231). Technical developments were supported by changes in organization. An élite infantry unit was created to match the superb cavalry composed of nobles that served Philip and acted as his "companions" (239–242). The infantry and cavalry were organized in territorial brigades under specific commanders and supplementary units were created from subject peoples to remedy deficiencies in Macedonian techniques (248–250). Greek immigrants were encouraged and created the urban society that seems so closely linked to effective heavy infantry in Greek social conditions. All of this seems to have been carried out at amazing speed and served to support a policy of expansion. Philip's victory over Thebes and Athens at Chaeronea in 338 brought him direct or indirect control over all of Macedonia, most of Greece, Thrace and a wide swath of territory stretching towards the Danube in one direction and the Bosporus in the other. Philip had devised the means to realize the potential of the first large territorial state in Europe, a potential that was far greater in manpower and other resources than any competing Greek power. In doing so he permanently altered the political balance in Greece and so began the decline of the city-state as a significant factor in the international balance of power.

ALEXANDER THE GREAT

When Philip was assassinated in 336 he had already taken steps to send a large force of mercenaries across to Asia Minor to prepare for an invasion of the Persian empire. The full extent of his plans will never be known. After a power struggle the details of which are unclear his son Alexander III came to the throne at the age of 20. The sources for the career of Alexander the Great are far better than for the reign of Philip. Alexander's extraordinary success and personality soon created a web of legend around him that makes it difficult at times to distinguish fact and invention. His ultimate objectives are perhaps the most obscure aspect of his reign.

After spending the first year and a half of his reign consolidating his power in Macedonia and Greece and strengthening his borders, Alexander launched his invasion of Asia Minor in the spring of 334 with a force of about 40,000 infantry and 6000 horse (255). The large number of cavalry was designed to counter Persian strength in that arm. This is not the place to trace Alexander's progress in detail. In four set-piece battles, at the Granicus in 334, the Issus in 333, Gaugamela-Arbela in 330 and the Hydaspes in northwestern India in 326, Alexander displayed an unrivaled tactical genius and improvisational skill. It was crucial to his success that Philip had created a superb army that he could work with. Another vital element in his success was that Macedonia possessed one of the few truly effective cavalry forces in Greece. It was so effective that Alexander was able to use it as his decisive offensive force, a great departure from traditional Greek practice. Gaugamela perhaps showed Alexander's improvisational skills to best effect. Confronted by the Persian king Darius III's superior numbers in infantry and cavalry he drew up a double phalanx able to form a protective square if he should be outflanked. In addition he used flank guards to equally good effect. He also used an oblique battle line, offering his right where he himself was stationed with the cavalry and refusing his left. Moving obliquely to the right he was able to extend the enemy so that an opening was created for his cavalry to break and roll up the Persian line. The battle typifies his ability to take traditional elements and wield them to produce a new and effective combination. This was true in engagements at every level (268–270).

His strategy is less clear. It appears that he neutralized Persian naval superiority by conquering its bases along the Mediterranean coasts of the empire and then struck inland to confront Darius. It seems that from the first he was not content to wrest land from the Persians but wanted to conquer all of its territory and assume the Persian crown himself. This meant that Alexander had to forge a policy that could join the unwieldy structure he created together. His administration copied Persian methods but for the most part substituted Macedonian personnel. This was not possible as far as his empire's military forces were concerned. There were simply too few Macedonian and Greek troops to meet his needs. By the end of his reign he appears to be have been planning to create an army drawn from Orientals and Greeks alike (262–265). Alexander does not seem to have been willing to cease his conquest when Persia was acquired. The end of his eastward march was due to the resistance of his army and not to any choice of his own. Though there has been debate about Alexander's "final aims," there is no reason to doubt that he planned further conquests.

THE HELLENISTIC PERIOD:
THE LEGACY OF ALEXANDER

Alexander's death in 323 ushered in a period of intense struggle among his generals for control of his empire. It was not until approximately 280 that a new and stable realignment of the balance of power emerged. Three successor kingdoms divided most of Alexander's heritage. All of them were in the control of descendants of Alexander's leading commanders; the house of Ptolemy in Egypt, the Seleucids with a heterogeneous kingdom stretching from western Asia Minor to northwestern India at its greatest extent, and the Antigonids in the ancestral Macedonian kingdom. Other second rank powers also emerged that included the Attalid kingdom in western Asia Minor with its capital at Pergamum which was carved out of former Seleucid territory, the island of Rhodes that emerged as a great seapower and in Greece two leagues, the Achaean and the Aetolian. The traditional city-state no longer had sufficient resources to compete in the international arena.

Except for Macedonia the monarchies were composed of heterogeneous mixtures of local and immigrant populations. Alexander had established a number of city colonies before his death to provide garrisons to hold down conquered territory. The successor kingdoms in Asia, except for Egypt, vastly expanded this practice to satisfy their needs for Greek administrators and soldiers. Between 320 and 250 a large-scale immigration from Greece took place that dispersed Greek-speaking populations and Greek culture around the shores of the eastern Mediterranean and far inland to the borders of India.

Even the smallest of these states had vast resources in comparison to earlier Greek states and the armies of the Hellenistic period were huge in comparison to earlier Greek forces. The major powers were able to field armies of between 70,000 and 80,000 men for major campaigns (**283, 291**). The preference for Greek and Macedonian armies, however, created problems in supplying men for these comparatively vast military establishments. Various expedients were resorted to try to attract and retain mercenaries in service. A system of land grants, contracts and incentives was used (**571–573**), the land grant being among the most popular as it tied the recipient physically (**295–296**). Economic conditions seem to have been poor enough to attract large numbers overseas. By 200 Greek manpower had largely been exhausted and the same system was used to attract recruits from other areas of the Mediterranean. Macedonia and the Greek leagues were the exceptions, having essentially national armies (**277, 288, 301–302**).

There was little tactical change in the aftermath of Alexander's death. For about seventy-five years cavalry remained as it had with Alexander, a major offensive weapon. But finances and access to horses eventually placed the greatest part of the offensive burden back on the heavy infantry. These were armed essentially as they had been under Alexander, though there was experimentation with the length of the sarissa to try to increase it effectiveness. What resulted was an ever more rigid and inflexible phalanx that needed very specific conditions to be effective (**278–279**).

The one major innovation was the introduction of elephants into European warfare. Alexander had encountered them in India and they had left a significant enough impression to create a major demand for them. The chief sources of supply were India and Africa south of Egypt. But the offensive promise of the animals never lived up to expectations. They were used on the battlefield and in siege warfare; however, they did not prosper in the European climate and presented vast logistical problems. Within about 150 years they disappeared from European battlefields forever (285–287).

FORTIFICATIONS AND THE FATE OF CITIES

The history of Greek fortifications is intimately tied to the progress of siege warfare. With the development of hoplite warfare as the mainstay of Greek military practice, siege warfare became extremely difficult to wage successfully. The hoplite ethic of man-to-man military confrontation as well as the unsuitability of hoplite equipment for such encounters meant that in general hoplite armies were ill-equipped to successfully carry out a siege. Whatever the motivations behind the massive cyclopean Bronze Age fortifications at Mycenae or Tiryns were, they had disappeared by the end of the Bronze Age. Until the fifth century Greek fortifications remained relatively simple and depended on a vertical barrier such as a wall or the joined façades of houses. For the most part the fortifications defended the acropolis, the civic and religious center of the city, which was also usually on a hill that made fortification easier and more effective. Under Near Eastern influence there were refinements in this vertical barrier. Towers were added to provide for flanking fire and to strengthen weak parts of the defensive wall. The whole of the urban area rather than just the acropolis was now fortified and defended. This change may reflect a difference in the conception of what was essential to the concept of the city. A crucial innovation of the mid-fifth century was the development of so-called long walls that connected a city with its harbor. Athens has the most famous example but there were others. This now meant that for naval powers the older strategy of starving a city into submission by controlling its agricultural territory was no longer valid. Even with the loss of a city's fields the population could now be fed on imported foodstuffs.

Despite the general simplicity of construction, the fortifications were more than adequate to the task. Despite evidence for the use of the ramp, ram and moveable sheds until the end of the fifth century a small but resolute garrison could successfully resist much larger besieging forces. The most effective technique that the besiegers had at hand was to promote treachery within and have the gates opened by a traitor. Otherwise it was necessary close the city off and starve it into submission. The process was long and costly and not resorted to unless there was no other remedy.

THE MECHANIZATION OF SIEGE WARFARE

By the beginning of the fourth century mechanical devices based on Near Eastern and Carthaginian models and original Greek inventions began to be constructed. The effort seems to have been most advanced in the West. The sources point to Dionysius I, tyrant of Syracuse, and Philip II as the individuals most responsible for these developments (**218, 220**). Of the Greek innovations perhaps the most important was the catapult which allowed much greater propulsive force to be given to missiles of various types (**219–223**). These weapons for the first time provided a direct threat to the integrity of the walls themselves. Near Eastern techniques comprising mining and moveable protective devices for the first time gave the offensive the advantage. The adoption of mechanical devices by the defense tended in the end to make the struggle more equal. Nevertheless, cities fell to siege much more frequently than they had earlier.

The cities that did fall were treated in a variety of ways. Massacre, enslavement or simple surrender and submission to the will of the victor were all possibilities (**168–169**). Gradually, perhaps in response to the greater xenophobia that resulted from the Persian invasion of the early fifth century, a growing repugnance was felt at least by some thinkers to enslaving or massacring Greeks as opposed to barbarians. The same sense of difference and varieties of treatment were visible on the battlefield. The reservations as developed were never sufficiently strong to end the taking of extreme measures where a Greek population was concerned (**173–175**).

TREATIES AND ALLIANCES

The same variety that governed the treatment of enemies also controlled the creation of alliances and friendship (**119–127**). Though all treaties of alliance observed certain formalities such as oaths to the gods, they display an astonishing variety depending on their purpose. Perhaps the most striking element is the absence of permanent alliances until quite late. Most were for a term of years and had to be renewed by annual oaths. This is a reflection of the idea that independent states were in natural opposition to each other and that peace was an exceptional state that had to be carefully specified and delineated.

EPILOGUE

The history of ancient Greek warfare is remarkably consistent despite major changes in technique. At its heart from the eighth century lay the dominance of the heavy armed infantryman, whether he was a hoplite or Macedonian phalangite. War always remained a major preoccupation and activity as well as a source of prestige and wealth. The competitive nature and scant resources available to Greek society were powerful incentives to war-making. It was only with the advent of Roman control that this situation ended and Greece enjoyed a peace that was not of her making. The competition between cities continued but it was now a matter of the award of status and benefactions controlled by others.

1

EARLY GREEK WARFARE
Homer and the Dark Ages

The importance of warfare in Greek society is nowhere better symbolized than by the fact that its first great literary product is a monumental epic poem, the *Iliad*, which is almost wholly concerned with warfare. Though set down in final form about 700 BC, the epic is the end product of a long period of oral composition with roots reaching back to the Mycenaean period of the Bronze Age in Greece (*c.* 1600–1200 BC). In addition to the material contained in the *Iliad* the Mycenaean period itself supplies artistic representations of warfare in various mediums, remains of actual weapons as well as a series of documentary palace records that deal in part with military matters, but which are difficult to interpret and offer no coherent picture of warfare. The most productive approach is to draw inferences from these archaeological remains and to compare them with the material contained in the poem. The technique of oral composition that resulted in this poem depended upon the development of a stock of poetic formulas and themes and a specialized poetic dialect that aided the non-literate poet by allowing him to concentrate on character and story-telling. The lack of limitation to his creativity or conceptual genius is evident in the final product.

The development of the poem's compositional elements represents a gradual accretion of material over many centuries. The tradition on which this poetry is based stretches from the Mycenaean period and the Dark Ages (1200–800 BC) down to the eighth century and includes the contemporary world of the poet who created the final version, and whom both we and the ancients call Homer. This method of composition has created a poem that is an amalgam of material relating to warfare, including weapons, tactics and codes of behavior from all of these periods. Much debate has raged over which period formed the background for Homer's world, with opinion divided on locating the historical setting of the world of the poem. Some scholars have felt that the world of the poems is an imaginary creation of the poet and the tradition in which he worked and so, in fact, never had a real existence. The picture has been complicated by the presence of the other great epic poem ascribed to Homer, the *Odyssey*. This work has been thought to have been composed somewhat later, about the first quarter of the seventh century, and it provides some interesting differences from and additions to the material found in the *Iliad*.

1

In assessing the poems as evidence for Greek military practice, it is crucial to remember that they are poetry and not historical treatments of warfare, even though Greek writers considered Homer the founder of tactical theory. There are inconsistencies in weaponry and tactics that result from heroic exaggeration and a mixture of material from different periods; they may bother us but they were of no importance to the poet. His concern was to present a convincing and compelling story of heroic warfare and the greatness of his achievement is evidence of his success.

The warfare Homer portrays appears to suit best the late Dark Ages and his own period (end of the eighth century BC), and the poems form our only roughly contemporary literary evidence for those periods. His contemporary audience and later generations of Greeks found it compelling enough as a portrayal of a "heroic" style of warfare and the poems were to have a lasting impact on Greek ideas of combat and heroism. Crucial to this must have been the fact that in the poem the dominant warrior on the battlefield was the heavily armed infantryman who was also to be the determining factor in Classical warfare. The remarks of the fourth-century philosopher Plato disparaging Homer's role as educator of Greece and his contemporary Xenophon's acknowledgment of the poet as "the master of those that know" emphasize the continuing impact of the poems in antiquity. The strength of the heroic ideal embodied in the poems is evident in the conscious imitation by later Greek conquerors such as Alexander the Great of Achilles, the preeminent hero of the *Iliad*. On first crossing to the Asian shore in his expedition against Persia, Alexander sacrificed to the spirit of Protesilaus, the first of the Greeks to fall at Troy, and then purposely exchanged his own armor for that allegedly borne by the heroes of that war.

The *Iliad* is an epic poem of about 15,000 lines covering a period of a few weeks in the tenth year of the siege of Troy. It is centered on a quarrel between the leader of the Greek forces Agamemnon, the king of Mycenae, and the greatest of the Greek heroes, Achilles. That quarrel leads to Achilles' refusal to participate in the war and to the difficulties that ensue for the Greeks until Achilles' return to battle after the death of Patroclus, his closest companion. It ends with the death of the Trojan champion Hector at Achilles' hands and the burial of his body by the Trojans. The action takes place at many levels, both human and divine. Though human warfare and the heroic code that governs it represent only some of the many intertwined themes and focuses of the poem, they are crucial ingredients for its structure and meaning.

The *Odyssey* is in some ways a sequel to the *Iliad*, recounting the ten-year-long journey of one of the heroes, Odysseus, from Troy to his home kingdom of Ithaca. Fighting occupies only a very small part of it. But it supplies a series of useful supplementary glimpses of the same heroic world as the *Iliad* but from a different perspective.

THE HERO AND THE HEROIC CODE

The *Iliad* centers on and celebrates the struggle of the hero as much as it focuses on any other matter. Its opening scenes, which set the outlines of the plot, show in the interchange of Agamemnon and Achilles the crucial function of the hero who stands at the center of the poem and of the warfare that forms its main action. The key to understanding the actions of the hero lies in the code which governs his interactions with his peers and determines his standing in a fiercely competitive society. The gods have a role to play and appear on the battlefield, most noticeably in their participation in battle after Achilles once again consents to fight the Trojans. But the real interest of the poem is centered on its human protagonists. These are the "kings" of Homer, men of high standing whose prime qualities are martial prowess and a sense of personal honor. The display of these characteristics is governed by what has been called a "shame culture." This is characterized by an intensely personal code which rests on the hero's fear of loss of status in the eyes of his peers. It is summed up in the injunction always to be the best; as the following selections make clear, this especially means the best or the most effective warrior. In addition to individual prowess in battle, the other admired quality praised is the ability to give good counsel to other chiefs.

The absolutes of the code are tempered in two ways. First there is a stress on the principle of descent which comes out most clearly in the position of Agamemnon who leads the host. His leadership is not based on his superior fulfillment of the code since it is clear that other heroes approach the ideal much more closely than he does. It is his superior hereditary position and the resources that result from it that give Agamemnon, the chief, his status as the most kingly leader and command over the expedition. Inherited position also appears to involve some ties and obligations to the community, most noticeably expressed in the interchange between Sarpedon and Glaukon (see no. 2). Sarpedon makes an explicit connection between lordship, its prerogatives and the willingness to bear the brunt of battle. Second, there are a series of limitations which arise from other considerations such as the ties of guest friendship which can also change relationships. There are further boundaries to the exercise of political power, most noticeably in the moral and physical inability of Agamemnon to control Achilles' behavior. Nonetheless the world of the poem is a world intensely focused on personal standing and achievement. The ordeal of battle provides the perfect setting in which to actualize the heroic code and to display its consequences.

The heroic code

The following passages illustrate the general outlines of the code, the sanctions that enforce it and the centrality of excellence of warfare as its most demanding imperative.

1. *Iliad* 11.401–410

Now spear-famed Odysseus was left alone and none of the Argives remained with him since they were all held in the grip of fear. Troubled, he spoke to his own proud spirit. What will become of me? It would be a terrible thing if I ran in fear of this multitude, yet it would be worse if I am caught alone. Zeus has instilled fear in the rest of the Greeks. Yet why do I debate this with myself? I know that cowards walk away from battle, but one who wants to be outstanding in battle must stand his ground strongly, and either strike or be struck down.

2. *Iliad* 12.310–328

A speech by Sarpedon, from Lycia in western Asia Minor, son of Zeus and one of the major figures on the Trojan side.

"Glaukos, why are we given the seat of honor, and choice meats and full wine cups in Lycia? Why do all look upon us as if we were gods? Why have we received a large estate by the banks of the Xanthus, fertile in orchards and good ploughland for the planting of wheat? We must now go and take our stand among the front ranks of the Lycians, and take our part in the heat of battle so that one of the well-armored Lycians might say, 'These men are not without fame, our lords who rule in Lycia, who drink choice wine and eat the best of the flocks. Most important is strength in them since they fight with the foremost of the Lycians.' My friend, if we could escape this strife and then live forever ageless and immortal, I would not fight again in the van of the battle nor would I press you into battle where fame is won. But now the thousand fated forms of death press upon us which a man cannot escape or evade. Let us advance and let the enemy gain glory from us or we from them."

3. *Iliad* 6.476–481 and 486–491

Hector is praying for his son.

"Zeus and you other gods, grant that this boy who is my son becomes as I am, conspicuous among the Trojans. Grant that he excel in his strength and rule Troy in his power. And may someone someday say he is a far better man than his father was, when he returns from the battle. Let him bear back the bloody spoils, after killing his enemy, as a joy to his mother's heart. . . . My darling [Andromache], why are you so deep in grief? For no man will cast me down to Hades against my fate. Neither good men nor evil ones can escape the fate born with them once it has been fixed."

The conduct of the hero

4. *Iliad* 6.206–210

These words addressed to the Greek hero Diomedes are spoken by the same Glaukos addressed by Sarpedon in no. 2. The repetition of such advice in the course of the poem stresses its importance to heroic conduct. Ephyre is probably the Homeric name for Corinth.

"Hippolochus bore me and I say that I am his son. He sent me to Troy and urged me repeatedly always to be the best and to hold my head above other men. He also enjoined me not to shame my ancestors who were by far the best in Ephyre and broad Lycia."

Other motivations for fighting

5. *Iliad* 1.148–170

The economic wealth that warfare generates is a constant preoccupation in the Homeric poems. Note the tension generated by rival claims of status and ability in this case personified by Agamemnon and Achilles. Agamemnon's power rests on his kingship which ultimately is grounded on the authority of Zeus. The issue centers on the interaction between the honor represented by the distribution of appropriate booty and its economic value. Both are inextricably linked. The central importance of honor and the standing it confers explains the intensity of the conflict.

Looking fiercely at him [Agamemnon], swift Achilles spoke. "You are a man wrapped in shamelessness, always greedy for profits. How can anyone of the Achaeans gladly obey you either to go on a journey or to fight strongly in battle? I did not come here to fight against the Trojan spearmen for their sake. They have done nothing to me. For they have never driven off my herds or horses, nor in my homeland where the rich soil breeds good men, have they laid waste my crops, since we are greatly separated by the shadowy mountains and the roaring sea. But you, O great shameless man, we have followed to please you and to win your honor and Menelaus' against the Trojans. This you ignore or forget. And now you threaten to deprive me of my prize which I got with great labor and which the sons of the Achaeans have given to me. I never have a prize equal to yours whenever the Achaeans sack some strong citadel of the Trojans: but it is I who always have the greater share of fighting. At the distribution of booty yours is much the larger share. But I take away some small, dear thing back to my ships."

6. *Odyssey* 11.401–403

These words are addressed by Odysseus to the shade of Agamemnon in the underworld. The assumption is that raiding for profit is a normal activity. At the end of the poem the same words are addressed by Agamemnon to Aphimedon, one of the suitors slain by Odysseus. The casualness of the inquiry is the point to notice and the lack of shame that such activities carried. Yet it remains a somewhat ambiguous activity that can on occasion be condemned, as it is later in the poem by Odysseus' swineherd Eumaeus.

"Did some enemy slay you on dry land as you were driving off some of their cattle or fleecy flocks of their sheep, or did you die fighting for their citadel or women?"

Command and preeminence

7. *Iliad* 1.275–296

Nestor, the elderly Pylian king, intervenes to try to restrain the developing feud between Agamemnon and Achilles over the retention of Achilles' female captive Briseis. The passage brings out clearly the conflict between status and personal prowess. In terms of individual achievement Achilles is unmatched. Agamemnon's position as the most "kingly" and the ruling commander of the

Greek forces is based on his inherited status as the ruler of the greatest of the Greek kingdoms involved.

"Both of you listen to my advice for it is better to do so. Do not deprive him [Achilles] of the girl though you are a great man, but leave things as they are. The girl was given first to him by the sons of the Achaeans as his share. Nor do you, son of Peleus, be desirous in your dispute with the king to be his equal since a sceptered king does not ever have an equal share of honor to those whom Zeus has given the glory. Granted that you are stronger since a goddess was your mother yet he is greater since his power over men is greater. Son of Atreus [Agamemnon] give over your anger. I ask that you cease in your anger against Achilles who is a great wall for the Achaeans in harsh battle." In answer great Agamemnon spoke, "All that you say old sir is true, but this man wants to stand above all others and to command and rule all. He wants to give all orders yet I think none will obey him, and even if the immortals have made him a spearman, have they given him the right to be insulting as well?" Interrupting him, godlike Achilles answered, "I am then a coward and a man of no account if I submit to your very command. Give your orders to others; I will no longer obey."

Social differentiation

The following passage illustrates the social cleavage in the society of the poems between the nobility and the rest. Ideologically the lower classes are defined as possessing the qualities that are the inverse of those of the nobility. Noble qualities are defined as lineage and the preeminent heroic qualities of prowess in battle and the giving of good counsel. The *Odyssey* appears to show that the cleavage, which is almost impassable, has an economic component. It is founded on the larger scale of the agricultural productive units (*oikoi*) owned by the aristocracy. In addition, materials unavailable locally were obtained by the nobility through a series of gift-exchanges. We know nothing about such exchanges among the rest of the population. These exchanges comprised a set of reciprocal transfers of goods, the most important of which involved metals, and were accompanied by the cementing of social ties. What happened lower down the social scale is less clear. Both the *Iliad* and the *Odyssey* stress the preeminence of the nobles in warfare; nonetheless the mass is certainly of importance in the course of battle.

8. *Iliad* 2.188–206

As a result of a poorly conceived plan to test the morale of his troops Agamemnon precipitates a stampede by the Greeks to their ships to leave. It required Odysseus' utmost efforts to stem the departure of the Greeks. It is revealing that it is excellence and warfare and noble lineage that are the key concepts of the speech.

Whenever he encountered a noble and prominent man, he restrained him with gentle words: "Friend, it is not fitting for you to be frightened like this. Sit down and restrain the people. You do not clearly understand the words of Agamemnon. He now makes test; soon he will press upon the sons of the Achaeans. Did we not all hear what he said in council? May he not in his anger harm some of the Achaeans? For the anger of a Zeus-bred king is great. Honor comes for him from the god and Zeus of the Counsels loves him." When he came upon some man of the people and saw him shouting, he struck him with the scepter and issued a sharp command to him. "Fool, be still and listen to others who are your betters, you who are useless in war and a coward. Not all Achaeans can be kings. Many lords are a bad thing. Let there be one leader, one king to whom devious Zeus gave the power to judge and to rule over his people."

WEAPONS AND PREPARATION FOR BATTLE

The Homeric poems are written in an artificial literary dialect. Unlike written poetry they are constructed from a series of phrase units that economically fit the demands of the poetic meter. These tools provide the flexibility for expansion and development by a composer of genius like the author of the *Iliad*. This is true not only at the level of language, but it is also used in the manipulation of certain standard scenes and themes. One of these standard scenes is the arming scene which usually precedes a set of striking exploits by the hero who is the subject of the scene. The *Iliad* provides us with four of these scenes, and though there is variation in detail the various items of armor and other equipment are taken up and put on in the same order in each of them. Some of this may be dictated by practical considerations. The donning of greaves to protect the shins before putting on the metal corselet to protect the warrior's upper body may be dictated by the fact that bending in the rigid corselet would have been difficult at best. The selection below describing the arming of Agamemnon is among the most elaborate of these scenes. It includes certain peculiar elements in the decoration of the king's arms and in the individual history of the pieces. In particular, the Gorgon head on his shield, which also is found on the aegis of Athena (5.738), appears to point towards the late eighth century for the passage when this motif enters Greek art.

Some elements in the description of armor and weapons in the poems are traceable to the Mycenaean period because of archaeological evidence. These elements are mostly connected with single objects or techniques. Certainly Homer is consistent in portraying all of his weapons and armor as being made exclusively of bronze, which fits the late Bronze Age context. But it is clear that this is part of an attempt to reconstruct heroic warfare and is not based on any deep knowledge. Even in this limited area there are problems. Though weapons and armor are made of bronze, agricultural implements and tools are usually of iron in the poems. This is the exact reverse of the sequence established by archaeology for the introduction of the latter metal. In fact, tools were the last implements to be made of iron. More important is the fact that basic political, social and cultural elements of the late Bronze Age are absent from these poems. The great palace fortresses of the period with their elaborate bureaucracies and writing have completely vanished from the poems. Even the terms for various offices and functions have, with few exceptions, either disappeared from the poems or survived in a changed context. One of the great problems connected with the survival of knowledge of the Mycenaean or late Bronze Age period is the question of chariot warfare which will be dealt with below.

But with all that has perished the archaeological record makes clear that a few details of Mycenaean weaponry were early on encapsulated in the formulae out of which the poems were constructed. Some, such as Nestor's dove cup or the metal inlay work on Agamemnon's armor, point back to the Mycenaean period, as does the knowledge of the wealth of Egyptian Thebes. But for the most part these references are confined to objects and lack any real social or political context.

The arming of Agamemnon

9. *Iliad* 11.15–46

This is the most elaborate of the four arming scenes in the *Iliad* and it serves to introduce a decisive turn in the action that will lead to Achilles' return to battle. Agamemnon's position as the most powerful of the Greek kings may explain the richness of his equipment. The corselet has possible parallels to Near Eastern models and some have seen a resemblance to the representations of corselets on Bronze Age Greek inventory tablets. The inlay work on the corselet has a parallel on an eighth-century statuette from Salamis in Cyprus. The elaborate shield is round in form, like that carried by several other warriors, and appears to have parallels with late Mycenaean types with a handle and a strap for suspension. The Gorgon on the shield is not attested as a decorative figure till later. His two throwing spears reflect the period after the Bronze Age when the throwing spear replaced the thrusting one as the major offensive weapon. Homer is often inconsistent about this.

The son of Atreus cried out and commanded the Argives to arm themselves. He himself put on his shining bronze. First he fastened his beautiful greaves with silver ankle straps. Then he buckled on the corselet which long ago Kinyras gave him as a guest-gift when the Achaeans were about to set sail for Troy, Kinyras, who had heard of his great fame in Cyprus. To please Agamemnon, he gave it to him as a gift. It had ten bands of dark enamel, twelve of gold and twenty of tin. Enamel snakes arched towards the neck of the piece, three on either side, like the rainbow which Zeus fixes firmly in the clouds as a sign for mortal men. About his shoulders he slung his sword, on which the hilt bore golden studs, and bands of silver were about the scabbard which was hooked to a gilt baldric. Then he took up his man-protecting skillfully wrought shield. It had ten circles of bronze; the twenty studs were of white tin around its rim. On its middle was a boss of dark enamel enclosed by the mouth of a ferocious Gorgon, and on each side of her were Fear and Panic. The strap for hanging the shield was of silver on which a dark blue serpent of three heads twined on one trunk. On his head he fitted a double-ridged helmet with four white crests of horsehair which nodded terrible above it. He took up his two sharp spears with heads of sharpened bronze.

Mycenaean relics

The boar's tusk helmet

10. *Iliad* 10.261–265

A number of representations of these helmets survive in Mycenaean art, most notably on the frescoes dated in the last third of the seventeenth century from Thera, a volcanic island to the north of Crete. The helmet most probably is a leather cap with rows of plates cut from boar's tusks and sewn in horizontally reversed bands. These plates have appeared on a number of Mycenaean sites guaranteeing the ubiquity of this type of helmet. It appears to have belonged exclusively to the Greek mainland. Evidence for it stretches from before the late Bronze Age till the very end of that period. It is not impossible that it entered the poetic tradition far later as an heirloom.

He placed on his head a helmet made of leather. On the inside it was lined with many tightly stretched thongs of leather: on the outside it had thickset white teeth of a sharp tusked boar artfully sewn right next to each other row upon row. In the center, felt was fitted.

Tower shield

There are clear references to the great tower shields which were used on both the mainland and Crete during the Bronze Age. Representations of them in hunting scenes have been found as early as the shaft graves at Mycenae of about 1500 BC. These great shields, which seem to have been about four feet in length, appear in two varieties. The first, which appears to be the one represented in the *Iliad* and is most commonly associated with the Greek hero Ajax, is rectangular in shape and seems to have had a rising curve on its top edge, perhaps as a further protection. The common form is the figure-eight shield. Neither variety seems to have had handles but was wielded with a strap worn over the left shoulder called a *telamon*. The shields were made of oxhide stretched over a wooden frame. They seem to have been used in warfare until about 1400, and after that the figure-eight type continues to appear often in a symbolic guise. The great size of the tower shield explains the problems that Hector and Periphetes have in managing them in the poem. The most common shield in the *Iliad* is in fact the smaller round shield with strap and handle mentioned in the passage on the arming of Agamemnon above (no. 9).

11. *Iliad* 15.644–647

Periphetes of Mycenae was son of the Kopreus who acted as herald for Eurysthenes, king of Mycenae. He was employed by the king as a go-between to Herakles since the king was too frightened to face the hero on his own.

For now he added to the glory of Hector. In turning backward he tripped against the rim of his shield that extended to his feet and which he carried as a barrier to spears.

Caught on it, he fell onto his back and his helmet clashed horribly about his temples as he went down.

The bow

The bow is not prominent among the weapons used by the heroes of the *Iliad*, though it is used by common soldiers on both sides, as is the case with the Locrians mentioned below. Only a few heroes used it: Pandarus and Paris on the Trojan side and Teucer on the Greek. In general it is a weapon held in low esteem in the poems, as is clear from the remarks of Diomedes below (no. 13). Archaeological evidence suggests that during the late Bronze Age archery did not play an important role in warfare. Arrowhead finds are rare, as are figured portrayals of the weapon. The typical Mycenaean bow was the self bow, made from a single stave of wood and of limited power and range. It was not until the eighth century that archery became more common, perhaps with the introduction of the Asiatic composite bow. The detailed description of Pandarus' bow seems to indicate such a composite bow, as does the description of Odysseus' bow in the *Odyssey*. But the Asiatic bow was a composite of wood, sinew and bone and this is not reflected in Homer's description. In fact the bow as described in the *Iliad* could never have been used.

12. *Iliad* 4.105–126

The passage suggests that the bow arms are simply of horn which would not give the required flexibility. It is doubtful if the bow as described by Homer could actually have been used since it would not have been sufficiently flexible to draw back any amount.

Straightway he took out the bow of polished horn from a wild goat which he himself, laying up in a hiding place, had once shot in the chest as it leaped down from a rock. The goat then fell backward on the rock. Its horns were a good four feet in length. The horn-worker working it bound it together. Smoothing it well the worker added a golden hook. Pandarus, leaning it upon the broad earth, strung it. His brave friends held their shields in front of him. . . . He drew the lid from the quiver and from it he selected an arrow never before shot – a bearer of sharp pain. He drew back the bow, holding the grooves and the bow string to his breast and the arrowhead to the bow. But when he stretched the great bow into a circle, the bow groaned, the string twanged and the sharp arrow flew striving to fly among the crowd.

13. *Iliad* 11.384–390

Unafraid, powerful Diomedes answered Paris, "Archer, scoundrel, pretty-boy with an eye for the girls, if you should try me face to face with weapons your bow would be of no use to you nor your thickly showered arrows. . . . This is the weak weapon of a coward, a good-for-nothing."

Marshaling for battle

Whatever the much disputed nature of Homeric combat was, it is clear that the battles in the poems begin with a marshaling of mass formations on each side. As passages establishing the battle orders make clear, the Greek and Trojan armies confront each other as organized formations. But, as one would expect in a poetic composition, the stress is on the effect of the mass and the drama of the marshaling, rather than on any detailed sense of how the units were formed. This passage is the one that comes closest to presenting a rational form of tactical organization, but there are problems with it. First it seems odd that the detailed advice it contains would only have been suggested after nine years of warfare. It creates the serious difficulty as to how the troops were ordered before this plan was put forward by Nestor. In the first full march-out of the army there is no reference to such an arrangement. During the course of battle we see groups coalesce around various leaders, and occasionally these leaders cooperate with their units but the organization of the mass for the most part operates without any description beyond one in very generalized terms. Terms denoting organized masses occur frequently. For much of the fighting battle lines exist, but the poet's lack of detail as to their function allows us to say very little about them. The passage can best be explained as a poetic device to prepare the audience for the *Catalogue of Ships* representing the Achaean forces that is to follow rather than an attempt at actual tactical dispositions. The meaning of the terms used by Nestor and translated as tribe and clan are disputed, and it may be possible that they are not kinship terms but are rather terms denoting the military formations of commoners.

14. *Iliad* 2.361–366

It has been pointed out that the advice is not in fact followed, not even among the troops of his own contingent. It is not improbable that Nestor's instructions serve as a dramatic means to impress the audience and that the poet has not given much thought to their military significance.

"What I say is not advice to be spurned. Set the men according to tribes and by nations, Agamemnon, so that clan can support clan and tribes support each other. If you do so and the Achaeans obey you, you will know who is a good leader of the people and who is a bad one. For they will fight in sight of each other."

THE PRACTICE OF HOMERIC WARFARE

The warfare of the *Iliad* consists of two types of combat: mass and individual. The major battles of the poem open with the mass encounter and these struggles reappear at intervals throughout the poems and involve both hand-to-hand combat and missile warfare. But as the battles develop the focus of the poem quickly changes to individual combat among heroes. These encounters follow a standard form but contain numerous variations in detail. Individual combats account for the majority of fighting depicted in the poems. This is in part a result of poetic requirements. Heroes are the dominant characters in the poems and it is their fates that preoccupy the reader. Such personal struggles give a veracity and immediacy to the poem that mass warfare cannot. There is also the problem that any poet would have in presenting a synoptic view of the field of action: attempting to combine the fates of individuals with that of the accompanying anonymous masses on the battlefield. Later historians faced the same problem and were often no more successful. There has been a prolonged debate as to which was really the effective force on the battlefield. The prevailing modern view envisions mass combat as decisive, but that must remain an open question. The effect of heroes such as Hector and Achilles on the course of the battle often appears definitive in the *Iliad*. For instance, Hector's death is taken to portend the destruction of Troy since he is no longer able to defend it. Progress in understanding the warfare of the *Iliad* has been made by emphasizing the idea that the onus of fighting rests upon individuals who place themselves in front of the battle line and so are called *forefighters*. It is they who undertake the majority of fighting and are crucial in determining the outcome of the battle. These are for the most part identical with the heroes upon whom the poet lavishes his attention. This conception still puts the weight of battle on the individual hero, and in a heroic poem that is where such weight ought to rest. In essence the Homeric picture is unclear and heroicized and so unavoidably clouds and impedes the interpretation of the course of battle.

The mass encounter

15. *Iliad* 4.446–456

This is the first mass encounter of Trojans and Greeks in the poem and forms the prelude and background to a series of exploits by individual heroes, culminating in those of Diomedes in the next book. This passage and others like it can be taken to be no more than a representation of closely massed ranks and need imply no particular type of warfare.

Then coming together in one place they encountered each other. They dashed together their shields and spears and the force of men armored in bronze. Then bossed shield struck against bossed shield and a great din of fighting ensued. Then arose the groans and shouts of triumph, of men killing and being killed. The ground ran with blood.

16. *Iliad* 16.210–220

This passage, in which Achilles marshals his Myrmidons for battle, is also one of those cited for evidence in Homer of the use of the heavily armed hoplite that is characteristic of later Greek warfare. The poet is anxious to stress the closeness of the formation and compares the Greek formation to a wall of stones closely set to keep out the wind. But the later description of the battle opens with a spear cast by the hero Patroclus and gives some indication that the poet has no very clear image in mind.

So speaking, he strengthened the courage and spirit of each man. When they heard their king, each rank fell in more closely. As when a man joins together the close stones of a high house wall that shields against the force of the winds, so they fitted together helmets and studded shields. They pressed shield upon shield, helmet upon helmet, and man upon man. Horsehair crests on their helmets brushed each other as the soldiers nodded standing in dense array next to each other. In front of the line two men stood in full armor, having one purpose: to open the fight in the van.

17. *Iliad* 16.772–775

As opposed to the densely packed formations, the more normal opening to encounters is a loose combat at a distance involving missile weapons with the foremost warriors freelancing between the masses of the opposing forces. Cebriones the brother of Hector has just been killed and the Trojans and Greeks are fighting over possession of his body, a frequent activity on the battlefield of the *Iliad*.

And so the Trojans and the Achaeans springing against each other engaged in the slaughter and neither side thought of harrowing panic. Many sharp spears stuck fast about Cebriones and feathered arrows sprung from bow strings, and many great throwing stones crashed against shields as they fought about him.

Individual combat

The most memorable warfare recounted in the poem consists in these individual encounters between noble heroes. Though part of this repetition is due to the nature of combat, it is clear that a major element is the result of the poetic technique of the poem. Often these individual combats take place in the context of a series of exploits that focus on the prowess of a single hero such as Diomedes in book 5. The vast majority of these encounters begin and end with a single death blow. These fights provide the real focus of the war narrative which serves to give scope for the individual heroes to display their prowess in the most important area of heroic excellence. For the most part the combats involve individual Trojans and Greeks in conflict with each other. Another major variant is one man against two others who are usually Trojans. The individual focus is heightened by challenges issued by name and by the giving of a pedigree to each hero as he is introduced. The battle is fought with various weapons including stones. At times there is a confusion concerning the weapons used, with heroes sometimes within the same fight having both a single thrusting spear and two javelins in succession. It is as if the poet unconsciously combines two styles of warfare without any particular concern over the details. One characteristic of Homeric descriptions of individual fighting is the concentration on the final wound. There is an almost infinite variety of wounds recounted, ranging in accuracy from the impossible to those which are highly anatomically correct. Often the victorious fighter strips and carries off the equipment of his victim, and the dead man's chariot may be driven off if possible. These patterns of combat can be woven into longer sequences to display the prowess of individual warriors such as Agamemnon at the beginning of book 11 or Achilles in books 20 and 21.

18. *Iliad* 5.37–68

This passage makes clear both the repetition and variations in detail that these combats contain. The fullest descriptions of wounds inflicted are those done by Menelaus and Meriones, the companion in arms of the Cretan king Idomeneus. It is generally to warriors like these of the second rank that the infliction of the most gruesome wounds is assigned.

Then the Danaans bent back the Trojans. Each of the leaders killed his man. First the lord of men Agamemnon hurled Odeus, the leader of the Halizones, from his chariot. As Odeus was turning, the spear was fixed in the middle of his back between the shoulders and then driven on through his chest. He fell with a thud and his armor clattered about him. Then Idomeneus killed Phaistos son of Maeonean Borus who had come from fertile Tarne. Spear-famed Idomeneus stabbed him in the right shoulder as he was mounting behind his horses and he fell from his chariot and hateful darkness seized him. The followers of Idomeneus stripped the armor from Phaistos while Menelaus the son of Atreus killed Scamandrios son of Strophios, skilled in the chase and himself a fine hunter with his sharp spear. For Artemis had taught him to strike down all the wild things that grow in the mountain forests. But Artemis who fills the air with arrows was of no use to him nor were the long spear casts in which he excelled. But spear-famed Menelaus stabbed him from behind as he was fleeing and the spear was driven through the back between the shoulders and it carried on through to his chest. He fell forward on his face and his armor rattled about him. Meriones then killed Phereclus, son of the smith Harmodius, who knew how to fashion with his hands all intricate things, since Pallas Athena had exceedingly favored him. . . . Meriones pursued this man and having over-taken him stabbed him in the right buttock. The spearhead passed straight through and went under the bone into the bladder. He dropped screaming to his knees and death enshrouded him.

The chariot

One of the crucial indices of the reality of Homeric warfare and its relation to that of the Mycenaean period has been seen in the use of the chariot in the *Iliad*. It is clear that it was known in Greece at the beginning of the Mycenaean period around 1500 BC. It is often represented pictorially in the late Bronze Age, but the evidence about its use is far from clear. The numerous representations that have survived are mostly of a ceremonial nature and so are of little use for determining its military purpose. In addition, it must be remembered that the mostly rough terrain of Greece is not suitable for mass chariot charges. When chariots are represented pictorially in warfare, they are almost without exception shown with the warrior dismounted and fighting on foot beside the chariot. This would imply the use of the chariot simply as a means of transport, a function attested in later Greek warfare.

Large numbers of chariots are registered in the inventories of certain Mycenaean palaces. The Linear B tablets at Cnossus in Crete indicate that palace could have fielded a force of some two hundred vehicles. Contemporary usage in the Near East presents a very different picture. In Egypt the chariot was used as a mobile firing platform for archers and operated in massed units in both the charge and pursuit. Hittite chariotry, which may have been the source of the Bronze Age Greek chariot, appears to have relied upon a heavy thrusting spear, but how the spear was used in conjunction with the vehicle is disputed. There is evidence that Near Eastern forces provided armor for their horses, as would have been essential in battle to keep the chariot functioning. In Homer the major function of the chariot was to serve as transport for a warrior who fights dismounted. In fact, a standard thematic situation in the *Iliad* is the encounter between a dismounted warrior and a pair of enemy warriors in a chariot. Often in battle the warrior's chariot remains close by him to provide a ready means of escape if things go badly. At times, it may also function as an ambulance to carry the wounded hero from the battle-field. The presence of the chariot in the middle of the mêlée appears to be an impossible use of the vehicle. If used solely for transport, the chariot would have been kept to the rear. It is difficult to envision a battlefield with chariots conveniently parked in the middle of the struggle. Certain passages show chariots used in a manner reminiscent of the Near East, as massed for the charge or fighting as a unit in the front rank. The Pylian king Nestor's advice about massing chariots does explicitly hark back to this as an ancient practice. Yet there are other passages that appear to show chariots engaged individually in close combat in the course of the Trojan War. These conflicting and in part unbelievable pictures seem to result from the fact that the poet was delib-erately invoking a style of warfare he conceived as ancient and heroic without clearly understanding the mechanics of that warfare. This evidence tends to support the general contention that the warfare of the poems owes more to heroic convention than reality.

19. *Iliad* 4.293–309

Nestor is the oldest of the Greek rulers at Troy. He figures prominently as advisor and counselor to Agamemnon and the other Greek leaders (see nos 7 and 14 above). Often the advice is accompanied by reminiscence and comparison with the days of Nestor's youth and is contrasted with current practice. For the most part this is a literary device. His advice often deals with tactics. Here he is arranging his own forces and often his tactics present problems. His dispositions divide the infantry and chariotry into two operational groups that have little parallel with the way they actually function in the rest of the poem, though they do make tactical sense. By ordering the chariots to act as a group in the van, he seems to imply that they will charge ahead of the infantry. Evidence for this independent use of infantry and chariots exists, but does not correspond to the normal methods of employing these troops in the rest of the poem. The massing of cowards in the middle of the infantry force is distinctly odd. The remark by Nestor that such dispositions are old-fashioned may point to their being based on a vague reminiscence of Near Eastern, perhaps Hittite practice, that may have been familiar to Mycenaean Greeks active in Asia Minor.

Then he [Agamemnon] came upon Nestor, that lucid speaker of Pylus, arranging his companions, great Pelagon and those with him, Alastor and Chromion and great Haimon and Baias, the shepherd of the people, and urging them to battle. First he placed the chariots with their horses, he then stationed the foot soldiers behind them, many and warlike, as a shield for battle. He then arranged the cowards in the middle so that even if they were unwilling they had to fight. First he gave orders to the horsemen to hold their horses in check and not to be entangled by the crowd: "Let no man relying on his horsemanship and courage in front of the line fight alone with the Trojans, nor let him give ground, for in that way you will be weaker. When a man from his own chariot encounters the enemy, let him stab with his spear since that way he will be more effective. So in olden times our ancestors sacked cities and fortifications with this spirit and purpose in their hearts."

20. *Iliad* 5.9–26

This is an example of the more detailed narrative of individual duels that are the most striking aspect of war in the poems. It is part of the Greek hero Diomedes' series of exploits in book 5. Series of successive successful combats are assigned to various prominent Homeric heroes such as Achilles and Agamemnon. The episode is built up from a number of repetitive motifs that are used to construct such encounters. The use of divine rescue is also repeated elsewhere. The problem that remains central to assessing Homeric warfare is the relation between these episodes and the general course of the battle. In the course of the poem it appears to be a single hero who determines the course of action. The safety of Troy is repeatedly said to depend on Hector's survival and abilities. It seems more than mere hyperbole.

There was a certain man among the Trojans, Dares, wealthy and good-hearted, a priest of Hephaestus. He had two sons, Phegeus and Idaeus, who were skilled in all manner of fighting. Separating themselves from the ranks they charged Diomedes in their chariot. He came on foot. Now they were close and advancing against each other. Phegeus cast his long spear first. The point of the spear flew over the left shoulder of Diomedes and missed him. Next the son of Tydeus threw and did not miss his mark, but struck the man's chest between the nipples and so Phegeus was hurled backwards from his team. Idaeus broke off the combat and, leaving the beautiful chariot, he did not dare to stand over his stricken brother. Even so he would not have escaped black death had not Hephaestus protected him, and saved him, covering him in dark night so that the old man, their father, would not be totally bereft. The great-hearted son of Tydeus, Diomedes, drove off their horses and entrusted them to his companions to take back to the hollow ships.

A later parallel to the use of the chariot in the Iliad

21. Aeneas Tacticus, 16.14–15

Cyrene and Barca are both in north Africa, in or bordering Libyan territory which was known in antiquity as good horse country. The Cyreneans employed vehicles in this way through the late fourth century. The parallel is not exact since wagons are also used. Though the troops dismount to fight like Homeric heroes, the vehicles are clearly only for transport and the fighting takes place in the massed and closed ranks characteristic of hoplite warfare. In essence these are mounted infantry. Aeneas was a mid-fourth-century writer of military treatises who probably had served as a commander of the Arcadian League's forces.

The inhabitants of Cyrene, Barca and some other states are said to bring long distance aid on wagon roads using two-horse chariots and wagons. After they arrive at the agreed upon place they first arrange the vehicles in order, and then the hoplites dismount and form up. Since they are fresh they attack the enemy immediately. States that have an abundance of transport enjoy this important advantage that they can move their troops to where they are needed and have them arrive unfatigued. The wagons can also be used as a defensive barrier for their camp and if there are wounded or they suffer some other misfortune they can be transported back to the city.

THE RESULTS OF WAR

One of the crucial means of obtaining goods, including slaves, was through warfare. It is frequently resorted to in the Homeric poems and probably employed throughout the Dark Ages as a communal activity and one which allowed a great deal of entrepreneurial activity to take place. The usual procedure on capturing a city was to exterminate the male population, enslave the women and children and then collect and carry off the moveable goods. This booty was then distributed according to rank and prowess. Such distributions played an important role as the amount given was a token of social standing. Further the successful completion of the enterprise created additional links through the distribution of booty between the leader and his men. The last passage given here is one of the most evocative in all Homer of the emotions that accompanied the fall of one's city.

22. *Odyssey* 9.39–42
Odysseus has just begun telling his audience on Phaeacia about his real identity and about his return from Troy. The treatment of the captured city has parallels elsewhere in the world of the poems. He gives much the same tale to his swineherd Eumaeus while concealing his identity by pretending to be a Cretan adventurer. The Cicones appear in the *Iliad* as allies of the Trojans and later sources place them in Thrace in the northern Aegean.

"From Troy the wind bore me to Ismarus on the shores of the Cicones. There I sacked the city and slaughtered the men; we collected the women and booty from the city and distributed them so that no one would be cheated of an equal share."

23. *Iliad* 1.121–129
This is the same problem dealt with in nos 5 and 7 above, concerning the handing over of Briseis to Agamemnon in compensation for his loss of a slave woman. The passages show the interplay of status and purely economic considerations.

Achilles in offering a three- or four-fold return draws clear attention to the second aspect. The passage also shows that there apparently was no central reserve of booty maintained. This also seems to be the case in the previous passage.

Then swift-footed godlike Achilles answered Agamemnon: "Oh son of Atreus most glorious, greediest of men, how shall the great-hearted Achaeans give a prize now? I do not know of any great common store lying about. What we took from the cities by storm has been distributed. It is not fitting for people to call back things already given. Return the girl to the god for now. But we Achaeans will repay you three- or four-fold if ever Zeus allows us to sack well-walled Troy."

24. *Iliad* 6.447–461
Hector's words to his wife Andromache are among the most striking in the poem and sum up poignantly not only the fate of the conquered city and its inhabitants, but also the crucial role that shame and honor play in the value system of the poem and its world.

"I know in my mind and heart that there will come a day when sacred Troy and Priam and the people of Priam of the strong ash spear will perish. But it is not so much the pain of the Trojans nor of my mother Hecuba nor of Priam himself that grieves me nor the thought of my brothers, though they be many and valiant and shall drop in the dust at the hands of those who hate them, as much as the thought of you, when you shall be led away in tears by some bronze corseleted Achaean who has deprived you of the day of freedom. Then you will work before the loom of another and carry water from the spring Messeis or Hypereia against your will under the bonds of strong necessity and some day someone seeing you crying will say, 'This was the wife of Hector, who was the best of the fighters among the horse-taming Trojans in the days when they fought about Troy.'"

THE DARK AGES

The period after 1200 BC saw vast changes in every aspect of life on the Greek mainland and islands. The great palace complexes of the late Bronze Age were destroyed or abandoned. With their disappearance went many of the skills, among them writing, that had been integral parts of their functioning. There appears to have been a general decline in technical skills. This was accompanied by a drastic fall in population and the abandonment of many previously occupied sites or the reoccupation of pre-existing sites but at much lower level of population. In addition, there seems to have been a process of fragmentation and loss of communication between various areas of the mainland. This is best evidenced by the contrast between the uniformity of pottery styles in the Mycenaean period and the proliferation of regional styles in the following period. Overseas contacts also were reduced to a minimum and at times appear to have been non-existent. Starting in the early eleventh century it was also a period of movement and turmoil. Large-scale immigration took place to the western coast of Asia Minor and some of the islands lying off that coast. These movements do not appear to have ended until the early ninth century, when again a measure of stability returned to the Greek mainland.

The world of the Dark Ages is obscured by our lack of source material. We have to depend heavily on archaeological evidence as a crucial aid to reconstruct a picture of the society of the period, including its military aspects. It is only towards the end of the period, that is from about 800 on, that human and animal figures reappear on pottery and provide an additional source of evidence. Scenes involving warfare are confined to an even narrower chronological period and spatial distribution. They are dated in the last half of the eighth century and come primarily from Athens.

Our literary sources also possess severe limitations. There are scattered references in later writers, often overlaid with a mythological gloss, which can only be used with great care. The basic source, especially for warfare, remains Homer, though as discussed earlier, caution must be used in evaluating the evidence contained in the poem. For the end of the period the Boeotian poet Hesiod provides further information from a totally different perspective from Homer, that of the small farmer.

The period of the late Dark Ages was hardly static; there is evidence for much development, yet the details of that development are now lost to view. There were innovations in pottery and burial customs, but of crucial importance for warfare is the introduction of iron in place of bronze as the major material for weapons. After a period of transition, in the late twelfth and eleventh century a few objects made of iron appear, but by about 1000 BC a complete shift to iron as the medium for tools and weapons was completed. The sword appears to be the first weapon made of iron; by the end of the century spears and other weapons were also being made from that material.

A further important change in weaponry is signaled at about 900 BC by evidence for the growing importance of missile warfare. Between 900 and 700 BC a normal warrior burial included two or three spears, indicating that missile warfare had become dominant. This development has no parallels in the preceding two centuries. The evidence of late Geometric pottery seems to support the importance of missile warfare for at least a part of the fighting. The chariot survived the Dark Ages and again appears on painted pottery made around 800. The same uncertainty exists about its use in the extant artistic representations from this period as in the case of the Homeric poems and Bronze Age depictions. Certainly the status value of the horse for Greek aristocrats around and after 900 BC is not in doubt. A magnificent burial discovered at Lefkandi in Euboea from that date contains four horses buried with their master as tokens of his prestige.

Aside from this magnificent burial and later burials in Cyprus the picture painted by the archaeological evidence is of poor small settled communities. If the evidence of the Homeric poems is accepted as applying to this period these settlements were headed by a class of aristocrats who dominated all major aspects of community life. Their power rested on birth and on their economic resources.

They depended, like the rest of their communities, on a basic social and economic unit: the *oikos*. This is best visualized as a household and not merely a family. It might contain several generations of family members as well as slaves and retainers. The latter were men who for various reasons attached themselves to a family unit other than their own. The *oikos* was also the basic unit of production in what was a completely rural economy. Though cereal and other crops were grown, there seems have been a stress on animal husbandry; wealth was counted in livestock. It was economically a largely self-sufficient unit. Commodities that were not immediately accessible to it were obtained, at least at the higher social levels, by a system of gift-exchange which hinged on the notion of reciprocity and also served the purpose of establishing and cementing social bonds. The other great mechanisms of acquisition were raiding and warfare which seem to have been constant activities in the Dark Ages.

Given the limited resources of the period, warfare must have been on a limited scale and have consisted mostly of the raiding of livestock and the pursuit of other booty under the leadership of aristocratic warriors who used it not only for the acquisition of goods, but also to build up a following to defend and, where possible, enhance their power.

The scale and style of fighting

The evident poverty and isolation of Greek communities until the middle of the eighth century makes the type of warfare depicted in the following selections probably typical of the period. The discussion by the fifth-century historian Thucydides correctly registers the local and desultory nature of warfare in this period. The limitations imposed by economic and social structures restricted the types of military cooperation possible and the objectives obtainable. The only apparent exception to this rule comes at the very end of the period, in the war between the cities of Chalchis and Eretria in Euboea for the possession of the fertile Lelantine Plain on which they both bordered. But the war's date and nature are obscure. Scattered references can be used to show a widespread net of allies on both sides, but it appears less a matter of two large coalitions in armed conflict than a series of limited border wars with their epicenter in the Lelantine Plain.

25. Thucydides, 1.15.2

This section of the fifth-century historian's work comes from those chapters detailing the early development of Greece down to the beginning of the Peloponnesian War in 431 and is designed to show that it was the greatest conflict engaged in by the Greeks. His proof is based on the contention that no units of any size or power emerged on land until the Spartans did so during the Persian War, and that up to that point Greek states were weak and isolated.

There was no war on land that led to the development of any considerable power. All wars were fought against neighboring peoples and the Greeks mounted no foreign expeditions with the aim of subduing others. The smaller communities did not ally with the most powerful nor did these less powerful states join on an equal basis to make expeditions in common. Rather warfare was waged between neighbors.

26. *Iliad* 11.670–684

This narrative of an incident from the Pylian king Nestor's youth is meant to contrast Achilles' sulking inactivity with Nestor's energetic action as a young warrior. The small-scale cattle raiding, reprisals and limited expeditions probably did characterize warfare for most of this period. The impression is strengthened because this initial raid of reprisal only caused a counter-raid to which Nestor responds by another expedition. The last in the series ends the sequence by so weakening the Eleans that they could not carry out any further actions. The acquisition of goods was central and the community, not just the king, played a central role in distributing that wealth. (Neleus was Nestor's father.)

"If only I were young and my vigor undiminished, as once when we had a quarrel with the Eleans over cattle-rustling. It was then that I killed Itymoneus, the noble son of Hypeirochus who dwelt in Elis, as I was driving off cattle in reprisal. As he was defending the cattle among the foremost, he was struck by my spear and fell. His herdsmen were in panic about him. We drove off a great deal of booty, fifty herds each of oxen, swine and goats. We took as many flocks of sheep. We also made off with one hundred and fifty bays, all female along with many of their colts. We drove them at night into Pylos, Neleus' land, into the fortress during the night. Neleus was pleased that I had gotten so much spoil though a youth. At dawn the heralds called loudly for all to appear who had a claim on rich Elis. At the assembly the leading men of Pylos apportioned the spoil. There were many claims against the Epeians as we in Pylos were few and so had been often wronged."

Dark Age weapons

These passages illustrate the use of the javelin in warfare. Such weapons become common in graves between 900 and 700 BC and indicate that the type of warfare illustrated here belongs to the last phase of the Dark Ages. The passage in which Thoas the Aetolian appears (no. 28), in particular, is an illustration of the type of warfare that appears on Attic painted pottery from *c.* 750 to *c.* 725. Though artistic conventions are often hard to interpret, a plausible style of fighting has been reconstructed in which we have what appears to be an initial phase of massed long-range fighting with the casting of spears; after this first phase the units broke up into smaller groups and engaged in close combat with swords. The basic difference between the vases and the Homeric poems is that the vases frequently show the use of archery and so imply that it possessed an importance that is absent from Homer. Archaeology supports the poems, as arrowheads are rare among the finds from the Greek mainland in this period.

27. *Odyssey* 9.47–61

This passage is part of the same speech by Odysseus cited above (no.22). The one anachronistic feature is the use of bronze for spearheads. By 900 iron had replaced bronze.

"Meanwhile, the Cicones summoned other Cicones who were their neighbors and who lived inland and were greater in numbers and better men. They knew how to fight men from horses and also on foot. They came then like leaves or flowers in season in the early morning. Then our luck from Zeus was bad and in our misfortune we suffered many evil pains. Both sides stood and fought the battle by the swift ships and they cast their bronze-headed spears at each other. As long as it was early and the sacred daylight increased, we stood our ground holding off the superior force. But when the sun had gone down to the time for the unyoking of cattle, then the Cicones began to rout us. From each ship we lost six of my strong-greaved companions, but the others escaped death and destruction."

28. *Iliad* 4.527–531

The sequence of the action in this passage closely mirrors the two phases of battle that appear on late Geometric vases. In this case the slashing of the stomach is in revenge for Peirus' own disemboweling of a comrade of Thoas' immediately before this encounter.

Then Thoas, the Aetolian, threw his spear at Peirus as he was retiring and struck him in the chest over the nipple. The bronze point stuck in his lung. Thoas came to close quarters and wrenched the heavy spear from his victim's chest. Drawing his sharp sword, he killed him with a thrust to the center of his belly. Then Peirus' breath left him in death.

Prevalence of piracy

Piracy has until recent times been endemic in the Mediterranean area. It has been a way of obtaining scarce resources and of building up a following. It is particularly prominent in the *Odyssey*. The *Odyssey* makes an explicit contrast between it and trade. While piracy is acceptable for an aristocrat, trade is seen as demeaning and carried on for the most part by non-Greeks. This would be typical before the spread of Greek trade in the course of the late eighth century. Later Greek writers noticed this feature of the world of the poems.

29. *Odyssey* 3.71–74

"Strangers, who are you? From where do you come sailing over the watery ways? Is it on some specific business, or without a determined destination do you wander over the salt sea like pirates, who hazard their lives as they wander bringing evil to foreign peoples?"

30. *Odyssey* 14.229–232

Odysseus is in conversation with his slave Eumaeus, but in disguise as a Cretan fallen on hard times. The passage is notable for its clear indication of piracy as an economic activity and its links to status in Homeric society.

"Before the sons of the Achaeans embarked for Troy, I was nine times a leader and I and my men went in speedy ships against foreigners. I gained much booty of which I took an abundant share for myself, but I also distributed much. My estate grew great, and then I was feared and respected by the Cretans."

The aristocratic attitude towards trade

31. *Odyssey* 8.158–166

The aristocrat's contempt for trade is visible throughout antiquity, though, depending on other factors, certain exceptions might be made because of the scale of the trade or the use of intermediaries. The aristocratic society of the poems makes every effort to disengage itself from contamination with trade. It is noticeable that it is not the gaining of wealth that is at issue but the acquisition of it by trade.

Then Euryalus answered him to his face and spoke, reviling him, "Stranger, I do not think that you are skilled in athletics, such as is the case with many men. But you seem to be like one who plies his trade with a many-locked ship and like a ruler of men who sails to trade. You appear to be one who is ever mindful of his own cargo and what he can get in exchange, with his mind on voracious gain. You certainly don't seem like an athlete." Scowling, wily Odysseus looking at him answered, "Friend you speak witlessly. You seem a fool."

The connection of the horse and the aristocracy

Certainly the chariot and the horse are the prerogative of the aristocrat in the *Iliad*. It seems likely now, especially in view of the burials at Lefkandi and Salamis in Cyprus (750–600), that the chariot survived the Dark Ages. Clearly horse-rearing continued to be an aristocratic activity and its value to the aristocracy for prestige purposes is attested by the prevalence of aristocratic names derived from words connected with the horse. Chariots engaged in warfare do occur on Geometric pottery and may have continued to play some role in actual combat, although they appear most often in ceremonial contexts. In the following selection Aristotle appears to be referring to cavalry and not to chariotry. But the mounted warriors who appear on Greek vases from the late eighth century into the seventh are more likely mounted heavy infantry rather than true cavalry. It may not have been until the sixth century that true cavalry developed. If such mounted aristocrats dominated the political structure of their communities there is little evidence besides the following passages in Aristotle and the burials. But the equation of horse-rearing and aristocratic status makes it likely. Certainly in some outlying areas such as Thessaly this remained true into much later phases of Greek history.

32. Aristotle, *Politics* 1289b27 and 1297b12

a. Among the rich there are differences according to wealth and the size of property such as in the raising of horses (for this activity is not easy for those who are not wealthy). It was for this reason that in many cities whose power consisted in cavalry, oligarchies were in control. The oligarchies used horses in war against their neighbors such as in the war between the Chalcidians and the Eretrians and the Magnesians (who live on the Maeander) and many other peoples in Asia.

Aristotle shares the traditional Greek view of a transition from monarchy in this early period. The same conception of early historical development is found in Thucydides with slight modifications. The transition was not universal, if indeed it really occurred, and perhaps the best-known exception is Sparta with its two kings.

b. The first political régime after the fall of the monarchies was composed of warriors and these originally came from cavalry, for strength and superiority in warfare belonged to the cavalry, since without order heavy infantry is useless. In early times there was neither sound empirical practice in warfare nor rules for it, and as a result mastery on the battlefield rested with the cavalry. When the cities increased in population and the number of citizens with arms became larger, they took a share in the governing process.

2

THE AGE OF HOPLITE WARFARE

INTRODUCTION

By the mid-eighth century BC there is archaeological evidence for a series of crucial political, economic and social changes in the Greek world. A surge in population accompanied a change from pasturage to cereal production as the dominant mode of food production. Overseas trade revived and with it foreign cultural elements and techniques were introduced into Greece. In the political sphere, monarchy disappeared to be replaced by aristocratic rule and finally by the development of a new form of community: the city-state. This last can best be described as an urban conglomeration centered on a defensible citadel which became its religious and political center and on an open space which developed into an agora. This was at first a public meeting place but later acquired some of the characteristics of a marketplace as well. These centers were rather small concentrations that had a dependent series of villages attached to them. This phenomenon was accompanied by the political change mentioned above that culminated in aristocratic government. This period from about 750 is one of the most remarkable in Greek history. It is extraordinary precisely for the Greek willingness to experiment that is visible in almost all areas of Greek life.

It is in the context of these momentous changes that a new style of warfare developed which was to be the determining factor in land warfare in Greece until the defeat of the Greek city-state before the arms of Macedonia at Chaeronea in 338. It was of course to undergo permutation and change in the course of the next three centuries, but for all the changes, it was to prove remarkably resilient in form and successful in practice.

This mode of warfare was based a group of heavily armed infantrymen organized in a phalanx formation. The phalanx can be defined as a body of heavy infantry drawn up in close rectangular formation at least several ranks deep. This usage of the term is found as early as Homer, but its later usage to denote a massed military formation became common only in the Macedonian period.

The heavily armed infantryman himself is called a hoplite, from the name of his shield (*hoplon*). His equipment followed a fairly standardized pattern.

25

Defensive armor consisted of a metal helmet which was to evolve in various patterns but the earliest and most widespread of which was the Corinthian helmet. From the available archaeological evidence it seems to have been developed around 700 and was a remarkable technical achievement since it was fabricated from a single sheet of bronze. It placed a premium on protection, fitting the whole head from the collar bone upwards. The cheek pieces swept forward, leaving only a T-shaped opening since the helmet had a nasal protector. The stress on protection impaired both hearing and vision; other forms of helmets were soon developed to remedy this deficiency. In addition to the helmet, the hoplite wore a bronze bell-shaped plate corselet composed of two sections, a breastplate and a back plate. Despite inconveniences, it endured for two centuries until lighter varieties were adopted just before the Persian Wars at the beginning of the fifth century. Greaves to protect shins and calves appeared about 675. Further there were sundry protective devices such as armor for ankles, forearms and thighs, but their use tended to be vary greatly among individual hoplites and they were gradually abandoned.

The single most important piece of defensive equipment was the shield, developed about 700. It was a large circular shield between three and four feet in diameter constructed from a wooden core initially covered in leather and rimmed with bronze, though later the entire shield tended to be faced with bronze. It was extremely convex in shape. Its most revolutionary aspect was the method of holding it. The shield had a detachable central armband, the *porpax*, through which the left arm was normally thrust up to the elbow. The left hand then grasped the second element, the *antilabe*, normally a leather thong which ran around the periphery of the shield's rim. This gripping mechanism allowed a firmer and more rigid grip than was possible with a single central handle and it distributed the weight of the shield more evenly between the elbow and the hand, allowing it to be held more securely and for a longer time in front of the body. But it created problems in protecting the right side of the body. This was a new and specifically Greek invention.

The major offensive weapon was the heavy thrusting spear, between six and one half and ten feet (two to three meters) in length. It had a heavy iron head and a butt spike both for supporting the spear in the ground at rest and as a secondary weapon in case the point was broken off. This did in fact tend to happen. As secondary armament, the hoplite carried a short stabbing sword useful for close fighting.

This equipment was subject to later variations but its use was generalized in the hoplite formations of the various Greek states. It is important to realize that this bronze armor was extremely expensive and severely limited the numbers of troops that any state could field since the individual fighter generally was responsible for supplying and paying for his own equipment.

The warfare that this phalanx-form style of fighting replaced has been described in the previous section. That form of warfare had been the preserve of the aristocrat. It was heavily dependent on the contribution of these individuals and their companions. The horse may have played a role, but not as true cavalry. Its main function appears to been as transport for aristocratic warriors to the field of battle. The personal valor and abilities of these aristocratic warriors were crucial even with the support of massed infantry. This is the style of fighting visible in Homer. It was also for the most part an affair of missile weapons with close combat only in the final stages.

The development of the classic phalanx style of warfare has been the subject of much scholarly debate, for it represented a different form of mass warfare from any that had preceded it. It substituted face-to-face combat for missile warfare and ended the predominance of the aristocracy on the battlefield. It was certainly in existence by about 650 BC, or perhaps earlier, based on the evidence of vase painting.

Two basic theoretical approaches have been taken to the explanation of the rise of hoplite warfare. The first and older view is that it is the product of a technical innovation – the introduction of the hoplite shield with its new grip. The nature of this shield led directly to the development of the phalanx as the shield had disadvantages compared with traditional forms outside of such a mutually supportive formation. The other view, now probably held by a majority of scholars, is that the phalanx is the product of a relatively long period of experimentation. The individual items of equipment were adopted initially by aristocrats because they were technically superior as single items. These adoptions predated the formation of the phalanx. The change in tactics came later in this model. The second view is inherently less plausible. One would expect those with resources and a fighting tradition to be the first to respond to military innovation. The archaeological evidence points in the same direction. But the crucial problem is still the shield. Though arguments can and have been made for its use by individuals, it is clearly less functional when used by an isolated warrior than the shield types it replaced. The most plausible reconstruction is that the hoplite shield was adopted at the same time as the phalanx. One was dependent upon the other. In the same way the Corinthian helmet with its limited field of vision also seems geared specifically for use in a phalanx rather than by independent warriors. The final model of fighting that emerged with the particular armored protection and offensive weapons of the phalanx was no doubt subject to development, and it must have taken some time before the form which was to persist for three centuries finally evolved. Even under the conditions of earlier aristocratic warfare there seem to have been infantry acting in formation.

The impetus for this form of warfare, which was to involve a larger section of the community than earlier forms, most probably stemmed from the aristocrats themselves. The formation depends upon mass for its effect and so it was natural to try to include all those who could afford the necessary equipment in the phalanx. This, except in the rather special case of Sparta, probably never included more than half of a state's adult male population. But it was an ideal formation for the protection of crops and farmland, that is the city's territory, in an era of expanding population. This use must have been a potent factor is persuading prosperous peasant farmers to undertake the expense and join in battle. It is hoplite warfare's military value in a specific context that explains its speedy and widespread adoption. It is important to remember, though, that there always remained areas like Thessaly and Aetolia that were not strongly affected by this innovation.

The spread of hoplite warfare has also been linked to the development of the city-state and to the end of the aristocratic predominance in the affected communities. There exists no necessary connection to the city-state, which could have equally well produced other forms of warfare. But there is a stronger case for a tie among the following phenomena: the introduction of the phalanx, the end of aristocratic predominance and the rise of tyrannies in various Greek states at about the same time. The evidence is not conclusive and depends very much on questions of mass psychology and class consciousness. But the possibility exists not least because of the chronological proximity of new political developments to this military change. Certainly new concepts of military virtue and new conceptual stresses in older views of the warrior did accompany the introduction of hoplite warfare.

Some literary evidence for the introduction of hoplite warfare

33. Tyrtaeus, Fragment 11 West

The biographical details of this poet are sketchy at best. He appears to have been a Spartan and to have been writing in connection with the outbreak of the Second Messenian War, which probably took place in the last third of the seventh century. Though the phalanx is attested by earlier archaeological evidence, his is the first sure literary testimony to it. It is important to note the stress on the necessity for holding formation, which is a characteristic of the phalanx formation. The poet exhorts the soldiers to attack either with spear or sword. This may be some evidence that the reliance of the phalanx on the heavy thrusting spear was not yet fixed. Some early vase paintings show hoplites with two spears, one obviously for throwing. It is probable that though the formation became fixed early, there was prior experimentation with various offensive weapons.

For those who, standing shoulder to shoulder, dare to come to close quarters and to fight among the foremost, fewer die and they preserve those behind them. All of the courage of cowards is dissipated. No one could make an end in telling each of the evils that befall a man if he learns cowardliness. For it is attractive to pierce from behind the back of a fleeing man in hard war. But shameful is the corpse lying in the dust with a spear point in his back. But with feet set well apart, firmly planted on the ground, endure biting your lip and covering thighs and legs below and chest and shoulders above in the hollow of your broad shield. Let each shake the mighty spear in his right hand and the frightening crest upon his head. Let each learn by practice to do the mighty deeds of war and not stand outside the range of the missiles with shield in hand. Rather everyone

28

should close up to his man with his great spear or sword and wound and kill his enemy. Standing leg to leg, resting shield against shield, crest beside crest, and helmet to helmet having drawn near, let him fight his man with his sword or great spear. And you, O light-armed fighters, crouching behind the shields on either side, hurl your great boulders.

The name of the hoplite

The Greek term for this type of heavy armed infantryman is *hoplites*, which is derived from the word *hoplon*. Though this word is used in both the singular and plural to signify armor and weapons, it is also occasionally used, as in the following passage, of the great shield which the hoplite bore, and this seems to be its basic meaning in this context. This derivation is further evidence for the connection of this shield to fighting in phalanx formation and so to the link between the equipment and the formation. The following passage deals with the reforms of the Athenian general Iphicrates in 374/373 BC. For the *pelta* see nos 65 and 66.

34. Diodorus Siculus, 15.44.3

Those who had previously been called hoplites, from the shield they carried, had their name changed to peltasts from the name of their new shield, the *pelta*.

The equipment of the hoplite

The shield

The importance of the hoplite shield has been stressed. What comes out clearly in these passages is the collective nature of hoplite warfare and the important place of the shield in it. This is particularly evident in the passage from Andocides, where the throwing away of the shield carries with it severe civil penalties, and in the saying of Demaratus. The hoplite shield was crucial to the success of phalanx tactics and these passages illustrate the close mutual dependence that its use required.

35. Plutarch, *Moralia* 220A, "Sayings of the Spartans"
Demaratus, one of the two Spartan kings, reigned from *c.* 510 to 491 BC. He was exiled and spent his remaining years at the Persian court. He appears frequently in the narrative of Herodotus, giving advice to Persians about Greek behavior.

When someone asked Demaratus why the Spartans disgrace those who throw away their shields but not those who abandon their breastplates or helmets, he said that they put the latter on for their own sakes but the shield for the sake of the whole line.

36. Andocides, *On The Mysteries* 74

This selection is from a speech given in self-defense at Athens in 400 BC. Probably by 405 the throwing away of one's shield had become a legal offense, as this speaker testifies.

A second kind of disenfranchisement was that for life, in which an individual retained the property he possessed. Men who fell under this penalty were those who left the line of battle or who avoided military service or were guilty of cowardice or who, being in charge of a warship, did not bring it into battle, or threw away their shield, or who bore false witness three times or who three times acted as a false witness to a summons or who mistreated their parents. All of these were disenfranchised though they retained their property.

The spear

This is the main offensive weapon of the classical phalanx. But it is clear that it had its limitations. In the tremendous onrush of opposing formations it was often shattered. Numerous holes in extant pieces of armor dedicated at Olympia and elsewhere show that it could be effective in piercing the corselet. It appears that the spear was thrust overhand with the main targets being the unprotected neck and genitals of the opponent. The sword was a secondary weapon that was used if the spear was unserviceable.

37. Diodorus Siculus, 15.86.2

The following incident is dated by Diodorus to the second battle of Mantinea in Arcadia in 362 BC.

And at first the Spartans and Boeotians struck at one another with their spears. But because of the frequency of the blows, the majority of the spears shattered and they then engaged each other with swords.

The cost of hoplite equipment

We have few indications of what the armor actually cost, but it is clear that it was expensive and so beyond the reach of the majority of the citizen population in most states. The following inscription and the passage in Aristophanes are our only sources on the cost of this equipment. Aristophanes' figure is for Athens in the late fifth century. Since the reference occurs in a comic poet, caution should be used about its accuracy.

38. Athenian Decree Concerning Samos, GHI² no. 14, ll. 9–10

This is the earliest Athenian decree extant. It probably dates from the late sixth century BC. It is a series of regulations for an Athenian citizen colony (cleruchy) on the island of Samos. The value of the arms specified is uncertain, because it is not known what equipment is here being required. As is almost universally the case, the citizen is responsible for providing his own equipment. The sum is a substantial one. A laborer would earn between a drachma and a drachma and a half per day in the late fifth century.

Each [colonist] is to provide arms himself to the value of thirty drachmae. When they are under arms, the archon shall pass the arms in review.

39. Aristophanes, *The Peace* 1224–1225 and 1250–1252
The comedy was produced in 422/421 BC.

Arms Seller: What use will I, in my wretched state, make of my 1000 drachma corselet wonderfully joined? . . . O hard-to-satisfy wretch, how you ruin me! What will we do now? Who will buy these helmets for which I paid a hundred drachmas?

Who were the hoplites?

40. Pseudo-Xenophon, *The Constitution of the Athenians* 2
The date of this treatise by a strongly oligarchical writer has been much debated. A date in the late 440s is most likely. What this passage as well as the following ones from Aristotle (*c.* 330) make clear is that the hoplite class was from the beginning composed of property owners. They were the farmers who had the means to provide their own equipment and formed, in Aristotle's conception of the correct constitution, a sort of middling class, though they are not at all a middle class in our sense of the term. This class obviously had a variegated composition and ranged from substantial property owners to those who were right on the margin necessary for bearing the expense of providing their own equipment. This always remained the situation except in special circumstances such as those at Sparta where the hoplite class was equivalent to the full citizen body. The ethical terms in the following passage are descriptive of economic class rather than moral worth.

First I can say this, that the poor and the people in general at Athens rightly have more than the well-born and the wealthy because they are the ones who man the ships and who make the city powerful: the steersmen, the boatswains and sub-boatswains, the look-out officers and the shipwrights – these are the ones who give strength to the city much more than the hoplites or the well-born or the good men.

41. Aristotle, *Politics* 1297b16–28
There is some dispute about the historical information contained in this passage, on the grounds that Aristotle would not have had evidence for the chronological relationship between the changes in political structure and warfare. But there is no reason to assume that the general scheme that he presents could not have been known without a detailed account being available. See no. 32.

The first political régime after the fall of the monarchies was composed of warriors and originally drawn from cavalry, for strength and superiority in warfare belonged to the cavalry. Without order heavy infantry is useless. In early times there was neither sound empirical practice in these matters nor rules for it, with the result that mastery on the battlefield rested with the cavalry. When the cities increased in population and the number with arms became larger, then they took a share in the governing process. For this reason the constitutions we now call polities the ancients called democracies, for the ancient constitutions were strictly oligarchies and kingships. For the middling class were few in number due to the smallness of the population, and consequently before this there was a small middling class, and given the form of contemporary military organization, the people more easily tolerated being commanded.

42. Aristotle, *Politics* 1279a37–b4

The passage is based on the notion of distributive justice common to Greek thinkers that insists that rights be accorded in proportion to the contribution the individual makes to the welfare of the state. Also inherent in this description is Aristotle's notion that such a class represents a mean which is the basis of goodness itself. The middling class is free from the excesses of the other groups that constitute the state.

Whenever the mass governs the city with a view to the general good, the name given to such a constitution is the name common to all types of constitutions – polity. There is good reason for this usage, for one man or a small number may excel in virtue, but it is difficult to expect perfection in all virtues, especially in that which pertains to war. That arises among the multitude. For this reason sovereignty rests in this constitution with those who are able to fight, and those who participate in it are those who bear arms (hoplites).

43. Thucydides, 2.13.6–7

The numbers in this passage have given rise to much discussion and emendation. But they provide us with some sense of the proportion of hoplites to the total Athenian population in 431 BC in a period when population in Attica was at a maximum. Athenians were liable for normal military service from the age of 18 to 60. It is generally assumed that the "oldest" and "youngest" mentioned by Thucydides correspond to men aged 18 to 19 and 50 to 60, and those who were unfit for normal service ought to be added to the age classes enumerated. The active field army was comprised of men aged 20 to 50. Metics are resident aliens who are not Athenian citizens, but still liable to taxes as well as military service and other duties. On the best estimates in 431, the adult male population of an age to serve numbered about 40,000. Out of a total metic population of approximately 28,000, 5500 were eligible for hoplite service out of a total of 9500 men of military age. This is quite a high proportion of hoplites.

It must be remembered that Athens had additional resources from her empire in 431 which enabled individuals to gain hoplite status, although they normally would have been unable to do so. For Boeotia, the percentage of hoplites to citizens is about one third of the available males, and this in an exceptionally prosperous agricultural area.

Pericles reassured them about their financial position. As for the army there were thirteen thousand hoplites not counting those in the garrisons and those defending the city. This was the number that was originally on guard in case of enemy attack, composed of the youngest and oldest citizen groups as well as those metics who possessed a hoplite rating. These in total amounted to sixteen thousand.

Sparta: an exceptional case

Sparta was the one state in which the army could truly to be said to be equivalent to the citizen body. A peculiar economic system based on the labor of an unfree class of agricultural dependents liberated the full Spartan from any economic concerns and allowed him to devote his full attention to the responsibilities of citizenship, the most important part of which was military service. After about 600 BC Sparta developed a complex educational system called the *agoge* designed to inculcate qualities necessary for military service. This system gave the Spartans the preeminent land army in Greece until their defeat by the Thebans at Leuctra in 371. Their peculiar system of education and social organization made them, in effect, the only large-scale body of professional soldiers in Greece until the fourth century.

44. Plato, *Laws* 666E
The term used can be translated as herds, but, in fact, the youths undergoing the *agoge* were divided by age into paramilitary units and the herd is best understood as the largest of these groups, equivalent to a regiment in a military formation. A Spartan is being addressed by an Athenian.

"I am hardly surprised at that. In fact, you have never attained the noblest type of song. Your cities are organized like armies, not like societies of town dwellers. You keep your youth in herds like so many colts at grass in one troop."

45. Plutarch, *Life of Lycurgus* 16.6

They [the Spartans] only learn as much of reading as is necessary. The goal of their education is to create ready obedience, hardiness in endurance and victory in battle.

46. Simonides 92D
Simonides (556–476) from the island of Ceos wrote in a number of poetic genres but is particularly known for his epitaphs. This, probably the most famous, is that of the three hundred Spartans who fell at the battle of Thermopylae in 480 BC. It gives an excellent summary of the Spartan ideal of military conduct.

Friend, go tell the Spartans that here we lie obedient to their orders.

The hoplite military ethic

The ethic of hoplite warfare is closely tied to the concept of citizenship. In essence, the warrior is equivalent to the citizen serving as a soldier. All citizens are liable to military service of some kind. The clearest example and logical end of this is represented by Sparta and at Athens by service as an ephebe (see nos 49 and 55). There was an identification made between citizenship and hoplite status. The hoplite's position is dependent on his being a landed proprietor and a head of a family. In such a context, service as a soldier then represents the fulfillment of the obligations of a citizen to his country and its gods. In this sense it is a privilege belonging only to the citizenry. The infrequent and exceptional enrollment of slaves in wartime is further evidence of this tie between citizen status and military service.

These concepts are reinforced by the idea, clear in the writings of Tyrtaeus, of the equality and dependence of the members of the hoplite phalanx. The stress, as opposed to the Homeric ethic, is not so much on personal excellence in war as on rendering unstinting service and on the importance of self-sacrifice for the sake of the common good. The funeral oration of Pericles in Thucydides as well as the other passages make this abundantly clear.

This idea of pooled or common effort is reflected in the constant stress on remaining at one's post for the common good. It is supported by military considerations insofar as such behavior is crucial to the success of the phalanx. The expression of this practical need is an ideology that subordinates individual glory to the common good. Rather what has happened is that the Homeric notion of individual prowess is subsumed and utilized in the hoplite style of warfare. Individual courage and success matter as profoundly as they did in the world of Homer, but now they are displayed as part of a common effort. This is evident in the continued giving of prizes for valor in war.

47. Tyrtaeus, Fragment 10 West

It is a noble thing for a brave man to fall fighting among the foremost, doing battle for his fatherland. . . . So let us fight for our land and let us die for our children without sparing ourselves. Young men, fight shoulder to shoulder and do not begin shameful flight or be afraid. Make your heart great and brave. Do not restrain yourselves in fighting the enemy or flee and abandon those from whom age has stolen agility. It is a disgrace for an old man to fall fighting in the van and lie there in front of the young men, his hair white and his beard gray, breathing out his brave soul in the dust and holding his bloody genitals in his hands. He is a shameful sight and his naked flesh a cause for indignation. This is suitable for the young man while he has the bloom of youth. He is a thing of admiration to men and desirable to women as long as he lives and he is fair when he falls as well. So let each stand his ground firmly with his feet well set apart and bite his lip.

48. Thucydides, 2.42.2–43.1

This is a section of a speech given in the winter of 431/430 by the Athenian statesman Pericles over those who had fallen in the first year of the Peloponnesian War.

"It seems to me that the death of these men has provided both a reminder and a final proof of manly courage. Even if they had their faults, we ought to give preference to the courage they displayed fighting on behalf of their native land. For they have blotted out what evil they have done by the good they have achieved, and they have done greater service to their country then any harm they might have done as private individuals. None of these men weakened by the prospect of the enjoyment of their wealth or by the hope that they might escape their poverty and become rich tried to put off their day of reckoning. They held vengeance upon the enemy as more desirable than those things. They considered it most glorious to undergo danger and to strike at the enemy while relinquishing all else. Success in battle they left in the hands of hope; they trusted in themselves in the face of battle. They considered that it was better to fight and suffer death than to save themselves by flight. So they fled a shameful reputation and endured the physical danger, and in a brief moment of time they were taken away from what was the height of their glory rather than their fear. So were these men worthy of their city. Those who remain should hope to escape their fate but must hold to the same brave spirit towards the enemy."

49. Oath of the Athenian Ephebes, GHI II no. 204

This inscription is from the second half of the fourth century. Athenian citizens from the mid-330s on served as ephebes for a two-year period from the age of 18 to 20. They were given military and civic training in their first year of service. They served during this first year as well on guard duty at the port of Athens. In their second year, they received the shield and spear of a hoplite at state expense, and then served on garrison duty on the Athenian frontiers. After this period they rejoined the regular citizen body. It is possible that the poorest Athenian citizens were not obliged to serve in this way. Some form of this institution existed at Athens much earlier, but evidence is scanty. This institution is an excellent example of the direct connection between citizenship and military service. The following oath illustrates the importance of group cohesion and the idea of military service as service to the state.

Gods. The priest of Ares and Athena Areia, Dion, son of Dion, set up this dedication.
    The ancestral oath of the ephebes which the ephebes must swear. I will not shame the sacred arms [I have been given] nor will I desert the man at my side wherever I am positioned in line. I shall defend what is sacred and holy and I will not pass on to my descendants a diminished homeland, but rather one greater and stronger as far as I am able and with the assistance of all. I will offer my ready obedience at any time to those who are exercising their authority prudently, and to the established laws and to those laws which will be·judiciously in force in the future.

Military training

Except for certain institutions like that of the ephebate connected to the transition to adult life and full citizenship, most Greek states gave little or no military training to their citizens. Sparta remained the great exception. This lack of training was made possible by the simplicity of tactics required by the hoplite phalanx. Athens, about which we have the most complete information, apparently required no formal military training for adults, though by the end of the fifth century there existed at Athens and elsewhere professionals who would give private instruction for a fee. In part, this may have been due to the close connections evidenced by many Greek thinkers between practice in athletics, hunting and dancing, and success in fighting. The prevalence of the gymnasium as a feature of Greek civic life must be linked not only with athletics but with the need to condition the body for fighting, a need which faced every Greek citizen of requisite means.

As simple as the tactics required by the phalanx formation were, there still must have been some training in marching and in maneuvering from one type of formation to another. The state must have provided basic training in these matters. Without them even the simple requirements of phalanx warfare could not be met.

50. Xenophon, *Oeconomicus* 4.2–4

The following passage indicates the traditional and close connection between warfare and agriculture. In many Greek states ownership of land was a perquisite not only for full citizenship, but also for its concomitant military service. The rhythm of Greek warfare was adjusted to that of the agricultural year. The virtues of farming as a promoter of the proper characteristics of the warrior became a truism in Greek and later in Roman thought. The arts mentioned are various crafts. Socrates is speaking.

"For the illiberal arts, as they are so-called, are condemned and rightly are disdained in our states. For they ruin the bodies of those who practice them and those who oversee them, since these arts compel men to sit and bind them to a sedentary life, and some among them force their practitioners to sit at a fire all day. The softening of their bodies also involves a pronounced weakening of their spirit. These arts leave little time for leisure and so for taking care of one's friends and city. The result is that such men are reputed poor at helping their friends and weak defenders of their countries. Also in some states, especially in those reputed to excel in warfare, no citizen is permitted to practice any of these arts." "But, Socrates, what sort of arts do you advise me to practice?" "Well," said Socrates, "should we be ashamed to imitate the king of the Persians? For they say that he considers that the noblest and most necessary arts are those of farming and warfare and he practices both most assiduously."

Hunting

51. Xenophon, *Cynegeticus* 12.1–4

Those who eagerly pursue the art of hunting will reap great benefits, for it creates a healthy body and improves sight and hearing. It also slows the aging process. It is especially useful as a preparation for war. First, men who hunt will not tire when they are making difficult marches under arms. They will bear up under such hardships because they are accustomed to the armed capture of wild beasts. Then they will be capable of sleeping in harsh conditions and of capably guarding their assigned position. In their attacks upon the enemy they will be able both to attack him and at the same time to carry out their orders because they do the same things on their own when hunting. Once assigned to their position in the front line they will not leave because they possess endurance. If the enemy flees, they will be able to pursue him correctly and safely in any type of territory because of their experience.

Athletics

52. Xenophon, *Memorabilia* 3.12.1–4

On noticing that one of his companions, although young, was in bad physical condition, Socrates said, "Epigenes, you look as if you are in need of physical training." The young man replied: "I am no athlete but a private citizen, Socrates." Socrates answered, "You need physical training no less than those who compete at Olympia; or does the life and death struggle with their enemies on which the Athenians will enter someday seem of little importance? Further, many men perish amid the dangers of war or are saved in some disgraceful way because of their bad physical condition. Many are captured alive and spend the rest of their lives, if this should happen to them, in harsh slavery for this very reason or falling into the most miserable straits they pay in ransom more than they possess and live the rest of their lives lacking necessities and in misery. Further, many gain an infamous reputation as their portion since they are thought cowards because of their physical weakness. Do you despise the disadvantages of the bad physical condition of such men and think you could easily bear up under such circumstances? I think that the man who takes care of his physical condition experiences an easier and more agreeable condition."

The value of military training

53. Aristotle, *Politics* 1338b24–29

Further we know that the Spartans, as long as they alone persisted in laborious practice, excelled the rest of the Greeks. But now both in gymnastic contests and in warfare they are bettered by others. Yet they were not superior because of the type of training they gave to their youth, but because they alone trained.

54. Plato, *Euthydemus* 271D
The first evidence for professional teachers of weapons training appears in the late fifth century. It is clear that there was some suspicion attached to such instruction at first, but it was later incorporated into ephebic training at Athens. The suspicion in part resulted from the taking of a fee and that practice introduced monetary concerns into an area where the Greeks were uneasy about it. There are parallels in other forms of paid instruction such as in oratorical training.

First, these men are extremely formidable physically and able to defeat anyone in fighting. They are also experts at fighting in armor and can teach that skill to another who will pay their fee.

55. Aristotle, *Constitution of the Athenians* 42.2–5
For the ephebic oath and the date of the institution, see no. 49.

After the ephebes have undergone official scrutiny, their fathers meet by tribes and under oath select three of their tribesmen over the age of forty who are considered to be the best and most suitable to oversee the ephebes. From these men the whole people elect one man from each tribe as *sophronistes* and one *kosmetes* from the rest to be in charge of the whole force. These men assemble the ephebes and first make a tour of the shrines. Then they make their way to the Piraeus and the young men serve as guards there, some at Munychia and some at Acte. They also elect two trainers for them and also instructors in hoplite fighting, archery, javelin throwing and catapult firing. . . . Each *sophronistes* buys provisions for all of his tribal members (for they eat by tribe) and is in charge of everything else. This is the way in which they pass the first year. In the second year a meeting of the assembly takes place in the theater and the ephebes hold a review of their maneuvers for the people and receive a shield and a spear from the city. They then patrol the countryside and spend their time in guard posts. . . . So they are on guard for two years and are free of all obligations. . . . After these two years are past they rejoin the rest of the citizen body.

ARMY ORGANIZATION

Our knowledge of Greek military organization is extremely sketchy. In part this results from the fact that the ancient historians who are our main sources have little interest in it, and references to military organization tend to be offhand and sporadic. It is the more technical writers who provide some help in this matter. But their information covers only a limited period and detailed descriptions are extant only for Athens and Sparta. Unfortunately, even these are incomplete and at times contradictory.

Athens

Service as a hoplite at Athens appears to have been based on the possession of a property rating that then led to entry of the individual's name in a list of all those eligible for service. Such eligibility extended from the age of 18 to 42. Before the latter half of the fourth century, citizens apparently served in turn. After that date selection for a campaign was done by calling up a specific series of age-classes.

The organization of the army appears to have been by tribes and we possess tribal casualty lists that support this view. The tribes were commanded by taxiarchs. The evidence for any unit smaller than the tribe is poor, but such a unit must have existed.

56. Aristophanes, *Knights* 1369–1371
There is some dispute as to whether there was a central register that contained census ratings for those eligible for military service.

"And furthermore, no man enrolled as a hoplite on the register will have his name altered through private influence. But he will remain so inscribed as his name was first entered."

57. Aristotle, *Constitution of the Athenians* 53.7

They use the year-classes also in the case of military service. Whenever they send out an age-group on campaign, they give public notice to those who must serve by specifying from what archon and what year-class to what archon and what year-class is under obligation.

58. Aristotle, *Constitution of the Athenians* 61.3

The [Athenians] elect ten taxiarchs, one from each of the tribes. These men are in command of the tribes and they appoint company commanders.

Sparta

Almost all of our evidence on the organization of the Spartan army dates from the late fifth to the mid-fourth century BC. There is little of it and, as the two passages below indicate, it contains contradictions. However these are resolved, it is clear that the Spartan tactical organization from at least the fifth century on and probably earlier was the most fully articulated of any Greek state, and Xenophon is correct in seeing its advantages. The Sciritae from Sciritis in Arcadia formed a separate unit of six hundred men. They were an élite unit involved in unusually hazardous tasks.

59. Thucydides, 5.68.3

The following battle took place at Mantinea in Arcadia in the summer of 418 and was one of the most important land battles of the Peloponnesian War. The structure of the army given here differs from that found in Xenophon (no. 60).

It is possible from the following considerations to estimate the number of Spartans present at the battle. There were seven regiments present, not counting the Sciritae who numbered six hundred. In each regiment there were four companies and in each company there were four platoons.

60. Xenophon, *Constitution of the Lacedaemonians* 11.4–5

Lycurgus is the legendary founder of the unusual Spartan political system and way of life. The size of the regiment of infantry is variously given in different writers, ranging between five hundred and six hundred. But the resulting size of the entire Spartan army seems too small and convincing arguments have been made for doubling the size of the unit.

[Lycurgus] divided the troops into six regiments of cavalry and hoplites. Each of the citizen regiments had a polemarch, four company commanders, eight platoon leaders and sixteen squad leaders. . . . Most think the hoplite formation of the Spartans is overly complicated but this is the very opposite of the truth. For in the Spartan arrangement the men in the front rank are all officers and each file has all that is needed to make it efficient.

Elite hoplite formations

Several other élite formations are attested in mainland Greece and in Sicily. It is not clear how widespread these units really were.

61. Plutarch, *Life of Pelopidas* 18–19.3

There is some evidence that the Sacred Band at Thebes was an old institution. What Plutarch may in fact be referring to is a reform or revival of the band after the expulsion of the Spartans from Thebes in 379. The battle of Tegyra in Boeotia in 375 was not important in itself but it was the first Spartan defeat on land in open battle and a forerunner of the great victory of the Thebans at Leuctra in 371. The Cadmea is the citadel of the city of Thebes.

It is said that it was Gorgidas who first constituted the Sacred Band from three hundred select men. The state provided them with training and supplies while they were encamped in the Cadmea, and because of this they were known as the band from the city. For in those days the cities were named after their acropoleis. Some say that this unit was composed of lovers and their beloved. . . . For a body of men linked together by mutual love is indissoluble and unbreakable. They support one another in danger since the lovers regard their beloved with affection and those who are loved are ashamed to disgrace their lovers. . . . Then it was natural that this band be called sacred since Plato calls the lover "a friend inspired by the divine." It is said that they remained undefeated until the battle at Chaeronea. . . . But Gorgidas, by placing these men in the first rank of the entire phalanx, did not allow their excellence to shine, as he made no use of them as a united force, since their strength was in this way dissipated and mixed with that of inferior troops. But Pelopidas, when they displayed their excellence at Tegyra while they were fighting by themselves and about him, no longer separated and scattered them but used them as a single unit and placed them in the van in the most serious struggles.

LIGHT-ARMED TROOPS

The presence of various types of light-armed troops on Greek battlefields is attested. They include archers both on foot and mounted, slingers, stone throwers, javelin men and a special variety of the latter: the peltast. For the most part their effect on the course of battle and warfare in general, except for certain special cases, was negligible in this period. On land the decisive arm continued to be the heavily equipped hoplite. The tasks assigned to the light-armed remained ancillary. They were used to ravage enemy territory and in foraging and plundering expeditions. On the battlefield they acted as a screen and often opened the battle by fighting opposing light-armed troops, but in general had little influence on the course of the battle. They could not deal with unbroken heavy infantry or cavalry. Their main tasks lay in ambushes and in the pursuit of broken hoplite armies when their speed and mobility would be of maximum value. They also proved useful in dealing with enemies who were strong in light-armed forces.

Except in Athens and in certain other Greek states, they appear to have lacked any formal organization and standardized equipment. The need for such forces was most often met by hiring them from outside the city-state, from areas that specialized in them because of their relative backwardness in urbanization and political organization. These included many of the peoples from central and northern Greece such as the Acharnanians and the Aetolians, who provided javelin throwers, or from areas peripheral to the main centers of power, like Crete and Rhodes, whose inhabitants developed specialized skills and training and provided a portion of their population with employment as mercenaries, much as the Swiss did in the Middle Ages. Non-Greeks were also utilized as allies or mercenaries. Best attested are the Thracians, who were a main source of mercenary peltasts in the Classical period.

The neglect to develop such troops who would seem well-suited to the broken and difficult terrain of much of Greece seems at first view surprising. Though they could not withstand hoplite forces on level ground, one would expect that they might be used by defenders to block entry-points into their territory. However, most of the major passes could be forced by hoplite infantry or bypassed by sea. Nonetheless it was in such country that light-armed troops would be especially useful, as Demosthenes' disaster in Aetolia (see no. 69) illustrates. If this type of terrain could be bypassed, then the hoplite formation, ideally suited to gain control of an enemy's agricultural land, and consequently to force his capitulation, remained a perfect instrument for war, and light-armed troops were largely irrelevant to such a task.

Other factors must have played a part in this lack of development. The social identification of light-armed formations with the lowest stratum of the population must have reinforced what appears to be a general social conservatism in military matters. Class identification was reflected and intensified by an ideology that placed maximum value on the close encounter as a test of manhood. More practical factors were probably as compelling. To be truly effective, light-armed troops needed prolonged training and a higher level of discipline due to their more open formations. Most Greeks states did not possess the resources or the need to engage in such training which also violated the notion that military service was not professional but a duty and privilege of citizenship. Finally, the basic nature and purpose of hoplite conflict – that is a short, sharp and ideally decisive encounter that was designed to limit the destructiveness and duration of war – must have acted as a brake on investment in formations whose value could only be realized fully under the conditions of prolonged combat.

62. Arrian, *Tactica* 3.1–4
Though written with Greek armies of the Hellenistic period in mind this passage presents standard Greek thinking on the division of infantry troops. For the sarrisa, a type of pike, see p. 169.

Infantry and cavalry formations and armaments are many and varied. To begin with, the armament of infantry is assigned to three types if we make the most basic distinctions.

41

Those three types are on the basis of their equipment: the hoplite, the light-armed and the peltasts. The heaviest armed are the hoplites, who have breastplates, shields, round or oval in shape, and swords and spears as the Greeks do or sarrisas as the Macedonians carry. The light-armed are equipped in a way that is the very opposite of the hoplites, because they do not have breastplates, shields, greaves or helmets. They also habitually use missile weapons. These include bows, javelins, slings and hand-thrown stones. The peltasts are more lightly armed than the hoplites, their shield is both smaller and lighter than that of the latter and their javelins are lighter than the spears or sarissas of the hoplites but they are heavier than the javelins of the light-armed.

63. Tyrtaeus, Fragment 11 West
This is our earliest attestation (sometime after 640 BC) of the use of light-armed troops. Notice that the light-armed appear to be brigaded with the hoplites rather than on the wings or to the rear as was normal later. The formation is rather difficult to picture.

But you, light-armed soldiers, crouching beneath your shields at various points in the line, hurl your great stones and cast your wooden javelins against the enemy, arrayed next to the heavy infantry.

64. Thucydides, 6.69.2
This picture by Thucydides of the first battle against the Syracusans in October 415 is a good illustration of the lack of importance of light-armed troops in hoplite encounters. Their actions are merely an overture to the actual battle and of no practical effect. It is the clash of hoplite armies that follows that decides the battle and results in an Athenian victory.

And first the stone throwers, slingers and archers fought each other in front of the main formations. Each side routed the other in turns as is normal in combat between light-armed troops.

Peltasts

These troops whom the Greeks classified as falling between light and heavy infantry seem initially to have been of Thracian origin. Their name is derived from their shield, the *pelte*, in the same way as the hoplite's stems from the designation of his shield, the *hoplon*. Our most detailed knowledge of the equipment of the Thracian peltast comes from representations on pottery. The *pelte* seems most often to have been crescent shaped and was held so that its tips pointed upwards. It provided the peltast's basic protection since he wore no body armor. His offensive weapons were usually two short javelins or a single long thrusting spear. As in the case of the hoplite, a sword or dagger served as a secondary armament.

Greek settlements along the northern coast of the Aegean seem to have been heavily influenced by this Thracian military tradition and to have developed troops of their own in imitation. Aside from the special shield and dress, they bore a great resemblance to warriors in the more backward areas of Greece. Yet tradition distinguishes them as a separate category. Thracian troops may have been used by the mid-sixth century by the Athenians. Later they became a practical necessity met, for the most part, by hiring mercenaries from Thrace or from Greek areas. By the time of the Peloponnesian War their importance increased.

65. Aristotle, *The Constitution of the Thessalians*, Fragment 498 Rose

The peltast's shield seems to have been more varied in shape and materials than Aristotle acknowledges. It appears in some paintings to have been made only of wicker and to have been faced with bronze and other metals. Its form also varied.

The *pelte* is a shield without a rim as Aristotle says in his *Constitution of the Thessalians*, writing that "the *pelte* is a shield without a rim nor is it covered with bronze and it is not cut round from oxhide but of goatskin or the like."

66. Herodotus, 7.75.1

This passage is from Herodotus' description of the Persian king Xerxes' army with which he invaded Greece in 480. The Thracians described here are from Bithynia in northern Asia Minor but their dress and equipment was basically the same as that of their European branch.

The Thracians marched with foxskins for headgear. They wore tunics with long, brightly colored cloaks over them. On their feet they had deerskin boots. They were armed with javelins and a *pelte* and, in addition, carried small daggers.

Other areas specializing in various light-armed troops

Cretan archers

67. Pausanias, 4.8.3

If Pausanias (writing in the mid-second century AD) is reliable, Cretan special-ization in archery and their characteristic employment as mercenaries reaches back to the eighth century. Archaeological evidence shows that archery for some reason had maintained its popularity in Crete during the Dark Ages when its use declined on the mainland. Like other areas that supplied mercenaries, Crete suffered from military and political instability as well as from excess population and endemic warfare. The Laconians are the Spartans.

The Laconians were far superior to the [Messenians] in the craft and practice of warfare as well as in numbers since they had the neighboring peoples as subjects and as allies in war. . . . They had a band of hired Cretan archers to fight the Messenian light-armed troops.

Rhodian slingers

68. Xenophon, *Anabasis* 3.3.16

This selection highlights the expertise of the Rhodians as slingers. They were hired specifically for their craft by the Athenians for the Sicilian expedition. The Acharnanians who lived in the northwestern portion of the mainland also had a reputation with this weapon. Slingers could serve as a complement to archers and, as this passage makes clear, their weapons could not only outrange the bow but they could also carry a larger supply of ammunition than the archers. Such troops required great expertise and an open formation to be used effectively. The army that Xenophon is referring to is the mercenary army of the ten thousand assembled in 401 by Cyrus the Younger.

But I hear that there are Rhodians in our army. It is said that most of them understand the use of the sling and that their sling bullet carries twice as far as that of the Persians. The latter have only a short range because they use only stones that fit the hand, while the Rhodians know how to use lead bullets in their slings.

The use of light-armed troops

69. Thucydides, 3.94.3–98.2

This campaign belongs to the summer of 426. The Athenian failure was the result of hoplites being unable to respond to the missile attacks of a light-armed and swiftly moving enemy in rugged country. If Demosthenes had waited for the Locrians, he would have had a force similar in equipment and style of fighting to the Aetolians and the outcome might have been different. Indeed, as long as the Athenian archers were able to fire and retain their cohesion they kept off the Aetolians.

About the same time Demosthenes was persuaded by the Messenians that it was worthwhile to attack the Aetolians since he had such a large force at his disposal and the Aetolians were hostile to Naupactus, and if he should conquer them he would easily cause the rest of the mainlanders in that area to go over to the Athenians. The Aetolians were a large and warlike nation, but they lived in unwalled villages that were widely scattered and they were only equipped as light-armed troops; the Messenians asserted that they could be conquered before they were united to defend themselves. Demosthenes made his base at Oineon in Locris. These Ozolian Locrians were allies of the Athenians. It was agreed that they with their entire force would meet him in the interior of Aetolia. Since they were neighbors of the Aetolians and equipped in the same manner, he expected that they would be a great help on the expedition because of their experience with the Aetolian method of making war and because of their knowledge of Aetolian territory. . . . These preparations did not escape the notice of the Aetolians, even when the expedition was first being planned. When the allied army entered their land they arrived with a large force drawn from their whole territory. The Messenians advised Demosthenes in the same way as they had done earlier, saying that the conquest of Aetolia would be easy. They counseled him to advance as quickly as possible against the villages and not to wait until the Aetolians had assembled their whole force, but to continue and to seize each village as he came to it. Demosthenes was persuaded by their advice and did not wait for the Locrians who were supposed to come to his aid since he was seriously deficient in light-armed javelin throwers. He proceeded against Aegytium and took it by assault. . . . The Aetolians, who by this time had come as far as Aegytium, began to attack the Athenians and their allies, running down from the surrounding hills in various places and hurling their javelins. When the Athenian army attacked them they gave way, and when the Athenians retreated they pursued them. The fighting, which consisted of alternate advances and retreats, went on for a long time and in both actions the Athenians came off the worse. But as long as the Athenian archers had arrows and were able to use them, they held out since the Aetolians were light-armed and retreated when they were shot at. But after the commander of the archers was killed, his men dispersed, and the hoplites were worn out through being subjected for a long time to the same fatiguing actions; the Aetolians pressed them and continued to shower them with javelins. The Athenians were thus routed and fled.

The Aetolians kept up their barrage of javelins and killed many of the Athenians at the spot where they were routed and others as they caught up with them since they were fast-moving and light-armed.

70. Thucydides, 4.32.2–35.1

The campaign in the summer of 425 of Cleon and Demosthenes at Pylos and Sphacteria was one of the key events of the first phase of the Peloponnesian War. The Athenian success there provided them with a base from which to harass Spartan territory and with Spartan prisoners as hostages. Its conduct reveals that Demosthenes had learnt from his experience in Aetolia (no. 69) about the effectiveness of light-armed troops in appropriate circumstances. It was particularly applicable in circumstances where Spartan hoplites were regarded as superior to any comparable Athenian force. Demosthenes showed his skill by capitalizing on the strength of this type of force in conjunction with hoplites. The use of combined forces foreshadows the changes in warfare that the fourth century would bring.

On the Athenian side there were eight hundred archers and not less than the same number of peltasts. This force consisted of the Messenians and the other troops from Pylos who were not required as a garrison for it. Under Demosthenes' orders they were divided into groups of approximately two hundred men and occupied the high ground. The purpose of this maneuver was that by having the enemy completely encircled he would not be able to form up against any one point but would be exposed at every point to great numbers of attackers. If the Spartans attacked the troops in front of them, they would be shot at from those in the rear; if they attacked one flank, they would be showered with missiles by the men on the other flank. In whichever direction the Spartans went, they would have enemies to their rear who were light-armed and impossible to overcome since they attacked with arrows, javelins, stones and slings from a distance and the Spartans could not get to close quarters with them.

This was the plan that Demosthenes devised and now carried out. The troops with Epitadas were the major Spartan force on the island, and when they saw that the first guard post had been taken and the enemy was coming against them, they arrayed themselves in battle order and advanced against the Athenian hoplites wanting to get to close quarters with them. The hoplites were to their front while the light-armed troops were on both their flanks and their rear. The Spartans could not make contact with the Athenian hoplites nor use their experience, for the light-armed troops kept them back by bombarding them from either side and heavy infantry did not advance against them but remained in position. They put to flight the light-armed at any point where they pressed their attack. But the former, being light-armed and assisted by the difficulty of the ground and its roughness because the area was uninhabited, were able to retreat easily and defend themselves as they were falling back. The Spartans were unable to pursue them because of the weight of their armor. For a little while the fight continued at long range, but when the Spartans were no longer able to run out quickly at whatever point they were attacked, the light-armed troops became aware that they were defending themselves more sluggishly, and were heartened by this since they knew that their force was much larger. Also they had now become accustomed to no longer regarding the Spartans as dangerous as they had before because they had not suffered by fighting them as they had expected to when they had first disembarked. They began to despise them and charged down on them shouting *en masse* and continued to hurl stones and javelins or shoot arrows at them. . . .

Their [Spartans'] felt headgear did not protect them against arrows and when they struck their spearheads broke off. They were unable to defend themselves since they could not see what was to their front. Further, the loudness of their enemies' cry prevented them from hearing orders. Danger beset them on every side, they were without any hope of defending and saving themselves. Finally, when many had now been wounded because they were constantly forced to remain in the same spot, they closed ranks and retreated to their last strong point on the island.

CAVALRY

Whatever may have been the role of the horse in warfare in the Dark Ages, there is little explicit evidence about the period when true cavalry was introduced into Greece. True cavalry can be defined as troops that use the horse as their fighting platform and do not dismount to fight. Our best evidence for the introduction comes from vase paintings on Attic and Corinthian pottery of the seventh and sixth centuries. Mounted troops are depicted from the seventh century on, but the paintings are ambiguous as to whether the rider dismounted to fight. It appears most likely that it was not till the late seventh century at Corinth and the early sixth at Athens that true cavalry appeared. It may well be that both uses of the horse in warfare, that is true cavalry and the mounted hoplite, existed side by side. As a parallel one might cite the continued use of the chariot in the sixth century to convey hoplites to battle in Cyrene and Cyprus. Even in the case of the best documented cavalry at Athens, the evidence for a standing true cavalry force does not appear until the mid-fifth century. Sparta had none until the 420s and even then such units were absent in other major states such as Corinth and Argos. It is safe to say that it is only in Thessaly that we can assert the definite use of true cavalry before the beginning of the fifth century.

There are excellent reasons for the late development and marginal position of cavalry in Greece as compared to some of the great cavalry peoples of the Near East. Of central importance is the fact that in Greece suitable pasture land for horses is confined to the area stretching northwards from the plain of Boeotia. Athens' own territory and much of Greece to the south of Attica is unsuitable. In particular, the limited water and fodder supply in most of Greece during the campaigning months of the summer limited the usefulness of cavalry. The contrast with the Greek colonies of the west, which had such resources, is clear from the archaeological record. The majority of finds of horse armor occur in Sicily and southern Italy; they are relatively rare in Greece itself. In general, most of the mainland states did not have the resources to devote to supporting horse-raising on a large scale or a social élite capable of monopolizing sufficient wealth to maintain large cavalry forces.

Greek cavalry suffered from technical limitations that further reduced its advantages as opposed to hoplite forces. Greek horses in the Classical period were small by both medieval and modern standards, and were limited in the weight they could carry. This obviously restricted the amount of armor carried by both horse and rider. In addition, the Greeks lacked stirrups and horseshoes. Their absence are liabilities in a land as rough as Greece. It is noticeable that Xenophon, an expert in cavalry matters, is very concerned with the feet of cavalry horses and the possibilities that horses would be lamed. These limitations tended to hamper the operational range of horses and to turn cavalry away from the use of shock weapons and to promote the employment of missile weapons such as the javelin and the bow.

Such troops could not ride down heavy-armed infantry as long as it kept its formation. But they were useful for flank or rear attacks on infantry and for protecting their own formations from similar enemy action. They were also effective against hoplites once their formation had been broken or in harassing them on the march and in cutting off stragglers. Cavalry could threaten the enemy's food supply by preventing foraging. Greek cavalry could hold its own against light-armed troops if properly handled. Further, its usefulness for reconnaissance, patrolling, guard duty and forming a cavalry screen for the main formations was recognized and utilized in this period.

Though relegated by its various limitations to a subsidiary role in the main engagements of the period, its usefulness, particularly in conjunction with other arms, led to the formation of cavalry units by the major military powers by the end of the fifth century or the beginning of the fourth.

71. Aristotle, *Politics* 1289b33–39
The strong association of horse-rearing and wealth is evident in Greek social and political thought. It appears in connection with Greek sport, where chariot racing was regarded as the most spectacular form of self-advertisement and as clear evidence of wealth and often of aristocratic background. This connection further emerges in the use of the word for horse in compounds forming the

names of Greek aristocrats and in the fact that some Greek aristocracies took their names from the connection with horse-rearing, such as the *hippobotae* or horse-rearers of Chalchis in Euboea. Such a link has analogs in other places and times, the European Middle Ages being an obvious example. Well into the nineteenth century membership in the cavalry regiments in many European armies carried aristocratic connotations.

There are differences among the notables as far as wealth and the extent of their property, as appears in the matter of raising horses, for this is no easy activity to engage in for those who are not wealthy. For this very reason, in ancient times those cities whose military power rested on cavalry were also oligarchies. They used cavalry in wars with their neighbors and as examples one may cite the Eretrians, Chalcidians, the Magnesians on the Maeander and many others in Asia.

72. Aristotle, *Politics* 1321a7–11

Thessaly is a case in point. It has a relatively large, open plain providing suitable pasturage as well as a sizable subject population, the *penestae*, who were an enslaved labor force used on large estates often owned by local dynasts.

In the same way that there are four divisions of the people, the farmers, the craftsmen, the retailers and the laborers, so there are four types of military men useful in warfare, that is, the cavalryman, the hoplite, the light-armed and the sailor. The formation of a strong oligarchy is natural where the countryside is suitable for the rearing of horses. For the safety of the inhabitants depends upon the use of cavalry and it is only men with ample means who can afford to breed and raise horses.

Thessaly

73. Plato, *Laws* 625D

Cleinias: "You see that the character of the entire countryside of Crete is not, as is the case of the Thessalians', level: that is why they especially use cavalry while we Cretans employ rapid infantry movements."

74. Aristotle, Fragment 498 Rose

The following two passages raise several problems. The selection from Aristotle leaves uncertain the extent of the districts mentioned as well as their constituent parts. Normally in time of war, the Thessalian states elected a commander-in-chief called the *tagos*. There were separatist tendencies and competition among the Thessalian aristocracies based in various areas, but the federal structure persisted as the fragment from Aristotle makes clear. Aleuas the Red was a descendant of Heracles and the ancestor of the important family of the Aleudae of Larissa. Many Thessalian constitutional arrangements are ascribed to him. This activity is in part legendary.

Aristotle says in his *Constitution of the Thessalians* that Aleuas divided up the cities and ordered that each furnish, according to lot, forty cavalry and eighty hoplites.

The Boeotians and Thebes

75. Thucydides, 4.72.4

Hipparchs appear in the sources as specific cavalry commanders presumably subordinated to the boeotarchs in the sources. But of the organization of the Boeotian cavalry we know nothing. This passage details a prolonged cavalry battle outside the walls of Megara in 424 during the Peloponnesian War. It is one of the few occasions on which Athenian cavalry defeated Boeotian. For the political and military organization of Boeotia in the late fifth century see no. 116.

The Athenian cavalry in turn charged the Boeotian and engaged them. The battle lasted a long time and both sides claimed victory. For the hipparch of the Boeotians and a few others who had gone forward as far as Nisaea itself had been killed and their bodies stripped by the Athenians, who, after they had gained control of the bodies, gave them back under truce and erected a trophy.

76. Xenophon, *Hipparch* 7.3

This selection emphasizes the generally poor quality of Athenian cavalry as compared to the Boeotian and highlights the unexpected victory in the preceding passage.

If the entire levy of the city should come out against such enemies in defense of its territory, the prospects are good. Our cavalry will be superior if they are cared for as they should be and the numbers of our hoplites will not be fewer, nor will they be physically inferior or less spirited if they are trained correctly with god's help. And the Athenians are not less proud of their ancestors than the Boeotians.

Sicily and Syracuse

77. Pindar, *Nemean Odes* 1.15–19

In general the cavalry forces of the western Greek states were more developed and effective than those of the homeland. The son of Cronus is Zeus.

The son of Cronus has honored Sicily, rich with the wealthy summits of its cities. In addition he has given a people of horsemen, suitors of bronze-armored war.

78. Thucydides, 6.64.1

The superiority of Syracusan cavalry was to play a vital role in the total defeat of the Athenian expedition in 413. This makes the small number (thirty) of the initial cavalry force sent by Athens something of a mystery. This excerpt illustrates the resulting difficulties. This is a description of part of the preliminaries to the Athenian victory on land outside Syracuse in the late summer of 415.

Since they were aware of these factors the Athenian generals wanted to bring out the Syracusan army at full strength as far as possible from the city, while they would sail during the night in their ships along the coast and occupy a suitable campsite at their leisure. They knew that they could not carry out their plans as easily if they disembarked from their ships or marched by land against a prepared enemy since their light-armed troops and camp followers would suffer greatly at the hands of the Syracusan cavalry who were numerous, while they themselves were without cavalry.

Sparta

79. Thucydides, 4.55.2
The Spartan formation, known as the *hippeis* or knights, despite their title fought on foot. Certainly this was true by Thucydides' time and it is doubtful if they ever fought as true cavalry. They were a corps of young men, three hundred in number, who served as an élite regiment and royal guard. The force mentioned here, established in 424, marks the first evidence for true cavalry at Sparta. Cythera is a strategically placed island off the southern Laconian coast.

Since Pylos was in enemy possession as well as Cythera and they were beset on every side by a war that required mobility and against which it was impossible to take precautions, the Spartans contrary to their usual custom established a force of four hundred cavalry as well as archers.

80. Xenophon, *Constitution of the Lacedaemonians* 11.4
Though Xenophon ascribes this reform to the early and mythical Lycurgus it obviously must postdate the first establishment of cavalry mentioned in no. 79. The reform must predate their appearance at the battle of Nemea in 394 but it is impossible to deduce an exact date. It is not clear that the cavalry at Mantinea on the Spartan side was actually Spartan cavalry. They are not named. The cavalry was under the command of a *hipparmostes*.

[Lycurgus] divided the army, so equipped, into six *morai* of infantry and six of cavalry.

Athens

Our information about the Athenian cavalry force is fuller than that for any other Greek state.

81. Andocides, *Oration* 3.5
The reference in this speech, delivered 393/392, is to the Thirty Years Peace concluded with the Spartans in 446/445. The Athenian cavalry, as in the late fifth century, appears to have been supported by funds made available through the growth of Athens' empire. Its institution is to be dated between 479 and 432/431. The exact year is not known, but it may be possible to connect it with the desertion of Athens by the Thessalian cavalry at the battle of Tanagra in 457. The number three hundred receives further support as the initial strength from the number of cavalry commanders on the inscription translated below (see no. 157). The three commanders mentioned would then each have been in charge of a force of one hundred troopers. The king is the Persian king.

I will show you how many benefits accrued to us on account of that peace. First, we fortified the Piraeus and the northern sections of the Long Walls. In place of triremes, which were old and unserviceable and with which we defeated the king and the barbarians in battle and freed the Greeks, we constructed a hundred new ships, and it was also at that time that we first established three hundred cavalry and hired three hundred Scythian archers.

82. Thucydides, 2.13.8

This is an extract from a speech made at the beginning of the Peloponnesian War in 431. As is clear from the following selections there were two hundred horse archers who had their own commander. See no. 81.

Pericles also pointed out that there were 1200 cavalry including mounted archers, 1600 foot archers and 300 seaworthy triremes.

83. Aristotle, *Constitution of the Athenians* 61.4–6

The number of hipparchs is confirmed in other fourth-century texts. Each of the two commanded five tribes. This facilitated their use as commanders on both wings of the line where the cavalry was normally stationed. They were subordinated to the generals who served as overall commanders. The statement in the passage concerning their equality with the generals is not then strictly accurate. Lemnos was taken by the Athenians in the 490s. It became the site of a cleruchy, a type of colony in which the colonists retained their original citizenship. It was lost at the end of the Peloponnesian War and regained in 392, and Athens' claims to the island were recognized by the King's Peace of 387/386. Lemnos was on the main grain route from the Black Sea to Athens, and was itself flat and exceptionally fertile and therefore excellent cavalry country. The date for the introduction of a hipparch to the island is uncertain; there is no evidence for such an officer before the fourth century, possibly as late as the 350s.

The Athenians also elect two cavalry commanders (hipparchs) from the entire citizen body. These men command the cavalry, each taking five tribes. They are in charge of the cavalry in the same manner as the generals are in charge of the hoplites. They are also subject to a vote of confidence.

Further, they elect the tribal cavalry commanders, one from each tribe, who command the cavalry just as the taxiarchs command the hoplites.

They elect as well a cavalry general for Lemnos who commands the cavalry there.

Cost, enrollment, administration and terms of service

84. Xenophon, *Hipparch* 1.19

This is Xenophon's estimate. It was issued to cover the grain allowance given to a cavalryman for himself and his mount, and could be withheld if the horse had not been properly cared for (see the next passage). It is first attested in an inscription dated to 410/409 but it may have been introduced in the mid-fifth century (see no. 102). The normal allowance was probably a drachma a day.

It is expedient to remind the [cavalry] that the state expends nearly forty talents a year in order to have a cavalry force available for immediate use in the event of a war.

85. Aristotle, *Constitution of the Athenians* 49.1–2

The *prodromoi* appear to be a selected body of light cavalry used for scouting and other purposes, who were the successors of the horse archers of the fifth and early fourth centuries. The *hamippoi*, who also existed among the Boeotian cavalry, are light infantry who were stationed with and fought alongside the cavalry. The use of light troops with cavalry is recommended by Xenophon but he does not mention the *hamippoi*. The Athenians may here have copied the Boeotians.

The Council also examines the horses, and if someone in possession of a sound horse is found to have poorly cared for it, they dock him his grant of fodder. Those horses which are unable to maintain formation either because of physical weakness or a bad disposition are branded on the jaw with a wheel. Any horse so marked is rejected for service. The Council also scrutinizes the *prodromoi* to see who is able to serve, and if they reject anyone, his service is at an end. Further, they examine the *hamippoi*, and if they reject any of them, that man's pay ceases. The registrars, who are ten men elected by the people, register the cavalrymen. They turn over the names of those they propose to enroll to the cavalry commanders and the tribal commanders. These take the register and present it to the Council. This body opens the sealed tablet on which is entered the names of the currently serving cavalry and deletes the name of any man who is in service and swears that he is incapable physically of carrying out his duties. They also call up those newly registered and, if someone of these swears that he is unable because of physical or financial incapacity to carry out his duties, they release him from liability to service. The councilors then take a vote as to whether those who have taken no oath are suitable for cavalry service or not. If they vote affirmatively, that man's name is entered on the tablet. If they reject him, they dismiss him.

The use of cavalry in battle

Major battles

The following passage illustrates the typical tactical disposition of cavalry in major battles involving large hoplite forces. They are stationed on the wings to provide a threat to the rear and flanks of the opposing force.

86. Thucydides, 4.93.4–94.1

Disposition from the battle of Delium in 424.

The Thebans and the others who composed their force held the right of the battle line. In the middle were the men from Haliartus and Coronea and Copais and others from around the lake. The Thespians, Tanagreans and the troops from Orchomenus formed the left. On each wing were the cavalry and light-armed troops. The Thebans were ranged twenty-five shields deep, and the troops from the other states were arrayed in their customary depth. This was the Boeotian army and its arrangement. The Athenians were ranged eight men deep, their number being equal to that of the enemy, and the cavalry was stationed on both wings.

87. Herodotus, 9.69.1.–2

At the battle of Plataea in the spring of 479 the Boeotian cavalry gave clear evidence of their effectiveness even at this early date. Herodotus in fact never mentions Athenian cavalry in connection with the Persian Wars. This passage illustrates the usefulness of cavalry against hoplites who have lost their cohesion and formation. These were troops from the center of the Greek battle line.

In the midst of this rout, it was announced to those Greeks who were stationed by the temple of Hera and had not taken part in the battle that battle had occurred and that Pausanias' forces had been victorious. On news of this and keeping no order, the Corinthians and those arrayed with them advanced, going up through the spurs of the mountains and the hills on the road that led straight past the temple of Demeter. Those in formation with the Megareans and the men of Phlius proceeded through the plain by the level route. When the Megareans and Phleasians were near the enemy they were seen advancing without any order by the Theban cavalry. The Thebans attacked them under the command of Asopodorus, the son of Timander. They charged them and killed six hundred of them and in their pursuit drove the remainder as far as Cithaeron.

88. Plato, *Symposium* 220E7–221C1

This passage conveys something of the personal experience of a hoplite retreat and of the value of cavalry in preserving those whose line has given way. It is a vivid picture of the service that the Athenian cavalry performed for its hoplites at Mantinea. Alcibiades is describing his experience. Laches was a prominent Athenian general and politician of the period.

"You should have seen Socrates, gentlemen, when the army retreated in flight from Delium. I was there serving in the cavalry and he was serving as a hoplite. He was retreating together with Laches when the army had disintegrated into disorder. I fell in with them, and catching sight of them, I told them to take heart and said that I would not abandon them. I once more observed Socrates' conduct in battle as I had at Potidaea, since I was mounted and I was less frightened. He seemed much more controlled than Laches. Further, Aristophanes, to quote your line: he made his way 'swaggering and looking from side to side', calmly glancing sideways at friends and foes. It was perfectly clear, even from a distance, that if he were attacked he would defend himself vigorously. Because of this, he and Laches got away safely. As a rule men who behave in this manner on the battlefield are not attacked, the enemy pursues those who flee recklessly."

Other functions of cavalry

89. Diodorus Siculus, 15.71.4–5

An illustration of another cavalry function. This time it involved the harassment of a line of infantry on the march. It took place during the unsuccessful

Boeotian invasion of 368 directed against Alexander, the ruler of Pherae in Thessaly. A second expedition, probably in the following year, forced Alexander to negotiate and to conclude a truce with them. Xenophon paints a very unpleasant portrait of him in the *Hellenica.*

While Autocles was sailing around Euboea, the Thebans invaded Thessaly. Since Alexander had assembled his infantry forces, and his cavalry were far superior in numbers to that of the Boeotians, the Thebans at first thought to force a decision by bringing about a major battle since they had the Thessalians as allies. But when the latter abandoned the Thebans, and the Athenians and other allies joined Alexander, and in addition their supplies failed, the boeotarchs decided to return home. When the Boeotians had broken camp and were making their way across level ground, the enemy followed close and attacked their rear rank. Many of the Boeotians perished, being bombarded repeatedly by javelins, while others fell wounded. Finally, they were reduced to such straits that they could neither move forward nor remain in place, and were without supplies.

90. Asclepiodotus, *Tactics* 7

The cavalry, like light-armed troops, assume their positions according to the attendant needs of battle. This is especially true of those troops that fight at a distance. These are the most suitable for being the first to draw blood, to goad the enemy to battle as well as to cause them to break formation, to repulse enemy cavalry and to occupy in advance the most advantageous locations and further to capture those places already occupied by the enemy, to reconnoiter ambushes and to set them. In a word, they are the best fit to open the conflict and then to support it. They do many great services because of their speed in battle.

Cavalry tactics

The following two passages sum up the basic tactics of the Classical period. Ironically they were written on the eve of the flowering of the Macedonian cavalry, which was to render them obsolete and to prove the value of shock tactics for the ancient cavalryman. The second passage is an illustration of the methods described and a recommendation by Xenophon as applied by experts. The professionalism of these mercenaries is evident.

91. Xenophon, *On Equitation* 8.12

If two armies are encamped opposite each other and the cavalry skirmish with one another, and if one side pursues the other as far as the enemy phalanx and then retreats back to its own infantry formation, it is good to know that as long as one is near the friendly line it is proper and safe to be among the first to wheel about and attack the enemy at full speed. But when one is close to the enemy formation, one must keep one's horse in hand. This is the way in which the most harm will be inflicted on the enemy with minimal losses.

92. Xenophon, *Hellenica* 7.1.20–21

These events took place in the summer of 369. The Spartans had been early supporters of Dionysius the Elder's tyranny at Syracuse and had sent help to him in the form of mercenaries in 398/397. He had returned the favor twice before. This is the third occasion mentioned by Xenophon. In this case Dionysius had prepaid the mercenaries' wages. This is the first reference to Celts serving as mercenaries in Greece. At the end of the summer they returned home with the Syracusan fleet.

At the same time as these events took place, the help sent by Dionysius to the Spartans reached them. There were more than twenty ships and they carried Celts and Iberians and about fifty cavalry. The next day the Thebans and their allies, forming up in separate units and filling the plain from the sea to hills near the city, began to destroy anything of use in the area. The cavalry and the Athenians and the Corinthians kept some way from the enemy's army noting its strength and numbers, but the cavalry sent by Dionysius, despite its numbers, rode separately along the enemy line and charged while casting their javelins. When the enemy advanced against them, they retreated and then turned and continued to cast their javelins. In the midst of these activities they dismounted and rested. If they were attacked while dismounted they would leap easily on their horses and retreat. If, in turn, some of the enemy pursued them far from their own forces they would harass their pursuers and cast their javelins at them with great effect while they were in retreat. The result was that they forced the entire enemy force to advance and retreat at their pleasure.

PROVISIONING AND SUPPLY ARMIES

Provisioning is central to the effective functioning of any army. Without adequate supplies, military forces become hard to control and disintegrate. At first, Greek hoplite armies undertook short campaigns, and the initial supplies were the responsibility of the citizen-soldier himself. At most the state was responsible for seeing that there were adequate supplies available for private purchase. This situation lasted well into the fifth century at Athens, as the passages from Aristophanes and Thucydides below make clear. Protracted campaigns required supplies to be provided beyond what could be transported by the army at the start of a campaign. If the campaign took place in friendly territory and was sufficiently close to home, a supply train could be organized. Again, if the army were in friendly or neutral territory, local cities might provide markets for troops to purchase their supplies. Alternately, merchants might accompany the expedition to sell supplies to the troops. If the army were isolated and cut off from ready access to supply, which was usually the case in prolonged campaigns, the normal recourse was to live off the enemy's land by plundering and ravaging it. But that of course created the danger that enemy cavalry or light-armed troops might attack and cut off foraging parties. By the end of the fifth century we begin to see the start of a magazine system.

93. Aristophanes, *The Peace* 312
The play was produced at Athens in the spring of 421. The proclamation is that of the Peace of Nicias that ended the first phase of the Peloponnesian War in 421.

Chorus: "But we were delighted when we heard a proclamation like this. For once it wasn't 'come with three days rations.'"

94. Lysias, *In Defense of Mantitheus* 14
The money must have been used for the purchase of supplies before and during the campaign. It is far too much for three days' rations.

When his demesmen had assembled before the expedition, he saw that some of them, though good citizens and eager, were without their own provisions. He said that those who were able ought to provide for those in straitened circumstances. He not only gave this advice to the others but also himself provided thirty drachmas to two of those in need.

95. Plutarch, *Lycurgus* 12.2
This passage provides us with some idea of the standard fare given to soldiers on an expedition. As in the Mediterranean diet in general, pride of place went to grain either in the form of gruel or bread. A handmill to grind it was standard equipment in an army's baggage.

The Spartans meet in groups of about fifteen, sometimes a few more, sometimes a few less. Each man brings to the mess each month ninety pints of barley, fifty-one quarts of wine, about five pounds of cheese and approximately two and one half pounds of figs. In addition, they also bring a small amount of money for garnishes.

Supply columns

96. Xenophon, *Anabasis* 1.10.18
The following events took place in 401. The Cyrus mentioned here is not Cyrus the Great, but Cyrus, the younger brother of the Persian king Artaxerxes II, who made an attempt on the throne and was defeated at the battle of Cunaxa in the same year. Notice that the wagons carried a reserve food supply. The normal method of supply was purchase from local cities or from merchants who accompanied the army.

They discovered that most of their property had been pillaged, especially the food and drink. The king's men had also pillaged the wagons loaded with meal and wine which Cyrus had prepared for distribution to the Greeks if ever the army should be in pressing need. It was said that there were four hundred of these wagons.

97. Thucydides, 6.22
The following passage is part of a speech delivered by the Athenian general Nicias in opposition to the proposed Sicilian expedition in the spring of 415. Nicias' expectation is that normally the army could have purchased its food locally.

"And we must have a superiority in the number of our ships in order that we can easily transport our supplies, that is grain from here and roasted barley, and bakers from the mills must be conscripted fairly and paid so that if for some reason we cannot sail, the army will still have its supplies. The reason for this is that the army is so large that not every city will be able to receive it."

Provision of markets

98. Thucydides 6.44

This is a description of the reception accorded the first Athenian expeditionary fleet in 415 on its way to Sicily. The reaction of the individual cities was the result of sympathy with the opposing side or fear of Athenian intentions.

The entire force put into land at the Iapygian peninsula and Tarentum and other points depending on how they fared. They sailed along the Italian coast until they arrived at Rhegium at the tip of Italy. But the cities along the way would not provide them with a market nor allow them within their walls, but did furnish them with water and an anchorage. The Tarentines and the Locrians would not even provide them with the latter. They assembled at Rhegium and encamped outside the city, in an area sacred to Artemis, as they were not permitted inside. There the people of Rhegium provided them with a market, and then, drawing their ships up on shore, they remained inactive.

Living off enemy territory

99. Thucydides, 4.6.1

During the Archidamian War the Spartans ravaged Attica every year between 431 and 425, the only exceptions being 429 and 426. This passage is clear evidence that though the Peloponnesians brought supplies with them (see no. 95) they also lived off their enemy's land.

The Peloponnesians who were in Attica when they learned of the capture of Pylos returned home quickly, since the Spartans and King Agis regarded the affair at Pylos as of vital concern to them. Also, they had invaded at the beginning of the spring when the grain was still green and were therefore short of provisions. Further, storms more severe than those usual at this time of year had afflicted the army. So for a number of reasons their army withdrew early and this was the shortest of all their invasions of Attica.

100. Onasander, *The General* 6.13

Though a late (mid-first century AD) and pedestrian compilation, Onasander's treatise on generalship is useful for its repetition of truisms which reflect conventional military thought, as in the following passage which depicts living off the enemy's land as a way of supplying an invading force.

After his army has been fully recruited the general should neither delay in his own territory nor in subject territories nor in the lands of an ally; for he will consume his own crops and so punish his friends more than his enemies. Rather let him lead his forces out as soon as possible, if affairs at home are in a satisfactory state. He will have unlimited support from the domain of the enemy if it is fertile and prosperous, but if it is not, at least he will not cause injury to friendly territory and also gain more from injuring that of the enemy.

Hoplite attendants

It was normal practice for Athenian and Spartan hoplites to have at least one servant while on campaign. Given the weight of their equipment and the supplies that they carried this is only to be expected. Normally the Athenian attendant appears to have been a slave and the Spartan a helot. The Athenians provided reimbursement for the attendant to his owner. The same situation must have held good for the hoplite armies of other states. Normally, there appears to have been one attendant for each hoplite even for the Spartan army, but most scholars accept the seven to one ratio attested for the Spartans at battle of Plataea. These attendants were employed in a variety of functions from carrying weapons and provisions to removing the wounded from the field of battle.

101. Thucydides, 7.75.5
A description of the Athenian retreat from Syracuse in the summer of 413.

Each Athenian personally carried as much as he could of what was useful. Even the hoplites and the cavalry carried their own food which was unusual. Some did so because they lacked attendants, others because they distrusted them.

MILITARY AND NAVAL PAY

The only state for which we have any information on military pay is Athens. There is a dearth of information on remuneration for any form of state service except at Athens. The general rule seems to have been that state service, including service in the military, was a normal duty attendant upon citizenship and therefore was not paid. The development of paid service seems to be connected with the financial resources made available by the growth of the Athenian empire and with the democracy which required some form of pay to permit state institutions to function democratically. Even in Athens, the payments were never lavish either for military or civilian service.

Military pay in the fifth century was primarily provided to enable the citizen soldiers to purchase their food while on campaign. It was not till the fourth century in the wake of the prolonged service resulting from the Peloponnesian War and the growth of mercenary forces that the vocabulary used clearly shows that pay had now developed to include two components. One part of it was still essentially a food allowance, but it is now supplemented by moneys which are conceived of as actual remuneration for military service for both citizen soldiers and mercenaries. Certainly, in the fourth century, the rates of pay when compared with that of a day laborer were low. Clearly the disturbed condition of Greece as well as the prospect of booty and plunder were the main incentives for mercenary service in that period.

Athens

102. Scholion on Demosthenes, *Oration* 13

The accuracy of this note on Demosthenes, written by a fourth-century AD rhetorician, has been questioned. Some have argued that it represents a confusion with the introduction of jury pay, but there is other evidence that would support the contention that compensation was given in this period to those on service with the fleet.

For Pericles was the first to assign pay, and he gave it to the people on military service.

Rates of pay

103. Thucydides, 8.45.2

These events are dated to the winter of 412/411. The passage has been used to argue that the rate of pay for sailors, and therefore for soldiers, was three obols a day or half a drachma. Other scholars support a drachma a day or double the former amount. On balance, the evidence of Thucydides is for a drachma a day for both land and sea forces. Tissaphernes was the Persian governor of the satrapy of Ionia and had already concluded a treaty with the Peloponnesians at the higher rate.

And [Alcibiades], when he was [Tissaphernes'] instructor in all things, cut the rate pay from an Attic drachma to three obols [a day] and that was not paid continuously. He instructed Tissaphernes to say to the Peloponnesians that for a long time the Athenians, who were knowledgeable in naval matters, had paid their own crews three obols.

104. Xenophon, *Anabasis* 7.6.1

We possess limited evidence on the rate of mercenary pay at the end of the fifth century. A daric was a Persian gold coin equal to twenty-five Attic drachmas so that the daily rate was five obols. This was most likely pay beyond subsistence, which seems to have been given to the troops in kind, and it appears from other passages to have been a normal rate in this period. This excerpt also gives us some of the pay differentials between officers and men.

At this time, when nearly two months had passed, Charminus, the Spartan, and Polynices arrived on a mission from Thibron. They said that the Spartans had decided to make an expedition against Tissaphernes, and that Thibron had sailed to make war, and so he had need of this army and he agreed that it should be paid at the rate of one daric per man each month, and that the *lochagoi* should receive double pay and the generals fourfold remuneration.

105. Xenophon, *Hellenica* 5.2.21

This meeting was held prior to the campaigning season of 382. It took place at an assembly of the Peloponnesian League to whose member states the terms refer. This expedition against the city of Olynthus ended in a serious Spartan defeat in the next year. The commutation of money for men is probably due to the increased use of mercenary forces dating from the Peloponnesian War. Sparta had employed them on long-distance expeditions as early as 424. After a blockade, the Olynthians finally made peace with Sparta in 379 on terms favorable to the latter. The differential between hoplites and cavalry is at the ratio of four to one.

As a result of the discussion it was agreed that any state that wished would be permitted to contribute money in place of men. The rate would be three Aeginetan obols per man, and if they provided cavalry they could discharge the obligation by providing two Aeginetan drachmas in place of each cavalryman.

MILITARY COMMAND

The growth of the city-state led to the replacement of kings and chiefs as military leaders by the most important executive magistrates in most city-states. At Sparta where kings continued to lead the state's military forces, one can see a tendency for kingship to be assimilated to the magistracies found in other Greek states by the imposition of various limitations on the king's authority. Even areas which remained rural, like Thessaly, tended in the same direction.

In fifth-century Athens, the generalship became the most important political office. Typically it combined the most important civil powers with the chief responsibility in military matters. The equation of civil and military leadership was, in part, the result of the fact that military leadership was simply a facet of overall command, in the same way that liability to service was a part of the duties of the individual citizen. This explains the resistance to military specialization among leaders until the watershed of the Peloponnesian War. The other factor which allowed the maintenance of this system of command was the relative simplicity of phalanx tactics. It is revealing that in most cases, after the initial dispositions were made, the commander fought in the battle, often in the most dangerous and therefore honorable section of the line. Leadership was an amalgam of tactical ability and encouragement through example. Few armies, except the Spartan, had the structure needed to allow major changes after the initial dispositions on the field had been made. This was, along with Sparta's relative professionalism, a crucial factor in her success. Unfortunately little is known about the command structure in other Greek states.

Athens

106. Aristotle, *Constitution of the Athenians* 3.1

The mythical Ion was the son of King Xuthus and King Erechtheus' daughter Creusa. He was made war leader of the Athenians and was victorious against the Thracians and the people of Eleusis. Draco's date varies in the tradition between 624/623 and 621/620. One expects the more specifically named polemarch to have been instituted after, rather than before, the archon. All of this is reconstruction and not documentary history.

And this was the arrangement of the Athenian constitution before Draco. Offices were filled on the basis of birth and wealth. At first, office was held for life, and then later for ten years. The first and most important of these offices were the basileus, the polemarch and the archon. The first of these was that of the basileus (this was the traditional office of ruler), and the office of polemarch was added second because some of the kings were unfit for war. It was on account of this that they sent for Ion when they were in need.

107. Aristotle, *Constitution of the Athenians* 22.2
It is possible that the office of general existed earlier as a tool for specific tasks and not as a standing magistracy.

First then, in the fifth year after this settlement in the archonship of Hermocreon (501/500), the Athenians made the Council of the Five Hundred swear the oath that they still swear. They then elected the generals by tribes, one from each of them, but the polemarch was the supreme commander of the entire army.

108. Herodotus 6.109.1–2 and 110
These incidents belong to the preliminaries of the battle of Marathon in 490. The relationship between the polemarch and the strategoi (generals) has been the subject of controversy. Some have seen the former acting in the role of a chairman, others have seen his precedence as merely honorary, with the real control being exercised by the strategoi.

The opinion of the Athenian strategoi was divided. Some favored avoiding battle with the Persians, since they were greatly outnumbered by them. The others, and especially Miltiades, wanted to offer battle. Since they were split in their views and the worse course of action was defeating the better, Miltiades approached Callimachus of the deme Aphidnae who by lot held the office of polemarch of the Athenians and had the eleventh vote (for the Athenians used to give an equal vote to the generals and the polemarch). ... The vote of the polemarch allowed the decision to attack to prevail. Afterwards, the generals who had voted for the attack when their day to command came round, turned it over to Miltiades. Though Miltiades took their offer, he did not attack until his own day for command came round.

109. Aristotle, *Constitution of the Athenians* 22.5
The date is 487/486. This change was obviously of significance in making the generalship the most important magistracy. Nevertheless whether the change was a consequence of the already existing weakness of the archonship, or whether that was the result of this reform is difficult to determine.

Immediately in the next year, in the archonship of Telesinus, they chose the nine archons by lot for the first time since the tyranny; before that, they had all been elected.

110. Thucydides, 6.8.2

These details are part of the preliminaries to the first Sicilian expedition in 415. The special powers granted were only within a restricted sphere, as ultimate authority resided in the Assembly. In this case it was clearly the distance and difficulty of communication that entailed this special grant to all three strategoi.

The Athenians held an assembly and listened to both their own ambassadors and those from Egesta. The speeches of the men from Egesta were attractive but untrue, especially concerning the statement that the Egestans had large sums of ready money in their treasury and temples. The Athenians voted to send a fleet of sixty ships to Sicily, and selected as generals with special powers (*autocratores*) for the expedition, Alcibiades, the son of Cleinias, Nicias, the son of Niceratus and Lamachus the son of Xenophanes.

111. Aristotle, *Constitution of the Athenians* 61.1, 5 and 6

This selection refers to the situation of the late fourth century. Originally, as no. 107 states, the generals were elected one from each tribe. The date when generals were elected without regard to tribe is debatable, but this was certainly the case by *c.* 360. It may not have been until the mid-fourth century that special commands were assigned to the generals. Munychia was a strategic hill in the eastern side of the Piraeus and Acte is part of a projecting peninsula in the southwestern section of the same harbor. The symmories were first created in 378/377. They were taxation units for the maintenance of the fleet. It had become too expensive for individual Athenians to maintain a ship – even when it had been built by the state – in service, that is to serve as trierarch, for an entire year. The lawsuits referred to are those brought by individuals who requested an exchange of property with those whom they considered to be richer and so more able to bear the expense. By the end of the third century all ten generals had regular postings. Lemnos had become an Athenian possession during the 490s. It was lost at the end of the Peloponnesian War in 404 but regained in 392/391.

They elect all of the magistracies connected with warfare, that is the ten generals, who were previously elected one from each tribe but are now selected from the whole citizen body. They assign them to specific duties by vote. One is in charge of the hoplites and is in command of them whenever they go on an expedition, one is responsible for the home territory and guards it. If war should break out at home, he is in charge. Two generals are assigned to the Piraeus, one of them to Munychia and the other to Acte. These have the duty of guarding the equipment in the Piraeus. One general is in charge of the symmories and enrolls the trierarchs and supervises their exchange suits and brings these suits to court. The other five are sent out on current business.

They also elect the two cavalry commanders from the whole of the citizen body. These men command the cavalry; each is in charge of five tribes. These officers have the same full authority over the cavalry as the generals do over the hoplites. . . . The phylarchs are elected as well, one from each tribe, and each controls the cavalry of that tribe in the same manner as the taxiarch controls the hoplites of a single tribe. . . .

They also elect a cavalry commander for Lemnos who is commander of the cavalry there.

Sparta

The kings and their staff

Unlike the Athenian commanders, the Spartans drew their supreme commanders from two hereditary lines of kings. In the same way as their Athenian counterparts, they combined civil and military authority, though in a different fashion. The hereditary nature of their office was a crucial difference. The priesthoods were connected with the Zeus who was associated especially with Sparta, and with Zeus as lord of the heavens. Herodotus' statement that the kings could wage war on anyone they wanted is not in fact true. It was the Spartan assembly which voted for war, and the ephors were responsible for the draft. If the kings were incapacitated or otherwise occupied, normally a relative was chosen to replace them in command. Occasionally advisors were appointed when there was dissatisfaction with a king's conduct. It is only during campaign that the king's formal powers became significant.

112. Herodotus, 6.56

The Spartans give the following privileges to their kings. They receive two priesthoods, that of Zeus Lacedaemonius and Zeus Uranius. Also they are able to wage war against any place that they wish and no Spartan is to interfere in this. If he does so, he falls under a curse. On an expedition the kings are the first to depart and the last to return. On a campaign one hundred select men are assigned to guard them.

113. Herodotus, 5.75.1–2

This change in command occurred in 506. But though problems of joint command were avoided, the kings still remained ultimately responsible to the state and could be fined or suffer other penalties for failure (see no. 130).

Just when they were on the point of going into action [against the Athenians], the unit from Corinth, after discussing among themselves and deciding that what they were doing was unjust, changed their minds and withdrew. Afterwards Demaratus, the son of Ariston, one of the two Spartan kings who were in joint command of the expedition, came to the same conclusion as the Corinthians although he had not previously been at variance with Cleomenes, the other king. Because of this dissension a law was passed in Sparta that both kings should not accompany an expeditionary force, although this had been the case until this incident.

114. Xenophon, *Constitution of Lacedaemonians* 13.1 and 7

For the Lycurgus mentioned here see no. 60. Xenophon is describing what he considered to be the "classical" Spartan state. Polemarchs controlled the largest units in the army under the king's supreme command. The staff are simply called "those about the public tent" by Xenophon. It is clear that there are two types of staff here. One, which includes the polemarchs, is a council of war, the other is really a body of functionaries who act to assist the king, as the passage indicates.

I will now describe the powers and honors that Lycurgus conferred upon the king when he is on an expedition. First, on active military service he and his staff are maintained at public expense. The polemarchs lodge together with the king so that they will be constantly at hand and thus able to take counsel with him if the need should arise. Also, three other full Spartans also share the king's tent. These men are in charge of all the supplies for the king and his staff in order to avoid any interruption in the king's attention to the conduct of the war. . . .

The (king's) staff consists of all full Spartans who are tent mates of the king and the diviners, doctors, flute players, commanding officers and any volunteers that might be present.

Other officers

115. Thucydides, 5.66.3

The chain of command at the battle of Mantinea in 418 is clearly laid out, though there are differences from Xenophon's account. Orders are passed down the line to the commanders of increasingly smaller units. How further orders were relayed once the actual movement of Spartan forces began is a mystery. Mounted dispatch riders are sometimes mentioned and there was a limited repertory of trumpet calls available.

When a king is in command of an army, all orders are given by him. He himself gives the necessary instructions to the polemarchs who in turn pass them on to the *lochagoi*. The latter transmit the order to the *penteconteres* who then give them to the *enomotarchs* who finally instruct their units.

Boeotian Confederation

116. *Hellenica Oxyrhynchia* 16.3–4

The author of these historical fragments is unknown and his identity is much disputed, though the work appears to belong to the first half of the fourth century. The system described here appears to belong to a constitutional arrangement instituted in 447 and in effect to 387. It appears that Thebes is the dominant city. Note the artificiality and careful numerical construction evident in the constitution of the federal league.

Boeotia was at that time organized in the following manner. All of the inhabitants were divided into eleven districts. Each of these districts provided a boeotarch. The Thebans contributed four, two on behalf of the city, and two for the Plataeans, Scolus, Erythrae, the Scaphae and the others which had previously shared in the citizenship of Plataea but were not dependent on Thebes. Orchomenus and Hysiae provided two, as did the Thespians in combination with Eutresis and Thisbae. The people of Tanagra contributed one, as did those of Haliartus, Lebdae and Coronea who sent one in rotation. In the same way the people of Acraephnion, Copae, and Chaeronea provided their assigned Boeotarch. So in that manner each of the areas provided magistrates. They also provided sixty councilors for each Boeotarch. The districts also paid their daily expenses. Each area provided one thousand hoplites and one hundred cavalry.

Generalship

These discussions of the art of generalship are for the most part self-explanatory. The first extended discussion of the requirements for exercising command is extant in the writings of Xenophon who had both practical experience and a theoretical interest in the subject. It is noticeable that it occurs in the context of a growing professionalism in the exercise of command in the fourth century. The presence of professional instructors in generalship and in individual hoplite fighting is part of this same general trend. Given the character of hoplite fighting and the limited nature of command exercised by a general, the stress on training in tactics is understandable. A common thread in all of these discussions is the greater stress on the moral qualities of the commander than would be found in a modern discussion of the subject. The one exception is the passage from Polybius, in which the acquisition of specialized knowledge is the central motif.

117. Xenophon, *Memorabilia* 3.1.1–6 and 3.2.2

This conversation takes place because of the philosopher's young friend's desire for office. It is revealing that Socrates has to prod his young friend to take specialized training.

Socrates said: "Tell us at what point he began to teach you about generalship so that, if we happen to serve as tribal or unit commander, we may be more knowledgeable in military matters." The lad replied: "We began and ended at the same point. He taught me tactics and nothing else." Socrates said: "But this is a very small part of generalship. For a general must be prepared to furnish military equipment and to provide supplies for his troops and he must be resourceful, active, exercise care and be hardy and clever. In addition, he must be friendly and harsh, open and devious, on his guard, but also ready to seize another's property, and lavish and avaricious. Further, he must be generous and grasping, cautious in defense and courageous in attack. Also there are many other qualities that a general either possesses naturally or acquires by training." . . .

For a king is not chosen to take good care of himself but so that those who choose him should be happy because of him. Men fight in order to live as happy a life as possible and they choose their generals for the same purpose: to lead them to this goal. So they choose the man who serves as general to perform this function for those who elected him. It is not easy to discover something more noble than this nor more shameful than its opposite. And so by examining what is the particular virtue of a good leader he [Socrates] dismissed from consideration all the other virtues except the power to make those he leads happy.

118. Polybius, 9.12.1–4 and 14.1–5

Polybius had written an earlier separate work on tactics that is lost. This discussion surely reflects that lost work. Note the stress on the intellectual and professional qualifications of the commander.

Those unforeseen circumstances which accompany military undertakings require thorough inquiry. Success is possible in each of them if one carries out one's plan with intelligence. It is easy for anyone to discern in past examples that what is done openly and by main force is of less moment than what is accomplished by strategy and through the use of opportunity. Further, it is not hard to recognize from past events that in the majority of those actions which depend upon opportunity, failure is more frequent than success. No one could doubt that the bulk of these errors are due to the ignorance or indifference of the commander. . . .

These [skills of generalship] which we have discussed are acquired by experience or by inquiry or by the systematic consideration of experience. It is best if the general knows the routes to and the place towards which he is moving, and the nature of the place and, in addition, through and with whom he will act. The less attractive alternative is to make careful inquiry and not to trust chance informants. The pledges given by the guides must always rest in the hands of those whom they lead. These and similar matters can be learnt by those in command through the routine experience of soldiering, that is partly by the leaders' own experience and partly by research. However experience needs to be supplemented by a scientific education, particularly in astronomy and geometry.

TREATIES OF ALLIANCE

The basic motivation for alliance in the Greek world always remained military security. The term which denoted an ally (*symmachos*) had as its basic meaning an ally in war. For the most part alliances were not only military in nature but directed towards specific military objectives. Given the rudimentary nature of the diplomatic machinery developed by the Greeks, alliances were contracted with a view to immediate advantage. In general, ideological motivation played only a minor role. There was an absence of elaborate and formal diplomatic procedures as well as of any permanent representatives stationed in other states.

Envoys were often limited in their power of discretion by the decisions of the state that had dispatched them. These decisions were often made in open political assembly and bargaining was almost precluded in these circumstances. It is noticeable that most alliances are so simple and straightforward in their phrasing that they required few amendments. In addition, the absence of a bureaucracy made for sharp changes in direction and little continuity in policy. There was hardly any secrecy possible under such circumstances and for the most part it was not attempted.

The most comprehensive agreement concluded was the *symmachia*: an offensive and defensive alliance whose basic term was the agreement between the contracting parties "to have the same friends and enemies." This wording first occurs in the early fifth century and becomes frequent. Normally before the fourth century an alliance specified a term of years, the longest one being one hundred, but sometimes it was of indefinite duration. Our earliest extant example of a Greek alliance, that between Sybaris and the Serdaeoi, is an alliance of indefinite duration. Such an alliance became the norm in the fourth century and after. These symmachies were of two types. The first class consisted of those which involved the subordination of one party to another, where the stronger party did not undertake reciprocal duties to the weaker. An example of this system of alliances is the one that the member states of the Peloponnesian League concluded with Sparta. The hegemony of Sparta was emphasized by adding a clause to the effect that the other contracting party would follow Sparta wherever she might lead them. The second type is one in which the formal arrangement is between the two parties that at least in theory stand on an equal footing. The use of the formula "to have the same friends and enemies" is rarer in this type of alliance than in those involving direct subordination. The original alliance forming the Delian League in 479 BC seems to have been of this type. It is obvious that such an arrangement could give rise to disputes about the interpretation of the respective commitments on both sides and that inequality of resources could easily change the second type of alliance into the first.

A second form of alliance which is attested for a short time in the late fifth century is the *epimachia*. As opposed to the symmachy, this type of alliance only committed the contracting parties to defend each other in case of attack by a third party. Its main function seems to have been to limit the commitments made by the participants. By the end of the fifth century the term ceased to be used as the alliances concluded from this time were normally defensive in character and so a special form of alliance was no longer necessary.

Military alliances by their nature raised problems connected with the sharing of expenses and the division of command. Various expedients were devised to deal with the first problem. In the earliest alliances, the party that solicited the aid bore the expense of the expedition. By the fifth century, we often see the costs shared equally for specified periods. Formulas were also developed to deal with the division of spoils in the event of a victory.

The other crucial question, of course, was the exercise of command. Here the basic dividing line was between the two types of symmachy noted above. If one party was in effect the controlling member of the alliance, command rested with it, as was normal in the Peloponnesian League where the Spartans monopolized command and in the Delian League where the Athenians occupied a similar position. Where the parties were equal, rotation might be used, as was the case in the Spartan–Athenian alliance of 369, or there might be a division of command with one power commanding on the sea while the other on land. Finally, as in the treaty of 420, command might devolve upon the state in whose territory operations were being conducted.

Offensive and defensive alliances

119. Treaty between Eleans and Heraeans GHI² no. 17, SV no. 110, IG I³ no. 11

This is the earliest known symmachy and it shows that the basic form of Greek alliance was for military purposes by its wording. Its term of one hundred years is paralleled in the treaty of 420 (see below, no. 126), but this tends to be the upper limit of such treaties. The length of the alliance seems to imply that it is essentially a permanent agreement. It is striking that it lacks the oaths and divine sanctions that normally accompanied a symmachy. The circumstances which gave rise to this treaty are unknown. Heraea lay in western Arcadia. The treaty itself was inscribed on a bronze tablet at Olympia.

This is the agreement between the Eleans and the Heraeans. There shall be an alliance for one hundred years and this is to be the first. If anything is needed in word or deed by either party, the other party will stand by them in everything but especially war. If they do not stand by each other, they shall pay a talent of silver to Olympian Zeus to be used in his service. If anyone mutilates this text, whether a private individual, magistrate or community, he shall be liable to the sacred fine written herein.

The Hellenic League

120. Herodotus, 7.145.1, 9.106.4 and 8.2.2–3

Despite elaborate Persian preparations to invade Greece, it was not until the fall of 481 that a group of envoys from various Greek states met, probably at Sparta, to concert opposition to Persia. The oath mentioned by Herodotus was probably to guarantee a common symmachy among these states. It may have been a perpetual alliance. The wording of the alliance can perhaps be glimpsed in the second paragraph of the passage below. Leadership on both land and sea was given to Sparta as the strongest Greek state and hegemon of the Peloponnesian League, which must have constituted the majority of members.

We know of no ancient name for the league beyond the simple appellation of "the Hellenes." The victory offering of a bronze column in the shape of three entwined serpents and surmounted by a golden tripod, dedicated at Delphi, bore the names of those Greek states that had fought against Persia in 480–479 but cannot be identical with the original membership of the league since some of those which appear, such as Naxos or Potidaea, were firmly under Persian control until 479. The league is recorded as meeting once more in the spring of 480 to hear an appeal of the Thessalians for aid, and acceded to their request. This is the first general league of Greek states attested since Homeric times.

The Greek states which were more confident about the future survival of Greece entered into discussions with one another and exchanged guarantees. Then they decided that the first matter in importance was to reconcile their disputes and end their fighting with one another. . . .

So the allies brought the Samians, Chians, Lesbians and the other islanders who were fighting alongside the Greeks into the alliance. These gave guarantees and oaths to wage war in concert and not to desert the common cause. . . .

The Spartans provided as the commander in charge Eurybiades, the son of Eurycleidas. For the allies would not agree to follow Athenian leaders: if a Spartan was not able to command, they preferred to disband the army. In the beginning, before the embassy was sent to Sicily to ask for an alliance, there was a proposal that the Athenians ought to command at sea. In the face of the allies' resistance to this proposal the Athenians yielded.

The Delian League

121. Thucydides, 1.96–97

Thucydides is here referring to the events of 478 when the Spartan regent Pausanias was sent out by his home government to command the fleet of the Hellenic League. After a series of victories culminating in the capture of Byzantium a movement developed in opposition to Pausanias' control that led to a transfer of leadership of the fleet to the Athenians and to the founding of the Delian League. The number and names of the original members in their entirety are beyond recovery. It is most likely that the league congress was composed of a single house and did not have a bicameral structure as the Peloponnesian League did. The *Hellenotamiai* were the treasurers of the alliance.

The Athenians took over control in this way with the agreement of the allies who were incensed at Pausanias. They settled which cities would provide money and which would provide ships against the Persians. The announced intention of the allies was to revenge themselves for what they had suffered at the hands of the Persians, by laying waste the territory of the Persian king. The *Hellenotamiai* were then first constituted by the Athenians, and these officers were the receivers of the *phoros*. That was the name given to the contribution of money. The first *phoros* was assessed at 460 talents. The treasury was located on the island of Delos and the meetings of the alliance took place at the temple there. They led allies who were at first autonomous and who reached their decisions by means of common deliberations.

122. Aristotle, *Constitution of the Athenians* 23.5

This passage clearly shows that the Delian League was a symmachy. It is, in fact, the first extant use of the formula "to have the same friends and enemies." The agreement belongs to the category of equal symmachies. The obvious interpretation of the section dealing with the sinking of the lumps of iron is that the alliance was meant to be permanent, but that seems in conflict with the limited objective of the alliance which was to liberate Greek states under Persian control and to exact revenge for Persian depredations. Aristeides was a prominent politician who had commanded the Athenian contingent at the decisive battle of Plataea and was well-connected at Athens.

For that reason it was [Aristeides] who first assessed the tribute of the cities in the third year after the naval battle at Salamis when Timothenes was archon [478/477], and he swore oaths to the Ionians that they should have the same enemies and friends. In confirmation of this they sunk lumps of iron in the sea.

Alliance of Athens and Leontini

123. GHI² no. 64; SV no. 163

Envoys from Leontini and Rhegium in Sicily arrived at Athens in 433/432. Their embassies were probably related to a possible threat to them from Syracuse that might result from a war between Athens and the Peloponnesian League.

The two symmachies which resulted were of the equal type, as the text makes clear. Much of the document has been lost in both cases, but this alliance and the one with Rhegium show the importance of the oaths that accompanied such an alliance, as well as the presence of conditions which gave each side an escape clause. These alliances are normally held to be renewals of alliances originally contracted in the 440s. That fact sheds some light on what the term "forever" means in this context.

Gods. The ambassadors from Leontini who concluded the alliance and took the oath were Timenor, the son of Agathocles, Sosis, the son of Glaucias, Gelon, the son of Execestus, and the secretary was Theotimus, the son of Tauriscus, in the archonship of Apseudes [433/432] and in the Council of which Critiades was secretary. The Council and people resolved in the prytany of Acmantis when Charias was the secretary and Timoxenus presided and Callias made the motion that there will be an alliance between the Athenians and the people of Leontini and they will exchange oaths. The Athenians will swear the following: "We will be forever faithful and guileless allies of the Leontinians." The Leontinians likewise will swear: "We will be forever faithful and guileless allies of the Athenians." . . .

A Spartan treaty with the Aetolians

124. GHI² no. 312

This is the first and so far the only example of an inscribed Spartan treaty from the Classical period. The inscription comes from the Spartan acropolis. It has been dated as early as the first half of the fifth century and as late as the second decade of the fourth. The most likely date is 426 or 425 after the Spartan débâcle at Pylos. It reflects a symmachy of the unequal type, typical of Spartan alliances within the Peloponnesian League. The other party to the treaty is the Erxadeis, who are perhaps Aetolians.

The agreement with the Aetolians will be on the following terms. There will be friendship and peace with the Aetolians and alliance . . . [they will] follow wherever the Spartans lead both on land and on sea. They will have the same friends and enemies as the Spartans and they will never make a settlement apart from the Spartans. But they will cease fighting when the Spartans do. They will not receive those exiled for their participation in misdeeds. If someone should attack the territory of Erxadeion with hostile intent, the Spartans will render all possible assistance. Likewise if someone attacks Spartan territory, the Erxadeis will give aid to the best of their ability.

Defensive alliances

125. Thucydides, 1.44.1

This is the first defensive alliance (433) recorded, and Thucydides makes clear the advantages of greater control over their own foreign policy that it allowed to the contracting states. The *epimachia* is a rare form of treaty and disappears by the end of the fifth century for the reasons mentioned in the introduction to this section.

After the Athenians had heard both sides [the Corinthians and the Corcyreans] they held two assemblies. In the first they were not less receptive to the arguments of the Corinthians, but in the second they changed their minds but did not make a full alliance with the Corcyreans so as to have the same enemies and friends. For if the Corcyreans called upon them to sail against Corinth they would be compelled to violate their treaty with the Peloponnesians. Rather, they made a defensive alliance to come to each other's aid, if someone attacked Corcyra or Athens or allies of the Athenians.

126. Alliance for One Hundred Years between Athens, Argos, Mantinea, and Elis, SV no. 193, Thucydides 5.47

Complicated maneuverings in the Peloponnese and the failure of an attempt by Spartans and Athenians to reconcile their differences led, in the summer of 420, to the formation of a triple alliance between the three Peloponnesian states of Argos, Elis and Mantinea with Athens. The fact that all four had constitutions that were democratic to varying degrees must have made the alliance easier. Since treaty relations had existed between the three powers prior to their alliance with Athens, they appear in the language of the treaty as a single entity as well as separately. The first portion of the document is a mutual non-aggression pact between the parties. The second is a defensive alliance which recalls some of the terms of the Spartan–Athenian alliance of the previous year. The terms of this alliance are especially interesting since they form the first extant treaty of which we know the mutual obligations in detail. The provision of rations by the city sending the aid requested included not only the thirty days in the territory of the host city, but also provisions for the round trip. The monetary amounts are for rations only and do not include pay. Three Aeginetan obols are approximately equal to four and one third Athenian obols; the figure is higher than the regular grain allowance for the Athenian hoplites and light-armed troops while on service (see no. 103). However, the cavalry ration seems low and, surprisingly, nothing is provided for attendants.

The problem of command is dealt with by using two of the methods detailed in the introduction to this section. Given the simplicity of Greek tactics such alternations were not as serious as they would be in other conditions. Thucydides' text, though it shows differences in language from the version preserved epigraphically, does not diverge seriously in matters of substance.

The Athenians, the Argives, the Mantineans and the Eleans have concluded a treaty with one another and on behalf of the allies that they lead for one hundred years without guile or violation of its terms by land and by sea. Neither the Argives nor the Eleans nor the Mantineans nor their allies are permitted to bear arms to the injury of the Athenians or their allies and neither are the Athenians or their allies permitted to bear arms against the Argives, Eleans, Mantineans or their allies or to injure them by any device or means. On the following terms the Athenians, Argives, Mantineans and Eleans will be allies for one hundred years. If an enemy state should invade the territory of the Athenians, the Argives,

Mantineans and Eleans will come to Athens to render aid as the Athenians request, in any way possible, and to the fullest extent of their ability. And if the enemy has laid waste the land and departed, the hostile state will be deemed an enemy by the Argives, Mantineans, Eleans and Athenians and will be punished by all of these states. None of the parties will conclude peace with a hostile state unless all of the allies are in agreement. The Athenians will render aid to the Argives, Mantineans and Eleans, if some state should proceed against the territory of the Argives, Mantineans or the Eleans with hostile intent as it is requested by these states, in any way it can and to the fullest extent of its ability. If after laying waste the territory the enemy should depart, that state will be considered as hostile by the Athenians, Argives, Mantineans and Eleans and will be punished by all of these states. Peace is not to be concluded with the hostile state by any of the allies unless all are in agreement. The allies are not to allow an armed expedition to pass through their own territory, that is the territories of the Athenians, Argives, Mantineans and Eleans or those of their allies, nor shall passage be allowed by sea, unless all of the allied cities vote to allow such passage. . . . The state which renders aid shall provide thirty days rations to its forces from the point of their arrival in the state requesting help and the same procedure shall be followed on their departure. If the state which requested aid wishes to retain the troops for a longer time than the thirty days, it shall provide rations to the hoplites, light-armed troops and archers at the rate of three Aeginetan obols per day, and at one drachma per day to the cavalry. The city which summons these troops shall command in whatever action takes place on its territory. If all of the contracting states decide to mount an expedition in common, command shall be shared out equally among all of them. The Athenians swore to abide by these terms on behalf of themselves and their allies. The Argives, Mantineans and Eleans and their allies will swear to this agreement in each of their states.

127. Alliance of the Athenians and Boeotians, SV no. 223; Tod no. 101

This treaty, concluded in 395 when hostilities against Sparta were looming for both states, is typical of the symmachies of the fourth century and later in its unlimited duration and because of its defensive character. The same language reappears with minor variations in most of the alliances of the period. Such a treaty gave states greater latitude to maneuver and to deal with conflicting sets of obligations.

Gods. . . . Alliance of the Boeotians and Athenians for all time. . . . If anyone shall proceed against the Athenians with hostile intent either by land or by sea, the Boeotians are to render assistance with all their strength as far as they are able in the manner requested by the Athenians. And if anyone proceeds against the Boeotians with hostile intent by land or by sea, the Athenians are to render assistance with all their strength, as far as they are able, in the manner requested by the Boeotians. If anything needs to be added or deleted [to this treaty], the Athenians and Boeotians deliberating in common.

HOPLITE BATTLES

Early hoplite battles

Our sources for early Greek hoplite battles of the seventh and sixth century are extremely fragmentary and it is impossible to reconstruct in detail the course of any Greek battle before Marathon in 490, nor is an accurate and detailed reconstruction of the course of any battle between hoplites possible until the Peloponnesian War. It is only with the appearance of the historians that coherent descriptions are available. The battles of the earliest period that appear to display the purest manifestations of hoplites tactics are now lost to us. Only the occasional anecdote or passing remark survives.

There is one type of battle that is attested, at least from the late eighth or early seventh century on, that loses its importance in later Greek warfare, but never completely disappears. It encapsulates some of the most important features of the Greek view of warfare and its roots reach far back into the Dark Ages. This is the agonal or ritual battle often manifested in the form of the *monomachia* or duel between selected individuals or groups. Frequently it took place during a pitched battle, but it could be used as a substitute for battle. It could be viewed by the participants as equivalent to full-scale warfare, as the example of the Battle of the Champions shows (see no. 129). This sort of battle is in later times closely connected with border disputes over territory whose acquisition bears little proportion to the expenditure of effort and the loss of lives involved. The engagement was delimited by a set of rules designed to confine the destructive effects to both sides.

The functions of such fighting are difficult to discern. It has been suggested that, since some of these wars between neighboring states have religious connections, the real purpose of these conflicts was to serve as a mechanism of social control. In this regard, these conflicts seem to be linked to initiation and other social rites and to the strengthening of internal cohesion. But the irregularity of these struggles tells against this view. It appears that they served as a ritual vindication of military superiority of the winning side and also as a justification of the social position of the hoplite. The elaborate restrictions on combat are simply a more stringent application of the formality of all hoplite conflicts in this period.

128. Herodotus, 7.9.2b–g

Though this passage is clearly Herodotus' thoughts, rather than that of the Persian Mardonius, on the customs and capabilities of Greeks in waging war, it does reflect the codified and ritual side of Greek military practice. This long remained a vital feature of Greek warfare. Mardonius' comments also reflect Herodotus' knowledge of Persian military practices and some of their strengths as compared to those of the Greeks. But given the assessment by Herodotus of the superior armament and training of Spartan infantry in comparison with the Persian, it creates in the reader's mind a paradoxical contrast and so cannot be regarded as a totally legitimate critique of Greek practice. Rather, it serves as an ironic commentary on the lack of realism in regard to Greek military superiority in heavy infantry of a Persian general who was to suffer most directly from its effects (see no. 138).

"And yet the Greeks are accustomed, as I have learned, to wage war in a most thoughtless manner because of their lack of sense and skill. Whenever they declare war on one another, they search out the finest and most level area they can find. Then they have their battle there. The result is that even the victors suffer great losses. As far as the losers, well I can't even begin to speak about the losers; they are totally destroyed. Surely, they ought to settle their differences by using heralds or messengers, since they speak the same language, or in any way rather than by fighting. If they really must come to blows, they ought to discover what is most disadvantageous to their opponent, and so conduct their fighting to that end."

129. Herodotus, 1.82

This battle is dated to *c.* 546. The area involved is a rather isolated but fertile plain which lies at the head of Cynouria, a narrow coastal strip along the eastern coast of Laconia that includes the island of Cythera. By the mid-sixth century, this region, except for the area of Thyrea, had been secured by the Spartans. Its fertility was important, but more crucial was its role as the access route from Laconia into the Argolid. Herodotus implies that it was still in Argive hands in the mid-sixth century, but this is hard to believe and the archaeological material does not support this contention. From the perspective of Sparta, maintaining control of Thyrea seems to be part of a rational strategy for sealing off the approaches to Laconia from the northeast. It would also be a sensible rounding out of that coastal strip that was already in Spartan hands. The passage in Herodotus makes it clear that it is Spartan expansion that brought about the conflict. The conflict between Sparta and Argos for possession of this district continued until Roman times. The reality of the Battle of the Champions has been doubted by some, but it seems that at least by the mid-fifth century it was taken as historical. Parallels from other areas make its truth possible if not probable. Despite the practical advantage of control there were other factors at work. This type of conflict is, in essence, a form of judicial war to establish control of the disputed territory. It may also have served as a form of regulation in the respective status of both of these states in the Peloponnese. This battle was one of the most celebrated in the poetic and literary tradition and was closely linked to important religious festivals. As so often happened, the judicial aspects of the contest were only resolved by a full-scale battle.

It so happened that at the same time the Spartans were involved in a dispute with the Argives concerning the area called Thyreatis. For the Spartans were in possession of this area which they had detached from Argive territory. This territory extends to the west of Argos as far as Cape Malea on the mainland; the island of Cythera and the remaining islands had also once belonged to the Argives. After the Argives had marched out in defense of the territory that the Spartans had appropriated, they entered into negotiations with the Spartans with the result that they both decided that three hundred from each side would fight and that the land would belong to the victor. They further agreed that the armies of both sides should withdraw to their own territories and not remain to witness the engagement so as to avoid their fighting in support of their own men, if they should appear to be losing. After concluding this agreement the armies departed, while the picked troops on either side fought it out. So closely contested was the battle and so equal the result that only three men were left alive out of the original six hundred; the Argives Alcenor and Chromus and the Spartan Othryades. What saved them was the arrival of darkness. The two Argives ran back to Argos to report their victory, while Othryades stripped the corpses and carried the armor back to his own camp while remaining under arms.

On the next day both sides came together after they had learned the results of the battle. For a while both sides claimed victory. The Argives asserted that they had the larger number of survivors, while the Spartans claimed that the Argives had left the field and their own man had remained and stripped the Argive dead. The result of this dispute was that both armies finally came to blows. Though many fell on each side, the Spartans emerged victorious.

The Classical hoplite battle: the first battle of Mantinea

130. Thucydides, 5.63–74

The Peace of Nicias, concluded in 421, had failed to satisfy many of the states engaged in the Peloponnesian War. The Spartans were unable to carry out several of the promises they had made and a number of states in the Spartan alliance during the Archidamian War, both inside and outside the Peloponnesian League, were dissatisfied with the terms of the peace and with the subsequent alliance between Sparta and Athens (see no. 260). Further crucial factors in the situation were the dissatisfaction of many of the Athenians with Sparta's compliance with the peace terms, and the rise of political opposition to the peace, particularly on the part of the Athenian politician Alcibiades. Finally, in 421 Argos' fifty-year peace with Sparta had ended, leaving relations between the two states in an uncertain position. The Spartans wanted a peaceful settlement with the Argives that would avoid any threat to their position in the Peloponnese and a way to stop those states dissatisfied with peace from forming a countervailing force. A series of complicated diplomatic maneuvers by all sides, further Spartan failure to satisfy Athens, and the desire of the Argives for allies to counter the Spartans, led, in the spring of 420, to the creation of a defensive alliance between Athens, Argos, Elis and Mantinea (for terms see no. 126).

In 419 the Argives began a campaign against the city of Epidaurus to secure themselves against any move originating in Corinth and to allow Athenian troops easier access to the Argolid from the island of Aegina. The Spartans garrisoned Epidaurus in response. Finally, in the next year, the Spartans under King Agis launched a major expedition against Argos, calling up the Corinthians and Boeotians in support. An intricate series of military maneuvers resulted in the Argive army being trapped between the converging columns of Sparta and her allies while deployed at Nemea. Instead of crushing the Argives, Agis concluded the truce referred to by Thucydides. Presumably this was done in the hope that Agis' Argive friends could bring the city over. The king was wrong. The Argives were persuaded by Alcibiades to resume the war. It was at this point that Orchomenus in Arcadia was captured by them and their allies. It was of strategic importance because it hampered Sparta's northern allies from joining her in campaigns.

This event marked the total failure of Agis' policy of rapprochement and explains the reaction of the Spartans towards him on his return. The allies decided to advance on Tegea, in opposition to the Eleans who then withdrew their force of at least three thousand hoplites. This created a numerical disparity between the two sides.

The threat to Tegea was both external and internal and the Spartans reacted with speed, mobilizing themselves and their helots. This speed shows the perceived magnitude of the threat to the Spartan position in the Peloponnese as well as to its borders.

The choice of Agis to command Sparta's force, despite the anger against him, must have been due to the discrediting of the other king, Pleistoanax, who had favored an alliance with Athens. Agis' past record must be a factor in assessing his conduct on this campaign. He had shown himself to be both unlucky and unskilled in war. His invasions of Attica had been unsuccessful. To this must be added the failure of his earlier expedition against Argos. Hence the selection of ten advisors to accompany him on this campaign. But their role is far from clear. In Thucydides' account the advisors do not play any role at all as a group. They must have exercised some general oversight over the campaign, while battlefield tactics were left to the king to avoid a division of command. Their appointment is unparalleled on a campaign conducted by a Spartan king.

Agis and his forces departed in late August 418. They appear to have marched up the Eurotas valley to the north-northwest, a route which assured an easier passage for the wagons and facilitated a meeting with the Arcadian allies. The choice of Oresthium, which appears to have been close to Megalopolis and the Arcadian border, as a stopping point, facilitated his juncture with them. The united army then crossed the southeast corner of the plain of that city. It must have been here that the king learned that the Eleans were not going to be present. This meant he would now have a numerical advantage and this allowed him to send one-sixth of his army back to garrison Sparta while still keeping his superiority in numbers.

There are problems with the account in Thucydides. First, though he goes through elaborate calculations to ascertain the size of the Spartan force, he fails to give totals for the other units serving with them and for most of the formations on the allied side. He does makes clear that the Spartans had the advantage in numbers. The best modern estimates are about ten to eleven thousand hop-lites on the Spartan side opposed by nine to ten thousand. The *Brasideioi* were the remnants of the of the troops that Brasidas had used in Thrace and were enfranchised helots who had been rewarded for their military service. The *neodamodeis* were also freed helots. Like certain other groups at Sparta, their position remains obscure. There are a number of topographical puzzles as well in Thucydides' account. It may be that he had never personally inspected the battlefield. The temple to Heracles which was the site of the Spartan camp was probably in the eastern side of the plain, at the foot of Mount Alesion, and it was on the lower slopes of this same mountain that the Argives originally encamped. It appears that, when he gave up his abortive attack on the Argive coalition, Agis decided that the only way to bring his opponents to battle was to divert the water of the major stream in the southern part of the plain, the Zanovistas, into the Sarandopotamus, which flowed into Mantinean territory and would flood that area when the rains of the approaching fall raised the water level in these streams, since the plain slopes downwards at its northern end. Presumably there was already in existence a channel which linked the two rivers. This could explain the speed of the operation, which took less than a day. Thucydides fails to clarify these preliminary actions. But the greatest puzzle of all is the surprise of the Spartan forces upon sighting the allies in the plain in battle order. Though observation posts were available for the Spartans from which they could see the northern end of the plain towards which Agis was marching, Agis may not have been overly concerned to use them. It was not uncommon for Greek forces to neglect such matters. But the plain in which the battle was fought is relatively featureless and Agis should have seen the enemy some distance away. One possible explanation is that, in Thucydides' time, there existed a wooded area called Pelagus and this wood screened the enemy from Agis until he emerged at its northern side. The wood certainly existed in the second century AD, but it is disturbing that it is not mentioned in Thucydides' account of the battle nor in accounts of later battles in this plain. It is always possible that this may be the case because the wood was not crucial to these descriptions.

The course of the battle, including Agis' strange maneuvers, is clearly explained. The real failure of the allies was their inability to exploit the gap opened in the Spartan line by Agis' tactics. Though there is some lack of clarity here, it seems that the Spartan right curled round the allied left and would have taken the allies on that side in the flank, if Agis had not decided to come to the aid of his defeated left. This flanking maneuver appears to have developed accidentally in this battle. But the Spartans perceived its effect and in the fourth century attempted consciously to use it to defeat enemy phalanxes.

When the Spartans returned from Argos after having concluded a four-month truce, they were outraged at Agis because he had not subjected Argos to them although he had been presented with an opportunity such as had, in their opinion, never occurred before, and since it would not be easy to assemble again allies in such numbers and of such high quality. But when they received the report that Orchomenus had been taken, they became far angrier than before and they immediately decided in assembly, under the influence of their anger which is not their normal fashion, that Agis' house should be demolished and that he should pay a fine of 10,000 drachmas. He begged them not to do these things. He said that he would atone for the grievances against him by some noble deed while on campaign and added that if he did not, they could do as they wished. The Spartans refrained from fining him and from destroying his house, but for the present they carried a motion which they had never done before to choose ten Spartans as advisors to him and in whose absence he was not to lead an army from the city.

While these events were going on, the news came to them from their friends in Tegea that unless they came quickly Tegea would revolt from them and join the Argives and their allies and that the Tegeans were on the point of doing so. At this juncture the Spartans, with all of their forces and their helots, sent aid faster than they had ever done before. The Spartans advanced to Orestheum in Maenalia and sent word to their allies in Arcadia to assemble and follow in their tracks to Tegea. The whole Spartan army proceeded as far as Orestheum. From there they sent home one-sixth of their force, composed of the youngest and oldest, to serve as a garrison for Sparta, and with the rest of their force they arrived at Tegea. In a short while their Arcadian allies arrived. They also sent a summons to the Boeotians, Corinthians, Phocians and Locrians to come to their aid with all possible speed. But this gave their allies little time, and it was not easy for them to pass through enemy territory unless they waited for each other and united their forces (since they were shut off from each other). Nevertheless they made haste. The Spartans joined with their Arcadians allies and invaded Mantinean territory. After encamping by the Heracleum, they laid waste to the area. When the Argives and their allies saw them they occupied a strong position, difficult of access, and arranged themselves for battle. The Spartans immediately advanced against them and came within a stone's throw or within javelin range. At this point one of the older men, seeing that they were advancing against a strong position, shouted out to Agis that he had it in mind to cure one evil with another by an unseasonable courage in wanting to make amends for his retreat from Argos for which he had been blamed. And Agis, whether on account of the shouted warning or some other reason or because of a sudden change of his view of the situation, hastily led the army back before it had come to grips with the enemy.

Coming into the territory of Tegea he diverted water into Mantinean land. This water had been a constant source of fighting between the Tegeans and Mantineans on account of the harm it does to wherever it flows. He wanted by this maneuver to bring the enemy down from the hill they were on when they found out about his diversion of the water, and so to bring about a battle on level ground. He stayed where he was that day and diverted the water.

The Argives and their allies were at first amazed by the speed of the Spartan retreat and at a loss as to what to make of it. But after the enemy withdrew and disappeared from sight they remained in position and did not pursue him. They then began to blame their generals because, as previously when the Spartans had been overtaken in a disadvantageous position in front of Argos, they had been allowed to escape and although they had run off there had been no pursuit. So now the Spartans were getting away at their leisure while their own army was being betrayed. The allied generals were immediately confused, but then led the army down from the hill and, marching into the plain, they encamped with the intention of attacking the enemy.

The next day the Argives and their allies formed up in the battle order with which they intended to attack if they opportunity arose. The Spartans were returning from their operations to divert the water to the same campsite they had previously occupied by the temple of Heracles when they saw the enemy a short distance away arrayed in battle formation after their descent from the hill. The Spartans were then more dismayed than at any other time in memory because they had only a short time to make their preparations.

Immediately they took their positions at full speed with the king giving his orders in the normal manner. When a king leads the army all orders are given by him and he personally gives the necessary instructions to the polemarchs who pass them on to the *lochagoi*, who in turn give them to the *pentekosteres* and then these pass them on to the leaders of the *enomotiai* who then instruct the troops in their unit. Orders are passed down the ranks when necessary in the same way and they go quickly. For almost the whole of the Spartan army consists of officers serving under other officers and many are responsible for carrying out an order.

The Sciritae occupied the left wing of the army. They alone of the Spartans have an assigned place in the line which they always occupied. Beside them were the soldiers who had served under Brasidas from Thrace and the *neodamodeis* with them. Then came the Spartan *lochoi* one after another, and beside them the Arcadians from Heraia, and after these the Arcadians from Maenalia. On the right wing were the Tegeans, and at the extreme end of this wing a few of the Spartans. Their cavalry was arrayed on both wings. This then was the battle order of the Spartans.

Their opponents' line was arranged in the following manner. The Mantineans formed the right wing because the battle was being fought in their territory. Beside them were the Arcadian allies and then the select Argive force of one thousand, who were given long training in warfare at public expense. Then came the rest of the Argives and next to them their allies, the men of Cleonae and Orneae. Finally, the Athenians held the extreme left of the line with their own cavalry unit.

These were the preparations and arrangement of each army. The Spartan force appeared larger, though I am not able with full accuracy to give the numbers of either army or of their various units. The reason in the Spartan case is their habitual secrecy, and as to the other troops engaged, it is the normal human tendency to boast about one's own numbers. One can, using the following method of calculation, estimate the number of Spartan troops present. There were seven *lochoi* present not counting the Sciritae who numbered six hundred. In each *lochos* there are four *pentecostyes*. In each *pentecostys* there are four *enomotiai*. Four men fought in the front rank of each *enomotia*. In depth they were arrayed unequally according to their *logachos'* choice but in general they were eight men deep. The first rank was thus for its entire length, without the Sciritae, 448 men.

When the armies were on the point of joining battle, the units of the individual states were given speeches of encouragement by their generals. The Mantineans were exhorted to keep in mind that the battle was on behalf of their country and that the issue was about power and subjection: that is of not losing power after their taste of it and of not lapsing again back into subjection to Sparta. The Argives were reminded of their old supremacy and of not being deprived for all time of their equal share in the Peloponnese. They were also urged to take revenge for the injustices they had suffered from men who were both their enemies and their neighbors. The Athenians were told that it would be a glorious achievement to be bested by none of their many brave allies, by whose side they were fighting, and that if they defeated the Spartans in the Peloponnese, Athens' empire would be more secure and powerful and no other state would again invade their land. These were the words of encouragement spoken to the Argives and their allies. The Spartans, among themselves, good men that they were, according to their customs in war were making the usual exhortation, which was simply a reminder of things they already knew. For they were aware that prolonged practice is a much more effective means of safety than the words of a hurried but effectively delivered speech of exhortation.

After these preliminaries the two sides met. The Argives and their allies advanced eagerly and with their emotions at fever pitch, while the Spartans came on slowly and to the measure of the many flute players in their ranks. The reason for this was not religious but to advance evenly with measured step so that the order of their ranks would remain undisturbed. Such a disturbance is usual in large armies while advancing. As the two armies were still advancing and not yet engaged, King Agis decided to carry out a maneuver. All armies behave in the following manner: when they are coming into action their right wings become unduly extended and so these wings overlap their opponents' left. The reason for this is that in fear each man protects his unarmed side as much as possible with the shield of the man on his right and thinks that he is best protected by the closest locking of shields. The man who is on the extreme right of the line is the one who bears the original responsibility for the drift to the right by constantly trying to keep his unarmed side away from the enemy. The rest follow his example because of the same fear. So now the wing formed by the troops from Mantinea extended far beyond the Sciritae, while on the opposite side the wing of the Spartans and Tegeans extended even farther beyond that of the Athenians as their army was larger. Agis became afraid that his left wing would be encircled and thought that the Mantineans were outflanking it too much. He signaled to the Sciritae and the *Brasideioi* to bring themselves in line with the Mantineans and ordered the polemarchs, Hipponoidas and Aristocles, with their *lochoi* to come up from the right wing and fill the gap thus created. By executing this maneuver, he thought he would retain sufficient superiority on his right, while strengthening his left against the Mantineans. What happened was that since the orders were given at short notice and while the armies were on the move the two polemarchs refused to obey. They were later exiled from Sparta on account of their action after being convicted of cowardice. But the enemy came to grips before the Sciritae could close the gap themselves. Agis had ordered the Sciritae themselves to do so when the two *lochoi* would not come up. But on this occasion, at the most crucial point, they showed themselves inferior in skill but nevertheless prevailed by their courage. After the fighting had begun the Mantineans on the right routed the Sciritae and *Brasideioi* opposed to them. The Mantineans and their allies and the picked Argive force of one thousand rushed into the gap in the Spartan line which remained open. They killed many Spartans and encircled them and drove them back to their wagons. They then killed some of the older men who had been posted there. On this part of the battlefield the Spartans were bested. But elsewhere and, especially in the center where King Agis and the so-called three hundred knights were stationed, they fell upon the older Argives, those called the five companies, the Cleoneans, the men of Oenae and the Athenians who were arrayed alongside them, and routed them. Many of them did not even wait to come to blows but immediately gave way as the Spartans advanced and there were some who were trampled in their haste to avoid being caught.

When the army of the Argives and their allies had given way at this point and the line had broken on each side of the center, simultaneously the right wing of the Spartans and the Tegeans encircled the Athenians with those of their troops that outflanked them. The Athenians were thus threatened with danger from both sides: on one side they were being encircled and on the other they had already been defeated. The Athenians would have suffered more seriously than any other part of the army but for their cavalry. Further, it happened that when Agis saw that his left wing, the one opposite the Mantineans and the thousand Argives, was in difficulties, he ordered the whole army to the aid of the defeated wing. While this was happening and as the Spartan army passed by them and their army inclined away from them, the Athenians and the defeated units of the Argives along with them got away unharassed. The Mantineans and the select Argives were no longer minded to keep up the pressure against those opposed to them, but seeing their own side defeated and the Spartans advancing, turned to flight. Then many of the Mantineans perished but the greater part of the select Argive force survived. Indeed, they were not pressed hard nor for long during their flight and retreat. For Spartans holding a position will fight long and stubborn battles until they rout the enemy, but once they have done so they do not pursue them for any great distance nor for long.

This account of the battle is as close as possible to what actually transpired. It was on an exceptionally large scale and involved a number of very important Greek states; it had been a very long time since a battle on this scale had been fought.

The Spartans piled up the arms of the enemy dead and immediately erected a trophy and stripped the corpses. They took up their own dead and carried them back to Tegea where they were buried and they gave back the enemy dead under truce. The Argives, Orneatae and Cleoneans lost seven hundred killed, while the Mantinean dead numbered two hundred and those of the Athenians with the Aeginetans were two hundred, along with the loss of the two Athenian generals. The allies of the Spartans suffered no noteworthy losses. But it is difficult to obtain information on the number of Spartan casualties; it is said that three hundred perished.

GREEKS AND NON-GREEKS IN BATTLE: THE PERSIAN WARS

By 546 the Greeks cities on the coast of Asia Minor had passed under Persian domination. The rise of Persia to imperial predominance in the Near East was extraordinarily swift. The Persian homeland in southwestern Iran near the Persian Gulf had been subject to a related group, the Medes. It had been a relatively minor client of the Median empire until the accession of Cyrus the Great in about 559. By the death of Cyrus in 530 most of the Near East had passed under Persian control through a rapid series of conquests. Under Cyrus' son Cambyses Egypt and parts of Libya including the Greek city of Cyrene were subjugated. Cambyses' reign ended in 522 with revolt in the Persian homeland and among the subject peoples. By 521 a king from a collateral branch of the Achaemenid family, Darius I, had reestablished central control and initiated a period of reorganization and a new phase of imperial expansion.

The surprising swiftness of Persian expansion calls for some explanation. It appears at least in part due to a fortuitous combination of several factors. Persian expansion took place in a period when other large imperial states were relatively weak and were unable to form effective combinations against the young and aggressive new power. Further, the Persians, unlike some earlier states, were relatively tolerant and supportive of local religious beliefs and customs. This won local support for them. Finally, existing governmental techniques and personnel were incorporated and assimilated. The governmental structure that seems to have been reorganized and refined under Darius (521–486) was typical of ancient

Near Eastern imperial states with a large scribal bureaucracy. It was staffed mostly by non-Persians, including Greeks, and centered on sites where the Persian king had located his treasuries; of these the most important were Susa, Ecbatana and Persepolis.

In theory all power rested with the king. The structure of the court, composed for the most part of the Persian nobility which tended to monopolize the crucial positions at the center, is obscure. As in all monarchical states those who served as advisors and in close proximity to the king were in the crucial positions of power. By the time of Darius the empire was divided into at least twenty large provinces called satrapies, mostly governed by members of the Persian nobility. Satraps had extensive authority with both civil and military powers, including the collection of taxes and the recruitment of military forces as needed. There were garrisons at important cities to insure local tranquillity and to act as some check on the extensive powers of the governor.

Our evidence for the organization of the Persian armed forces is scanty. The core of the standing army was provided by a corps of ten thousand infantry, known as the Immortals, as the number was always kept up to strength. This élite unit was mostly Persian though the closely related Medes and Elamites from southern Iran are also known to have been members. One thousand of these troops served as the king's personal bodyguard and were always in attendance on him. Cavalry units of the same type and strength (ten thousand and one thousand) are also attested as part of the standing army. These forces, like those recruited for particular expeditions, were organized on a decimal basis and units between ten and ten thousand are noted in the sources. There were also standing forces in the satrapies, which served in attendance on the governor or as the garrisons for crucial strong points. Unlike the Immortals they were often raised from native peoples and included mercenaries. In addition to the standing army military contingents were raised for major expeditions or special situations. Herodotus provides us with our fullest list for the expedition of Xerxes in 480. He lists forty-five peoples organized in twenty-nine commands and in six army corps. In addition to the standing army there was also a standing navy with the trireme as the standard ship-of-the-line. The naval contingents were recruited from peoples with a maritime tradition, primarily from the Phoenician cities, Cyprus and Egypt. Technically the Persians appear to have been adept especially in logistics, siege warfare and diplomatic maneuvering. But the very size and variety of Persian forces were a potential source of difficulty on major expeditions. On land there is also the question of how effective troops other than Persians were in battle.

Darius continued the policy of Achaemenid expansion on both the eastern and western borders of his empire. Active elsewhere, his major effort was directed towards the West. Before 513 the major Greek islands of Samos, Lesbos and Chios passed under Persian control. In that same year Darius himself crossed over into Europe and began the conquest of Thrace as far north as the Danube. After Darius' return the conquest was completed and Persian control was extended as far as Macedonia. Diplomatic relations were entered into with mainland Greek states at the same time.

There seems to no reason to doubt that Darius intended the conquest of Greece and the Aegean. This should be seen in the context of the normal dynamic of expansion that had marked the reigns of his predecessors. In 499 his forces made an attempt to capture Naxos and begin the penetration and conquest of the Cyclades. The expedition ended in failure and recrimination. Its most important effect was to serve as the catalyst for a revolt by the Ionian Greeks on the coast of Asia Minor. The causes of the revolt lay in the unhappy state of the area under Persian rule. Persian domination had led to economic problems created by disruption of trade and lost opportunities for mercenary service. In addition, the imposition of tyrants by the Persians added political resentment.

The revolt lasted from 499 to 493 and initially the Greeks were surprisingly successful. This appears in part to have been due to the slowness of Persian mobilization. The Ionians solicited aid in mainland Greece, but only Athens with twenty ships and Eretria with five responded and they soon departed as the fortunes of war shifted to the Persians. Severe losses by the Greeks and their allies were followed by a definitive naval defeat at island of Lade in 494. In the next year the key city of Miletus was taken and sacked and the rest of the Ionian cities were reduced one by one, often in a harsh manner.

In the aftermath of the revolt the Persians continued small-scale military action and then restructured the governments of the Ionian cities as a first step towards consolidating their position in the northern Aegean and preparing for an eventual invasion of Greece. In 492 Mardonius, a son-in-law of Darius, campaigned in Thrace, solidifying the Persian position there and readying the way for a possible future invasion.

By 491 the attack was imminent. Its approach was heralded by the construction of a large invasion fleet including horse transports and a demand for surrender sent to most of the major states of the Greek mainland. The strongest land power in Greece, Sparta, not only refused submission but executed the heralds, as did the Athenians. By so doing they gave public expression to a relentless will to resist. The Persian commanders Datis and Artaphernes made their first landing at Naxos, which they took in the high summer of 490. The Persians then landed in southern Euboea and proceeded against Eretria which had fought against them as Athens had. After a violent siege the city fell. It was devastated and the population deported. The Persians then landed on the plain of Marathon in northeastern Attica. It not only offered abundant supplies and a safe anchorage but also suitable country for cavalry. The Athenians made the decision to face the enemy in field and sent their field army of eight thousand which was joined by a levy of one thousand from their ally Plataea. The Athenian commanders were divided on whether to wait for promised Spartan aid before engaging but finally, under the prodding of Miltiades, decided to engage. The result was a total victory that showed the superiority of Greek infantry in close fighting in conditions where they could come to grips with their opponent and avoid prolonged exposure to enemy missiles. Herodotus remarks that it was the first Greek land victory over the Persians. The Athenians soon surrounded the victory with an enduring mythology about the victory of Greek freedom over Oriental despotism. The expedition seems to have resulted in a change in Persian strategy and a return to the use of a land route along the coast of Thrace.

Darius seems to have interpreted the defeat at Marathon as a signal that a larger and more formidable expedition was needed. But an Egyptian rebellion intervened in 486, the last year of the king's life. Before any foreign adventures could be undertaken it was vital to subdue this key province. Darius' son and successor Xerxes required three years to do so, completing its conquest in 483.

A decision was then made to invade the Greek mainland with a combined force by sea and land. Close cooperation between the two was vital. The fleet would allow the Persians to bypass formidable natural obstacles on land. In the confined spaces of Greece the Persian army would be at a disadvantage in equipment and training, as Marathon had shown. The land forces were vital to provide anchorage for the fleet, given the limited range of ancient warships. This mutual dependence lay at the center of Persian strategy. Preparations for the expedition against Greece then began. They illustrate a Persian expertise in logistics and engineering that appears to surpass anything the Greeks were capable of at this point. A canal requiring a vast expenditure of effort was built in three years around Mount Athos to avoid the danger of the storms, but the most impressive engineering feat was the construction of a double bridge of boats over the Hellespont to avoid the time-consuming ferrying of the Persian troops. Troops were assembled in the course of 481. The size of these forces is much disputed. The land forces have been estimated at somewhere between two to three hundred thousand fighting men with the most important being a core of twenty-four thousand Persian troops. The fleet may have consisted of about seven hundred triremes or fighting ships. It exceeded anything in Greek experience. During the latter part of 481 Xerxes sent embassies to the Greek states in his path requesting tokens of submission.

Those Greek states who were determined to oppose the Persian invasion had already met and formed an association in the fall of 481. The key states were Athens and Sparta. There was little unity among the Greeks: some were prepared to resist with all of their strength, but other states were divided internally or prepared to gain local advantages by allying with the invader. The leadership on both land and sea was given to the Spartans, perhaps in part because their allies constituted the majority of allied states. When Xerxes set out with his army in the spring of 480 the league met in May 480, and its first item of business was to answer an appeal from pro-Greek Thessalians for support in resisting the Persians. Thessalian cavalry would be especially valuable given known Persian strengths. An expedition of ten thousand was sent north to guard the pass into Thessaly at Tempe. The measure was not a success. Local support was weak at best and the pass could be turned from the west. The hastily assembled force retreated. This failure led in June to a decision to select a position where the fleet and the army could act jointly. The obvious point to defend against a combined naval and land operation was chosen: Thermopylae on land and Artemesium on the sea. This line offered the advantages to the Greeks of ready communication between land and sea forces, confined spaces that favored their naval tactics of ramming as well as their infantry methods, and it was far enough north to protect important states in central Greece. With reinforcements the Greek fleet was to total 368 ships of which 324 were triremes. The great majority (180) were Athenian though overall command rested with the Spartans. On land, command again rested with the Spartans under Leonidas, one of the kings, though the Spartans supplied only a nominal contingent of three hundred. Total forces numbered about seven thousand hoplites who took up their position within the pass at Thermopylae to block the Persians. Greek strategy is not totally clear but it appears that they anticipated that the major decision was to be on the sea. In practice it mattered little. If Xerxes could be held on either element his forces would not be able to sustain themselves and retreat would have been inevitable. On the sea the Persians suffered from the weather, losing a number of ships, and they seem to have come off worse in their first two engagements in the narrow sea at the northern end of Euboea. In the third things were more equal, and in any case the Greek fleet was forced to retreat as their position on land had been turned. Repeating the mistake of Tempe the Greeks had not sufficiently reconnoitered their position or given enough thought to the possibility of the Persians using a known alternative route around the pass. It was this route that turned the pass and caused the disintegration of the Greek position on land and the death of Leonidas and his Spartan contingent. The Greeks were forced to retreat south and a significant area of central Greece was opened to the Persians by mid-September.

In the immediate aftermath of the defeat the Greeks were disorganized and divided in their plans for resistance as Persians advanced on and sacked Athens while their fleet took up a position opposite the Greeks at the Bay of Phalerum on the Attic coast. The Greek fleet had at the request of the Athenians aided in the evacuation of Athenian civilians to the island of Salamis off the coast, and lay at anchor there when Xerxes arrived. The Peloponnesians including the Spartans wanted to withdraw and to cover the men fortifying the Isthmus. The Athenians and others north of Isthmus opposed withdrawal from the narrows at Salamis where the Greeks would again have the obvious advantage of a confined space. A major role was played by the Athenians with their 180 ships and by their commander Themistocles who was to enjoy the credit for having brought about the battle. Under pressure the Peloponnesians agreed to fight. The Greek allies possessed 378 ships. The Greeks believed the Persian fleet to be much larger but it appears that the forces were relatively equal in numbers. The critical encounter came late in September. The constricted channel between the mainland and Salamis favored the Greeks. The Persian fleet fell into disorder and the Greeks, using their tactic of ramming, scored a decisive victory over the enemy. Persian casualties were heavy and the morale of the fleet was broken. Xerxes was also afraid of the effect that the news of his defeat might have on the Ionian Greeks. In addition, the year was too advanced to begin another fleet on the same scale.

The Persian army now left Attica and retreated north while the fleet sailed to watch the Greeks in Asia Minor. To break off the campaign at this point would have been too damaging to Xerxes' reputation. There was also the possibility that rivalry and disunion among the Greeks could be exploited to good effect. At the very least there remained the possibility that the Greek army could be enticed to face the Persians on a battlefield that would favor eastern tactics. Xerxes selected his most experienced general Mardonius and decided to use a select force to carry out his purpose. The size of the army he left with Mardonius is again a problem. The best evidence is provided by the fact that in the final battle with the Greeks his forces seem to be of the same size as theirs. An estimate of 120,000 troops of all kinds including local Greek forces would seem reasonable. Mardonius wintered with his troops in Thessaly where there were loyal supporters and excellent supplies for his men and forage for his horses. Xerxes himself marched north to the Hellespont accompanied by his other senior commander, Artabazus, who was to return with his army to support Mardonius after the king had crossed to Asia.

The period between the fall of 480 and the summer of 479 was spent by Mardonius in trying to detach the Athenians from the alliance and so provide the Persians with a way around the Isthmus fortifications which effectively blocked them. The Athenians, supreme at sea, needed to defeat the Persians on land to free Attica from the threat of invasion. Despite tempting offers the initial negotiations with Mardonius proved fruitless for the Persians and in an attempt to bring pressure to bear on the Athenians and perhaps to lure the Peloponnesians out of their fortifications Mardonius and his forces moved south into Attica. With the Persians once again in control of Attica the Athenians finally threatened desertion to the Persian side. The importance of Athens' fleet was demonstrated by the immediate dispatch of a force of ten thousand, half of which consisted of Spartan soldiers.

Mardonius withdrew into Boeotia at the approach of the Greeks. It offered him a friendly base, abundant supplies and excellent cavalry country north of the Asopus River. He stationed his forces on the north bank of the river and built a stockade as a defensive measure. The Greek army moved north under the command of the Spartan Pausanias, nephew of the Leonidas who had perished at Thermopylae and regent for the son of Leonidas, Pleistonax. The Greek army, comprising 38,700 hoplites and about 70,000 light-armed men, crossed the main pass from Attica into Boeotia and encamped on the south bank of the Asopus in the foothills of the mountain range that separates Attica and Boeotia. The position offered abundant water, fairly easy supply from the south and broken country that was unsuitable for cavalry.

The course and details of the long period of waiting and battle that followed have been the subject of much dispute. What is clear is that there was a prolonged period of delay, with each side trying to draw the other onto terrain favorable to it. The Persians suffered some important losses but finally by intercepting supplies and fouling the springs upon which the Greeks depended forced them out of position and nearer Plataea and the pass that was used by the Greeks for their supplies. The Greek forces were intercepted by the Persians and a series of separate battles developed. The determining struggle was that of the Spartans and the troops on the Greek right wing who after a prolonged and fierce battle killed Mardonius and put the Persians to flight. The Greek forces then combined with the Athenians to attack the stockade where the Persians had fled. It was breached and the battle degenerated into a slaughter. Most of the Persian forces were killed or captured, though a remnant was able to flee north and to make its way home.

Plataea was the last defensive battle. Soon after, with a major Greek victory at Mycale in Asia Minor, the tide had turned. The initiative shifted to the Greeks who now went on the offensive. The victory in the war was decisive and ended permanently any threat of direct invasion of the Greek mainland by the Persians. The victory was due in part to poor choices by the Persians insofar as the season was so advanced that any serious setback would necessitate a change in the overall strategy they had adopted. Most serious had been their inability to win a victory on sea. That failure meant that they were deprived of the choice of battlefield where their cavalry and archery might prevail. They were forced to fight the crucial battle on a field that favored the superior defensive armament of the Greek hoplite. Persian infantry simply could not match this superiority under such conditions. But Persia was to remain a important factor in Greek politics; its role, especially as an arbiter of Greek politics and an employer of Greek mercenaries, was to grow in importance in the course of the fourth century until the Macedonians intervened and destroyed their empire.

The effect of the Persians extended into the ideological sphere as well. The war made the Greeks conscious of their cultural and ethnic identity as no earlier event had done. It gave rise to various intellectual and cultural movements that stressed the uniqueness of the Greek people and their way of life. Such currents were to play an important role in the world of literature as well as in political life.

Greek views of the Persians

131. Herodotus, 7.102.1–104.5

The speaker, Demaratus, figures as one of Darius' principal advisors in Herodotus. It is impossible to know his actual relationship to the king. Involved in a conflict with the other Spartan king, Cleomenes, in 491 he had fled for asylum as other Greeks had done to the Persian court. He accompanied Xerxes on his expedition in 480 and was later rewarded by him and died in Persia. He often seems to serve as a spokesman for Herodotus' thoughts. His words reiterate two themes that dominate the tradition about the war in Herodotus and in other Greek writers. The first is the connection between Greek military superiority and Greek freedom. Oriental despotism robs its subjects, who are slaves, of the basis for courage. The second theme is the portrayal of Xerxes as an Oriental despot that occurs in Herodotus and elsewhere.

"My king, you command that I speak the whole truth and in so speaking to say nothing that will be discovered by you to be untrue. Poverty has always been Greece's companion; her virtue was acquired. It is by her use of wisdom and the power of the law that she keeps off poverty and despotism." . . . Xerxes laughed on hearing what Demaratus said. . . . "How could a thousand, ten thousand or even fifty thousand, especially since they are free and not under the command of one man, stand against so great an army? Possibly if they were under the control of one man as our troops are, in fear of him they might show themselves more courageous than they really are and compelled by the lash attack a force larger than their own. But if they abandoned themselves to freedom they would do none of these things." . . . Demaratus answered the king as follows . . . "So it is with the Spartans, struggling by themselves they are a match for any, but fighting as a group they have no equals. They are free but not completely so; the law is their master, they are more thoroughly subject to it than are your men to you. They do what this master commands and his command never varies, it is to never flee any group of men in battle but remaining in position to conquer or die."

132. Plato, *Menexenus* 245C–D

Written in the 380s this dialogue is in all essentials a praise of Athens' past achievements in the form of a funeral speech delivered over Athenian war dead. Its attitude of superiority towards the Persians is typical of much fourth-century writing, as is its stress on intrinsic differences between Greeks and non-Greeks. The references to Pelops and the other mythological figures are to Asiatic or Egyptian settlers of various areas of Greece. The Athenians had a long-standing tradition that they had always inhabited Attica. The reference to the surrender of fellow Greeks is to agreements concluded between Sparta and the Persian king towards the end of the Peloponnesian War in which in return for financial and military support the Spartans conceded that the King had authority over the Greek cities of Asia Minor.

"So noble, free, stable and healthy is our city, and a hater of barbarians by nature, because we are pure Greeks unmixed with the barbarians. For we are not the descendants of Pelops, Cadmus, Aegyptus or Danaus nor any of the many others who are barbarians by race though Greeks by convention. We are true Greeks, pure, and so an unalloyed hate has sunk deeply into the city for foreigners. Despite our views we have become isolated again through our unwillingness to commit the shameful and unholy act of surrendering our fellow Greeks to barbarians."

The reasons for the war

133. Aeschylus, *The Persians*, 101–108

This play provides our earliest literary evidence for the war and was written by a participant. There were other contemporary plays dealing with the war but only Aeschylus' has survived. It was produced in the spring of 472. The prime cause of the war for the playwright is the destiny of expansion decreed by the gods for the Persians that will end by divine dispensation in disaster. In Xerxes' case the process is accelerated because expansion leads to insolent pride (*hubris*) which precipitates the anger of the gods and the disasters that follow.

Darius: "The divine destiny long ago imposed upon the Persians the waging of rampart-destroying wars and the turmoil of cavalry in battle and the overturning of cities."
The Queen: "Raging Xerxes learned this behavior by associating with evil men. They said that you had gained great wealth for your children in war and that he fought as a kept warrior and in no way increased his paternal wealth. Frequently hearing such reproaches from these evil men he devised the idea of an expedition against Greece."

134. Herodotus, 7.8a–d1

This council that Xerxes and his advisors called to decide whether to invade Greece is fictional but it does contain some Persian elements. The basic ideas of the speakers are Greek. They reflect two fundamental strands in Herodotus' thoughts on the reasons for the war. At one level the war is part of a divine plan, as Xerxes makes clear. On the other it is Xerxes' own personal decision. His cast of mind reflects the unbounded desire for expansion that will lead to disaster. They find a parallel in the selection from Aeschylus' *Persians* (no. 133). Astyages was the last Median king defeated in battle by the founder of the Persian empire, Cyrus, in about 550. The burning of Sardis probably occurred in 498 in the course of the unsuccessful revolt by the Ionian Greeks. Darius' expedition was the one defeated by the Athenians at Marathon in 490.

After they had assembled Xerxes said, "Persians, I will not be the first to institute this custom among you but I have inherited it and I intend to follow it. As I learned from the older of you, we have never remained passive since the time when we took over rule from the Medes when Cyrus deposed Astyages. God directs us this way and our following it has led to great benefits. I do not need to tell you, since you are well aware of the peoples that Cyrus and my father Darius conquered and added to our empire. When I succeeded to this throne I was mindful of not falling short of my predecessors in honor and of how to add not less than they to Persian power. In my considerations on these matters I discovered not only a glory which will accrue to us but also that what we add will not be smaller nor less productive than what we already have. At the same time we will obtain punishment and satisfaction for past wrongs. I have called this meeting to ask for advice on what I intend to do. My plan is to bridge the Hellespont and to lead an army through Europe against Greece to punish the Athenians for what they have done to my own father and to the Persians in general. Recently you saw my father Darius preparing to march against these men, but he died and so was unable to carry out his revenge. For his sake and the sake of the Persians I will not stop until I capture Athens and burn it. They began the feud by wronging us by first attacking Sardis with our slave Aristagoras of Miletus and burning its sacred groves and temples. Then they repelled our forces under the command of Datis and Artaphernes when they landed in their land, as you well know. As a result of all this I am now prepared to make war upon them.

In my thought about these matters I have discovered a number of advantages if we conquer the Athenians and their neighbors the Peloponnesians. We will make the land of the Persians as extensive as the heavens. The sun will look on no land bordering our own, but all will be added to our empire as I proceed through all Europe. There will be no city or people left of those I know that will be able to meet us in battle if these are removed. The guilty and the innocent will both be under the yoke of slavery."

The equipment of the Persian troops

For the Greeks the essential Persian weapon was the bow. Herodotus tells us that only three things were taught to Persian boys: to ride, to shoot straight and to tell the truth. The Persians used the spear as well as the bow, and that fact was recognized by the Greeks, but it was subordinated to the bow for the sake of emphasizing the contrast between Greek and Persian.

135. Aeschylus, *The Persians* 140–148

"Come Persians, seating ourselves on the steps of this ancient structure, let us consider wisely and deeply – the need is pressing – how it goes with Xerxes the king, son of Darius of the ancestral line that has given us our name, whether the draw of the bow is victorious or the iron-headed spear."

Infantry

136. Herodotus, 7.61.1

Representations of the élite Immortals that illustrate this passage have survived from the royal palace at Susa. There is some doubt among scholars as to whether the average Persian soldier wore a scale tunic. The normal view is that it would have been too expensive to supply it to all troops and that the normal body armor was provided by a quilted corselet. The wicker shield which was made to be set upright in the ground may have been covered with leather, and the spears were certainly shorter than those of the Greek hoplites and put the Persians at a disadvantage.

The peoples who composed the expedition were these. The Persians were equipped in the following manner: on their heads they had soft felt caps they call tiaras, multi-colored, sleeved tunics, a corselet made of iron scales like those of a fish, and trousers. They carried wicker shields for protection, low-slung quivers, short spears and great bows with cane arrows. In addition, they had daggers hanging from their belts near the right thigh.

Cavalry

137. Herodotus, 7.84.1–2

It is likely that a proportion of the Persian cavalry wore metal helmets and were equipped with quilted corselets covered with metal scales. Those could prove almost impenetrable to Greek weapons. Offensive weapons shown on reliefs and in paintings include cutlasses and axes. As with Greek cavalry they did not use stirrups or a saddle and cavalry seem to have functioned as mobile missile platforms, though they could on occasion close with other cavalry. Their advantages lay in the superior breeds of horses available to the Persians to outride their opponents and in more effective cavalry spears. In combat the cavalry appear to have been the most effective Persian force. On many occasions the Greeks display reluctance to face or to move across open spaces where it might be deployed against them.

The Persian cavalry was equipped in the same way as their infantry except for the following. Certain horsemen wore helmets of beaten bronze or iron. There is a nomadic people, the Sagartians, who are ethnically and linguistically Persian and whose dress is halfway between the Persian and the Pactyan, who provided eight thousand troops. They carried no metal weapons except daggers. Rather they used lassos plaited from leather thongs.

Persians and Greeks in battle: Plataea

The battle which marked the final end to the Persian campaign in Greece took place in July 479. Its course has been briefly described in the introduction to this section. The forces massed on both sides seem to have been approximately equal. The combined Greek forces under the Spartan regent Pausanias mustered 38,700 hoplites and approximately 70,000 light-armed troops for a total of about 110,000 men. It is a remarkable total of hoplites and far exceeded in numbers any earlier forces that the Greek states fielded. The Persian troops under the overall command of Mardonius, with a separate force under his nominal subordinate Artabazus, consisted of about 60,000 men directly under Mardonius' command with an additional 40,000 under Artabazus. To these troops must be added perhaps 20,000 Greeks who fought with the Persians. Both armies were in the field for an extended period of time for the final and decisive encounter. This took place on the thirteenth day after the arrival of the Greek forces. Despite what appears to be the normal superiority of the Persians in organization and logistics, the Greek army was successfully supplied by wagon convoys from the south. It was when the Persian cavalry threatened Greek supplies that their army was forced to change position to keep their supply line open. Mardonius also had to bring his supplies over a considerable distance from Thebes. Both sides showed a remarkable ability to feed masses of men over a considerable period of time and move supplies for substantial distances.

The importance of Persian cavalry in the course of the struggle is obvious. It determined the positions of both armies. Mardonius encamped north of the Asopus River to take advantage of the plain to its north where his cavalry could operate unhindered, while the Greek forces chose all three of their positions in the course of the battle with an eye to selecting hilly and broken country unsuitable for cavalry operations. The following passages make clear that missiles in the form of arrows and javelins were the predominant offensive weapons of the cavalry, though on occasion they could fight at close quarters. They seem to have attacked in squadron, keeping up a constant barrage of missiles which could cause serious losses among the Greek heavy-armed troops who except for the Athenians lacked specialized missile firing troops who might have provided a counter. The cavalry were especially effective against disorganized troops or those caught in the line of march. Persian tactics seemed to center on the use of missiles to disorganize and soften up the enemy, then a final rush of cavalry and infantry at close quarters to complete the defeat of the enemy.

138. Herodotus, 9.49.2–63

Mardonius, delighted and elated by his illusory victory, ordered a cavalry attack. When the cavalry attacked they began to cause casualties among the Greeks by their archery and use of the javelins since they were horse archers and were difficult to engage. The cavalry destroyed and filled in with dirt the spring of Gargaphia from which the entire Greek army drew its water. Only the Lacedaemonians were stationed by the spring; it was some distance from the other Greek forces stationed in their various positions near the Asopus. Since the Greeks were kept from the Asopus because of the Persian cavalry's bows, they were forced to use the spring for water.

Since the army was deprived of its water supply and harassed by the enemy's cavalry the Greek generals met and then went in a body to Pausanias who was on the army's right to discuss these and other matters. The generals were also upset about other matters as well, though these were bad enough. They were still without food and the servants who had been sent to the Peloponnese to bring food were cut off by the Persian cavalry and could not reach the camp. The generals decided to withdraw to a place known as the Island if the Persians let the day go by without a battle. . . . They chose this spot to have an unlimited water supply and to prevent the enemy's cavalry from harming them as they did when they were exposed to them. It was decided to change position during the night at the second watch to avoid the Persians catching sight of them as they set out and pursuing and harassing them. . . .

The final phase of the struggle on the right of the Greek line shows the standard Persian infantry tactic of creating a barrier of shields behind which those archers on foot could deploy and fire their arrows. It also makes clear that once Persian infantry became immobile they were hopelessly outclassed in terms of their defensive and offensive equipment.

After Mardonius had said these things he led the Persians forward at top speed across the Asopus in the tracks of who they thought were running away. His attack was launched only against the Lacedaemonians and the Tegeans as he was unable to see the Athenians who had turned into the plain and were hidden by hills. The other commanders of the various barbarian units saw that the Persians had begun to move in pursuit of the Greeks and immediately began to set their forces in motion as fast as they could without any order or discipline. They attacked yelling and shouting, thinking that they could take the Greeks easily. . . .

So the Lacedaemonians and the Tegeans were isolated; the former numbered fifty thousand with their light-armed troops while the latter totaled three thousand men (they would not allow themselves to be separated from the Lacedaemonians in any way). When they were about to launch their attack against Mardonius and his army they made a sacrifice. The sacrifice was not favorable and so they could not move. While this was going on many were killed and even more were wounded. The Persians planted their shields in a defensive wall and continually discharged their arrows. . . . While Pausanias was still praying the Tegeans rose up first and moved to the attack against the barbarians and immediately after the prayer of Pausanias the omens turned out favorably. The Lacedaemonians now also advanced against the Persians who put aside their bows and were ready to meet them. The combat began around the shield wall. When it had been breached a sharp engagement took place around the shrine of Demeter and lasted for some time at close quarters. The enemy would grab hold of the Greek spears and break them. The Persians were not inferior in courage and strength, but they lacked armor, were poorly trained and greatly inferior in skill to their opponents. They broke ranks, and darting forwards individually in groups of ten – sometimes more, sometimes fewer – they fell upon the Spartan line and were killed. Mardonius was on the field fighting from a white charger with an élite unit of a thousand. As long as Mardonius survived they kept up the struggle and struck down many of the Lacedaemonians; but when he and his personal guard (the finest Persian troops) were killed, the rest gave way to the Lacedaemonians and fled. The crucial factor in their defeat was that they were unprotected, unarmed men fighting against heavily armored infantry.

Why the Greeks won and the Persians lost

The Persian War was a critical event in forging a strong sense of Greek cultural and ethnic identity that was to contribute to an abiding sense that Greeks and "barbarians" were separated by an almost unbridgable gulf. It was quickly conceptualized as a struggle of despotism against freedom, luxury against poverty. It soon took on mythic proportions and its importance is marked by the fact that it is associated with the development of the building on a large scale of the first permanent victory monuments, as well as with a flood of poetry and plays celebrating and glorifying the Greek victory. Its lasting significance is demonstrated by the fact that almost a half century later Athenian speakers could point to their service in the war against the Persians as a justification for their imperial position over other Greek states.

139. Herodotus, 7.139
Herodotus was writing for a Greek audience at a point in time when Athens had acquired an empire and had become very unpopular as a result. Despite his claims of the importance of Athens' role in the Greek achievement, Herodotus gives due credit to the Spartans and recognizes that Plataea was essentially a

Spartan victory. His assertiveness may here may be explained by the existence of rival views one of which ascribed victory to the Persians' own mistakes.

At this point I think it necessary to give my opinion and although most might object, nevertheless I will not hold back since it appears to be the truth. If the Athenians in fear of the impending danger had left their homes or if they had not left it but remained and surrendered to Xerxes, the Greeks would not have attempted to resist the King at sea. And if no one had opposed Xerxes by sea, then the result on land would have been the following: even if many fortification walls been constructed across the Isthmus by the Peloponnesians, nonetheless the Lacedaemonians would have been betrayed by their allies that served under compulsion and these cities would have been taken one by one by the barbarian fleet. The Lacedaemonians, now isolated after performing prodigious feats, would have died nobly. Either this is what would have happened or, seeing the other Greeks go over, they would have surrendered to Xerxes. Either way Greece would have become subject to him. I cannot see what benefit there would be in fortifying the Isthmus if the King controlled the sea. If someone should call the Athenians the saviors of Greece he would be speaking the truth. Whichever side they chose was bound to prevail. They first chose that Greece should continue to exist and be free and then rallied those Greeks who had not already gone over to the Persians and with the gods' help repelled the invader.

140. Plutarch, *On the Malice of Herodotus* 874A–B

This prolonged attack on Herodotus, written at the beginning of the second century AD, was motivated by local Boeotian patriotism and a view of history as a form of moral exhortation. Herodotus obviously did not give much support to either point of view. Plutarch voices one of the common views of the war, that saw the Greek victory as the result of superior valor and virtue. The cause of victory was moral and it represented the superiority of the Greek way of life.

What is there that is glorious or great that resulted from this battle if the Lacedaemonians fought with unprotected men, if the other Greeks were unaware that a battle was being fought, if the common burial honored by the descendants of each is empty, the tripods that stand as dedications are covered with lies, and Herodotus alone knows the truth, and that all other men who have heard the account of the Greeks have been deceived by the tradition that these successes were remarkable accomplishments?

THE AFTERMATH OF BATTLE

At the conclusion of most hoplite battles the scene must have differed considerably from the modern battlefield. The highest concentration of dead would normally be in the area where the two hostile forces had come into contact. There the bodies might be piled several high, as in the aftermath of Leuctra in 371. On the losing side the casualties would then spread back along the track of their flight or retreat. The numbers of dead would normally be considerably fewer as the distance from the initial point of collision increased. But occasionally, when a victorious army had good cavalry support, the countryside might be filled with the bodies of hoplites struck down as they fled in panic, lost their cohesion and so were most vulnerable to attack by light-armed or cavalry forces.

But in general, pursuit was carried out only for a short distance in the absence of effective light-armed and cavalry support in the major hoplite battles. Hoplite equipment was not suited to swift or lengthy pursuit and the basic concept in Greek warfare was domination of the battlefield and not the extermination of the enemy. Both of these factors mitigated the impulse to destroy the fleeing enemy. Unlike on a modern battlefield, the bodies of the dead would be relatively intact and the manner of their death more obvious.

There were wounded as well as the dead. The wounded, including those with flesh wounds, simple fractures or concussions, would be helped off the battlefield, and would have had a good chance of survival so long as infection could be avoided. But the more seriously injured, with deep penetration wounds or severe blows to the head, especially where internal bleeding was involved, could not expect to survive despite the rudimentary medical services provided by some armies. Contemporary medicine was simply incapable of dealing with a trauma of this magnitude. So, as in modern warfare, casualties might still be accumulating in the weeks following the battle.

The numbers killed varied greatly with the type of enemy encountered. At Marathon Herodotus tells us that 6400 Persian troops were killed at the cost of 192 Athenian casualties. In the battle of Cunaxa, none of the Greeks was killed or indeed wounded except for one possible minor wound due to an arrow. These numbers are for the most part due to the superior defensive and offensive equipment of the hoplite as opposed to other infantry.

In clashes between Greek hoplites casualties normally ran much higher. On the average the winners had a 5 per cent mortality rate for their forces as against about 14 per cent for the defeated. Of course there was great variation due to the skill, experience and cohesion of the troops involved. The Spartans emerged from major battles such as Nemea with very few fatalities. But even for the victors, given the small size of the populations of Greek city-states, the strain could be severe. Among the losers, especially the smaller states, disaster could be the result. So at Delium in 424 the losses of the Thespians were so great that Thebans were able to annex them and destroy their fortifications.

Casualties

141. Xenophon, *Agesilaus* 2.14

Xenophon presents a moving portrait of the aftermath of the particularly fierce clash between the Thebans and the Spartans at Coronea in 394. The possession of the enemy dead is necessary to prompt a request for burial which served as a formal admission of defeat.

After the fighting had ceased one could see that where they had clashed with each other the earth was stained with blood and the corpses of friends and enemies lay side by side.

There were shattered shields, spears broken in pieces and unsheathed daggers, some lying on the ground, some stuck in bodies and others still gripped to strike even in death. The Spartans dragged the enemy dead within their formation and then ate and slept.

142. Xenophon, *Hellenica* 4.4.11–12

This action was fought near Lechaeum, Corinth's harbor on the Corinthian Gulf. It took place either in 392 or 391. It serves as an excellent illustration of the weaknesses of hoplite equipment and the result of the disintegration of a hoplite formation. There is some exaggeration in the description: human corpses can pile to the height of two or three, but hardly to the height of heaps of grain or stone.

The Corinthian exiles had defeated the men posted opposite them and had slipped through further to the south towards [Corinth], and were now close to the circuit of the city walls. The Spartans, when they saw that the area held by the Sicyonians had been taken by the enemy, came out in support, keeping the stockade to their left. When the Argives heard that the Spartans were behind them, they turned around and ran out of the stockade on the double. Those on the extreme right of the Argives were struck on their unshielded side by the Spartans and were killed. Those on the side where the wall was, fell back in a disorderly mass to the city. When they encountered the Corinthian exiles and recognized them as hostile they turned back again. Some mounted the fortification and then jumped down and were killed. Others were pushed back by the enemy to the steps and were struck down. Still others were trampled by their own men and suffocated.

The Spartans were not at a loss as to whom to kill next. For the gods had given them an opportunity they could not have prayed for. A mass of the enemy struck dumb by fear were delivered into their hands. Moreover, these men had exposed their unarmored side and were unprepared to fight. Everything contributed to their destruction. How could it not be the result of divine intervention? In a short time, so many of the enemy fell that their corpses were piled up like heaps of grain, wood or stone.

143. Athenian Casualty List of the Erechtheid Tribe, GHI² no. 33

This is one of the casualty lists (460 or 459 BC) from the monuments in the public burial area described by Thucydides and Pausanias. Often the names of all the dead of a campaigning season were listed on a single stele or on an adjoining set of stelai fashioned into a monumental whole. One other monument to the dead of a single tribe has been found. The earliest monument dates to 464. These monuments are closely connected with the public oration and burial described by Thucydides (see no. 148) and also with the games held in honor of the dead at the same time. These lists, in conjunction with the conduct of the Athenian general Nicias (see no. 144) illustrate the care shown at Athens for the individual dead, and give us some idea of the total casualties suffered. This behavior strengthens the presumption of accuracy for the numbers of casualties given by Greek authors. At Athens it appears that not only hoplites but all citizens were listed – as well as non-Athenians who formed a part of the Athenian forces, as the foreign names on the stele of the archers indicate. Allied troops appear to have been given their own separate memorial.

Of the Erechtheid tribe the following died in the war in Cyprus, in Egypt, in Phoenicia, in Hales, at Aegina and at Megara in the same year:
Of the generals:

Ph[ryni]chus	Phanyllus	Acryptus
P[ant]aleon	Ch[..]nius	Timocrates
Polystratus	Al[c]ippus	Euthycrates

The list continues in three columns

General:	In Egypt
Hippodamus	
Euthymachus	
Eumelus	Telenicus
Androsthenes	seer
archers Phrynus	
Taurus	
Theodorus	
Aleximachus	

144. Plutarch, *Nicias* 6.4–5

These casualties were incurred as a result of an encounter between Athenian and Corinthian forces after the Athenians disembarked in Corinthian territory. The action took place on the beach in front of Solygia and on the hill itself in the summer of 425. The Athenians won the battle, but had to evacuate their position when enemy reinforcements arrived. The passage shows the care that was devoted to gathering and identifying the dead. This supports the value of the casualty lists as accurate evidence for those killed.

Disembarking in Corinthian territory, Nicias defeated them in battle, inflicting heavy casualties on them and killing their general Lycophron. It happened that when he was taking up his dead for burial he missed two of them. When he realized this, he immediately halted his fleet and sent a herald to the enemy to ask for the two bodies.

Admission of defeat

The aim of most hoplite warfare was not the destruction of the enemy but the winning of possession of the field of battle. If this was achieved it often exposed the losing side to the possible loss of their food supply and affected their prestige sufficiently to make it impossible, or at least unprofitable, to continue the fighting. The casualties of the losing side in major engagements were often enough to seriously deplete their military manpower and to make it difficult for them to sustain further combat.

Hoplite warfare was a way of concentrating conflict and so limiting the overall effect of warfare on the Greek states. To serve this function, it needed to clearly identify the victor. A symbolic system was developed to provide unambiguous confirmation of the results. The first sign was the possession of the enemy dead by the victor. Since Greeks considered burial of the dead as a necessity the losing side had to ask by herald for a truce to obtain back the bodies of their dead. This request and its acceptance by the other side served as a clear signal as to who had won and who had lost. The bodies of the losers became hostages with which to exact a formal recognition of defeat. Further unambiguous evidence was provided by the erection of a trophy which was tangible evidence of victory. One of the great differences between ancient Greek and modern warfare is this strict system of rules and rituals that was developed to avoid prolonged conflict and to prevent the total destruction of the defeated enemy.

145. Xenophon, *Hellenica* 7.5.26–27

Xenophon is here referring to the indecisive result of the second battle of Mantinea in 362, which was a Theban tactical victory but a strategic failure in that it did not clearly establish Theban leadership in Greece. In this case he makes evident the clear links between the actual result of battle and its reflection on the symbolic level of the burial truce and the trophy.

After the completion of this battle affairs turned out opposite to what most men supposed they would. Since almost all the Greeks had marshaled their forces against one another, there was no one who did not think that if it should come to battle, the victor would become the ruling power and the vanquished would be reduced to a dependent role. But the divinity so brought it about that both armies erected trophies as though each side had been victorious and neither side prevented the other from doing this. Both sides, as if they were victors, returned the enemy dead under truce and took back their own dead under truce as if they had lost.

146. Plutarch, *Nicias* 6.5

According to unwritten law and normal usage the side that took up their dead under truce was thought to have given up its claim to victory and once they had obtained their request were not entitled to set up a trophy of victory. For those who were victorious were, by definition, those left in control of the battlefield. Those who have to make such a request show that they are not victors, since they cannot take what they want.

Burial of the Fallen

The necessity of burial for the dead, particularly for those who died in battle, was unqualified in Greek thought. As a result the dead of the defeated army were useful as hostages to ensure the open acknowledgment of victory. Sophocles' *Antigone* is perhaps the most famous portrayal of the imperative to bury the dead. Denial of burial or disinterment and the casting out of the corpses were only resorted to in order to punish sacrilegious or treasonous conduct, as detailed in the passage from Thucydides below. Occasionally purification of a temple area, like that carried out by the Athenians in 426 on Delos for Apollo, could result in disinterment of remains, but these were reburied with appropriate ceremony as happened with the remains from Delos.

147. Euripides, *Suppliants* 522–527

I do not set war in motion,
nor did I invade the land of Cadmus with these men.
But I judge it right to bury these lifeless corpses,
I bring no harm to your city nor do I bring to it man-destroying strife,
but I simply follow the custom of all Greeks. Where is the wrong in this?

Athenian practice

The Athenians seem to be the only Greeks that consistently practised burial at home and not on or near the field of battle as had been the custom from Homeric times. Other Greek states usually buried their dead on the field or in the closest friendly town.

148. Thucydides, 2.34.1–7

The first mass burial of Athenian dead in the Peloponnesian War occurred at the end of the first year of the war in the winter of 431. This type of burial probably did not occur on a fixed date but simply at the end of each year's campaigning season and so might fall as late as the spring of the following year. Games were celebrated in honor of the dead under the direction of the polemarch as the military representative of the city. The exact date for the introduction of this method of interment of the dead at Athens in a reserved area of especial beauty is a subject of scholarly controversy. The sources point either to the period of the Persian Wars or perhaps around 470–464.

In the same winter the Athenians in accord with their ancestral practice buried at public expense in the following manner those who were the first to die in this war. Their custom is the following: they erect a tent and assemble the bones of the dead in it for three days before burial and each Athenian can offer to their own dead whatever they wish. Then a funeral procession takes place in which wagons bear coffins of cypress wood, one for each of the tribes. In each are the bones of the men of that tribe. There is one empty bier decorated for those who are missing and whose bodies could not be recovered. Anyone, either citizen or foreigner, can join the procession and there are women who are relations of the dead who wail at their tombs. They are laid to rest in the public cemetery which is in the most beautiful suburb of the city. That is where those who die in war are always buried, except those who died at Marathon. The courage of those men was judged outstanding and they were buried on the field of battle. Whenever they perform the burial, a man is chosen by the city who is an able speaker and of outstanding reputation and he praises the dead in a speech in an appropriate manner. After this they depart. This is how they buried men who had died in this way and throughout the whole of the war. Whenever it was necessary they followed this custom.

Spartan practice

Though the Spartans must have kept a record of the names and numbers of the dead, if only to establish the size of their military forces and to provide for the fulfillment of other obligations such as membership in a soldier's mess, their practice with regard to the dead was to avoid a public burial and the public mourning that accompanied it. There is no evidence of festivals, cults or games for the dead. It accords with the general absence of militarism in Spartan life and the anonymity of the individual characterized by the epitaph of those who had fallen at Thermopylae (see no. 46).

149. Plutarch, *Agesilaus* 40.3

This is the general but not inevitable Spartan practice, as the burial of the Spartan dead after Mantinea indicates. The kings received elaborate public funeral rites which are described by Herodotus (6.58.59).

It is the Spartan custom in the case of those who have died abroad to attend to their funeral rites and to leave their bodies where they died. However, they carry the bodies of their kings home.

150. Xenophon, *Hellenica* 6.4.16

These events form a sequel to the battle of Leuctra in 371 in which four hundred out of seven hundred Spartiates perished and perhaps a total of a thousand from all of Laconia. It was a major and almost catastrophic defeat, and so throws the restraint that was normal Spartan practice into bolder relief. The Gymnopaedeia was an initiation festival for young men that focused on combat and warfare.

After the battle the messenger who had been sent to Sparta to announce the disaster arrived on the last day of the festival of Gymnopaedeia when the men's chorus was in the theater. When the ephors heard of the disaster they were grieved as they ought to have been, but they did not end the festival and allowed the contest to continue. They gave the names of each of the fallen to their relations. They also instructed the women not to wail in mourning but to bear their suffering in silence. On the following day one could see the relations of those who had died going about openly happy and cheerful, while you could see only a few of those who were relatives of the survivors, and these were sad and dejected.

Trophies and dedications

Trophies

Trophies reflect the formalism that is an essential part of the hoplite battle. Trophies are erected on the field of battle as visible evidence of the victor's success and serve to mark the termination of the battle. The trophy has both psychological and social value. Its psychological value is the prestige that its erection gives to the victor, while its social value is derived from its function of sharply delimiting combat through strengthening the notion that victory depends upon possession of a plot of ground and not in the extermination of the opposing force. The other use of the term is to denote a permanent memorial in the city of the victor, or at one of the international religious sanctuaries such as Olympia or Delphi. This meaning appears to be derivative from the first.

The trophy may well have a magical or religious origin, but if so, the only real evidence for it comes from its dedication to Zeus as god of battles. Some trophies, especially those of the Persian Wars, did have games and other rituals attached to them. Since its form was essentially a set of cross-poles with enemy armor and weaponry mounted on them, as if an armed mannequin were being created, there may have been some notion of magical power or the manifestation of the divine will of god in battles at the decisive moment resident in them. It can be seen as a symbolic way of returning to the god what he has delivered over, that is the enemy. Certainly, its value as a symbol of prestige and its use to mark the termination of combat were uppermost in the minds of the Greeks in the period for which we have documentation. These uses are evidenced by the fact that it could be and was erected for an action of any size or scope, though its religious associations still persisted in the customary prohibition against its violation, if properly erected.

The trophy was constructed occasionally out of more permanent materials than wood. Though there are traditions about trophies reaching as far back as the eighth and seventh centuries, it is probable that these examples are anachronistic and that the first securely attested trophies belong to the period of the Persian Wars. The first use of the term occurs in the first half of the fifth century. The practice flowered in the course of the Persian Wars and occurred sporadically afterwards. It is not clear whether the Persian Wars produced monuments which were meant to be of a more lasting nature because of being a conflict with non-Greeks. After the battle of Leuctra, when we are told that the first permanent stone trophy was erected by the Boeotians, it is said to have become far more common. But the evidence is far from compelling. It may be that the less durable wooden form was the norm and that in territories that could be dominated for some time by the victorious power a more durable form of trophy was erected. Thus what was essentially a contemporaneous development was seen as a serial one.

With the decline of hoplite battle and the rise of monarchy after the emergence of Macedonia as the dominant power in Greece, the trophy began to take on a personal character as a memorial to the victorious king or commander.

151. *Etymologicum Magnum* s.v. Tropaion
The derivation of the word from the Greek noun used to express the turning point of the battle is generally accepted.

Those tokens of victory which we set up are named from the turning and pursuit of the enemy.

152. Diodorus Siculus, 13.51.7
These events took place in the aftermath of the combined land and sea victories of the Athenians over the Spartan fleet under Mindarus and over the combined land forces of the Peloponnesians under Clearchus and Persian troops under the Persian governor of the Hellespontine region Pharnabazus at Cyzicus in the

winter of 410 BC. It was a decisive turning point in the early stages of the last part of the Peloponnesian War.

The Athenians pursued the enemy for some distance. When they learned that Pharnabazus was hastening at full speed with a large force of cavalry, they retired to their ships, and after they had taken [Cyzicus], they erected two trophies for both of their victories: for the one at sea on the island of Polydorus and for the infantry battle where they had first routed the enemy.

Material and form

Later Greek tradition claimed that battlefield trophies were expressly made out of perishable material as a way to reduce the duration of the hostility that it might cause after the battle. Since in the Persian Wars permanent trophies did exist, at least, for victories over the Persians, it would be necessary to posit a difference of practice in wars fought against Greek enemies and those with non-Greeks. If it existed, this distinction was occasionally violated. Yet by the time of Cicero (mid-first century BC) the tradition existed that the Thebans were the first to build a permanent battlefield trophy.

153. Diodorus Siculus, 13.24.3–6

The passage is from a speech by a Syracusan arguing for lenient treatment for Athenian prisoners of war in the aftermath of the Athenian débâcle in Sicily in 413.

For hatred between Greeks should only last until the moment of victory, and punishment only until the enemy is subdued. For whoever revenges himself on those who have been conquered and are appealing to the reasonableness of the conqueror is no longer punishing his enemy, but rather commits an injustice against human weakness. One could cite in relation to the harshness of opponents of this type the sayings of the men of old, "Man, do not be presumptuous, but know yourselves." Remember that fortune is king in all things. So the ancestors of the Greeks ordained that trophies for victory in war should be constructed of whatever wood was available and not in stone. Was this not done so that these trophies should last but a short time and that these memorials to enmity should then disappear?

154. Cicero, *On Invention* 2.23, 69–70

The Amphyctions were the group of Greek states that regulated and controlled the Delphic sanctuary.

It was the almost universal custom among the Greeks when they fought each other that the victor should erect some sort of trophy on their boundaries to commemorate their victory only for the present but not in perpetuity. But the Thebans after their victory over the Spartans erected a trophy of bronze. They were accused before the Amphyctions. The charge was that they ought not have done it. The defense was they should have done so. The point at issue was whether it ought to have been done. The defendants alleged that it was by valor that they obtained such a victory and that they wanted to leave an eternal monument to it for their descendants. The plaintiff's rebuttal was that Greeks should not set up an eternal memorial to their enmity with other Greeks.

155. Vergil, *Aeneid* 11.4–11

This is probably the most detailed reference we possess to the form and appearance of the trophy. The trophy was erected from the captured arms of the enemy. These included not only the dead, but also armor captured from prisoners as well. The mannequin form is clear in these lines and the treatment of the armor, particularly of the Etruscan Mezentius, has strong Homeric parallels.

At earliest dawn, the victor first fulfilled his vows to the gods,
he sets up a great oak on a mound with its branches all lopped off,
and clothes it with shining arms,
the spoils of Mezentius, the enemy leader, as a trophy. Oh great in war,
he fastens to it the helmet crests dripping with blood and the man's broken javelins,
the corselet twelve times struck at and pierced,
he binds the bronze shield to its left hand and he hangs the sword with ivory hilt.

Dedications

The custom of making dedications in commemoration of a victory in the form of first fruit offerings to the gods is closely related to the custom of setting up trophies. These dedications might consist of actual spoils from battle such as weapons and armor, or in a sea battle, the prow of a ship. It might also take the form of a work of art paid for out of the proceeds of the booty taken in the battle. Such dedications are often found at the great Panhellenic sanctuaries like Olympia and Delphi and had the same psychological value as the trophy as an advertisement of victory. Their importance can best be seen in the occasional disputes that broke out over the right to make such dedications and the provisions in some treaties for sharing the costs and honors of making them among the allying parties.

156. Athenian Thank-offering for Marathon, GHI² no. 19

This inscription comes from a limestone base set up against the front of the south wall of the Athenian treasury at Delphi. Pausanias claims that the entire treasury was built from the spoils of Marathon. But some scholars have preferred an earlier date for its construction. The term "first fruits" is the normal one in this context.

The Athenians [dedicate] to Apollo the first fruits of the spoils [taken] from the Persians from the battle of Marathon.

157. Thank-offering for the Victory of Tanagra, GHI² no. 36

Pausanias describes the shield as gilded and decorated with a gorgon's head in his account of Olympia. The most likely date for the battle of Tanagra is 457.

We possess a monument in the public burial area in Athens for the Argives who fell in this battle. The Ionians were members of the Athenian empire.

The shrine has the golden shield from [Tanagra]
the Spartans] and (their) alliance dedicated it as a [gift (taken) from the Argives, Athe]nians, and [Ionians],
[the tenth of the spoils] on account of their [victory] in the war.
. . . Corinthi[ans].

The fate of the vanquished

In dealing with Greek treatment of the defeated it is important to recognize that there existed no recognized and independent concept of the prisoner of war as an individual with a special status. The victory of one side automatically placed those on the losing side at its mercy. In essence, victory eliminated the distinction on the losing side between slave and free and between goods and individuals. The treatment of the fruits of war depended upon the needs and desires of the conquerors. Hence a variety of terms developed in Greek which generally corresponded to the kinds of treatment that the conquered received.

The treatment of armies defeated in the field could run, especially in the later period, from enrollment among the forces of the victor to outright massacre. In general, three categories fit the treatment accorded such groups in the Classical period: massacre, enslavement and detention with the prospect of ransom and eventual freedom. The extant evidence indicates that ransom and release were the most frequent outcomes. This is certainly due to technical limitations in the destructive power of Greek forces and to long-standing conceptions about the limitations of combat that prevailed. The other types of treatment seem to have occurred in periods of stress such as the Peloponnesian War.

The victor's purposes fall into three major categories: military-political, economic and psychological. The primary aim behind the first was to end the possibility of any further military threat from the defeated enemy. This could best be achieved through massacre, slavery, detention and even enrollment in the victor's forces. There are extant examples of all of these solutions.

The maximization of profit for the victor came either through ransom or the sale of captured members of the enemy force. Those motives are clear in the case of the defeated Athenian forces in Sicily in 413. Thucydides claims that so many soldiers were enslaved by the victorious army that Sicily was filled with them. Often enslavement was less a means of economic gain than a way of meeting war expenses. In general, slaves were the most valuable booty, though, as in the Sicilian campaign, a glut on the market could seriously lower profits.

Psychological causes were also operative. This factor might appear as an irrational hatred of the enemy such as that between Sybaris and Croton or the settling old scores. The violation of religious taboos sometimes played a part.

The variation of treatment and its connection with practical motives is evident. The role of Panhellenic sentiment is less clear. Though literary evidence

104

for the view that moderation ought to be observed in wars between Greeks generally increases in the course of this period, it is hard to discern any practical effect that resulted from it.

Massacre

158. Diodorus Siculus, 12.9.1–10.1

This massacre, dated to 511, is the earliest attested in Greek history. The wealthy Achaean colony of Sybaris in southern Italy was founded about 720 in a fertile alluvial plain. It had access to fisheries and an extensive coastline. Despite its wealth the city was rent by internal faction. There was a long tradition of enmity with Croton which may have been exacerbated by political differences between the two Achaean colonies. But the real cause of Crotonite behavior remains unknown. The troop figure is, of course, impossibly high.

The settlement [of Sybaris] increased rapidly on account of the fertility of the soil. Since it lay between two rivers, the Crathis and the Sybaris from which it took its name, its inhabitants gained great wealth by working their large and productive territory. Through their numerous grants of citizenship they came to be the first of the Italian cities. Their population was so large that it numbered 300,000 citizens.

There arose a popular leader among them whose name was Telus and he, by making accusations against the wealthiest and most powerful citizens, persuaded the Sybarites to exile five hundred of them and to confiscate their property. These exiles fled to Croton where they took refuge at the altars in the marketplace. Telus sent an embassy to Croton with instructions to tell the citizens of Croton to either hand over the exiles or to prepare for war. . . . So the Sybarites marched against them and in response the Crotonites, under the command of the athlete Milo, arrayed their army against the invader's forces which numbered 300,000. Milo because of his superior physical strength was the first to rout the enemy arrayed opposite him. . . . He thus won the admiration of his fellow citizens as being responsible for their victory.

The troops of Croton in their anger decided to spare no one. They killed all those who fell into their power. They cut down the majority of the Sybarites, and then plundered the city and made it a total wasteland.

159. Xenophon, *Hellenica* 2.1.31–32

This victory by Lysander in the late summer of 405 led directly to the final defeat of Athens in the Peloponnesian War. After capturing and destroying the Athenian fleet at Aegospotamoi Lysander called a public assembly of Sparta's allies and used it to justify the execution of the captured Athenian sailors. Earlier Athenian violations of custom in naval warfare played a part in justifying this action, but it is likely that Lysander already was planning for the narrow oligarchy he would install at Athens after its surrender and had a political purpose in mind. Later sources place the number of Athenians executed at three or four thousand. The numbers actually involved must remain uncertain given the state of our sources. The Paralus was one of the Athenian state ships. Note should be taken of the consciousness expressed in Lysander's question to Philocles of the assumption of an accepted code of behavior for the treatment of other Greeks.

Then Lysander called together the allies and asked them to consider the question of the fate of the captives. Many accusations were made against the Athenians, both about the previous acts of lawlessness that they had committed and against their decree to cut off the right hands of their captives in the event of a victory at sea. In addition, there was the fact that when they had captured two warships, one from Corinth and the other from Andros, they had thrown the entire ships' crews into the sea. Philocles was the Athenian general who had done this. Many further matters were raised and it was decided to kill all of the Athenians among the captives except for Adeimantus because he alone had spoken in the assembly against the decree to amputate the right hands of captive sailors. But some accuse him of betraying the fleet. Lysander first asked Philocles, who had drowned the Andrians and Corinthians, what should be the penalty for one who first committed unjust acts against his fellow Greeks, and then executed him.

Enslavement

160. Thucydides, 7.85.2–87

For other references to the Sicilian expedition see nos 97, 110 and 180. This is clearly a case of formal enslavement used as a means to achieve the complete destruction of the expeditionary force. The motivation seems to be the need to insure that Athens would not be able to mount another expedition against Syracuse. To this motive must be added the sequestering of prisoners by the soldiers themselves for their own financial gain. Even granting Athenian and allied losses, the figure of seven thousand seems low and may be the result of dispersal of prisoners among private individuals. A certain number survived their enslavement and made their way home.

And now Gylippus ordered them to take prisoners and the Syracusans assembled the remainder of those still alive, as many as had not been hidden by their own troops, and in addition the three hundred who had broken through the Syracusan guard during the night, who had been pursued and taken. When the prisoners were assembled their number was rather small as a great number had been taken over by their immediate captors and all Sicily was full of them since the troops of [Nicias] had not surrendered under agreement as had the troops of Demosthenes. Also, a large number had been killed, as many as had perished in any action in this war. . . . Nevertheless, many escaped immediately and others after being enslaved ran away. They made their way to Catana.

The Syracusans and their allies assembled the prisoners and took them and all the booty that they could back to the Syracuse. They placed all of their Athenian and allied prisoners in the stone quarries since they thought they could watch them there most safely. . . . The Syracusans at first treated those in the quarries very harshly, for there were many of them and they were confined in a narrow pit. The stifling heat of the sun continued to affect them badly because the place had no cover. The cold autumnal nights that followed by their contrast brought on sickness. All of their natural functions were carried out on one spot because of the narrowness of the place, and further the bodies of those who had died from their wounds, or changes in weather or from some such cause were piled upon each other. The smell was unbearable, they were oppressed by hunger and thirst . . . and they suffered all of the other evils that men who have been imprisoned in such a place could experience. So for seventy days they continued to live this way. Then, except for the Athenians and all of their allies from Sicily or Italy, they were sold as slaves. It is not easy to state with accuracy the number of prisoners but it was not under seven thousand. . . . In every way they were completely subdued and there was no evil they did not endure. The destruction was, as they say, total. They lost their army and ships, everything was destroyed. Only a few of the many who had set out returned home.

SIEGE WARFARE

The Greek hoplite was ill-equipped to deal with the difficulties of taking fortified positions except under exceptionally favorable circumstances such as surprise or treachery. Both the ethic of hoplite combat and the practical restrictions imposed by his heavy equipment imposed severe limitations. These factors favored set-piece battles in open country. The equation between hoplite status and citizenship also made the rate of casualties a significant political consideration and this factor was magnified by the relatively small citizen populations of many of the Greek states. Since the assault of fortified positions generally imposed the greatest number of losses, there was a tendency to shun such operations unless unavoidable.

The approach to siege warfare that the Greeks developed to deal with these problems was determined by these conditions. The central task was the defense of the city's territory rather than its urban core. The close dependence of the city on its surrounding countryside made such a strategy of controlling the city by gaining dominance over its countryside possible. If a city could be deprived of its territory, then it was faced with a threat to its food supply both for the present and with the prospect of repeated invasion in the future as well. This type of strategy is clearly evident in the annual invasions of Athenian territory by the Spartans at the beginning of the Peloponnesian War. Though recent work seems to indicate that the ravaging of a city's territory was not as effective as once thought, nonetheless it not only had a practical impact but a psychological one as well. The behavior and feelings of the Athenians in reaction to these invasions by the Spartans clearly displayed these psychological consequences. This is not to deny the political and religious importance of the urban core, but to underline the fact that, given the limitations of tactics and ideology, territorial invasion could achieve the needed result by bringing about a set battle at a far lower cost than a direct assault. Further, practical considerations in the form of the expense of siege warfare also limited its use. The most effective tactics and techniques for siege warfare were developed by the large territorial Near Eastern monarchies that possessed and were able to mobilize the necessary resources.

These difficulties persisted into the early fourth century and are reflected in the slow development of Greek fortifications as compared to those of the Near

East. Greek city fortifications before the fifth century tended to be simple and to rely on the fortification wall itself as a vertical barrier whose main purpose was to counter hoplite attack. This was often enough to preclude a direct assault. There may have been some influence on the design of fortifications by existing Bronze Age walls, but the predominant influences appear to have come from the Near East. The preponderant change over time was the use of mudbrick on a stone plinth to replace the earlier all stone construction. The traces of the walls appear to have been curved outwards in a simple pattern with the gates defended by overlapping the curtain walls. The construction was simple but massive, to guarantee the physical integrity of the vertical barrier. Selection of terrain played an important part in these defenses. Frequently such fortifications were confined to the acropolis of the city. Often the fortification of the urban center outside of the acropolis was the result of the urban agglomeration itself with house walls acting in place of a city's walls. The practice continued into the Classical period and even later. By the Archaic period, many Greek cities in the homeland and overseas had begun to be surrounded by simple curtain fortifications with sporadic jogs to provide opportunities for flanking fire. They were designed to take as much advantage as possible of the natural defenses of the site. Around 500 BC a major innovation, perhaps borrowed from Asiatic sources, appears with the addition of towers at intervals along the wall to provide more convenient and numerous opportunities for flanking fire. These towers were rectangular in shape in accordance with eastern practice. Fortifications now began to include the whole inhabited area, though financial considerations often limited the size of their circuit. The concept of defending the whole of an urban area replaced the notion of a defensible strong point like an acropolis. In the Classical period the acropoleis of Greek cities were no longer fortified.

The walls of Athens, built in 479 with their thicker plinth and more frequent use of towers, set a higher standard for fortification which was followed in other constructions of the period. Another developmental factor seems to have been the expansion of the size of Greek cities. They now extended into areas without natural defenses and the curtain wall thus became more important. In addition to towers, crenellation was often provided for the walls though the upper works were often still made of wood.

Such fortifications became general on the mainland for larger sites in the wake of the Greek experience of the Persian invasion and then the growth of hegemonic leagues like the Athenian empire that were capable of deploying the far larger resources necessary for the expensive business of siege warfare. The first half of the fifth century also saw the growth of a new form of fortification in the long wall which connected a city to its port or ports. Perhaps the most famous example was at Athens, completed in 459. Such walls, as the Spartans were to discover, could make a Greek city independent of its territory and so not amenable to the traditional strategy. Such fortifications produced a new strategy associated with the name of Pericles which changed the defensive emphasis from the protection of territory to that of the urban center. Such a strategy was the realization, at least at Athens, of the increasing independence of the urban core with respect to its surrounding countryside.

Till the end of the fifth century the balance lay with the defense. Even a small garrison behind reasonable fortifications could withstand the attack of a much larger force. This was due in part to limited offensive techniques, consisting of hand-thrown missile weapons or the bow. What technical innovations there were favored the attackers over the defenders. By the end of the Peloponnesian War there is evidence for the use of the ramp, the ram and, perhaps earlier in the 440s, a moveable shed to protect the crews working the rams, the use of rudimentary sapping and at Delium the use of a primitive flame-thrower against wooden defenses.

This period is marked by one further development: the fortified outpost of which the most famous example was that at Decelea established by the Spartans in 413. It allowed the attacker to cut off the defenders from their territory for an indefinite period with the use of relatively few troops.

City walls

161. Thucydides, 1.8.3

This passage forms part of Thucydides' speculative reconstruction of Greek historical and economic development that serves as a justification for his assertion that his subject, the Peloponnesian War, was the greatest of all wars. Fortifications are seen by Thucydides as an essential part of the city and an indicator of civilized life.

The peoples living on the seacoast, since they had now amassed a greater surplus of wealth, lived a more settled existence and the more wealthy among them built walls for their cities.

162. Plato, *Laws* 778D4–779A7

Plato's attitude in the *Laws* towards the use of fortifications is linked to his notion that one facet of virtue is to be found in the traditional agonal contest of hoplites facing each other in open battle. The use of walls as a protection is therefore "unnatural" and can only lead to the deterioration of the moral character of the citizens of his state. It is an attitude found in other aristocratic writers as well, such as Xenophon and Isocrates. It appears in part to relate to Plato's negative evaluation in the *Laws* of sea power and its moral effects. It is based on the example of Athenian democracy and its reliance on fortification to allow it to devote its efforts to the aggrandizement of its navy and of its democratic form of government. The poet mentioned is unknown but the sentiment was a commonplace by Plato's time. The reference to sending young men out to fortify the utopia's countryside sounds as if it was influenced by the contemporary Athenian institution of the ephebe, on which see nos 49 and 55.

Concerning walls, Megillus, I would allow them to lie still and not awake them, just as your Sparta does, for the following reasons: it is well said by the poet, who deals with these matters, that bronze and iron ought to be a city's wall and not brick. And further, we should be justly laughed at, if after sending out our youth annually to open country, to keep off the enemy by digging defensive ditches, entrenchments and various other structures, all with the purpose of not allowing the enemy inside of our borders, if we should surround our city with walls. First, they are not conducive to the health of cities and, in addition, they allow those who live behind them to develop a cowardly character. Such fortifications invite cowardly behavior by allowing the citizens to seek shelter behind them and to avoid having to ward off the enemy in open battle. They permit them to relax their vigilance at night and to assure their safety during the day. Further, they incline the citizens to think that they are safe behind these walls and gates and so to take their ease, since they suppose they are protected by such artificial devices. They become lazy and ignorant of the fact that true strength comes from one's exertions rather than from shameful indolence and cowardice, and so create difficulties.

Siege warfare till the end of the Peloponnesian War

The siege of Plataea

163. Thucydides, 2.75–78 and 3.52.1–2

About the middle of May 429 the Spartans, deterred by the plague from invading Attica and with a view to placating their Theban allies, launched an attack on Plataea. After a series of unsuccessful negotiations, filled with sophistries and specious arguments on the Spartan side, designed to bring about a voluntary surrender by the Plataeans, the Spartans began their siege of the city. Before settling down to blockade the town the Spartans tried a number of expedients to take the town by assault. This in itself was unusual. Towns as well-protected by natural defenses as Plataea were not normally assaulted. These attempts may have been the product of Sparta's constant financial difficulties and her need to release troops for service elsewhere.

Their efforts belie the reputation that Herodotus assigns to the Spartans of being especially ineffective in siege warfare. The siege of Plataea shows their acquaintance with the most developed offensive techniques of their day and their ability to use them. Thucydides' account of the siege of Plataea is the first evidence we have for the use of a ramp for assault as well as the first recorded use of rams to break down fortifications. The defenders also employed what appear to be, if not novel, at least developed techniques of mining to prevent the Spartan siege mound from being successfully completed, and of the use of heavy wooden beams to break the tips of the enemy's rams. Thucydides' interest in the technical details of the siege, of which he gives an unusually full description, may have been the result of the novelty of the tactics of both sides at Plataea. The failure of the Spartans to take the city led to their building what may be the most complex wall of circumvallation constructed by a Greek army.

The siege provides revealing evidence of the real weakness of Greek siege warfare. All of the elaborate measures were undertaken against a body of defenders consisting of 400 Plataeans, 80 Athenians and 100 women left as cooks for this garrison. This is a clear indication of the difficulties that still stood in the way of capturing a prepared and well-fortified city during the Peloponnesian War, even with the latest techniques available. The city finally surrendered from hunger in the summer of 427 after a considerable proportion of the garrison had escaped and rendered the city no longer defensible.

After his invocation to the gods, [King Archidamus] brought his army into action. First, they built a wooden palisade around the city out of the trees which they had cut down to prevent any exit from the city. Then the Spartan forces began to throw up an embankment of earth abutting the city wall in the expectation that their army would take the city very quickly this way. They cut down timber from Mount Cithaeron and built a wooden framework in place of walls to keep the earthen mound from spreading. Next, they constructed the mound itself from the wood, stone, earth and anything else they could bring up. This work was carried on continuously for seventy days and nights since the troops worked in relays: while some were working on the mound, others would be sleeping or eating. Spartan officers who were regularly in command of allied Peloponnesian contingents were in charge and kept them at their work.

The Plataeans, as they saw the mound rising, put together a wooden wall and placed it on top of their fortifications where the mound was rising. They built inside it a wall of bricks taken from the neighboring houses that had been demolished for this purpose. The wood served as a bond to keep the structure strong as its height rose. They protected it with skins and hides to prevent both the workers and the structure itself from suffering from the effects of fire arrows. The fortification rose to a great height and the mound kept pace with it. In this situation the Plataeans hit upon the following expedient. They opened their wall where it abutted the mound and carried into the city the dirt from the mound. The Peloponnesians noticed this and so packed the earth in a framework of reeds into the gap to avoid further removal of the earth. The Plataeans, since they were thus prevented from utilizing this maneuver, gave it up, but instead began digging a mine from the city to a calculated point under the mound and began removing material from there. They avoided detection for some time, so that though the enemy kept up piling material on the mound, little progress was made since material was being constantly removed from the base of the mound by the Plataeans and the remainder settled into the empty space in the structure. Nevertheless, the Plataeans were afraid that, given their small number, they could not hold out against the superior strength of the enemy arrayed against them and devised a further stratagem. They stopped working on the large wall they had constructed against the mound and began to erect on both sides of it a counter wall and they built behind it a new crescent-shaped wall within the circuit of the original city wall. The purpose of this was that even if the large wall were taken by the enemy this second wall would still protect them and their enemies would still have to build another siege mound against it and in their advance would have to double the labor and simultaneously expose their flanks.

At the same time as they were engaged in constructing the mound, the Peloponnesians brought up siege engines against the city. One section of the large wall against the siege mound was shaken by them and was brought down for a considerable length. The Plataeans were now afraid. But they threw nooses around the machines operating at other points along the wall and turned them aside. Further, they suspended large beams linked together by iron chains at the ends of two poles which they suspended horizontally from the top of the wall. Wherever a machine was brought up, they let go the beam by loosening the chains and as it fell its force snapped off the tip of the battering ram.

After all this, when the Peloponnesians saw that their machines had achieved nothing and the counter-fortification had nullified their mound, they were at a loss at what to do since they thought that they could not take the city by assault and so began to build a wall of circumvallation. First, they decided to try an attack with fire and to see if with the aid of the wind they might burn the city down because it was small. They considered every idea in their effort to avoid the expense of a long siege. They brought up bundles of faggots and threw them down from the mound into the space between the first wall and the mound. The work proceeded quickly, since they had abundant manpower. Further, they heaped up more wood from the top of the mound to reach as much of the city as possible. They then set fire to the wood by throwing on it brimstone and pitch. The result was a man-made fire that had no precedent. Certainly, there have been great forest fires in mountainous areas brought on by the friction of the wood caused by the winds and with their flames extending over a wide area. But this was indeed a large fire and the Plataeans who had foiled the their enemy's other stratagems almost succumbed to it. They could not even get near a substantial portion of the city because of the fire and, if a favoring wind had arisen as their opponents expected, they would have been destroyed. But it did not and it is said that a heavy rain along with frequent thunder by coincidence quenched the fire and ended the danger.

The Peloponnesians, when they saw that this course had failed as well, left a portion of their army behind after they had let the majority of the troops go and began to construct a wall of circumvallation around the city, assigning different portions of its construction to various states. There were ditches both inside and outside the wall from which they obtained the material they made into bricks for the construction of the wall. When the project was completed (it was about the middle of September) they left behind guards for half of the wall and the Boeotians provided them for the other half; the rest of the Peloponnesian army left and the various contingents returned to their homes.

The Plataeans had previously sent away the children, women and the oldest as well as those useless in these circumstances to Athens. Those left behind to endure the siege were 400 Plataeans, along with 80 Athenians. In addition there were 10 women and 100 bakers. This was the sum total of those under siege and there were no others either free or slave in the city. In this manner the siege of Plataea began.

About the same time, during this summer [427], the Plataeans, now without food and incapable of sustaining the siege further, came to terms with the Peloponnesians. The latter had stormed the wall and it was clear that the Plataeans could no longer put up a defense. But the Spartan commander, though he was aware of their weakness, did not want to capture Plataea by assault. He had received instructions from Sparta which were framed with a view to any future peace with the Athenians that would specify that each side should return those places captured in war. Plataea would not have to be returned, if there were grounds for arguing that it had come over voluntarily. He sent a herald to the Plataeans to announce that, if they willingly handed over their city to the Spartans, the Spartans would serve as their judges and, though punishing those who had committed wrong, would not cause any to suffer unjustly. The Plataeans, since they were in a very weakened condition, handed over their city.

Offensive bases in enemy territory

The development of a fortified base from which to maintain a constant presence on enemy soil in order to do the maximum amount of damage appears to be a development of the Peloponnesian War and to have its roots in an attempt to deal with a city like Athens which was relatively immune from the normal techniques of ravaging and provocation to battle. It allowed the attacker to extend his normally seasonal operation of ravaging to the entire year, and so inflict much greater privation on the defenders. It may well be that the success of the Athenian strong point at Pylos, established in 425, had made them appreciate its advantages.

164. Thucydides, 7.27.3–28.1

Decelea lay about fourteen miles northeast of Athens. The site itself is on hard high stony ground and it dominates a major route over Mount Parnes into Boeotia. It remained of strategic importance after the Peloponnesian War and was fortified by the Athenians in the fourth century. There are problems with Thucydides' figure for the number of slave deserters.

Since Decelea had been first fortified by the whole Peloponnesian army in the course of this summer and later garrisoned by the cities in successive contingents, the Athenians had suffered severely. It was a prime cause of Athens' decline because of the destruction of property and loss of manpower that it caused. The previous invasions had been short and the Athenians had not been kept from enjoying their land during the rest of the time. Now they were under pressure continually. At times they were attacked by additional troops sent to supplement the garrison; on other occasions it was the garrison itself that overran the country and committed depredations to secure its own supplies. Further, the Spartan king Agis was present and he did not conduct the war as an amateur affair. The result of all of this was that the Athenians suffered great harm. They were deprived of their entire territory and more than twenty thousand slaves deserted, the majority of these being craftsmen. In addition, they lost all of their sheep and yoke animals. Since the cavalry rode out daily to conduct raids against Decelea and to act as a guard for the countryside, it lost many horses, some lamed by the rough ground or by their continual exertions, others wounded in combat. Further, supplies from Euboea, which had previously come from Oropus by the quicker land route, now had to come by sea and this greatly increased their cost. The city now had to import everything it needed and had been converted into a fortress.

Assault

In general, assaults on cities or prepared positions were avoided by the Greeks because of their lack of proper equipment and the cost in citizen lives that such an assault would entail. Successful assaults against defended positions only succeeded if the defense was inadequate due to the temporary nature of the fortifications, as at the Athenian camp at Delium taken by the Boeotians in 424, or to a lack preparations due to surprise. Often such defenses were not kept in a state of readiness and so facilitated the attackers' task.

165. Thucydides, 7.29.2–3

The attack on Mycalessus was almost an accident. In the spring of 413 three hundred Thracian mercenary peltasts arrived in Athens too late to accompany the second Athenian expedition to Sicily. To avoid the expense of maintaining them, the Athenians sent them home under the command of Diitrephes who was instructed to use them to inflict such harm on the enemy as he could. His second raid into Boeotia fell upon this militarily insignificant and totally unprepared town. Surprise was total and lack of preparation by the defenders made it easy to take, as Thucydides' description indicates. He betrays his prejudices by ascribing the ferocity of the attack to the natural savagery of the barbarian attackers. The massacre seems to have given rise to great bitterness among Athens' enemies. Xenophon mentions the Athenians' fear in 404 that if they surrendered they might suffer as they had caused small Greek towns to suffer while Athenian power was still intact.

[Diitrephes] led the [Thracians] against Mycalessus. He encamped unobserved during the night near the temple of Hermes (this was about two miles from the city). At daybreak he began his assault against the small city and captured it because it was unguarded and its population was unprepared. They had never thought that the enemy would come so far from the sea to attack them. Further, the fortification wall was weak and had fallen down in places (it had been built hurriedly) and the gates were open because of the populace's false sense of security.

Treachery

166. Aeneas Tacticus, *On Siegecraft* 1.3–7 and 11.1–2

Aeneas' work dates from around 355 and seems to be based on personal experience. He has sometimes been identified with the general Aeneas of Stymphalus in Arcadia who had control of the acropolis of Sicyon in 367. Despite advances in technique in the fourth century with the introduction of siege towers and artillery, the major preoccupation of Aeneas remains the threat of betrayal. Given the increase in internal strife in the fourth century, it is revealing to see how the author uses political sentiments as a criterion for the selection of persons for important military service.

Those forces which are engaged in guarding the fortifications and the citizens from within . . . should be arranged so as to guard positions in the city and to face impending danger. First, one must select the most sensible and those who have the most experience in warfare to serve with the commanders. Then from the rest, those whose bodies are most capable of physical exertion are to be chosen and then divided up and assigned to companies and, thus brigaded, can be used for the purpose of making sallies, patrolling the city, giving aid to those hard pressed or for some other similar task. These men should be well-disposed and satisfied with the existing arrangement of political affairs. A large group like this is like a citadel against the designs of others. It will be a terror to those in the city who want change. The leader and commander of these forces should be someone who is prudent and in his prime, and for whom the greatest dangers would result from a change in the existing constitution. . . . Further, one must be watchful of those [untrust-worthy] citizens and for this reason not readily accept their advice.

The beginnings of the mechanization of siegecraft

It was in Sicily at the beginning of the fourth century that the mechanization of Greek siege warfare began. There had been improvements in siege technique in the fifth century, probably under Eastern influence. The final stages of this influence were to lead to the next phase in the development of Greek siege technique. Again, the impetus appears to have come from Greeks fighting with a power of Eastern background and possessed of relatively advanced siege techniques – Carthage. By the end of the fifth century there had emerged at Syracuse a tyranny under Dionysius I which had the ability to be responsive to new techniques and which possessed sufficient wealth to allow it to develop technologies that were a real advance over previous Greek siegecraft. The sieges of Selinus and Himera in 409, as part of a concerted Carthaginian attack on the Greeks of eastern Sicily which ended in the peace of 405, are the first sieges in which the techniques of siege towers and mining are mentioned by our sources as effectively employed.

167. Diodorus Siculus, 13.59.4–9

Hannibal broke camp and departed with his entire army after destroying the walls of Silenus since he was especially anxious to capture Himera. His father had been exiled because of his failure there and his grandfather Hamilcar, outgeneraled by Gelon near its walls, had perished along with 250,000 of his soldiers. No fewer had been taken captive as well. Burning with desire to take revenge, Hannibal encamped with his army of 40,000 not far from the city on some hills. With the remainder of his force he invested the city along with the 20,000 Siceli and Sicani who had joined him. Setting up his siege engines against the walls in many places, he shook them and kept up a continual pressure on the defenders because, given the great numbers of his troops, he sent them forward in waves and his men were elated by their successes. Further he began to undermine the walls and then shore them up with wood so that when the wood was set on fire a great section of the wall collapsed. It was then that the fiercest action of the battle ensued, the one side trying to force its way inside the fallen section of the wall and their opponents fighting in fear of suffering what had befallen the Selinuntines. They were making a final stand for their children, parents and the fatherland for which all men will fight. The barbarians were pushed back and they quickly rebuilt the fallen section of the wall.

The capture of cities

It is arguably correct to separate the capture of cities in Greece from victories in pitched battles. First, the capture of the city center raised the question of the political survival of a state. So the consequences of the capture of a city were potentially much more severe. Second, the taking of a city involved the acquisition not only of enemy soldiers but also non-combatants such as women, children and men past the age for military service. The task of dealing with the vanquished in these circumstances was far more complex. Economically, the lucrative opportunities for the sale of human and other booty normally exceeded those taken in the field. Finally, in all ages, siege warfare has been normally a more difficult, costly and exasperating undertaking than normal battle and these factors have tended to influence the victors' treatment of a captured city. The general rule in Greek warfare was that human and other booty was at the complete disposal of the victor. It is hard to argue for the humanity of the treatment meted out to Greek cities by Greeks, though the literature, especially of the fourth century and after, in part reflects an attempt to delimit the boundaries of acceptable violence in the taking of Greek cities.

In the period between 335 and 223 there are no recorded cases of the enslavement or massacre of Greek towns, though often survivors were allowed to depart with so little that their future prospects must have been bleak. This may partially be the result of defective sources, but it is hard to believe that it does not mirror reality. The wars of Alexander's successors depended on victory in the field and, with the lesser importance of Greek cities as political centers, there was less to be gained by massacre and enslavement. Major motives in determining treatment in these cases can be characterized in the same way as those used for set battles. But economic motives as well as imperial control play a larger role in the case of cities, as might be expected.

Massacre

168. Thucydides, 4.120.1, 122.4–6 and 5.32.1

The treatment of Scione, a small city in the Chalcidice, was influenced by a number of factors. The people of Scione rose in open rebellion against Athens in the summer of 423. This was shortly before the news of a truce that had already been concluded between Athens and Sparta reached the area. The Scionians gave full support to the Spartan general Brasidas who had been unusually successful in detaching towns in that area from Athens. It was a region that had been a constant focus of difficulties for the Athenians. All of these factors impelled Athens towards making an example of the town when it was captured in the summer of 421.

About the time the delegates were approaching the various states at war, Scione, a city in Pallene, revolted from the Athenians and joined Brasidas. . . .

When Aristonymus announced the refusal [of Brasidas to hand back Scione] to the Athenians, they were immediately ready to send a force against it. The Spartans sent an embassy to Athens which made the claim that Athens would violate the armistice by so doing and, believing Brasidas, they claimed the city for themselves and were ready to submit to arbitration in the matter. But the Athenians did not want to risk arbitration; they wished to march against the place as soon as possible, since they were angry at the possibility that even those who were islanders were now ready to revolt from them and to rely upon Spartan land power which would do them no good. Also the truth about the revolt justified the Athenian position since the Scionians had revolted two days after the truce. The Athenians passed a decree in accordance with the motion of Cleon that the city should be captured and its inhabitants executed. They remained inactive otherwise, but made their preparations to this end. . . .

About the same time, during this summer the Athenians brought about the capitulation of Scione by siege. They killed all of the males capable of bearing arms and enslaved the women and children. They then gave the land to the Plataeans to cultivate.

Enslavement

169. Diodorus Siculus, 11.65.2–65.5
According to Diodorus these events are to be dated to 468 and this is probably correct, though he fails to set the capture of Mycenae in its broader context of an attempt by Argos, now recovered from the battle of Sepeia, to challenge Spartan supremacy once again.

In this year a war broke out between the Argives and the men of Mycenae for the following reasons. The Mycenaeans, in their pride at the ancient prestige of their own state, were not obeying the Argives as were the other cities in the Argolid, rather they maintained their independence and did not heed them. They were involved in a continuing dispute with Argos over the shrine of Hera and they thought that they had the right to conduct the Nemean Games. Further, when the Argives voted not to ally themselves to the Spartans at the battle of Thermopylae unless they received a portion of the command, the Mycenaeans alone of the cities of the Argolid fought beside the Spartans. In sum, the Argives suspected that if the Mycenaeans became stronger they would contest the mastery of the Argives on the basis of the ancient repute of their city. For these reasons these cities were at odds with one another; for a long time the Argives had been anxious to seize the city, but they judged that the opportune moment was at hand since the Spartans were in difficulties and could not come to the aid of Mycenae.

They assembled a sizeable force from Argos itself and its allied cities and marched against Mycenae. They defeated the Mycenaeans in battle and then laid siege to their city after enclosing it by siege walls. For a while, the Mycenaeans vigorously defended themselves against the besiegers, but later they began losing the fight, and the Spartans could not come to their aid because of their own wars and on account of the devastation that was the result of an earthquake, and further there were no other allies available to them. Finally, bereft of aid, the city fell by assault.

The Argives enslaved the Mycenaeans and dedicated a tithe of the spoil to the god and razed the city to the ground.

Exchange and ransoming of prisoners

It is hard to know how general the exchange or ransoming of prisoners was in the Archaic and Classical periods. The most pressing obligation to ransom fell on the captive's family and kin. An example of this obligation is provided by the legal code of Gortyn in Crete, in which the obligation to ransom falls explicitly on the kin group, but the liberated man was required to remain in the service of his ransomer until his cost had been repaid. Friendly individuals or powers could ransom or intercede on behalf of captives of another state. The practice of exchange and ransoming of Greek prisoners may have grown in the fourth century when there seems to have been a greater reluctance to keep Greeks captured in war in a state of slavery to their fellow Greeks.

170. Androtion, *FGrH* 324 frg. 44

This embassy, which took place in 409/408, had a far wider scope than merely the question of ransom and exchange of prisoners and dealt with the possibility of ending the war itself in the wake of Athenian successes in Ionian waters.

"To ransom for a mina." The Athenians and the Spartans in their war against each other made an agreement to ransom prisoners of war for a mina each. Androtion mentions this agreement: "Euctemon from the deme of Cudathena. In his archonship the envoys came from Sparta to Athens on this matter. Their names were Megillus, Endius and Philocharidas." He adds that they gave back the surplus of prisoners at the ransom of one mina per man. He states in addition that this had been the previously agreed upon ransom for captives.

171. Decree in Honor of Epicerdes, IG II² no. 174

The following is dated to soon after 413 on the basis of its lettering and by the fact that the recipient gave the money to ransom Athenians captured in Sicily in that year. One hundred minas is a substantial amount for a man of moderate means. Epicerdes was a metic and so did not possess the right to own real property, so the right to own land and a building is a substantial privilege.

Epicerdes the Cyrenaean
Bene[factor]
It was decreed by the council and people . . .]
[. . . is held the prytany . . .]
   . . . on account of his virtue and pos-]
[itive disposition towards the Athenians is to have immunity]
[and the right of owning a house and]
   . . . at Athens and other privileges as an Athenian]
[It has been announced that a herald shall proclaim this at the very next] [festival in the city that Epicerdes]
[the Cyrenaean has contributed]
one hundred minas for the Athenian prisoners and the Athenians have crowned him on account of his virtue and favorable disposition towards the Athenians.
This decree shall be erected by the secretary of the council on the acropolis on a stone stele, space [Arche[. . . proposed. The rest just as the council . . .]

Capitulation

172. Thucydides, 2.70.1–4

Potidaea, located on the isthmus of Pallene, finally surrendered to the Athenians in the winter of 430/429 after a siege of two and one-half years. The terms of capitulation have many parallels in other agreements of surrender. They include the departure of the conquered from their city – that is, essentially a form of civic suicide. It is hard to resist the impression that it was a situation which was little better than slavery.

During the same winter, the Potidaeans began discussions about an agreement with the Athenian generals assigned to the besieging forces, that is Xenophon, the son of Euripides, and Hestiodorus, the son of Aristocleides, and Phanomachus, the son of Callimachus. They were no longer able to endure the siege and the Peloponnesian invasions of Attica had not distracted the Athenians. Further, their food was exhausted and famine had brought in its wake its attendant evils extending even to cannibalism. The generals were ready for discussions since they saw that their army was in an exposed position, suffering from the cold, and in addition that two thousand talents had already been expended on the siege. Both sides came to terms as follows: the Potidaeans along with their wives, children and auxiliaries would be permitted to depart. The men were allowed to take one garment, the women two. They were also allowed to take a fixed amount of money for travel expenses. The Potidaeans left for the Chalcidice or anywhere else they could find to go.

However, the Athenians were angry with their generals because they had come to terms without consulting them and they thought that a surrender could have been made on any terms they wanted to impose. Later they sent out Athenian colonists to Potidaea and resettled it.

Greek opinion

From the fifth century a number of authors, often in accordance with what were termed the laws of the Greeks, favored some limitations on the rights of victors to do as they pleased when the defeated were Greeks. This concept of a special status for fellow Greeks continues into later centuries, as Plato and subsequently Polybius demonstrate. But, as this selection demonstrates, there was a great deal of diversity among various authors on the question and it is unclear what effect if any these thoughts had in limiting permissible conduct in actual warfare.

173. Euripides, *Heracleidae* 961–966
The reference is to a captured Greek.

Chorus: It is not possible for you to kill this man.
Messenger: Then we have captured him in vain.
Alcmena: What law forbids his death?
Chorus: Those who rule this land do not approve.
Alcmena: Why is this? Is it shameful to kill their enemies?
Chorus: Not one that they capture alive in battle.

174. Plato, *Republic* 471A

"Will they not then in their disputes with Greeks consider it internal strife and not call it war?"

"Certainly."

"And certainly they will quarrel but always with an eye to reconciliation?"

"Surely."

"Will they not behave with well-tempered moderation by exacting punishment so as not to enslave or to destroy but rather acting as men who are moderate and not in fact enemies?"

"Indeed."

"So then those who are Greeks will not ravage nor burn down dwellings nor agree that in each city all the inhabitants are their enemies, that is the men, women and children. But they will acknowledge that only a few are their enemies and are responsible for the dispute. So based on all of these considerations they will not want to ravage the enemy's territory, since it belongs to a majority who are friends, nor to destroy houses. They will only pursue their dispute until those who are answerable are forced to pay the penalty by the burden of the suffering of the innocent."

175. Polybius, *Histories* 5.11.3–6

It is one thing to seize and destroy the enemy's guard posts, harbors, cities, men, ships, crops and all other similar things through which one can weaken an opponent and at the same time strengthen one's own resources and the force of one's assaults. The customs and usages of war compel us to do so. But for no obvious advantage in our own affairs nor any detriment to the enemy in an ongoing war, but from excess, to damage their temples and statues and all such constructions of this type is surely the act of a frenzied and furious mind. For good men do not make war on wrongdoers to destroy and exterminate them, but to correct and reform those who err. They ought not to involve the guiltless in the affairs of the guilty; rather they ought to preserve and help those whom they think guilty along with the innocent. It is the act of a tyrant to do evil in order to rule the unwilling by fear. He hates and is hated by those subordinated to him, but it is the role of a king to benefit all by his benefactions and humanity and so being beloved to rule and to command willing subjects.

GREEKS AND NON-GREEKS

The conception of Greece as a cultural and ethnic unity is a development of the period of the Persian Wars and the years that followed it after Greece had for the first time been faced with a serious external threat. The reality of this Panhellenism receded as the Persian menace retreated, though it remained an educational and emotional ideal. Allied to it from the time of Aeschylus on was an attitude of racial superiority. Though it has been argued that ideas of racial superiority had little influence on the actual course of relations between Greeks and non-Greeks, except perhaps in the wars against Carthage of the Sicilian Greeks, it is hard to accept this view. Some traces of prejudice are visible as early as the Peloponnesian War. Cruel treatment of native peoples appeared during Sparta's campaign against the Persians in the early fourth century. For the Greek view of the Persians see nos 131 and 132.

176. Gorgias, *Fragmente der Vorsokratiker* Diehls II no. 84 5b

This passage by Gorgias of Leontini, one of the most famous of the sophists, was written in the last third of the fifth century and is one of the earliest statements we have that expresses the view that warfare among Greeks is equivalent to civil war and that wars between Greeks and barbarians is praiseworthy.

Victories over barbarians require trophies, while those over Greeks demand funeral lamentations.

177. Xenophon, *Anabasis* 3.1.23

This view of Xenophon's seems to be connected to ideas put forward in the fifth century by the Hippocratic school of medicine on the island of Cos about the effects of climate on physique and temperament. It emerges most clearly in the treatise *Airs, Water and Places.* The enemy is the Persians and their Asiatic allies.

In my view we can approach this struggle with much greater confidence than our enemies can. In addition, we have bodies that are superior in warfare to theirs and souls better able to put up with heat and toil. Further, our souls are superior on account of the gods, and our enemies are more liable to be wounded or killed if the gods grant us victory as they did before.

178. Aristotle, *Politics* 1252b5–9

The view Aristotle develops here and in the next passage is the logical outcome of the Platonic attitude with a theoretical foundation added by the former. It is not in formal disagreement with the view expressed in no. 181 that in essence the conquered, no matter what their origin, are at the victor's disposal.

Among barbarians the feminine and the slave occupy the same rank. The reason for this is that the barbarians lack the faculty of natural rule, so their marriage unions are those of two slaves; male and female. It is for this reason that the poets say that "it is right that Greeks rule barbarians" on the basis that the slave and the barbarian are by nature the same.

THE SPOILS OF WAR

From the recorded beginnings of Greek warfare, economic gain was always a major motive. It is a central component in the Homeric poems where there is no clear line drawn between plunder and legitimate trading activities. The same ideas seem to hold in the early Archaic period as well. The normal Greek view was that the conquered and their possessions passed into the hands of the conquerors to do with as they wished. At times, the desire to acquire wealth might be as openly expressed as it was by some of the Athenians on the eve of their expedition to Syracuse in 415, but its implicit existence was a normal accompaniment of warfare. Provisions for the division of plunder among allies in various treaties (see nos 188 and 189) indicate the normal expectation of the profits that victory and then pillage would bring.

In this quest for enrichment, the greatest profits came from the sale of the defeated into slavery or their ransoming. The sale of captured livestock was also a valuable source of profits. Captives could be easily moved and might offer a state a large pool of labor for carrying out public projects. Land was, of course, also of prime importance, but its appropriation was much rarer since it required the means and suitable methods of control beyond the capacities of most Greek states.

The economic rewards of warfare had to be supervised and controlled. The force that dispersed to plunder and pillage could often be defeated as a result of its disorganization. There was thus the need for control of the army in such situations. In addition, in the era of the city-state, the state's interest had to be safeguarded. There developed a distinction between the booty taken in common and that captured by private individuals. The Greek city-state never sufficiently subordinated its military force so that it could totally eliminate the private taking of booty, but it did manage to reserve the majority of the booty for itself. In doing so, it vested important responsibilities in its commander to collect and forward booty to the responsible state authorities. In some states like Athens and Sparta there existed regular state officials charged with the disposal of booty and with auditing accounts.

It was in the fourth century that violence and pillaging in the Classical period reached their peak. A number of cities were sacked and plundered. This may have been the result of the greater use of mercenary forces and the general economic difficulties of some of the major combatants in this period. The following Hellenistic era, given the size of the forces involved, was one of worsening conditions. Later the Romans continued in the long tradition of war as a profit-making enterprise.

One aspect of the capture of wealth was the accompanying acquisition of prestige. This function is evident in both private and public dedications placed in local temples or in Panhellenic sanctuaries like Olympia and Delphi. The erection of the Theban treasury at Delphi as a result of Thebes' victory over Sparta at Leuctra in 371 was both an honor to the god and a concrete memorial to Thebes' victory.

The economic motive

179. Archilochus, Fragment 2 West

This is a transparent expression of the freebooting mentality of the Homeric world and the Archaic period. At issue is not mercenary activity, but rather the plunder obtained in wars against the Thracians. It is only fitting that Archilochus died fighting in battle, in one of the wars between his place of birth, Paros, and the Naxians. Ismarus is a city on the Thracian coast not far from Thasos. Its wines are referred to by Homer and later writers.

My spear gives me my kneaded barley-bread, my spear gives me my Ismaric wine, I lean on my spear as I drink.

180. Thucydides, 6.24.3

Thucydides is here describing the feelings of the Athenians of the eve of the first Sicilian expedition in 415.

A desire surged up inside all of them to sail. In the case of the older men it was motivated by the belief that either they would conquer the objectives against which they sailed or, with so great a force, would come to no harm. The men of military age felt a desire to see and experience a distant place and were confident of their safety. The common crowd who remained at home and the members of the expedition thought only of drawing their pay for the present and of adding a possession to the empire which would provide permanent pay for the future.

181. Aristotle, *Nicomachean Ethics* 1160a14–17

The use of war as a natural mode of acquisition is also referred to by Aristotle in the *Politics*. Some have taken this as a reference to early Athenian law on associations formed for profit, but it seems to be a generalizing statement about particular types of associations and does not have a specific context.

Other associations [than the political] have as their purpose some portion of the advantageous. So associations of sailors are formed for a voyage aimed at the making of profits or something similar, and so those of soldiers in warfare seek booty or victory or the capture of a city.

182. Treaty for Mutual Legal Assistance between Oiantheia and Chaleion, SV no. 146

This treaty seems to have been concluded about 450 or a little later by these two small Locrian states. It is the earliest extant example of a treaty limiting the rights of seizure between two states. It appears to envision action by private individuals engaged in freebooting.

No one shall remove an Oianthian stranger from the territory of Chaleion, nor shall anyone remove a Chaleian stranger from that of the Oianthians nor his personal property. But it is permitted to capture a man engaged in such seizure with impunity. Carrying off foreign property on the open sea is permitted except within the harbors of the contracting states. If someone makes an unjust seizure, [the penalty shall be] four drachmas. If the seized goods are retained longer than ten days, the person who seized them shall be liable for one and half times their value. If a man from Chaleion resides in Oiantheia more than a month or if a man from Oiantheia remains in Chaleion for the same period, he will be liable to the laws of his place of residence.

The collection of booty

183. Aeneas Tacticus, 16.4–8

It is necessary for you to understand that an enemy who goes to war with intelligence and knowledge first advances with the strongest part of his forces in expectation of attack by the defenders and so is ready to defend himself. Some of these forces will scatter and ravage the countryside, another part will place itself in ambush in expectation of a disordered counterattack on your part. At that point you should not follow them closely and press them, but first allow them to grow bold and to despise you. They will then proceed to pillaging and to sating their greed. These men, filled with food and drink and intoxicated, will become careless and disobedient to their officers. The result of this is that they are likely to fight badly and to retreat if you attack at the right moment.

After your defensive force has been concentrated in a specified place and the enemy are dispersed in search of plunder, now is the time to attack them, to cut off their routes of retreat with cavalry and to form ambushes composed of select troops. Screen your forces with light-armed troops and bring up your hoplites in battle order close behind the leading divisions of troops.

Attack the enemy where you are not unwilling to give battle and in doing so you will suffer no disadvantage. From my previous discussion you can see that it is advantageous to allow the enemy to plunder as much of your territory as possible, so that plundering and burdened with booty, he will be readily open to your vengeance and all that has been taken can be recovered and those who have committed aggression will receive just what they deserve.

184. The Amphipolis Code, Moretti no. 114

This badly damaged inscription from the city of Amphipolis in Thrace, recording regulations issued during the reign of Philip V, is of either late third- or early second-century date. The *spheira* was a unit of about 250 men; a tetrarch commanded a unit of about sixty. The central concern here is to maintain order and discipline even in cases of private pillaging. It has been suggested that the provision to meet the plunderers at a distance of almost a half mile from camp is designed to decrease the possibility that booty would be hidden before it was taken over by the commander for the common stock. The need to maintain discipline must have been a factor. Fights might break out among troops as they pressed their own claims. See also no. 236.

Maintaining discipline during the collection of booty: If some soldiers should bring plunder to the camp, let the generals along with the spheirarchs and tetrarchs and the remaining officers accompanied by sufficient servants meet them at a distance of three stades in front of the camp. And if the officers should not turn over the booty to those who had seized it; and if some violation of military discipline results, the [commanders] and the spheirarchs and the tetrarchs and the *archhyperetai* shall pay the assessed value of those things which they owe.

The division of the booty

185. Diodorus Siculus, 11.25.1

Gelon, the tyrant of Syracuse, had the right to dispose of the booty after his victory at the battle of Himera against the Carthaginians in 480. An extra portion of the booty was set aside for Gelon because he had been in command. The passage again illustrates the relative freedom of the commander in such circumstances as well as the two important categories into which the booty was divided. The first is destined to reward soldiers who displayed especial prowess in battle. The second is the use of booty as a thank-offering to the gods. The part of the passage concerning Acragas shows the state claiming the lion's share of the booty and it also illustrates one function of booty: the acquisition of a labor pool for public works. A fourth-century law of Tegea specifies that the proceeds from the sale of booty were to be used for any public works damaged in war or whose construction was interrupted by it. The formula of distribution according to the number of combatants is dealt with below (see no. 188).

Gelon after his victory honored with gifts not only those cavalry who had killed Hamilcar, but also others who had distinguished themselves in the battle. He put aside the best of the booty to decorate the temples of Syracuse. Of the remainder, he nailed much of it to the most magnificent temples of Himera and the rest along with the captives he distributed to his allies according to the number of their soldiers who had fought with him. The cities chained their prisoners and used them to build public works. The men of Acragas received a great number of them and used their labor to beautify their territory. So great was the number of prisoners that many private citizens had five hundred of them in their homes. The number of slaves was so large because the men of Acragas had sent many soldiers to join in the fight and, after the rout, many of those who were in flight retreated inland into the territory of Acragas. All of these were taken alive by the Acragantines so that the city was full of them. Many were handed over to the state and some of them worked in the quarries cutting stone from which were built not only the largest temples of the gods but also the underground conduits which drew water off from the city.

The sale of the booty

In general it was the responsibility of the commander to organize the sale of booty, though at Sparta and probably at Athens as well as in other states there were special officials who assisted him in this task. Merchants often followed in the train of an army and provided a ready market for the booty. Such sales did not always go smoothly. The number of captives and the amount of other booty might saturate the local market, as it did after the surrender of the Athenian army in Sicily in 413, and result in low prices and a lack of customers. When Philip V's successful Peloponnesian campaign in the summer of 218 resulted in such a great overflow of prisoners he took them to Leucas in western Greece for sale because the local market was flooded.

At Athens there appears to have been a process by which the accounts connected with the sale of booty were scrutinized. The most valuable items were slaves and livestock. It may be that the sale of Greeks and barbarians captured in warfare was a major means of obtaining slaves in the Classical period.

186. Diodorus Siculus, 14.111.4

These events are dated by Diodorus to 387. The surrender of Rhegium after an eleven-month siege helped ensure Dionysius' control of the Straits of Messina. Ransom and sale by the state are used here to supplement each other.

Overcome by the magnitude of their hardships, the Rhegians surrendered unconditionally to the tyrant. Dionysius discovered in the city heaps of corpses of those who had perished because of the lack of food. Those he took alive were like dead men and physically weak. He brought the survivors together and they numbered more than 6000. He sent them back to Syracuse and ordered the Syracusans to free those who could raise a ransom of a silver mina and to sell into slavery those who could not.

The sharing of booty between allied states

The division of booty between allied states created special problems and tensions that might rupture an alliance. To avoid this problem terms for disposal of booty were included in treaties of alliance. Occasionally there may not have been a formal agreement but rather a pact.

Perhaps the most common method employed was the sharing of booty in proportion to the forces provided by each of the allies. This was taken as a rough gauge of their contribution to the final victory. Of course, this method was possible only in case of movable booty. Other types of divisions of plunder were used. There might be a division between movable and immovable property. Expenses incurred were also factored into the division as in the alliance in 347/346 between Sparta and Athens against the Phocians. There might also be a striking disproportion in the division of plunder dictated by the differential of power between two states, such as the case of the Rhodians and the Hierapytnians of Crete (see no. 188). The frequency of these provisions and the variety of mechanisms testify to the importance of the acquisition of booty.

187. Herodotus, 9.81.1
This passage illustrates the normal process, which was to first set aside a tenth of the booty for the gods and of a special grant for the commander (not mentioned here) and then to distribute the remaining booty. The central problem in this selection is what Herodotus means when he makes the amount of booty given to each state proportional to the worth of the individual state in the war. On the most likely interpretation it refers to the contribution of forces in terms of numbers of troops and not to a simple subjective assessment of the contribution of each member of the alliance to the victory.

The Greeks gathered together the plunder and they chose a tithe for Delphian Apollo from which they dedicated the golden tripod which stands on the three-headed snake next to the altar, and they also set apart a tithe for Olympian Zeus from which they erected a bronze Zeus, fifteen feet tall, and also made a dedication at the Isthmus of a bronze Poseidon nine and one-half feet tall. Taking the rest of the booty, they distributed it and each received the amount they were deemed worthy of. The spoil included Persian concubines, gold, silver and other valuables as well as draft animals.

Sharing in proportion to forces engaged

188. A Treaty between the Cities of Hierapytnia and Priansus, *Inscriptiones Creticae* vol. 3, III.4, ll. 53–58

This treaty between these two cities in eastern Crete seems to be dated to the beginning of the second century. The provision for distribution is simply one of a number of clauses where common rights are shared between the two states.

If in accordance with the will of the gods we seize some plunder from our enemies, either campaigning in common, or if some private citizens from either party either on land or sea shall take plunder, each side shall receive its share according to the number of men taking part. In the same way they shall share the tithe.

Sharing according to the relative strength of the allies

189. A Treaty between the City of Hierapytnia and Rhodes, *Inscriptiones Creticae* vol. 3, III.3, ll. 51–58

This treaty appears to be dated on historical and epigraphical grounds to the beginning of the second century. It was made in the course of an exhausting struggle between Rhodes and Philip V and various Cretan allies. The difference of the strength of the two sides is openly expressed. Hierapytnia lies on the southeast coast of Crete.

If piracy should occur in Crete and the Rhodians are in action against the pirates or those who receive them or who act in concert with them, the Hierapytnians shall fight with them by land and sea with all their strength as they are able at their own expense. And the captured pirates and ships shall be given to the Rhodians. The remainder of the booty shall be divided between them.

TRUCES AND PEACE TREATIES

Truces

Unlike the request for a truce to allow the losing side to recover its dead, other forms of truce were simply an agreement for a temporary cessation of hostilities, but did not mark a formal end to the conflict. However, they did perform various other functions and the truces themselves fall into certain clearly defined categories.

Among them were the general truces among Greek states connected with the great Panhellenic festivals like those at Olympia or Delphi. As the time for the festival approached, heralds were sent out to proclaim the truce and it was considered a sacrilegious act to fail to observe it. The point of a cessation of hostilities for religious gatherings may be that they were closely associated with the idea that religious ceremonies were conducted under the protection of the gods and so should not be violated by men. This idea is probably also connected with the inviolability of sacred places in time of war and the fact that the most frequent terms connected with truces and peace treaties are derived from the religious ceremonies that served as rites of sanctification and as a guarantee for the observance of these agreements.

Other truces had a more practical character with a definite political or military aim in mind. They were a method of limiting in the first case, or temporarily ending in the second, the hostilities between the two parties in order to provide time for a more permanent agreement to be reached. Sometimes truces were made on the field by the commanders to allow for embassies to be sent to their home governments to discuss the matters at issue.

Finally, truces could serve as a way of avoiding the conclusion of a more permanent end to hostilities while preserving appearances. After the Peace of Nicias in 421 between Sparta and Athens, the Boeotians refused to join it as a signatory to the peace but resorted to ten day truces with Athens that were constantly renewed. The Corinthians did the same on an informal basis. Both in language and intent there is a continuum in Greek thinking between this type of arrangement and the treaty of peace.

190. Isocrates, *Panegyricus* 43
The stress in this speech, finished in 380, is on the Panhellenic nature of these truces, the opportunity they offered for settlement of disputes among Greek states, and on the reaffirmation of a common cultural heritage. It should be read in the context of a call for Greek unity under the leadership of Athens and Sparta.

Those who have established our great common festivals have been justly praised for passing on to us the custom of proclaiming a truce and settling current disputes when we assemble together. After doing these things, we pray and sacrifice in common, thereby calling to mind our kinship with each other, and so we are better disposed towards each other for the future; we revive old friendships and create new ones.

191. Thucydides, 4.15.2–16.2, SV no. 176
The immediate impetus for this truce of 425, as for the later one of 423, came from the Spartans who in this case were trying to find a means to rescue the 420 hoplites cut off by the Athenians on Sphacteria. Given the small numbers of Spartan troops, this force represented a sizable fraction of Sparta's available manpower and it was also significant that a substantial number of these men came from the most important families. It seems clear from Spartan actions that this truce was concluded, as the later one of 423, to provide time to negotiate a more permanent settlement acceptable to both sides.

It seemed best to the Spartans to conclude a truce with the Athenian generals if the latter would do so, and then to send an embassy to Athens to conclude a truce over Pylos and get their men back as soon as possible. But they had little to offer beyond vague promises of good will without sufficient guarantees for it. The failure of the Spartan embassy to Athens led to the end of truce twenty days after it came into effect, as both parties had agreed. The ships were not returned by the Athenians, on the grounds that the Spartans had violated the armistice.

The [Athenian] generals accepted the Spartan proposal and a truce was arranged on the following terms: the Spartans were to hand over to the Athenians all of the warships that had taken part in the battle as well as all others that were in Laconia and were not to attack the fort at Pylos by land or sea. The Athenians would oversee the provisioning of those on the island and there were to be no voyages to the island in secret. The Athenians were to keep watch on the island as they had done previously though they could not land on it. Further they were not to attack the Peloponnesian army by land or sea. If either side violated these terms in any way the truce would be terminated. It was to last until the return of the Spartan embassy from Athens. The Athenians were to convoy the envoys and bring them back again. Upon their return, the truce would be ended and the Athenians were to return the ships they had received in the same condition in which they had accepted them.

Peace treaties

Peace treaties are separated from truces, for the most part, by their duration and not by any conceptual difference. Greek diplomatic vocabulary did not possess a specific set of concepts relating to the conclusion of peace treaties. They were not technically differentiated from other public and private agreements. The terms used with reference to such agreements fall into two classes, those that stress the contractual nature of the relationship and those derived from the religious acts which accompanied the conclusion of the agreements.

It was not until the 360s that the word which expressed a state of peace as opposed to war occurred in Greek treaties. The late appearance of this language is to be linked with another facet of the Greek peace treaty: the conclusion of peace for a definite term of years. One hundred years is the longest known, but thirty- and fifty-year periods are fairly standard as the periods of time during which a peace was to be valid. In addition, we often find a provision, as in the Peace of Nicias of 421, for an annual renewal of the oaths which had been taken at the original conclusion of the treaty. The key to understanding these actions lies in the idea that they were undertaken to legitimize and to maintain an abnormal state that could not be expected to last indefinitely. That state was peace. A hostile relationship was assumed to be the norm between Greek states.

What separated peace treaties from truces was less their form than their effect, though they did have to be validated by the sovereign authority of the state, while truces did not. More importantly they brought the state of hostilities to a definite end and, in doing so, usually encapsulated the power relationships existing between the two sides at the end of the conflict. However, many possessed a clause which allowed for arbitration and a mutual accord on change of terms.

Any treaty required some form of guarantee that both sides would abide by it. This created the need for sanctions, and various types were invoked. There were first of all practical guarantees. The most important was the generally unspoken one of the relative strength of the parties. Arbitration of a mutually-agreed-upon third party was also invoked as a means to settle disputes short of the resumption of hostilities. But the retention of surities, especially hostages whose number and social status were specified, was considered crucial in enforcing compliance.

Besides these practical guarantees there were a number of other steps taken to help assure the effectiveness of the treaty. The treaty, of course, needed public approval by the sovereign political body of each state. After such authorization, the treaty would be inscribed on bronze or stone pillars and set up in a prominent location in the home territory of the contracting parties as well as at the great Panhellenic sanctuaries. In addition, oaths were exchanged by prominent individuals on both sides to respect the terms of the treaty. These oaths had the purpose of invoking the gods as guarantors of the treaty. In the long run the final guarantor of peace among the Greek states was to be an external power who possessed the military force sufficient to exact compliance.

192. Thucydides, 5.18.1–20.1

The Peace of Nicias, which was concluded for fifty years but lasted for six years and ten months, was the outcome of long and laborious negotiations between Athens and Sparta as well as the fortuitous death of the main proponents for the continuation of the war on both sides. Certainly on the Athenian side, Nicias, after whom the peace is conventionally named, was now able to take a major role in peace negotiations. Athens' war weariness was plain; the Spartans remained as anxious as ever to recover their men captured on Sphacteria (see no. 70). These two major powers imposed the peace on their respective allies. Several of Sparta's allies who were more independent, like Boeotia and Corinth, refused to ratify it and contented themselves with renewable truces. But most of the Greeks as well as the Spartans and the Athenians greeted its conclusion with great joy. Thucydides was not deceived and calls it a suspect truce.

The main basis of the crucial territorial clauses which were to play a central role in discrediting the treaty was that of the *status quo ante*. Vital for Athens was the return of her most important possession in Thrace, Amphipolis. The other central promise in Athenian eyes was the return of the fortress of Panactum which helped secure Athens' northern border against Boeotia. Sparta's inability to carry out these provisions of the treaty was to be the most exasperating factor in its relations with the Athenians. In order to get them, Athens conceded a fair amount in the Thracian area of her empire. She granted a reduction of tribute to six cities in there. In addition, these cities were to be autonomous and allied to neither side unless the Athenians could persuade them to join her alliance. Autonomy as a term of Greek treaties of this period is perhaps best described as the freedom of a state to conduct its own internal affairs, but the concept was not applied to freedom in foreign affairs and thus could be reconciled with a situation in which the state's foreign policy was controlled by a ruling power. It was less the content of the term autonomy than its emotive force that mattered. It is important to note that captured cities had to be returned, but those who could claim to have willingly surrendered remained in the hands of their occupiers, as was the case for Plataea (see no. 160).

For the Spartans the most important provisions were those which gave back Pylos and islands off the Laconian coast which had served as Athenian bases against Sparta. Further, there was a crucial provision that freed the Spartan prisoners at Athens who had served as hostages against Spartan invasion of Attica. This was subsumed in a general exchange of prisoners.

The peace failed to endure because it rested on the fulfillment of terms which could not be carried out. Sparta could not or would not restore Amphipolis and Panactum. Further, on both sides there were those who were profoundly dissatisfied with the stalemate that had produced the peace and who were looking for the first opportunity to break the peace.

The Athenians and the Spartans and their allies have concluded peace on the following terms and sworn to it city by city.

In the matter of Panhellenic sanctuaries anyone who wishes can sacrifice at them, visit them, consult their oracles and watch the games held at them according to his ancestral custom. The shrine and temple of Apollo at Delphi and the Delphians are to be autonomous, that is they are not to pay tribute and are to administer their own justice among themselves and in their own territory according to their ancestral usage without external interference.

This peace is to be in force for fifty years without deceit or damage by land or sea between the Athenians and their allies and the Spartans and their allies.

Neither the Athenians or their allies nor the Spartans or their allies are permitted to bear arms with hostile intent against the other by any means or device.

If some dispute should arise, they shall act justly and in accordance with their oaths on what they shall agree upon.

The Spartans and their allies shall return Amphipolis to the Athenians. It will be permitted to all of the inhabitants of the cities that the Spartans return to the Athenians to go where they wish and to retain their own property. These cities will pay their tribute according to the assessment of Aristeides and will be autonomous. Neither the Athenians nor their allies are allowed to attack these places while they pay the agreed tribute after this peace is concluded. These cities are Argilus, Stagirus, Acanthus, Scolus, Olynthus and Spartolus. They are to be allies of neither the Spartans nor the Athenians. But if the Athenians win them over, they are allowed to be Athenian allies.

The Mecynernaeans, the Sanaeans and Singaeans shall inhabit their own cities just as the Olynthians and Acanthians do.

The Spartans and their allies are to return Panactum to the Athenians, while the Athenians are to give back to the Spartans Coryphasium, Cythera, Methana, Pteleum and Atalante.

The Athenians are to give back all Spartans held in public custody at Athens or in any territory under Athenian control. They are also to release those Peloponnesians who are besieged at Scione as well as other allies of the Spartans who are there along with any of Brasidas' men in the city. They shall also release any Spartan ally in public custody at Athens or in any territory under Athenian control.

The Spartans and their allies shall give back any of the Athenians or Athenian allies that they hold according to the same conditions.

The Athenians are free to make whatever arrangements they wish with respect to the Scionians, Toroneans and Sermulians or any city which they control.

The Athenians are to give their oaths to the Spartans and their allies in each of their cities. On each side seventeen men are to swear their most binding native oath. The oath for the Athenians will be the following: "I shall abide by these agreements and this treaty justly and without guile." Likewise, this will be the oath of the Spartans and their allies to the Athenians. Both sides will renew their oaths annually. Markers recording this treaty shall be erected at Olympia, Delphi, the Isthmus, on the acropolis at Athens and at the temple at Amyclae in Sparta.

If either side has forgotten any point on any matter, it is allowed to either party honorably and in accordance with their oaths to change any provision by mutual agreement.

This treaty comes into effect at Sparta on the 27th of Artemesias in the ephorate of Peistolas and at Athens on the 25th of Elaphebolion in the archonship of Alcaeus.

Those who took the oath and made the libations were as follows: For the Spartans: Pleistonax, Agis, Peistolas, Damagetus, Chionis, Metagenes, Acanthus, Daithus, Ischagoras, Philocharidas, Zeuxidas, Antippus, Tellis, Acinidas, Empedias, Menas and Laphilas. For the Athenians: Lampon, Isthmionicus, Nicias, Laches, Euthydemus, Procles, Pythodorus, Hagnon, Myrtilus, Thrasycles, Theagenes, Aristocrates, Iolcius, Timocrates, Leon, Lamachus and Demosthenes.

Unequal peace treaties

In form these agreements differed little from treaties concluded for wars that ended without any decisive result. But they seem to have had certain stipulations in common. The defensive capability of the losing side was often severely weakened by a compulsory dismantling of fortifications. Also its offensive capabilities were diminished or eliminated by forcing the surrender of arms or ships. It was less usual, as was the case under the Romans, for the losing side to pay an indemnity, as Samos did after the failure of its revolt against Athens in 440/439 BC. Internal constitutional arrangements often were changed to make sure that the supporters of the victor state on the losing side, if they existed, were maintained in power. In foreign affairs it was usual for the losing side to be forced into membership in a league if its opponent was the head of a hegemonic empire like Athens or Sparta. It could also be forced to cede land or territory to the winning side.

193. A Peace Treaty between Athens and Selymbria, GHI² no. 87 and SV no. 207

Selymbria on the north shore of the Propontis appears in Athenian tribute lists from 451/450–430/429 and seems to have formed a sensitive border point in Athenian contacts with the Thracians. By 410 it was in revolt from Athens and was recaptured by Alcibiades in 408. The following document is clearly designed to be conciliatory. This appears in the arrangements made for the return of hostages and in the terms for the indemnification of Athenians for property losses. The treaty was incorporated in and ratified as part of a proposal in the Athenian Assembly by Alcibiades in 407.

The Athenians are to return the hostages which they hold and for the future to refrain from taking more. The Selymbrians are to be autonomous and will be able to establish their constitution in whatever way they think best. . . . All property that was lost in the war, either of the Athenians or of their allies, or if anything was owed or deposited which the magistrates exacted, will be exempt from claim, except for land and dwellings. All other agreements which were formerly concluded between private individuals, or between a private individual and the state, or between the state and a private individual, or in any other manner, are to be regarded as settled. Matters that can be subject to dispute are those arising from disputes based on contractual agreements, that is those inscribed on the stelai in the temple. . . . The oaths of the Athenians have been sworn by the generals, trierarchs and the hoplites and any other Athenians present. All of the Selymbrians took the oath. Alcibiades made the motion that the agreement of the Selymbrians and the Athenians should be in force and that the agreement should be inscribed and set up on the acropolis by the generals together with the secretary of the Council . . . on a marble stele at their own expense together with a copy of this decree. . . .

194. The Peace between Sparta and Athens of 404, SV no. 211

After the decisive defeat of the Athenian fleet of 180 ships at Aegospotami in 405, it was only a matter of time before Athens was blockaded by the Spartans and forced into a total surrender. Sealing the straits to prevent further grain ships from reaching Athens, Lysander began mopping up remaining opposition. Instead of executing Athenians captured while on garrison duty or simply caught abroad by the campaign, he let them return to Athens. His conduct was probably governed by his desire to increase the besieged population as much as possible and so accelerate the effect of famine. By doing this he hoped to hasten the city's surrender. By October 405 he was in the Aegean and on his way to Athens with a fleet of 150 ships. The siege of the city was to be a joint operation of the entire Peloponnesian League levy serving under the command of the Spartan king Pausanias combined with the troops serving at Decelea under the other Spartan king, Agis. They would cut Athens off by land while Lysander blockaded the Piraeus. Athens was now totally isolated.

But it refused to yield. The Athenians were afraid to suffer the same fate that they had meted out to recalcitrant cities during the war. In response to this show of resistance, the main Spartan army retreated, leaving the siege to Agis' force, while Lysander sailed off to force the surrender of Samos, the only city still loyal to Athens.

Finally in November Sparta called a congress of her allies to discuss Athens' fate. The Athenians could not have been heartened by the determination of some of Sparta's most prominent allies, such as Thebes and Corinth, to bring about her total destruction. The pressing question for the Athenians now became their very survival. That goal was aided by the perception by the Spartans that the real effect of the destruction of Athens would be to the advantage of Athens' northern neighbor Thebes and not to their own. Sparta would be better served by a weakened and subservient Athens that could serve as a buffer against future Theban ambition. Hence the settlement, finally ratified by the Athenian assembly in March 404, guaranteed the survival of the city.

The magistrates of the Spartans decreed the following: "Demolish the Piraeus and the Long Walls, and leave all of the cities [of your empire] and retain only your own land. If you do all of these things which are requested of you and recall your exiles, you may have peace. In the matter of the number of your ships, comply with what is decided by our officials on the spot." The Athenians accepted these terms on the advice of Theramenes, the son of Hagnon.

195. Xenophon, *Hellenica* 2.2.20

We need not believe the noble goals that Xenophon, a pro-Spartan writer, enunciates. Power politics seems to have played a dominant role. The last clause is the standard one that the Spartans imposed on all members of the Peloponnesian League.

The Spartans said they would not allow the enslavement of a Greek city which had rendered great benefits to Greece in the midst of the most serious dangers. They offered peace on the following terms: the dismantling of the Long Walls and the Piraeus; the surrender of all ships except for twelve; the reception of exiles; and that the Athenians were to have the same friends and enemies as the Spartans and were to follow the Spartans by land or sea, wherever they might lead.

3

THE FOURTH CENTURY

The developments in the art of war in the fourth century have their genesis in the experience of the Peloponnesian War. In its length, in the methods used by the combatants to carry on the conflict, and in its political, social and economic effects it had no earlier parallel in Greek history. Most later changes in tactics or strategy that appear in the fourth century seem to grow out of experiments initiated during this conflict.

The traditional seasonal nature of Greek warfare had been determined by the fact that the majority of the troops engaged were also farmers. Soon after the Peloponnesian War started operations began to be undertaken for the entire year. This feature, added to the prolongation of military activity over a number of years, clearly hindered the participation of those who would have engaged in normal warfare. Further evidence for the changes that the war introduced can be seen in the effectiveness of what had been the traditional means of deciding conflict between Greek states – the hoplite battle. Though capable of resolving certain political problems, as the victory at Mantinea in 418 did for the Spartans, it did not dominate the course of the war as it had earlier. It was not hoplites that decided the struggle but a Spartan naval ascendancy that forced an already weakened foe to surrender or to face annihilation.

At Syracuse, as earlier at Sphacteria in 425, the final destruction of the enemy had been brought about by hoplites operating in conjunction with light-armed troops and cavalry. The fourth century was to see a refinement of this technique, though in the course of the century this method – the use of combined forces – remained limited to small-scale encounters until the rise of Macedonia.

These divergences from past practice seem to have made Greek commanders more ready to experiment with the deployment of the traditional phalanx as well as to find more effective ways to deploy light-armed troops whose effectiveness had now been made clear. This may have been facilitated by a lightening of hoplite equipment that made the heavy infantry more closely resemble traditional light-armed soldiers. By the fifth century the linen corselet predominated in place of plate bronze, and greaves begin to go out of use. Perhaps already by the Peloponnesian War or the beginning of the fourth century it appears that the hoplite had become lightly equipped and relied on his shield for defense since he had abandoned body armor. Mobility became more important than protection. These changes in equipment made it easier to use hoplites in conjunction with other troops. It may also have given the opportunity to commanders to experiment with a hoplite battle line that had traditionally placed its hopes in massed forces and in a single sharp encounter. The mobility may have first been exploited by the best organized of Greek armies, the Spartans, who now tried to use the right to outflank and to roll up their enemies' line from left to right. This had been an accidental occurrence at Mantinea (see no. 130) in 418 but it appears to have become purposeful by the battle of Nemea in 394. This produced a reflex action by the 370s at Thebes and led to more flexible uses of the traditional heavy infantry line by giving a commander the possibility of selecting the parts of his battle line where he wanted to seek a decision.

The stress on the use of light-armed troops created a need for them. The Peloponnesian War provided an opportunity because its magnitude and scope made the use of mercenary forces possible. The Peloponnesians were the first to use them and they were for the most part hoplites. Their numbers increased in the course of the war and by 415 the Athenians were also using them as hoplites but more frequently for specialist forces such as archers and slingers. The war showed the value of such specialist corps. It was far cheaper and easier to hire such troops than to train them. Their style of fighting was more difficult to master and required forms of command not congenial to citizen armies. There were areas such as Thrace, Crete and Rhodes that specialized in training in the use of these weapons and provided a hiring pool. Mercenary hoplites still came in general from the less developed areas of the Peloponnese. The Spartan experience against the Persians as well as Athenian successes during the Corinthian War reinforced the demand for the services of such troops. The dislocation and devastation of the war, as well as the establishment of dominant powers in Greece such as Sparta dependent on moneys from Persia (also a feature of the Peloponnesian War), created a ready supply of men prepared to earn a living this way. It also kept the prices for their services depressed to the point that even small states could afford them. Because of their training and sense of cohesion they tended to displace citizen troops on service and to create a rift in the traditional link between citizenship and military service. Warfare gradually became more professionalized. This trend was also visible in the appearance of a number of professional military commanders, and in men like Lamachus at Athens who held traditional offices because of their military expertise, and also in the growing number of manuals and handbooks purporting to teach the art of war.

This professionalism is also clear in siege warfare. The adoption of techniques from the East through Carthage as well as the invention of effective siege artillery in the fourth century was closely linked with men who were experts in mechanical technique. It was in this area that the greatest innovations took place. Unlike open conflict on the battlefield siege warfare became heavily mechanized and the offense developed an advantage. Cities lost much of their security at the same time as the scale and shape of war was changing to their disadvantage. It was developing into a conflict in which armies of mixed and specialized troops would replace hoplite armies and where city fortifications had lost a great deal of their defensive worth. The financial burdens of war as well as its requirements for manpower were beginning to surpass the ability of traditional city-states to meet them. The techniques of warfare were in flux in this transitional period before the appearance of Macedonia on the political stage set in motion fresh forms of political organization to meet these demands.

TACTICAL DEVELOPMENTS

From 378 BC Thebes and Athens engaged in intermittent and indecisive war against Sparta and her allies. Thebes had been the main beneficiary of this struggle. Despite Spartan opposition Thebes had managed to re-establish her ascendancy in Boeotia and to recreate the Boeotian League under her own direction. She had once again become a major power and wanted recognition of that fact. Probably from 373 the Spartans and their allies under the Spartan king Cleombrotus had maintained substantial forces based in Phocis and around Orchomenus in northwest Boeotia, thus conjuring up the possibility of an invasion from that direction. Despite Sparta's supposed supremacy, the 370s had seen her strength erode in the wake of border disputes, the loss of allies in central Greece accompanied by the disaffection of many who remained, a series of naval defeats, and more ominously by a defeat by Thebes on land at Tegyra near Orchomenus which bore some resemblance to later encounters. Athens, the other major power she was in alliance with, had cleared the sea of Spartan ships but was exhausted by the demands that naval warfare made on her financial resources. All sides seemed ready for a peace.

In 371 with Persian support a peace conference was convened at Sparta. The treaty contained an autonomy clause from which by mutual agreement Sparta's and Athens' allies were excluded. The Theban delegation on which Epaminondas served as boeotarch (see no. 116) at first swore separately, acknowledging the end of the Boeotian League, but then thought better of the matter and requested its oath to be taken on behalf of all of the members of the Boeotian League. The Spartans refused to allow this and so isolated Thebes. It seems clear that some of the Spartans were determined to neutralize Theban power by dismantling the league. Under Epaminondas' urging the Thebans refused to comply. An ultimatum was sent to Thebes to sign the treaty under the terms offered or to face military action. The Spartan troops in northwestern Boeotia under King Cleombrotus invaded Boeotia from the north down the valley of the Kephisos River.

Learning of the attack the Thebans and the other members of the Boeotian League encamped their forces at Coronea to block Cleombrotus' most obvious southern invasion route. Learning of this Cleombrotus turned away and marched to the western coastal area, turning Coronea and securing his communications with the Peloponnese. He then turned inland and advanced as far as the flat plain of Leuctra and encamped there on some low-lying hills on the southern edge of the plain. His forces now posed the threat of an invasion of Boeotia or a more direct threat against Thebes itself. Epaminondas and the rest of the boeotarchs reacted to the news by marching hurriedly to the rescue. They reached the hills that rim the northern edge of the plain and encamped opposite the Spartans. The plain is about three-quarters of a mile in breadth and slopes gently towards the south. It is for the most part featureless and little could have happened in the plain without its being observed from either encampment.

The ancient sources are in disagreement about numbers beyond the fact that the Spartans and their allies outnumbered the Boeotians. The figures generally accepted would give the Spartan army a total of nine to ten thousand hoplites and between eight hundred and a thousand cavalry. Lacedaemonians supplied between a quarter and a half of the infantry. The Boeotian army, which included no allied contingents, was composed of about six to seven thousand hoplites, four thousand of whom were Thebans, and one thousand cavalry.

Neither side was eager for battle. The Spartan king given his numerical superiority and his past lack of success against the Boeotians feared that a refusal to fight might be seen as treasonable. Some of the Boeotian commanders were also reluctant as they felt that open battle in a level plain would give the advantage to the Spartans because of their numbers. But Epaminondas finally was able to persuade a majority to vote for battle. Three main accounts of the battle have been preserved. The only contemporary one, written by Xenophon, fails to mention Epaminondas or any peculiarity in the tactics of the battle except for the extraordinary depth of the Theban battle formation which was arrayed fifty men deep against the more normal Spartan depth of twelve. The other accounts are much later though they appear to go back to fourth-century sources and can be used to supplement Xenophon, who seems to have been more concerned to account for the Spartan defeat than to explain the Theban victory. What emerges from the sources is that Epaminondas enlarged upon and developed certain features that were traditional elements in hoplite combat in combination with a peculiarity of Theban hoplite tactics. The Thebans had traditionally arrayed their troops in an unusually deep formation. At Delium they had been twenty-five deep. Now this tendency culminated in a fifty shield depth at Leuctra. Secondly, he again utilized in a purposeful manner a normal characteristic of hoplite warfare – the decision on one wing, usually the right. Epaminondas stationed his main strength on his left wing and positioned his line obliquely so that he offered his left wing for battle while keeping his center and right refused. He intended that the mass on his left would meet the Spartan army at the point where Cleombrotus was and break the Spartan line before it had a chance to encircle his left. The very depth of that left would slow the completion by the Spartans of their encircling movement. The élite Sacred Band would serve as the cutting edge of the Theban line.

Less than ten years later these tactics were to be repeated with less success at

Mantinea. Nevertheless, the development of these tactics prolonged the useful-ness of hoplite infantry by building on its inherent traits to transform it from a direct confrontation of two lines into a more flexible affair where force could be applied at chosen points, so that elements which themselves all had precedents in previous practice were combined in a new and tactically effective way.

Spartan casualties were heavy with four hundred out of a total of seven hundred killed, and politically the effects of the victory were immense. Sparta lost much prestige by simply showing that she could be beaten on the field of battle. Her losses were so high that she was thrown back on the defensive and allowed Thebes to establish her domination of Boeotia as well as detach the Arcadians from the Spartans in the Peloponnese. These developments eventually led to the loss of territories crucial to maintaining Sparta's position as a major power.

196. Xenophon, *Hellenica* 6.4.8–15

Xenophon's version of these events is the only contemporary account we have but it raises serious problems. It takes no note of tactical innovation as a key feature of this battle. Perhaps the best explanation is that Xenophon was really interested in giving an account of the reasons for Sparta's defeat and failed to recognize the genius of Epaminondas.

Certainly in this battle all went badly for the Spartans, but for Thebans everything turned out well as they had luck on their side. After breakfast Cleombrotus held his final council about the coming battle. At midday the Spartans had been drinking and it is said that the wine acted as a stimulant.

When both sides were arming and it was obvious that a battle was about to take place, those who had been providing a market for the Boeotian forces, as well as baggage carriers and those who were not willing to fight, began to leave the Boeotian army. But the mercenaries under Hero, the peltasts from Phocea and the Heraclean and Phliasian cavalry surrounded this group and began to attack them. They turned them back and pursued them as far as the Boeotian camp. The net result was that they made the Boeotian army more numerous and compact than it had been before.

Then since the ground between the Spartans and their allies and the Boeotians was level the Spartans ordered their cavalry to take a position in front of their phalanx and the Thebans instructed their cavalry to take up a position opposite the Spartans. The Theban cavalry were well-trained because of the war against Orchomenus and Thespiae, but the Spartan cavalry at this period was of the poorest quality. The rich raised the horses. But it was only at call up that the assigned cavalryman appeared. Receiving his horse and whatever arms were available the trooper took to the field immediately. The least physically capable and those without ambition found their way into the cavalry. This was the state of each side's cavalry forces.

As far as the heavy infantry were concerned, the Spartans marched their companies three abreast so that their line was no more than twelve men deep. But the Theban phalanx were arrayed not less than fifty men deep, because they thought that if they could prevail against the king and his bodyguard the rest would be easy.

At this point Cleombrotus began to move forward against the enemy even before his own troops perceived the movement. Now the cavalry of both sides encountered one another and the Spartans were quickly defeated; in their flight they entangled themselves with some of their own infantry and then the Thebans struck. Nevertheless at first Cleombrotus and his bodyguard were superior in the battle as the following evidence makes clear: the Spartans would not have been able to take up the wounded king's body and carry him off while he was still alive unless those fighting in front of him had been victorious up until that point. Then the polemarch Deinon fell, and Sphodrias from those in attendance on the king's tent and his son Cleonymus were killed while the knights, the so-called companions of the polemarch and other troops were pushed back by the weight of the Thebans and gave ground. When they saw this, the Lacedaemonian troops of the left wing gave way. Nonetheless, after they had crossed the ditch in front of their camp, they halted and ground arms at the place from which they had begun their attack. The camp was not situated on perfectly level ground but was on a slight rise. Some of the Spartans who found the thought of the enemy's victory unbearable asserted that the Spartans had to stop the Boeotians from erecting a trophy and further demanded that the bodies of the fallen be recovered not by a truce but by renewing the fighting. The Spartan polemarchs, noting that the Lacedaemonians had lost a thousand men of whom approximately four hundred out of seven hundred were Spartans, and also that the allies had lost heart for the fight (indeed, some were not unhappy with the result), took counsel from the most suitable individuals as to what needed to be done. When all had decided to seek the bodies of their fallen comrades under truce, they sent a herald to discuss the terms for a truce. After this the Thebans returned the bodies under truce and erected a trophy.

197. Plutarch, *Pelopidas* 23.1

Plutarch's account of the battle is now generally thought to be based on the late fourth-century historian Callisthenes. It most probably came from his *Hellenica*, a history of Greek affairs between 387 and 357 BC. Some scholars have gone so far as to suggest it is a manufactured tradition of the later fourth century.

In the battle Epaminondas advanced towards the left with his phalanx drawn up obliquely, in order that the Spartan right wing should be separated as far as possible from the rest of the army and also to force Cleombrotus back by falling upon him in mass on his wing. When the enemy saw what they were doing they began to change their formation and they extended their right and led it around to encircle and surround Epaminondas with their mass. But at this point Pelopidas, after he had collected his force of three hundred, ran forward to anticipate Cleombrotus' attempt to extend his line or to return to his earlier formation and close his front. His attack fell upon men who were not yet in position but still in disorder. This happened although the Spartans, master craftsmen in the art of war, had practised and accustomed themselves to nothing so much as to maintaining their positions and not disturbing their ranks during a change of formation, but to accept anyone as either a rank-mate or file-mate and to control and form compactly and to fight with equal intensity wherever there was danger.

But this time the phalanx of Epaminondas was coming at them and avoiding the rest of their army and Pelopidas attacked with unbelievable daring and quickness. All of this confounded their skill and plan and so the result was an unparalleled flight and slaughter of the Spartans. Through these actions Pelopidas who was not boeotarch as Epaminondas was and commanded only a small portion of the Boeotian forces, gained a reputation equal to the latter.

THE USE OF LIGHT-ARMED TROOPS

In the same way that the first half of the century saw experimentation in the tactics of heavy infantry, it also witnessed a limited change in the way light-armed troops, especially peltasts, were used. The reasons for this change are not totally clear, but some of the following factors seem to have influenced this trend.

In the Peloponnesian War on several occasions in smaller battles light-armed troops, especially javelin men, destroyed hoplite forces. The classic actions here were the Athenian disaster in Aetolia in 426 (see no. 69) and the spectacular success against Spartan hoplites on Sphacteria in the following year (see no. 70). In the majority of cases in which light-armed troops prevailed they operated in conjunction with other arms, especially hoplites and cavalry. It is noticeable that operating alone against other arms the peltasts often suffered heavily. At the center of these changes were experiments on a small scale with groups of diversely equipped troops.

The Peloponnesian War's devastation and dislocation were responsible for other trends in the same direction. The drain on manpower and on productive capacities led to the greater use of mercenaries. The recruitment of such groups was made easier as the war progressed. The continuous nature of the war made it possible and perhaps necessary for more individuals to pursue a career in mercenary service. This applied to both light-armed troops and to hoplites. The devastation caused by the conflict made such service attractive, even though the average wage was small. Other benefits awaited the successful mercenary. So a large floating population of professional soldiers seeking hire was created. It is a symptom of the situation created by the war that we hear for the first time of a Theban, Coeritadas, wandering around Greece hawking his skills as a general to the highest bidder.

A further result of this situation was the probable decline in the number of hoplites due to casualties and property losses sustained in the course of the war. It may have been to make use of groups like this that the Athenian commander Thrasyllus recruited a force of some eight thousand peltasts from among Athenian citizens and used them to make successful coastal raids on hostile areas in Asia Minor in the spring of 408.

The last phase of the Peloponnesian War also saw the involvement of the Persians in the war on a grand scale, though primarily through the provision of subsidies to the Peloponnesians. This infusion of money allowed mercenary forces to be employed on a far larger scale and for more prolonged periods than any Greek state could possibly have afforded.

The victory over Athens deprived large numbers of mercenaries of employment. It was again the Persians, this time in the form of an attempted coup by Cyrus the Younger against the Persian throne, who offered enticing prospects for vast numbers of these unemployed mercenaries. It was the success of the retreat of this force after the death of Cyrus that showed the superiority of the Greek hoplite as heavy infantry against any Persian force. At the same time it became

141

obvious that fighting in Asia required more than simply heavy infantry. To overcome the limitations of hoplites, light-armed troops including archers, slingers and cavalry needed to act in combination with each other. The Spartans in their campaign in Asia against the Persians in the first years of the fourth century took the lesson to heart.

Under these conditions there developed a series of experiments in the use of mixed arms at the level of raiding, skirmishing and the small-scale encounter. The major contests involved such troops but were still dominated by the traditional heavily armed foot soldier. It seems to have been the growth of professionalism in military life that allowed experimentation with combined arms. These experiments were to finally bear fruit in the use of such forces by the Macedonians under Philip II of Macedon and his son Alexander the Great.

Greek campaigns against the Persians in western Asia Minor showed the Greeks the advantages and the necessity in certain situations of employing light-armed troops and cavalry in addition to hoplite forces. Persian wealth and the spoils resulting from the Spartan campaigns provided the money and the constant service that allowed a level of training to be achieved characteristic of a professional force. Even though such troops played a larger role in the decisive battles on Greek soil in the fourth century, the basic arm of combat remained the heavy infantry. Integrated large-scale forces of difficult arms were not to evolve until the rise of Macedonia. The fourth century saw the increasing use in smaller scale actions of mixed forces and the growing use of the professional soldier.

Mixed formations of cavalry and infantry

More than any other arm cavalry was influenced by the Greek contact with the Persians. It may well be that Athens was induced to establish its first permanent cavalry formation by its experience in the Persian Wars (see p. 00). But Sparta resisted creating a cavalry corps until the 420s. Part of this reluctance to use cavalry on any scale was the absence of suitable grazing land for horses in most states. Cavalry might be useful in certain situations, especially when well handled in conjunction with other types of units against unmassed infantry, but it was not to be a dominant factor until Philip and Alexander.

After 399 the Spartans reacted to an attempt by the Persians to reassert control over the Greek cities of coastal Asia Minor by sending an expeditionary force at the cities' request to aid them against the Persians. From that date the Spartans were engaged in operations in this area. In 396 one of the two Spartan kings, Agesilaus, took control of Spartan forces there. The troops that he commanded were almost all infantry. He realized that to have any hope of real success he needed to vastly increase his own force of cavalry to counter the Persians. As a means of raising such a force he took a census of the richest Greeks in the area and demanded cavalry service or a commutation to supply a horse, arms and a trooper. This was readily accepted and in the spring of 395 his cavalry was ready to take the field. The first year's campaign culminated in the battle at Sardis in which a Persian force composed only of cavalry was routed by a combined force of hoplites, peltasts and cavalry.

198. Xenophon, *Hellenica* 3.4.21–24

Any account of the battle of Sardis in the spring and early summer of 395 is bedeviled by serious problems of reconstruction. There are at least two separate major traditions about the battle, the main difference being the use and importance of an ambush which is found in the tradition opposed to Xenophon's account.

Agesilaus was not dissimulating about the point of his invasion, but invaded the country around Sardis just as he had announced. For three days his army advanced through territory empty of the enemy and it provided his army with abundant supplies, but on the fourth day enemy cavalry appeared. Agesilaus told the officer in charge of the tent bearers to cross the Pactolus River with his men and set up camp. The Persian cavalry noticed and then killed many of the Greek camp followers who had dispersed in search of plunder.

When Agesilaus saw what was happening he ordered his cavalry to go to their aid. When the Persians saw this they massed together and formed up against their attackers in battle line with all of their cavalry squadrons. At that point, Agesilaus became aware that the enemy was without their infantry, while he had all of his forces present. He decided that this was the opportune time to join battle if he could. After he had performed the appropriate sacrifices he led his phalanx forward against the formation of the enemy's cavalry; at the same time he ordered the hoplites in the 20–30 age-group to run and close with them and also issued orders for the peltasts to follow them on the run. He also commanded the cavalry to charge and he followed with his entire army.

The Persians initially stood up to the cavalry charge but then gave way when they were faced by the threat of the entire army. Some fell immediately as they crossed the river, the others fled. The Greeks followed close on them and captured their camp. The peltasts as they normally do turned to plundering, but Agesilaus made a cordon around everything and every one friendly or hostile. A great deal of money was captured, which was found to be more than seventy talents, and the camels which Agesilaus later brought back to Greece were taken in this action.

Peltasts and other arms

For a general description of the equipment and fighting style of peltasts see p. 42–3 above. They were the most typical and probably the most effective light-armed troops during the first half of the century. Several incidents in its course show that to be really effective these mixed formations needed troops armed with missile weapons and cavalry. But even without them they could achieve remarkable success against less mobile hoplites. The key to the effectiveness of peltasts in combination with hoplites was the ability of the latter to hold the enemy in formation by their presence. This restricted the mobility of an enemy infantry already over-burdened with a heavy hoplite shield to chase and catch lightly armed peltasts who could continue to inflict losses from a safe range with their javelins. Peltasts could also be useful to hoplites in capturing and defending passes. Such troops were also more adept at foraging and raiding. Finally they were extremely useful in setting ambushes in difficult country. A force of 1200 peltasts under the Athenian general Iphicrates successfully ambushed a mixed Spartan force of hoplites and light-armed troops descending from a pass near Abydus on the Hellespont in the summer of 389.

Iphicrates and the peltasts at Corinth

Perhaps the incident involving light-armed troops that had the most far-reaching repercussions was the destruction of a Spartan *mora* of about six hundred men at Lechaeum near Corinth by a company of peltasts in Athenian employ and under the command of one of the most celebrated of Athenian commanders, Iphicrates, in conjunction with a unit of Athenian hoplites led by the general Callias. It is clear from fourth-century orators and from the citation below from Cornelius Nepos, a Roman biographer of the first century, that it became a famous military success, mentioned along with Thermopylae and Salamis by Athenian authors later in the century. It was clear evidence of what combined light- and heavy-armed troops could do in lesser engagements.

199. Androtion, *FGrH* 324 frg. 48

This mercenary unit was well known enough to be mentioned as a normal state expense by the comic writer Aristophanes in his play *Plutus*, produced in 388. The unit, if we follow this fragment, was established by the Athenian admiral Conon, who was in Persian service, after his naval victory over the Spartans at Cnidus in 394. It ethnic composition cannot be determined. It numbered about 1200 peltasts. This unit is first heard of in 392 when it held the right of the allied line against the Spartans in a battle within the Corinthian Long Walls. It was apparently disbanded at the end of the Corinthian War in 387/386.

The mercenary unit in Corinth. Conon first formed it. Later Iphicrates and Chabrias took it over. It was used under the command of Iphicrates and Callias to cut down the Spartan *mora*.

200. Cornelius Nepos, *Iphicrates* 2.1

Iphicrates, in contrast to most fifth-century generals, was from a humble background and was probably born about 415. His age makes it most unlikely that he was a general at this time, being less than 30. The tradition is consistent that he was a strict and at times fierce disciplinarian. The absence of any difficulty with his force seems to indicate that the troops were well paid. His success must have been due in part to the continued existence and *esprit de corps* of the peltasts. His career was one of almost constant military service, though rarely with the dramatic success he achieved in Corinth.

Iphicrates commanded his force at Corinth so that no Greek force was ever better trained or better disciplined. Iphicrates established the practice that at the general's command to begin battle the force deployed itself without the aid of its commander so correctly that it seemed that each man had been assigned his post by the most experienced of commanders.

The Spartan disaster at Lechaeum

After the battle of the Long Walls in 392 the Corinthian War was transformed into a series of skirmishes. The most important victory was gained by Agesilaus who captured Lechaeum, Corinth's port on the Corinthian Gulf, in 391. Other sucesses followed. But the Spartans' success in the field appears to have blinded them to certain weaknesses in organization, particularly in light troops. In fact, the Spartans were never very successful in leading mercenary troops of this type.

The professional force of peltasts that Iphicrates commanded had already successfully ambushed a force from Phlius sent to stop his plundering their territory. The same unit had also mounted a number of raids against enemy cities in Arcadia for plunder. They were so feared that Arcadian hoplites refused to face them in battle. Against the Spartans they had been less successful as the Spartan tactic of sending the younger hoplites in pursuit had on one occasion led to the death of a number of peltasts caught in the chase. This reinforced what must have been the normal Spartan disdain for such troops.

The disaster that befell the Spartan *mora* garrisoned in Lechaeum in the summer of 390 was totally unexpected. Xenophon's account is the only one worth credence. Xenophon is clear in indicating that the action fell into two parts. The *mora* was attacked by the peltasts with missile weapons in such a way as to avoid hand-to-hand combat with the hoplites and to inflict continuous casualties on it by missile weapons. Though in the course of the battle supporting cavalry came up, it was handled so badly by its commander that it was totally ineffective. The second and final phase of the battle occurred when the Spartan hoplites, at a loss as to what to do, retreated to a small hillock and then broke at the approach of the Athenian hoplite force.

The action re-emphasized what had already been established, and that was that under the right conditions a force of light infantry armed with javelins could wear down and render unfit a force of hoplites, even Spartan ones. It is important to remember that in this case those conditions were partly the result of the exceptional nature of the peltast force and the incompetence of the Spartan commander. It also was to have an important effect on the reputation of the peltast for success in war. It is in the half century following this encounter that the reputation of the peltast and the use of such troops reached its peak. It is also noticeable that this was a transitory state of affairs. In succeeding periods peltasts were once again reduced to marginal status.

201. Xenophon, *Hellenica* 4.5.11–18

The disaster to this *mora* happened in the following way. The men of Amyclae, even if they are on campaign or absent from home for some other reason, always return home for the festival of the Hyacinthia to sing the paean. At that time [390] Agesilaus had left all of the Amyclaeans in the army at Lechaeum. The garrison commander there ordered allied troops to guard the walls while he escorted the Amyclaeans past the city of Corinth with a *mora* of hoplites and a *mora* of cavalry. When the group was about three or four miles from Sicyon, the garrison commander returned with his force of about six hundred hoplites, but ordered the commander of his cavalry to follow him with his régiment after escorting the Amyclaeans as far as they had requested. The Spartans were fully aware that there were many enemy peltasts and hoplites in Corinth. But they contemptuously assumed that no one would dare to attack them because of past Spartan successes.

The Athenian commanders in the city, Callias the general in charge of the Athenian hoplite forces and Iphicrates who led the peltasts, seeing that the Spartan force was small and without cavalry or peltasts, thought it would be safe to attack them with their force of peltasts. For if the Spartans continued on their way they could be destroyed by javelins cast at their unshielded side and even if they should attempt to pursue their attackers, it would be easy for peltasts to avoid the hoplites on account of their speed. With these considerations in mind, the generals marched out from Corinth.

Callias deployed his troops close to the city, while Iphicrates took his force of peltasts and attacked the *mora*. Some of the Spartans were wounded or killed and the shield bearers were instructed to pick them up and carry them back to Lechaeum. These alone of the unit came through the ordeal with unblemished reputations. The polemarch ordered the hoplites between ages 20 and 30 to run out and pursue the light-armed troops. But as they were hoplites in pursuit of peltasts who had the lead of a javelin's throw they caught no one, as Iphicrates had ordered his troops to retreat before the hoplites came close to them. But when the Spartan hoplites returned to their unit, in no formation since each of them had pursued the enemy as quickly as he could, the peltasts turned about and some threw their javelins at them from behind, while others running alongside of them attacked their unshielded side. In the course of the first pursuit they shot down nine or ten. As a result, the peltasts pressed their attack more boldly. As the Spartans again began to come under attack and suffer losses the polemarch ordered a pursuit by troops aged 20 to 35. During their return from this pursuit the Spartans lost more men than they had the first time. After the best of them had already been killed, the cavalry came up with them and they again launched a pursuit in concert with the hoplites. When the peltasts gave way, the cavalry were poorly handled in their pursuit of them. For they did not give chase until they had killed some of them but kept pace with the hoplites riding in pursuit with them and turning back when they turned back.

The repetition of this process made the depleted number of Spartan troops who survived less bold, while the enemy became still more adventuresome and more of them joined in the attack. Finally, when they were at the end of their tether they closed ranks on top of a small hill about a third of a mile from the Corinthian Gulf and about a mile from Lechaeum. The troops who were garrisoning Lechaeum saw what was happening and, boarding small boats, sailed along the shore until they were level with the hill. The Spartans on the hill at this point were at a loss for what to do except to suffer and to die, and now seeing the Athenian hoplites moving up gave way. Some of them plunged into the sea and a few of the remainder made their way with the cavalry to Lechaeum. During the entire action Spartan losses were about 250 men.

Reforms in peltast equipment by Iphicrates

The passage from Nepos below provides our fullest reference to Iphicrates' activities, although other sources give a different picture. The only date that we have is supplied by a passage in Diodorus; this is placed under the events of the year 374, which appears likely. The date is the least of the problems associated with these reforms. The most fruitful approach is to see it as linked with Iphicrates' service with the Persians in Egypt. Egyptian infantry traditionally fought with long spears, as Xenophon acknowledges. The sword may be of Persian origin. These facts appear to mark a convergence of two separate streams of development, Greek and Persian. The increasing prestige of the peltast seems at least in some writers to have made the term a generic one for light-armed troops but these men appear to actually have been peltasts. Iphicrates needed troops who could close with the enemy. He took his Greek or Greek-trained infantry who had some experience with this type of fighting and equipped them as the tradition indicates. This made them essentially into the equivalent of light-armed hoplites. This would then explain the confusion in the tradition which saw it as a generalized replacement of hoplites by troops equipped this way.

202. Cornelius Nepos, *Iphicrates* 1.3–4

Iphicrates was extremely experienced in war, he was often in command of armies and never displayed poor leadership. He always prevailed because of his planning and was so skilled that he made many innovations and improvements in military technique. He changed infantry equipment. Before he was in command the Greek infantry were accustomed to using very large round shields, short thrusting spears and small swords. He substituted *peltae* for the round shield (because of this change the troops became known as peltast infantry) so that the troops would have more mobility on the battlefield and in their encounter with the enemy. He doubled the length of the spear and lengthened their swords. At the same time he substituted linen corselets for linked bronze ones. By these reforms he made the soldiers still more mobile for he took care to provide sufficient security for their bodies at the same time as he lightened that protection.

MERCENARIES

Soldiers who are long-term professionals and fight for pay are a constant feature in Greek history. What changed over time was the relationship of mercenary forces to citizen troops and the tasks for which such professional troops were employed. These factors were largely determined by the ability of Greek states to control the scope and intensity of their warfare and by the strength of the identification between citizen and soldier.

The first phase of Greek mercenary service extends from the seventh century until the Peloponnesian War. The primary employers were various Eastern monarchs, with Egypt attested as the only continuous employer. It is no accident that it coincides with the introduction of hoplite warfare and its associated equipment. During this period the Greeks of Ionia along with the Carians of southwestern Asia Minor supplied effective heavy infantry that was either lacking or of inferior quality in the eastern monarchies. It was also in the East that sufficient wealth existed to make employment attractive and to allow fairly substantial numbers to be employed. But with the growth of Persian power in the last half of the sixth century and the absorption of Egypt and other older monarchies into the Persian empire these markets dried up and disappeared, until the Persians themselves began to hire Greek mercenaries towards the end of the fifth century.

Within Greece itself, there were only very limited numbers of such troops, given the absence of the means to employ them and the widespread notion that fighting was a citizen's duty. They are mostly associated with the spread of tyrants on the Greek mainland or on the islands. Their function was clear: to establish and support a base of power for the tyrant that was not dependent in any way on his political rivals but was exclusively subordinated to himself.

By the beginning of the fifth century most of the tyrannies on mainland Greece had disappeared. The oligarchic or democratic states that evolved, as well as the nature of hoplite warfare and the fiscal systems of most Greek city-states, provided little incentive for use of mercenaries until the last third of the century. It was only in Sicily that mercenaries were employed on a large scale in the earlier fifth century. By 481 it seems possible that Gelon, tyrant of Syracuse, maintained an army that included as many as fifteen thousand mercenaries. They presumably constituted a significant part of the army that won the decisive victory over the Carthaginians at Himera.

The important turning point in the use of mercenary forces in Greece itself came with the Peloponnesian War. An increasing use of mercenary forces led to the substantial replacement of citizen troops in combat by such forces. The Peloponnesian states were the first to use them, but both sides employed them by the end of the war.

The reasons for their employment were many. The war was a prolonged affair involving the continuous use of forces in small-scale engagements. Such warfare was often easier and cheaper to conduct with mercenaries. It must have been fostered at least on the Athenian side by the large numbers of paid rowers in the fleet and the use of pay as recompense for a citizen's military service. This introduced the notion of a commercial transaction, which allowed an easy transition to paying a professional instead of a citizen. The warfare of this period required troops with specialized skills which were often difficult for an amateur to acquire, such as expertise with the sling or bow.

Such action was made possible by another feature of this period that is rare earlier: the presence of states with enough resources to employ mercenaries over a prolonged period. This type of prosperity offered the possibility and supplied the inducement to spend on hiring soldiers.

The war supplied further impetus for the use of such troops in the dislocation, hardship and distress that it caused. But despite this, the majority of mercenaries for most of the war period came from certain definite and limited recruiting areas. The Peloponnese, especially the territories of Arcadia and Achaea, were the major suppliers of hoplite professionals. These areas were somewhat marginal economically and their prime export was mercenaries. Other disturbed areas like Crete or Aetolia also supplied specialist troops. Non-Greek Thracians were recruited as peltasts along with Scythians as bowmen and other barbarian troops.

The end of the Peloponnesian War did not see an end to the use of these troops but rather the beginning of widespread employment of mercenaries. This seems to have been the result of the dislocation and devastation caused by the war. In some areas traditional peasant agriculture was threatened by the losses entailed by the war as well as by competition from imported food-stuffs. Those dispossessed were often unable to compete with metics as artisans or to find any employment at all. There appears to have been in the course of the century a gradual impoverishment which is best seen at Athens. These economic difficulties were accompanied by internal social and political crises which led to a growing number of exiles and displaced persons. It was the inter-section of an increasing demand with this expanding supply that led to the widening dominance of mercenaries as the preferred troops in fourth-century warfare. Demand grew as the result of increasing use by the Persians of Greek mercenary forces as heavy infantry. One modern estimate is that approximately twenty thousand Greeks as mercenaries served in the East during most of the fourth century. The West and Sicily likewise saw an increase in demand for mercenaries.

At home the increasingly diverse nature of warfare with the need for specialist units and hoplite supplements made it much more economical to employ mercenaries than to train and keep in being units of a state's own citizens. The first major battle in which mercenary hoplites were used on Greek soil was at Coronea. These were men brought back from campaigns in Asia Minor. The conditions that brought states to use mercenaries also pushed the states to maintain them, as was the case with Iphicrates' peltasts during the Corinthian War (see no. 200 above). Mercenary troops begin to take on a semi-permanent character with a commander who was essentially a professional as well. This development was reinforced by the general superiority in skill of mercenary over citizen formations and led to their further replacement.

The financing of war, an activity of little importance until the Peloponnesian War, now became a major problem. The new methods of financing war and a growing preference for the use of mercenaries are on view in the action taken by the Spartans in 383 when they allowed members of the Peloponnesian League to substitute money payments for military service. All of these factors led to a peak use of mercenary service by mid-century. The succeeding Hellenistic period was to see further developments in the same direction.

The importance of this type of service as a profession is clear from the fact that recruitment as the century progressed appears not to have been linked to a specific geographic or ethnic area. Mercenaries were produced in all Greek cities.

The social and economic needs that underlay mercenary service in this period are evidenced by rates of pay that fluctuate but are generally low and unattractive when compared to the little we know of wages in other areas of employment. The great hope of these men must have been the taking of plunder and so it was at best an uncertain source of income. By the later fourth century the mercenary had become a necessity in Greek warfare and a recognized social type whose interests often diverged from the civilians around him and sometimes from his employer. The mechanisms whereby the Greek city-state had been able to conduct limited hoplite contests which moderated the total effect of war on society had finally broken down.

Early service in the East

Greek mercenary service is attested first outside Greece in the eastern Mediterranean. It coincides in time with internal economic and social problems in the seventh century and also with the introduction of hoplite warfare. This gave the Greeks a skill to export which was lacking in the East.

203. Herodotus, 2.152.1–154.4

Egypt provides us with the earliest example of Greeks serving outside of Greece as mercenaries. Such service is first attested in the reign of Egyptian king Psammetichus I (664–610 BC). Although bronze armor was known to the Egyptians, it was scale armor sewn on to leather, and the Greeks with their plate bronze armor made a striking impression.

Then Psammetichus sent an inquiry to the oracle in the city of Buto (this is the most trustworthy of Egyptian oracles) and received the reply that revenge would come from the sea when men of bronze appeared. He thought it very unlikely that such an event would ever happen. But within a short time, some Ionians and Carians who were engaged in raiding were forced for some reason during their voyage to land on the Egyptian coast. One of the Egyptians saw them as they disembarked in their armor and came to Psammetichus who was in the marshes to inform him of this. Since he had not before seen men armored in bronze he said that bronze men had arrived from the sea and were plundering the plain.

Psammetichus realized that this was the fulfillment of the oracle and concluded a treaty of friendship with the Ionians and Carians and by making lavish promises enlisted their aid. After this, with Egyptians on his side and foreign allies, he subdued the other kings and gained control of all Egypt. . . .

Psammetichus gave land to the Ionians and Carians who had aided him to live opposite each other, separated only by the Nile; the area became known as the Camp. . . . They were later moved to Memphis by King Amasis to serve as a guard for him against the Egyptians. . . . They were the first foreigners to be settled in Egypt.

204. Alcaeus, Fragment 350 Capmbell

These lines are from a poem of welcome by Alcaeus in honor of his brother who perhaps served as a mercenary during the campaigns of the Chaldaean king

Nebuchadnezzar in Palestine at the beginning of the sixth century. The warrior mentioned was about 8 ft 4 in. in height.

You have come from the ends of the earth,
with sword hilt of ivory bound with gold.
As an ally of the Babylonians you have performed a great feat,
rescuing them from trouble by killing a warrior,
one palm's breadth less than five royal cubits.

Mercenaries in the service of Greek tyrants

205. Herodotus, 1.64.1

According to Herodotus this was in the period after Peisistratus' second unsuccessful attempt to establish himself as tyrant at Athens in 556. After leaving Athens he seems to have taken up residence near the gold mines of Mount Pangaeum in Thrace. Perhaps by mining he was able to hire a number of mercenaries from Argos, and with the support of other Greek states like Thebes he prepared his return. In 546 he landed in Attica and at Pallene defeated the Athenian aristocracy. The Strymon River marked the later boundary between Macedonia and Thrace.

Now that the Athenians were reduced to obedience, Peisistratus held the tyranny for the third time and he secured his rule by the use of numerous mercenaries and by acquiring many sources of revenue, some from Athens and others from the territory around the Strymon River.

206. Aristotle, *Politics* 1286b28–40

The following discussion is placed by Aristotle in the context of his analysis of one form of kingship, the absolute, and in the immediate passage he deals with problems germane to kingship such as hereditary transmission and its basis for enforcing sovereignty and guaranteeing the monarch's security. Some sort of guard is not only mentioned as a normal accompaniment but also as a necessity of absolute power. Earlier Aristotle had defined an *aisymnetia* as an elective form of tyranny that is non-hereditary. The office could be held for a term of years, for life, or to perform a specific function.

But there is an additional question about the monarch's power and that is: Should the individual who is going to exercise kingship have a bodyguard with which he can compel those who will not obey, or in what manner ought he to receive control of affairs? If he becomes sovereign legally and does nothing to satisfy his own desires at the expense of the laws, nevertheless he will need sufficient power to safeguard the laws. In the situation of a kingship of this type, it is perhaps not hard to settle the matter. For he who holds it needs enough power so as to be the superior of any one individual or group of individuals, but less than that of the body politic, just as was the case among the ancients who gave a bodyguard to those whom they established as *asymnetes* or tyrant, and so it was the number of his bodyguard that someone advised the Syracusans to assign to Dionysius that was of importance.

151

The use of mercenaries in the Peloponnesian War

The Peloponnesian War marked a turning point in the employment of mercenary troops on the Greek mainland. Between 500 and the outbreak of the war in 431 mercenaries were rare. The war changed all of this. Its length, nature, intensity and innovations, all outlined above, opened the way for the employment of mercenaries on a much larger scale.

Mercenaries in Peloponnesian service

The Peloponnesians were the first to use mercenary troops in the war, probably due to their access to the prime recruiting grounds for hoplite troops in Arcadia and Achaea.

207. Thucydides, 1.60.1–3

This force made its way north in the early summer of 432 when Corinth was not yet technically in a state of war with Athens, and so these Corinthians came as volunteers. The mercenaries, Peloponnesian volunteers, must be hoplites and Aristeus could expect a favorable reception in an area where peltasts were plentiful.

Also at that time the Corinthians, after the revolt of Potidaea and while the Athenian ships were stationed in Macedonia afraid for Potidaea, and feeling that this was a matter [the fate of Potidaea] that touched them personally, sent out a force composed of Corinthian volunteers and Peloponnesian mercenaries to the number of 1600 hoplites and 400 light-armed troops. Their commander was Aristeus, the son of Adeimantus, and not the least important reason for the presence of Corinthian volunteers was the friendship they felt for him; he was always well-disposed towards Potidaea. Their force arrived in the Thraceward region forty days after the revolt of Potidaea.

Mercenaries in Athenian service

208. Thucydides, 7.27

These Thracian peltasts were to join the relief expedition to Syracuse in the summer of 413 but arrived too late to sail. They and other light-armed troops were sent in response to the effectiveness of the Syracusan cavalry against Athenian hoplites. Their rate of pay appears to have been the same as that of an Athenian hoplite, though its relation to their expenses is unclear. Their tribe belonged to Thracians who inhabited the Rhodope mountain range. For the savage treatment of the small Boeotian town of Mycalessus on their way home see no. 165.

There then arrived at Athens that same summer 1300 peltasts from one of the short sword-bearing Thracian tribes, the Dii. They were to have sailed with Demosthenes to Sicily. But they arrived too late and the Athenians decided to send them home. They seemed to be too expensive to use (for each got a drachma a day) against the post at Decelea.

The fourth century

The Ten Thousand

The expedition of the Ten Thousand, which was to serve as a watershed in the employment of mercenaries and in Greco-Persian relations, arose out of the disappointment and resentment of Cyrus, a younger brother of the Persian king Artaxerxes. In 403 and 402 BC he came to secret agreements with various Greeks to raise mercenary contingents. The nucleus of these contingents was formed from his own bodyguard of Greek mercenaries. Using this as a base he was able to raise an unprecedented number of Greek hoplites, over ten thousand, to give him a superiority in heavy infantry. He at first deceived these Greeks as to his real intention and then revealed his true goal. Despite initial reluctance the Greeks were persuaded by pay and the prospect of booty to stay with him. In the late summer or early autumn of 401 Cyrus was killed in the battle and the Greeks found themselves isolated in northern Mesopotamia. The story of their adventures was written by an important participant, the Athenian Xenophon. It is the one ancient eyewitness account of a mercenary force in action that we possess. The Greek force successfully returned home despite constant pressures from the Persians and harsh local conditions. Their feat not only displayed Persia's weakness (see p. 182), but also clearly demonstrated the effectiveness of such mercenary forces. Interestingly it provides the first clear indication of semi-permanent mercenary forces under their own commanders.

209. Xenophon, *Anabasis* 6.4.8
This passage is not totally logical in its description of the motives for joining Cyrus. There is an attempt to elevate the standing of Xenophon's fellow soldiers by denying their commercial motivation. Most of the soldiers were from areas that had traditionally supplied mercenaries and where gain was the central issue.

The majority of the soldiers had not sailed from Greece to undertake this mercenary service on account of their neediness, but because of the report of Cyrus' character that they had heard; some brought others with them, while others had spent money of their own on this undertaking and others had abandoned fathers, mothers or children with the intention of earning money for them and returning once more since they had heard that those who served with Cyrus had enjoyed many benefits.

210. Isocrates, *Philip* 5.96
In this open letter of 346 Isocrates tried to persuade Philip II of Macedonia to end internal Greek troubles by uniting the Greeks in support of an invasion of a weakened Persian empire. Its picture of a comparatively settled Greece at the end of the Peloponnesian War appears exaggerated.

You [Philip] will have as many soldiers as you wish at your disposal, for the present state of Greece is such that it is easier to assemble a larger and more effective army from those wandering in exile than from men who are still citizens. At the time of the Ten

Thousand there was no standing body of mercenaries but one had to collect mercenaries from various cities, spending more in bounty for the recruiters than in pay for the soldiers.

211. Xenophon, *Anabasis* 1.2.9

This selection from Xenophon gives us some idea of the diversity of the mercenary force that Cyrus assembled. It falls into two broad categories: specialist troops and a majority from the traditional areas of hoplite recruitment. There was also a smaller number from other areas which shows a gradual change in the sources of recruitment. Larger and larger areas of Greece were utilized. Celaenae is in west central Asia Minor and is strategically sighted at a road junction between the coast and the interior of Asia Minor.

Cyrus remained in Celaenae for thirty days. Clearchus, the Spartan exile, arrived with 1000 hoplites, 800 Thracian peltasts and 200 Cretan archers. Also at the same time Sosis from Syracuse came with 300 hoplites and Agias the Arcadian with 1000 heavy infantry. Cyrus held a review there and counting his Greek forces in the pleasure park he found that the total of hoplites was 11,000 and there were about 2000 peltasts.

212. Xenophon, *Anabasis* 2.6.1–5

This appreciation of Clearchus (see also nos 152 and 211) points to the increasing professionalization and prestige of military leadership. It is visible within city states such as Athens in the deification of Iphicrates, and is clearest in the case of mercenary leaders. Some of these were, as Clearchus, former officers and officials in traditional states who had lost their positions and were now selling their expertise. The professionalization of commanders must have been furthered by the growing use of mercenaries and mercenary bands, leading to their becoming quasi-permanent. This trend appears to accelerate in the second half of the century. The daric was the standard Persian gold coin of 8.4 grams.

The generals were taken prisoner and conveyed to the king and were beheaded. One of them was Clearchus who was considered by all who knew him to be a man both fit for and in love with war. As long as the war between the Athenians and the Peloponnesians lasted he fought for his city. After peace was concluded he persuaded his state that the Thracians were committing acts of injustice against the Greeks and after he had obtained from the ephors what he could he sailed off to fight the Thracians who lived beyond the Chersonese and the city of Perinthus. When the ephors had for some reason changed their minds after he had left, and tried to turn him back at the Isthmus of Corinth, he refused further obedience and left, sailing to the Hellespont. He was then condemned to death as a consequence of his disobedience. As an exile he approached Cyrus and won him over with the arguments I have recorded elsewhere and received ten thousand darics from him. He took the money but did not take things easy. Using the money he collected an army and made war on the Thracians. He defeated them and from this point on he fought, harried and plundered them in every way possible until Cyrus needed his army. At Cyrus' summons Clearchus joined him to make war at his side.

213. Xenophon, *Hellenica* 6.2.6

These events in the Corcyrean campaign are part of the hostilities resulting from a breakdown in the peace of 375 between Athens and Sparta. Mnasippus was the Spartan admiral sent out in that year to attack Corcyra with a fleet of sixty ships. It was to be the last major overseas expedition by the Spartans. It provides a concrete and specific picture of the dynamics of commanding a mercenary force and the importance of mercenaries to the Spartans in this period.

Seeing these things Mnasippus thought that Corcyra was practically his and began to make changes in his mercenaries' conditions of service. Some he discharged from his service, the rest who remained in service had their pay two months in arrears. This was not the result of a lack of money, as was said, for many states had sent him cash instead of men since the campaign was overseas.

The besieged, noting that the guard posts were more poorly manned than before and that the enemy was scattered over the countryside, made a sortie and captured some of the enemy and also cut down others. When Mnasippus saw what was happening he armed himself and came to the aid of his men with all of the hoplites that he had, while ordering the *lochagoi* and taxiarchs to bring up the mercenaries. When some of his officers answered that it would not be easy to get the mercenaries to obey since they had not been given their provisions, he struck one of them with a stick and another with the butt-spike of his spear. The end of it was that all who came out from camp with him were in low spirits and hated him. Neither feeling is an advantage in battle.

The prevalence of mercenaries

214. Xenophon *Hellenica* 5.2.21

This meeting in 382 between Sparta and the members of the Peloponnesian League was summoned in response to a plea for help against Olynthus by various cities in the Chalcidice. The Spartans were reacting to their fear of a possible alliance between this powerful city and its other major Greek opponents Athens and Thebes. The great distance that the Peloponnesian forces would have to travel may have played a role in the desire of the allies to commute men for money and for Sparta's readiness to allow them to do so. The Spartans played an important role in introducing mercenary forces into Greek warfare. Agesilaus at Coronea in 394 was the first to use sizeable mercenary forces, and the Spartans continued to employ them in increasing numbers in the course of the century. The rate of commutation is lower than that paid to the Thracian mercenaries thirty years before at Athens. But the rate for infantry is the same as that specified in 420 between Mantinea, Argos, Elis and Athens in their treaty of alliance (see no. 128 above). The rate for a cavalry man is a third higher. An Aeginetan drachma was worth approximately 1.4 Athenian drachmas.

After their speech the Lacedaemonians allowed their allies to speak and asked them to give their counsel as to what they considered the best course of action for the Peloponnesus and for the allies as a whole. Given this, many who spoke counseled that an army ought to be assembled, especially those who wanted to do the Lacedaemonians a favor, and the assembly decided to send troops to the army from each of the allied states to form a force of ten thousand. A discussion arose as to whether those states that wished could contribute money in place of men at the rate of three Aeginetan obols per man for the infantry, and in place of cavalry the amount should be at the rate of the pay of four hoplites per trooper.

215. Diodorus Siculus, 18.21.1–2

The increased hiring of mercenaries created marketplaces where the mercenary soldier or troop could sell their services. The most famous of these was at Cape Taenarum (today Cape Matapan) in southern Laconia, which was difficult of access from the land and, in addition, possessed two harbors. It was the most active of these markets at the end of the fourth century. In Asia Minor Ephesus also was known as a center for the hire of mercenaries. The Thibron mentioned here was a Spartan. He had managed to gain control of considerable funds and had involved himself in internal struggles in the city of Cyrene in Libya. The date is 322 BC.

Although Thibron had experienced a major misfortune nevertheless he kept on with the war. Choosing the most suitable of his friends he sent them to the Peloponnese to hire the mercenaries who were waiting about near Taenarum; for many of the discharged mercenaries were wandering about looking for employers and at that time there were more than 2500 in the neighborhood of Taenarum. Thibron's agents hired them and all set sail for Cyrene.

The virtues of mercenaries

Mercenaries were increasingly attractive as war ceased being a single decisive encounter between heavy infantry phalanxes and began to assume the shape of a prolonged war of attrition. Such a struggle demanded the retention of troops in the field, as with Iphicrates' peltasts at Corinth, for a number of years (see no. 200). This was an impractical proposition for a citizen army whose productive and other skills were needed at home.

This type of war demanded the use of a much more diverse army with various specialized troops including archers, slingers and cavalry. It was cheaper and more efficient for a state to hire professionals from areas where training in these arms was traditional rather than go to the expense of training these men itself. The rates were low enough for much of the century to justify such a course. Further, one could exercise discipline much more fiercely and consistently with mercenary than with citizen forces. Such discipline became all the more necessary as troops fighting in open formation began to enjoy an importance, at least in small-scale war, close to hoplite forces.

Despite doubts about the loyalties of mercenary forces, their expertise, *esprit de corps* and discipline compensated for the fact that they were not citizens of the states for which they fought. If pay or the lack of it could sway their loyalty, citizen troops with their lack of expertise and the political divisions of the period did not necessarily enjoy any advantage.

216. Xenophon, *Hipparch* 9.3–4

The poor quality of Spartan cavalry before they started employing mercenary forces was noted by Xenophon as part of his explanation for the defeat of the Spartans at Leuctra (see no. 196) in 371. Xenophon appears have been extremely impressed by the performance of a troop of mercenary cavalry sent by Dionysius I of Syracuse in 369/368 to aid the Spartans against the Thebans. He contrasts unfavorably the performance of the citizen cavalry of Athens and Corinth with the skill and professionalism of Dionysius' mercenary force.

I assert that the full complement of the cavalry force [one thousand] would be reached far more easily and with less burden to the citizens if we hire two hundred mercenary cavalry. My opinion is that the addition of these men would make the whole of the cavalry force more obedient and would foster rivalry among the force's members in the display of courage. I think the Lacedaemonian cavalry began to be an effective force when they added mercenary cavalry. In all the states at present I can see that mercenary cavalry have an excellent reputation. For need produces great enthusiasm.

217. Aristotle, *Nicomachean Ethics* 1116b3–23

The battle at the temple of Hermes occurred in 353 between the Phocians and the Thebans. In general, Aristotle makes all of the points made above that support the superiority of mercenary troops. His one exception is that he rates the staying power of citizen soldiers as superior to mercenaries.

Again experience of particular danger is accounted as courage. It is from this fact that Socrates thought that knowledge is courage. This is displayed by various groups in different ways and especially in warfare by mercenaries. War seems filled with empty alarms that these men particularly have become knowledgeable about. They appear courageous because the rest do not share their knowledge. So they are able to be effective and to avoid suffering especially because of their experience. They know how to use their equipment and know best of all how to use it to attack and to defend themselves. It is the same as when armed men fight with unarmed and athletes vie with inexperienced. For not even in athletic contests do the bravest men make the best fighters, but those who are strongest and are in the best shape. But mercenary soldiers become cowards whenever the danger appears excessive and they are deficient with respect to the enemy in numbers and equipment. They are the first to run while citizen soldiers stand their ground and die, as happened at the battle at the temple of Hermes. Citizen soldiers think flight disgraceful and prefer death to safety achieved at such a cost. But mercenaries from the start take their risks in the belief that their numbers are greater and, discovering they are outnumbered, they flee. They fear death more than shame.

SIEGE WARFARE

The last years of the fifth century had witnessed important changes in the techniques used by the Greeks in siege warfare. Until this point the advantage had generally rested with the besieged. But this situation began to undergo a rapid change that started in Sicily under Dionysius, the tyrant of Syracuse. The wealth and resources available to Dionysius allowed him to set in motion an unalterable process of mechanizing siege warfare and of shifting the balance in favor of the besiegers.

This mechanization took two forms. The first was the adoption, presumably from Carthaginian sources, of devices such as the ram or siege tower. These machines had long been familiar in the Near East (see p. 82). The second advance appears to have been developed by the Greeks themselves and to have been stimulated by the access to greater resources available to tyrants like Dionysius. This was the development of the catapult or mechanical propulsive device that would eventually threaten fortifications by the sheer amount of force it could produce. Our best and most detailed source assigns the invention of the catapult to Dionysius I of Syracuse and dates it to 399 BC at the time when Dionysius was preparing to continue his expansion in Sicily. Dionysius played an active role in encouraging innovation among his craftsmen, and he had taken care to assemble a group of workers large enough to provide a broad range of expertise.

The catapult that was developed in 399 appears to have been what the Greeks called a "belly-shooter," that is in essence a magnified composite bow fixed to a pipe which was grooved to receive a dart and was cocked by the operator resting his stomach in a groove and pressing forward on the bow until it reached maximum extension. Later a winch was added to allow more powerful versions to be cocked. The new invention was tried out at the siege of Motya in western Sicily in 398. Its effect along with other new techniques resulted in the fall of the city in the next year. The use of the weapon spread rapidly. By 370/369 it is attested in an Athenian inventory, and we find it used in battle by Samians defending against the Athenians by the middle of the 360s. The casual mention of the use of catapults in Aeneas Tacticus' work on siegecraft, written in the 350s, implies that they have become commonplace. Despite the gain for the offense long sieges were still a fact of military life, and treason and ruses remained important elements in siege warfare. Later tradition could quote Philip II of Macedon as claiming that any fortification could be taken as long as an ass loaded with gold could reach it. This seems especially true of the fourth century when internal problems made treason an omnipresent possibility. That is a preoccupation of Aeneas' work.

By the end of the century a further technical problem had been mastered. This was the invention of torsion powered artillery whose energy was provided by springs made of hair or sinew and which was able to concentrate far more force than the "belly-shooter" and to allow that force to be released far more evenly and therefore accurately. This made it an eminently suitable device for attacking large fortifications and greatly increased the opportunities for taking a city by storm.

If the evidence for the belly-shooter is exiguous it is even worse in the case of the torsion catapult. All that can be said is that such devices did exist by 307/306, but when and where they were invented is less clear. The most likely place was at the court of the Macedonian king Philip II between the years 345 and 341. This solution is made likely by the fact that Philip was interested not only in military tactics in general but in siegecraft in particular. Our first clear evidence for the use of stone-throwing catapults is provided by Alexander's siege of Halicarnassus in the summer of 334. Since Alexander's reign was at this point barely two years old and had already involved substantial warfare it is unlikely that he had the time or inclination to create conditions for the new technical development of such artillery.

218. Diodorus Siculus, 14.41.2–4

These events are datable to 399 and the preparation by Dionysius I of Syracuse for war against the Carthaginians. One cannot rule out the possibility that the catapult mentioned here was powered by torsion springs, but it is more likely that it was a belly-shooter or giant crossbow. With a bolt for a projectile its range may have been of the order of 250 yards. Later improvements may have raised the range to 300 yards by mid-century.

[Dionysius I] thinking that it was a favorable occasion for war [against the Carthaginians] judged it necessary to first make his preparations. He anticipated that the war would be on a grand scale and of long duration as he would be fighting against one of the most powerful states. So he immediately began to gather craftsmen from his subject cities by order and by enticing them from Italy, Greece and even from the sphere of Carthaginian power by high wages. . . . Indeed, the catapult was invented at this time in Syracuse since the most skilled workmen had been assembled there in one place. The size of the rewards and the number of competitive prizes for the most skilled craftsmen stimulated the workmen.

219. Diodorus Siculus, 14.50.4

Motya in western Sicily was Dionysius' first goal in his attack upon Carthaginian possessions in the island. The siege was significant in several respects. It showed that Dionysius had successfully mastered Carthaginian techniques and further integrated the newly invented catapult with them to produce a new and much more active and effective technique of siege warfare. Catapults were also used for the first time in this action *en masse*. The surprise of the Carthaginians supports the tradition that the belly shooter was a Greek invention.

Himilco's attack on the Greek ships was held off by a multitude of missiles since a crowd of archers and slingers was on board the ships, and on land the Syracusans, by employing sharp-pointed bolts from catapults, destroyed many of the enemy. This last form of missile especially created consternation among the enemy as this was the first time they had seen such a device.

220. Aeneas Tacticus, *On Siegecraft* 32.8

This is the only mention in Aeneas' work of catapults, though it seems fairly clear that the pre-torsion catapults were widespread when he was writing in the 350s. Such a casual approach confirms our other evidence that by mid-century the catapult had become an accepted part of siege warfare. This may be correlated with the growing numbers of outworks included in the fortifications of Greek cities into the Hellenistic era. They were designed as far as possible to prevent catapults and siege devices from moving into a position from which they could be effective against a city's walls.

Further, against the large siege devices on which many men are brought up and from which missiles are shot and on which there are catapults, slings and incendiary arrows effective against the thatched roofs of houses, it is necessary for the defenders in the city to excavate a ditch in secret along the line of the machine's approach to cause the wheels of the device to sink into it and fall into the pits. In addition, inside the wall at the point at which the approach is made there should be constructed a strong point from baskets filled with sand and from nearby stones that will overtop the device and make the enemy's missiles useless.

221. Athenaeus Mechanicus, 10.1

Athenaeus was a technical writer of the late first century writing in Rome, probably under the patronage of Octavia, the sister of Augustus. His work which dealt with siege machines appears to be heavily indebted to an early first-century source. This passage, which appears to have a sound foundation in fact, indicates a parallelism between Dionysius and Philip that helps support the idea that both played a role in the invention of different forms of catapults. It also is a witness to Philip's interest in the technical side of war.

The making of siege devices progressed greatly in the reign of Dionysius, the tyrant of Syracuse, and during the reign of Philip, the son of Amyntas, when he was besieging Byzantium. At that time Polyidus, the Thessalian, and his pupils, Diades and Charias, took part in Alexander's campaign.

222. Inventory from the Erechtheum for 307/306, IG II² no. 1487B, ll. 84–99

This is the earliest indisputable evidence for the existence of the torsion catapult. The fact that it is now an ordinary item in the inventory of Athenian weapons presupposes some time for diffusion and further supports a date during Philip's reign for its origin. The cubit mentioned here appears to be the normal one of one and two thirds feet.

A stone-throwing and arrow-shooting catapult of four cubits complete, the work of Bromius. Another catapult three cubits, for stone-throwing, in serviceable condition. Another catapult, three cubits, torsion with apertures also in serviceable condition. Another catapult, three spans, torsion in fit condition.

223. Arrian, *Anabasis of Alexander* 1.22.2

This siege in the summer of 334 is the first definite evidence for the use of the stone-throwing catapult that was to become a standard part of siege equipment in the Hellenistic period. The force of the catapults implies that they are torsion powered and again supports a date for the invention of the torsion catapult under Alexander's father, Philip.

A few days later Alexander again brought his siege engines to the inner brick wall and himself took charge of operations. There then took place a full-scale sally from the city at the place where the wall had been breached and Alexander himself was stationed. . . . The troops around Alexander attacked the enemy forcefully and by using siege machines placed on towers that hurled large stones and showering them with darts easily repelled them, and the Halicarnassans fled back into the city.

4

THE RISE OF MACEDONIA
Philip and Alexander

For most of its existence Macedonia played only a peripheral role in the politics and warfare of the Greek city-states that have formed the focus of our attention. In its marginal status it bore some resemblance to the less urbanized areas of Greece such as Achaea and Aetolia. It resembled them as well in the fact that it preserved earlier and less sophisticated political structures and like them it suffered from internal disunity. Both the land and its population had the potential under favorable conditions of developing a state whose power far exceeded other Greek powers.

Geographically Macedonia consisted of two separate areas, Lower and Upper Macedonia. The core of Lower Macedonia as well as the later center of the kingdom was a large and fertile coastal plain watered by two major rivers, the Axius and the Haliacmon, that flow into the Thermaic Gulf. It was bounded on the east by the Strymon River. It was a strategically important center of routes leading northwards out of Greece towards the Danube, and also the nexus of another series of routes to the northwest and northeast. One of its continuing problems in antiquity was the constant pressure it faced from the tribal peoples to the north and the Greek city-states to the south. It was often cast in the role of an unwilling buffer for the Greeks on its southern borders against invaders from central and eastern Europe.

Separated from Lower Macedonia by a ring of hills is the upland area of Upper Macedonia. It consists of plains and valleys that are protected by major mountain ranges on all but their eastern side. Yet despite its relative geographical isolation it was frequently attacked by its neighbors.

The flat coastal plain of Lower Macedonia also differed in climate and apparently in economy from the upland areas. It enjoyed a Mediterranean climate with extensive tracts of fertile land suitable for the growing of cereal crops and providing good pasturage for horse and sheep raising. The upland areas with their continental climate also possessed some good land for cereal crops, but seem to have been particularly well adapted to sheep herding and horse rearing.

Agriculturally Macedonia as a whole possessed far greater potential than any contemporary Greek state and its capacity to be a source of mounted troops was unrivaled by any area except for Thessaly. In addition, Macedonia possessed extensive tracts of forest that provided excellent timber for shipbuilding, a commodity in short supply in most of Greece. Within and near its eastern border were important gold and silver mines that formed a significant source of royal revenue.

By Greek standards it was an exceptionally favored area. This allowed it to support a relatively dense population. Though any estimate of ancient populations is subject to a great deal of qualification, the figures given for Macedonian armies suggest a total population of about 150,000 adult males of whom about 80,000 would be available in theory for military service. Total Macedonian resources were on a scale that would dwarf any of the southern Greek states if it could be unified and provided with a stable political structure.

Contrary to allegations by fourth-century opponents of the expanding Macedonian monarchy, its nomenclature and language were Greek but, as might be expected, it had dialectical peculiarities. The absence of urban centers that set it off sharply from the area of Greece dominated by city-states is shared with other northern and western Greek peoples. The creation of the Macedonian state was the result of expansion of the controlling dynasty of the coastal plain, the Aegeadae, from their capital on the lower Haliacmon at Aegae which most scholars now identify with modern Vergina. This movement, perhaps beginning in the mid-seventh century, resulted in their control of most of the lowland plain, and by the beginning of the fifth century they asserted overlordship of the small cantons of Upper Macedonia as well. These territories had local dynasties and aristocracies that had claims of their own, and it appears that the dynasty of Lower Macedonia had only a very nebulous hold on the area.

Even within Lower Macedonia it is unclear as to how much authority individual kings could exert. In theory they had absolute power in almost all areas, but it appears that their authority was limited by their own nobility. In addition, there were tribal and geographic limitations. Though great importers of Greek culture, Macedonian kings before the mid-fourth century did little to create the urban substructure in which such culture flourished.

Their power was limited as well by constant external threats that often ended in bloody defeats or exhausting victories, and internal struggles that resulted from the kingdom's lack of formal political structures and in part were exacerbated by external powers. In the fifth and fourth centuries the Athenians and other Greek states intervened in internal dynastic struggles and weakened the stability of Macedonia. It is not accidental that it was in the last half of the fourth century when the major Greek powers were weak and beset by difficulties that an extraordinary king, Philip II, was able to unify the whole of the region and produce a military power that no Greek state could rival.

THE EARLY MACEDONIAN ARMY

Little is known of the Macedonian army before the reign of Philip II. Certainly, the area from which the earlier Macedonian kings drew their recruits was limited only to lowland Macedonia. The only effective arm appears to have been cavalry. These horsemen, generally acknowledged as the best in Greece, were drawn from the local nobility. The numbers involved must have been small, of the order of several hundred.

These nobles' estates must have been located in various regions of Macedonia. But it must be assumed that they were recruited for personal and political reasons since they enjoyed a close personal relationship to the king physically and politically. It was their personal qualities that counted. They served the king not only in war and ceremony, but also as his informal body of advisors and presumably as his executive agents. The king bound them to himself by the distribution of wealth, land and power. We can see these "Companions" acting out one of their functions on many occasions, that is as a council during Alexander's reign. The king's power was most evident in time of war when he held undisputed command over the Macedonian army. But he could and did occasionally delegate it to others. It is clear that down to the reign of Philip II the Macedonian infantry levies were generally ineffective on the battlefield. It is possible that a levy consisted of the smaller property owners and dependants of the nobles, perhaps actually recruited by them, and who were given no specific military training. Quotas were probably fixed on a regional basis. We can see regional units in operation under Philip. They did not rely on mass formations in battle, but appear to have fought more or less independently of each other. The only really effective infantry in this period appears to have been drawn from southern Greeks settled within Macedonia's borders who fought as hoplites. They came from cities along the coast such as Pydna and Strepsa on the Thermaic Gulf.

224. Thucydides, 2.100.4–5

Perdiccas II's reign (c. 452–413) was weakened by internal problems till the late 430s, but he then managed to consolidate his power. A major problem for Perdiccas was an expansionist Thracian dynasty, the Odrysian to the east. Support and encouragement for it came from the Athenians. These disputes finally erupted into war in 429 when Sitalkes the Odrysian king invaded.

Sitalkes had entered Macedonia from the north after crossing the Strymon River and captured most of the major towns in the northern part of Lower Macedonia. He proceeded down the right bank of the river, passing west of Pella and Cyrrhus; he then turned eastward and ravaged the areas named by Thucydides. It is in this context that the Thucydidean passage is to be placed. A lack of supplies and some astute diplomacy by Perdiccas led to a Thracian withdrawal. The importance of the passage is in its depiction of an armed force whose only effective arm is its cavalry.

Then the Thracians advanced towards the remainder of Macedonia that lay to the left of Pella and Cyrrhus; they did not advance further into Bottiaea and Pieria, but laid waste Mygdonia, Grestonia and Anthemous. The Macedonians did not even consider resisting them with infantry, but summoned cavalry from their upland allies. They attacked the Thracian army, though the Macedonians were few, wherever they could. Their enemy gave way where they made their attack since they were excellent horsemen and armed with breastplates. But hemmed in by the vastly superior numbers, they were in danger and so finally desisted from their attacks, considering that their numbers were insufficient to resist the invaders.

225. Thucydides, 2.100.1–2

Archelaus (413–399 BC), Perdiccas II's son, was able to pursue a policy of accommodation with an Athens severely weakened by war. He also tried to remedy some of the defects of the military system in Lower Macedonia. He consolidated and increased his territory, especially in the north and northeast. The road system that Thucydides mentions is best explained as a response to military needs. This goes along with the provisions for improving horses and weapons. It is uncertain if there is a reference to some change in the Macedonian infantry levy in this passage. Some have seen Archelaus as the founder of the Macedonian phalanx, though this is unlikely. It may be that it is a matter of some sort of provision of arms at state expense. But whatever improvements Archelaus made in the military situation were lost in the chaos of the next half century. The passage deals with the same Thracian invasion as no. 224 does.

So the Macedonians were incapable of resistance to the Thracians because of the size of the invading army and thus withdrew to the natural strong points or fortifications they possessed. These were not many, but a little later when Archelaus, the son of Perdiccas, became king he constructed the present strong points; he also constructed straight roads and he managed his military resources – horses, arms and everything else – in a manner that surpassed any of his eight predecessors.

PHILIP II AND THE DEVELOPMENT OF THE MACEDONIAN ARMY

The kingdom that Philip succeeded to in 359 was tottering on the verge of ruin, threatened by foreign invasion and internal division. On his death he left his son Alexander the wealthiest and most powerful of the Balkan states and a superb army. There is no doubt that much of the credit belongs to the man himself. He was able to capitalize on Macedonia's strength and through force, adroit diplomacy and bribery realize the full potential of his kingdom. His one great advantage was the failure of his enemies to ally themselves at a time when all of the major Greek states including Athens were in a terribly weakened state.

The problem that faced Philip, as it had many of his predecessors, was to create the stability and security necessary for these advantages to be put to the use. Philip saw that the key to it was the army. He also recognized that for that army to be effective it had to develop in new directions. In particular, no doubt influenced by his experience in Thebes when he was a hostage there in the early 360s, he saw the importance of developing suitable heavy infantry to supplement the magnificent cavalry. Such an army reform would also serve a further function:

to act as a centralizing force against local particularism within his kingdom. The peasants, now subordinate to the king, would have their ties to the local nobility weakened.

The exact stages by which Philip created this army are unclear. He seems to have been able to raise an army of ten thousand infantry within a year of his succession. So substantial a number after the severe Macedonian defeat of 359 seems to indicate that earlier Macedonian kings had not fully utilized the manpower available to them. He not only raised a large-scale heavy infantry force, but also showed his ability to organize and innovate in military affairs. A major new offensive infantry weapon – the sarissa – appears to have been his invention, or at least owes its adoption to him. He saw its value and potential both in multiplying the offensive force of his phalanx and in its use as a defensive weapon as well. This enabled him to lighten his troops' defensive equipment and so increase their mobility, and further lower costs and so create the opportunity to raise more troops.

This army allowed Philip to create a ring of conquered states in the north that guaranteed his kingdom's security. It also provided him with immense wealth and access to subject allies to further enhance his military effectiveness. This wealth allowed him to husband his resources and to use mercenaries for certain types of service. It also made it possible for him develop expensive weapons systems, especially siege artillery.

His genius for organization and tactical innovation is evidenced in his adoption of the wedge formation for cavalry and the command structure he developed for his heavy infantry. What in the end resulted was the culmination of a trend that had shown itself increasingly in Greek warfare in the course of the fourth century: a growing complexity in the composition of military forces now made up of contingents fighting with diverse types of equipment and carrying out specialized tasks. Before Philip no Greek state had the capability of doing this on any large scale. Philip possessed the means to develop a force of this kind which could operate in set-piece battles with each other and in conjunction with the specialist troops that were made available by his wealth. It was a superb instrument that was ready at his death to pass on to his son whose conquests owe much to the mechanisms that Philip had created.

226. Theopompus *FGrH* 115, F27
Theopompus was a mid-fourth century historian who wrote a history of Philip's reign, the *Philippica*, that was sharply critical of him.

Theopompus in the beginning of his work on Philip says that he was impelled towards undertaking his work because Europe had never produced a man at all like Philip.

227. Arrian, *Anabasis of Alexander* 7.9.2–4
The following is a speech of Alexander made in 324 in an attempt to justify his conduct and quiet his native Macedonian troops who had begun to suspect that he was growing increasingly alienated from them.

I will start my speech reasonably enough with my father Philip. Philip inherited you when you were wanderers and penniless, the majority of you dressed in skins, pasturing your few animals up in the mountains and ineffectively defending them from the Illyrians, Triballians and those Thracian tribes that border our land. He gave you cloaks to wear instead of those skins and brought you down from the hills into the plain. He made you into warriors who were a match for the barbarians who border our country so that you trusted for your safety to your native courage and not the roughness of land. He established cities for you to live in and provided you with good laws and customs. He made you masters instead of the subjects and slaves of those very barbarians who plundered and carried off you and your possessions.

228. Plutarch, *Pelopidas* 26.4–8

Philip had served as a hostage for his older brother Alexander II among the Illyrians soon after that brother's accession in 370. Alexander soon embroiled himself in Thessalian politics and was at the same time unable to face a rival for the throne, Ptolemy son of Alorus. Strong Theban military action under Pelopidas settled the situation. Alexander was reconciled to Ptolemy, who recognized him as king. In addition, Alexander concluded an alliance with Thebes, apparently dictated by Pelopidas, one of whose conditions was the surrender of Philip again as a hostage, this time into Theban hands. The exile apparently lasted for three years, with Philip returning home in 365.

In many ways Philip was unusually fortunate in the time and place of his exile. Pammenes was a close associate of Epaminondas who was then in the process of reorienting hoplite tactics. He was also a soldier in his own right who exercised independent command under Epaminondas and had led Boeotian forces after the latter's death in 362. It is clear that the experience was to have a profound effect on Philip's development as a commander after he came to the throne.

Pelopidas departed for Macedonia where Ptolemy was at war with the king of the Macedonians, Alexander. Both sides had summoned him as a mediator and arbiter, to serve as an ally and a helper to the rightly aggrieved party. He arrived and settled the matters in dispute and brought back the exiles. He took as hostages the king's brother, Philip, and thirty other youths from the best families and brought them to Thebes. In doing this he showed the Greeks how far the authority of Thebes extended by the report of its power and the faith in its fairness. This Philip was the one who fought the Greeks over their freedom. At that time he was a boy and while in Thebes he stayed at the house of Pammenes. Some think that it was as a result of this that he became an imitator of Epaminondas in matters pertaining to war and generalship, but such activities were only a small part of the man's excellence.

229. Diodorus Siculus, 16.3.1–3

At Philip's accession in 359 Macedonia was in a disastrous state. Four thousand soldiers had just been slain and Philip's predecessor, his older brother Perdiccas III, had been defeated and killed. The large losses in this battle against the Illyrians left Macedonia exposed. This situation was the culmination of the continuous weakness of the Macedonian royal house in the first quarter of the fourth century. After the defeat the army had sustained it was in no condition to defend Macedonia's borders. By an astute combination of diplomacy and bribery Philip created a situation in which he could face existing threats sequentially, ending with the most serious: the Illyrians. From the first he devoted much of his attention to the army, both because of his immediate military needs and because it could serve as a unifying force to counteract separatist tendencies. Diodorus states that Philip was the originator of the Macedonian infantry phalanx. This is certainly not true, but is reasonable to see that statement as a reflection of the fact that it was Philip who first gave Macedonia an effective heavy infantry. How soon innovations like the sarissa and the Macedonian shield were introduced is less clear. All of this could not have been done within his first year on the throne, and there must be considerable telescoping of events in the narrative. It is more likely that the most immediate effect of Philip's efforts led to improvement in discipline and training and to the capability of utilizing existing assets to the full. He faced the Illyrians in his first year with ten thousand infantry and five hundred cavalry and beat them.

The Macedonians were at their wit's end on account of their disastrous defeat in battle and the dangers looming over them. But Philip, despite the extent of the dangers and their fears, was not overwhelmed by their magnitude; he held continual assemblies and by the brilliance of his oratory he encouraged them and rekindled their bravery. He improved their military organization and provided them with the necessary weaponry. He held continuous competitive maneuvers and contests. He also devised the dense formation for heavy infantry and its equipment by following the model of the close formation of the heroes who fought at Troy and so was the first to create the Macedonian phalanx.

230. Polyaenus, *Stratagems* 4.2.10

Training was a key element, as this selection and the previous one make clear. Three hundred stadia is the equivalent of a march of about thirty-five miles. This is an unusually demanding regimen. Mobility, as is clear from Philip's approach to war, was more important than individual protection.

Philip used to train the Macedonians before they were at war. He frequently had them march three hundred stadia under arms with their helmets, shields, greaves, pikes and also their provisions and the equipment necessary for their daily needs.

231. Frontinus, *Stratagems* 4.1.6

This passage again emphasizes the premium placed on mobility and reducing non-essential personnel that is characteristic of Philip's approach to war. It may in part reflect the concern that any Macedonian monarch must have had about meeting nearly simultaneous threats on what were relatively widely spaced frontiers.

When Philip first organized his army, he forbade the use of wagons to all. He allowed cavalrymen one servant apiece and the infantry one for every ten men. It was the servants' task to carry a flour mill and tent ropes. He ordered the troops, when going out on summer campaigns, to carry thirty days of flour rations themselves.

The equipment of the Macedonian phalanx under Philip

The crucial change in equipment was the adoption of the sarissa or pike which was between sixteen and eighteen feet long and became the main offensive weapon of the phalanx. Its length and weight required it to be held with two hands and thus rendered the conventional hoplite shield obsolete. It was replaced by a much smaller shield that could be suspended from the shoulder and swung round to protect the left side of the soldier's chest. The corselet was sacrificed as well. This is in part the result of general developments in hoplite equipment, but it may reflect two other factors: that of technological change and economic limitations. A denser formation was now possible because of the reduction in the diameter of the shield. In addition the phalanx itself offered more protection than the conventional hoplite formation by forming a wall of sarissas. The equipment was relatively cheap and easily provided so that far larger numbers of soldiers could be raised than if they paid for their own equipment as Greek hoplites did. These changes greatly increased the offensive power of the heavy infantry by significantly increasing the number of pikeheads projecting from the front of the phalanx and extending the killing range of the phalanx.

The sarissa

This characteristic weapon of the Macedonian infantry was composed of a long shaft of cornel wood, a hard wood used for such weapons by the Macedonians, and an iron head to which the shaft was attached by a socket. Its other end was attached to an iron butt-spike. The shaft was of two-piece construction fitted together by an iron coupling sleeve. It was no doubt dismantled for travel. As finds from the graves at Vergina indicate, the sarissa varied greatly in length from sixteen to eighteen feet in the fourth century. Later it tended to grow in length so that by the second century we hear of sarissas of up to twenty-four feet in length.

232. Theophrastus, *History of Plants* 3.12.2

Theophrastus is describing the nature of the wood and the length of the cornelian cherry tree. Twelve cubits should equal approximately eighteen feet. He was in Macedonia with his teacher Aristotle and so had first-hand knowledge of the weapon.

The height of the male tree is approximately twelve cubits, the length of the longest sarissa.

233. Polybius, *Histories* 18.29.1–30.4

The phalanx of Philip V's time (beginning of the second century) seems to be arrayed in a depth of eight. By the time of Polybius' description (the last half of the second century) the normal depth had grown to sixteen and the formation had lost some of its flexibility.

169

It is easy to understand that, for many reasons, when the phalanx has its characteristic qualities and force nothing is able to face it nor withstand its charge. For each soldier in it with his weapons occupies a space of three feet when it is compacted and the sarissa is according to its original design sixteen cubits in length, though adapted to current practice it is fourteen cubits. From this length one must subtract the distance between the hands as they grasp it and the counter-weight behind the projecting portion. Thus each sarissa point projects ten cubits in front of body of each soldier whenever he charges and comes to grips with the enemy. The result of this is that the sarissas of the men in the second, third and fourth rank extend further beyond the troops of the front line, and even the sarissas of the fifth line extend two cubits beyond the front when the phalanx is arranged in its normal manner and with its customary closeness in respect to depth and width. . . . Those ranks beyond the fifth cannot use their sarissas to take part in the encounter, but hold their sarissas slanting in the air above the shoulders of the men in front and so protect the whole formation by keeping off missiles by means of the thick cover formed by their sarissas. Also by pressing with the weight of their bodies on those in front during the charge, they create a stronger impetus and it is impossible for the foremost ranks of the phalanx to face about.

The shield

The Macedonian shield appears to have been a small bronze shield about two feet in diameter and to have been suspended from the user's neck over his left shoulder by a thong. It may also have had a small handle through which the left arm passed and fixed it in place when using the sarissa.

234. Asclepiodotus, *Tactics* 5.1
A palm is about three inches.

The best shield for the phalanx is the Macedonian one; it is bronze and eight palms in diameter and it is not excessively convex.

235. Plutarch, *Aemilius Paulus* 19.2
Plutarch is recounting the battle of Pydna that took place on 22 June 168 and that resulted in a defeat for the Macedonian phalanx which essentially ended the Third Macedonian War. Plutarch remarks about the Roman commander's fear and astonishment at the power of the phalanx's advance. L. Aemilius Paulus was consul for the second time in this year and he brought to a brilliant conclusion the rather lackluster performance of the Romans in the Third Macedonian War during the previous three years.

As the attack began, Aemilius was present and saw . . . that the rest of the Macedonians were pulling around their shields which were suspended from their shoulders and with their sarissas were, as ordered, resisting his shield-bearing troops.

Other equipment

236. The Amphipolis Code, Moretti no. 114

For the date and circumstances see no. 184. The code's list of equipment agrees with that found in Polyaenus' anecdote (no. 230 above). The corselet seems to have served a double purpose: it denoted rank and, if file leaders were included as officers, must have offered additional protection to the first rank of the phalanx.

B1 Those who do not have their required equipment shall be fined according to the following written schedule: two obols for a protective belt for the lower stomach, two obols for a helmet, three obols for a sarissa, the same for a sword, two obols for greaves and a drachma for a shield. In the case of officers the fines are doubled and in addition the absence of a corselet is fined at the rate of two drachmas and a half-corselet at the rate of one drachma.

Organization

237. Arrian, *Anabasis of Alexander* 3.11.9

These are the dispositions of Alexander the Great's phalanx before the battle of Gaugamela in the fall of 331, but it is not unreasonable to infer the nature of Philip's army from that of his son in most respects. The battalions in Alexander's army appear to have had a paper strength of 1500 men. They seem to have been levied by geographical areas, in all perhaps anywhere between twelve and fourteen areas of Upper and Lower Macedonia. It is generally agreed that these commanders were often from the region in which the *taxis* or battalion was raised. In Alexander's army they appear have been functionally known by their commander's name.

Then came the successive battalions of the phalanx; the first of them was that of Coenus, the son of Polemocrates. Next in line was the battalion of Perdiccas, son of Orontes, then that of Meleager, son of Neoptolemus, next the battalion of Polyperchon, son of Simmias, and then that of Amyntas, the son of Philip. But Simmias was in command of this unit since Amyntas had be dispatched to levy troops in Macedonia.

238. Arrian, *Anabasis of Alexander* 7.23.3

The smallest unit known in the Macedonian army was the decad of sixteen men. Early on in Philip's reign it may have consisted of ten men, as its name implies, and then been enlarged to a multiple of eight for the purpose of more easily forming the normal depth of the line which was based on multiples of eight men. Also attested by Alexander's time and probably going back to Philip is the *lochos*, a unit of 250 men. Arrian is referring to events after Alexander's return to Babylon in 323 when he attempted to expand his army with Oriental troops. The selection is evidence for the decad as a unit, and also for pay differentials: presumably the differentials are from the time of Philip though the rates are those of Alexander's reign. The rates of the rankers compare favorably with

Athenian hoplites in the fifth century. A stater is equal to four drachmas. This goes some way to show that the added incentives of promotion and pay were used. This system must be in part the effect of differentials in mercenary pay in the fourth century and hardly fits the notions of a conventional citizen army.

Alexander enrolled the Persians in the Macedonian formations. There was a Macedonian as commander of each decad and next to him a Macedonian on double pay, then a ten-stater man whose name came from his rate of pay which was less than double pay but higher than the amount paid to private soldiers. Behind these men he added twelve Persians and the rear of the decad was brought up by a ten-stater man.

The formation of the Foot Companions

In its original sense the king's Companions formed the nucleus of his court and entourage (see above, p. 164). They existed in theory only at the king's behest, but it seems likely that, at least in their developed form, the Companions were made up in part from a group of aristocratic landowning families. The king had the power to add to their number and presumably to diminish it as well. Their functions corresponded to the needs of the king: they served as advisors, functionaries and as an élite force, originally of cavalry, that fought with the king and served as his commanders and officers.

In the later Macedonian army the term assumed a different meaning, denoting an élite unit within the Macedonian army, and by Alexander the Great's reign the whole of the Macedonian phalanx.

239. Demosthenes, *Olynthiacs* 2.17
This speech, delivered in 349, is part of a tendentious attempt by Demosthenes to foster support for the Chalcidic League in its struggle with Macedon and Philip.

The attitude of the majority of Macedonians to Philip can be easily gauged from the following: the mercenaries and foot guards in his immediate entourage enjoy a great reputation as soldiers and are well trained in military matters; but I have heard from a man who lived in Macedonia and is honest that they are no better than the other troops.

240. Theopompus, *FGrH* 115, F348
For Theopompus see no. 226.

Theopompus says that men, chosen as tallest and strongest, served as a bodyguard to the king and were called the Foot Companions.

241. Anaximenes, *FGrH* 72, F4
Anaximenes was an approximate contemporary of Theopompus and his historical works bear the same titles as the latter's. He was also a rhetorician and there is a tradition, though not a terribly trustworthy one, that he was a teacher of Alexander. His work on Philip has been conjectured to date from about 330.

Anaximenes in the first book of his *Philippica*, speaking about Alexander, says the following: "Then having trained the aristocracy as cavalry he gave them the title of Companions. He assigned the rest, that is the majority who were infantry, to companies, decads and other units and gave them the name of Foot Companions. The reason for this was that by providing a share in the royal companionship they would remain exceptionally loyal.

The cavalry

Under Philip and Alexander the single most important unit remained the Macedonian cavalry. At the beginning of Philip's reign it consisted of those noble retainers who were the king's Companions. Though it served as a cavalry unit it was also a collection of nobles and notables in the king's service. Though expanded it remained the unit with the highest prestige and rewards. By Philip's period, if not sooner, Macedonia utilized native cavalry of various types, both light and heavy.

The most important unit among the cavalry remained the heavy cavalry of the Companions, whose equipment was essentially that of the Greek heavy cavalry trooper and consisted of corselet, open-faced helmets, boots and perhaps additional protection in the form of an leather apron for the thighs. There is some evidence for the use of a shield but it is certainly the most questionable piece of equipment. Xenophon had recommended against it. The main offensive weapon was a strong and relatively long cornel wood spear.

The use of other cavalry units from various Balkan peoples and the Macedonians themselves increased in the course of Philip's reign. The area from which he drew was noticeably enlarged by the acquisition of Upper Macedonia, and later his overlordship of Thessaly greatly assisted the maintenance of the cavalry as the decisive arm in Alexander's army which, given the lack of information on Philip's, has to be used as a parallel. The same must also be true of the organization of the Companion cavalry.

242. Theopompus, *FGrH* 115, F224–225

The Companion cavalry that Theopompus is describing are probably those of the early 340s. The number of troops fits with the number of Companion cavalry that we would expect to find at this date. Theopompus is clearly exaggerating the wealth of the Companions in order to blacken Philip's reputation. This passage confirms that non-Macedonians could be admitted to the group. Often the grants of land and other revenues mentioned were in newly acquired areas.

When Philip had gained control of a great deal of money, he did not spend it quickly but threw it out and cast it away for he was the worst possible manager of his own wealth, and also none of his companions knew how to live correctly or how to manage a household. . . . His companions had come together from many places, some from Macedonia, others from Thessaly, still others from the rest of Greece. They were not selected on account of their excellence. But if a Greek or barbarian had a lecherous, repulsive or rough character he gathered with others of a similar character and was given the title of a Companion of Philip. . . . I think that the number of Companions was no more than eight hundred at that time, yet they enjoyed the revenues of not less than ten thousand Greek owners of the best and most productive land.

243. Diodorus Siculus, 16.85.5

This is a report of the forces available to Philip before the battle of Chaeronea in August 338. The total probably includes some allies, but the numbers of both infantry and cavalry remain close to normal figures for Alexander's forces and probably represent the approximate maximum cavalry strength available by the end of Philip's reign. Some must have been light horse. If the proportions in Alexander's army are used we get 2400 Companion cavalry and 600 light. In 334 Alexander had a total of 3300 combined.

After this, though Philip failed in gaining an alliance with the Boeotians he was no less determined to seek a decision against both allies. After waiting for his laggard allies he moved forward to Boeotia with more than thirty thousand infantry and more than three thousand horse.

244. Arrian, *Anabasis of Alexander* 3.11.8

This is an account of the disposition of forces for the battle of Gaugamela in 331. Though the major sources on it differ it remains the best known of Alexander's major battles. It shows the Companion cavalry at its normal location to the right of the battle line. The squadrons or *ilai* that Alexander took with him to Asia numbered eight. One of these is the so-called Royal Squadron or Agema of three hundred. The other squadrons appear to be approximately two hundred strong. Counting the cavalry left behind in Europe there were about fourteen or fifteen such squadrons in total. They were named either after their commander or the territory in which they were raised. We hear of at least four territories, all in land recently acquired. After Philotas' execution in 328 the Companion cavalry ceased to have a unified command and was divided between two commanders.

Alexander's army was arrayed in the following way. The right wing consisted of the Companion cavalry with the royal squadron posted at the front. It was commanded by Cleitus the son of Dropides. Then came the squadrons of Glaucias, Aristo, Sopolis the son of Hermodorus and Heracleides the son of Antiochus. They were followed in turn by the units of Demetrius the son of Althaemenes, Meleager, and the last squadron was that of Hegelochus son of Hippostratus. The whole of the Companion cavalry was led by Philotas the son of Parmenio.

Armament of the Companion cavalry

245. Arrian, *Anabasis of Alexander* 1.15.4–8

This event took place at the battle of the Granicus in spring 334. It shows not only the primary armament of thrusting spear but also the secondary armament of a sword which the trooper carried. Spithridates was the Persian governor of

Lydia and Ionia in 334. Cleitus commanded the Royal Squadron at Gaugamela and probably did so at the Granicus. Shields may have been carried but the evidence is against it.

Though it was a cavalry battle it resembled an infantry engagement more. Horses and men were entangled with each other in the struggle, the Macedonians trying to thrust the Persians once and for all from the river bank and down into the plain, while the Persians attempted to stop their crossing and to thrust the Macedonians back again into the river. In this encounter Alexander's force was prevailing not only because of their strength and experience, but also because they fought with cornel wood lances against javelins. . . . Spithridates had now raised his saber against Alexander from behind, but Cleitus son of Dropides anticipated him and struck him in the shoulder with his sword and cut it off.

Thessalian cavalry

The Thessalian cavalry was normally the second most important heavy cavalry unit in the Macedonian army. Their numbers, at least on Alexander's Persian expedition, were equal to those of the Companion cavalry. They formed along with the Agrianians the non-Macedonian units most constantly employed. Thessaly had essentially been annexed to Macedonia by Philip who had from the start of his reign involved himself in its affairs. He was elected *tagos*, the head of the Thessalian League, and safeguarded his position through the use of garrisons and by administrative reorganization. This cavalry furnished the crucial offensive element on the left side of the battle line in the major battles that Alexander fought, as the Companion cavalry did the right.

246. Diodorus Siculus, 17.17.4

The overall command of the Thessalian cavalry was always vested in a Macedonian. Its organization paralleled the Companions. It was divided into squadrons or *ilai* on a regional basis. The squadron from Pharsalus seems to have served with the commander in a role analogous to the Royal Squadron in the Companion cavalry. Their equipment was presumably the standard outfit of Greek heavy cavalry.

There were 1800 Macedonian cavalry under the command of Philotas the son of Parmenion and 1800 Thessalian cavalry led by Callas the son of Harpalus.

Tactical formations

This is another area in which Philip displayed his ingenuity. One of his striking chracteristics as a commander was his receptiveness to new or unusual technology. Parallel to this was his ability to develop new and effective tactics. The units and arrangements he instituted inside the phalanx may have been totally new. For the cavalry his innovation was the development of a new tactical formation, the wedge, that allowed him to successfully utilize the shock effect of his Macedonian cavalry. Though like all ancient cavalry it operated without stirrups or effective saddles and so could not break infantry in formation, it was sufficiently disciplined and trained to break enemy cavalry and then take its infantry in the flank.

247. Arrian, *Tactics* 16.6–7

We hear that the Scythians especially use the wedge-shaped formation, as do the Thracians, having learned of it from the Scythians. Philip of Macedon and the Macedonians practiced its use. This formation seems especially useful in that the leaders are arranged in a circle and the front of the wedge converges to a point. This makes it easy to cut through any enemy formation. It also allows the formation to wheel towards or away from an opponent quickly.

Light-armed troops

Philip's light-armed troops, foot and horse, formed the final element in a well-balanced combination of arms and marked a decided advance over earlier Greek practice (see p. 141 above). Demosthenes mentions their importance along with mercenaries and cavalry as key factors in Philip's expansionist activities. Our evidence is more impressionistic than accurate, but does show that light-armed troops played an important role in the Macedonian army. The dearth of sources, however, prevents us from seeing them in action. Under Alexander their presence and activities are often mentioned and so a clearer picture of the composition and employment of these forces emerges. There is reason to assume that Alexander's practice essentially recapitulated Philip's use of such troops.

In terms of origin it is easiest to divide light-armed troops of various arms into Macedonian soldiers and allied or mercenary troops. Troops who were ethnic Macedonians appear in the reign of Alexander as slingers, archers and javelin men who are similar to Thracian peltasts. It is the archers who figure most prominently and this may be the result of their ability to support all types of attacks by either cavalry or infantry. The total number of such troops appears to have been small. This may be explained by the absence among the Macedonians of the necessary skills. Even with troops using less specialized equipment such as javelin men, the Macedonians expanded into areas where it was easier to levy native troops than to try to train their own. Finally, the decline in the level of wealth necessary to obtain hoplite status had the effect of making native light-armed troops into heavy infantry. It appears to have been the Balkan states that were in some way subject to Macedonian authority that supplied the majority of light troops. The light-armed foot were drawn from Thracians, Illyrians and Triballians. The most important contingent was made up of Agrianians from the upper Strymon valley who formed under Alexander an élite corps of javelin men commanded by their king Langarus and were used as specialist and shock troops. They may have numbered five hundred under Philip and at the beginning of the Asian campaign.

The final source of light troops, especially for archers and slingers, were the mercenary Cretans and Rhodians who had supplied such specialist soldiers since the beginning of the fourth century. In contrast to earlier Greek practice these troops played a significant role in the major battles.

248. Arrian, *Anabasis of Alexander* 1.2.4–5

In the spring 335, in the wake of problems in Greece, Alexander needed to assert his authority on the northern borders of his kingdom. One of the people he moved against were the Triballians, located just south of the Danube. This victory shows the skillful combined use of heavy and light-armed troops which recalls earlier Athenian practice and probably reflects the tactics of Philip as well. The archers and slingers appear to have been Macedonians, as Arrian fails to label them.

When Alexander learned of their move, he turned back to attack the Triballians and came upon them while they were encamping. Caught in this situation they formed their line by the grove along the river. But Alexander formed his phalanx in deep formation and led it against them. He ordered the archers and slingers to run out and use their missiles against the barbarians to try and incite them to come out of the trees and into the open.

When the Triballians were within missile range and were being hit by their opponents they ran out against the archers to come to close quarters with them since they were unarmed as archers usually are. When Alexander had drawn them out of the wood he ordered Philotas to take the Companion cavalry of Upper Macedonia and charge their right wing where they had come farthest forward in their rush forward.

Allies

As mentioned above the Agrianian javelin men formed an élite contingent under their king Langarus in Alexander's army, and they clearly played an important role in Philip's time. Their tasks encompassed special duties as well as taking part in set-piece battles. They were often used for assignments requiring great speed of movement. In Alexander's Balkan camapign of 335 a flying column of the Agrianians was used in conjunction with other infantry and horsemen to safeguard the baggage train from attack by Glaucias the king of the Taulantians.

249. Appian, *Illyrian Wars* 14

The [Paeonians] have been famous since the time of the Macedonians on account of the Agrianians who rendered great services to Philip and Alexander and are Paeonians of Lower Paeonia, neighbors of the Illyrians.

250. Arrian, *Anabasis of Alexander* 3.12.2

These dispositions are for Gaugamela in the autumn of 331.

On the right wing next to the Royal Squadron were placed half of the Agrianians under Attalus and with them the Macedonian archers led by Brison. . . . On the left the Thracians were deployed at an angle commanded by Sitalkes, and then the allied horse under Coeranus. After them came the Odrysian horse under the command of Agathon the son of Trimmas. . . . . Thracian infantry were deployed to guard the baggage.

Mercenaries

Philip and Alexander both employed mercenary forces. Given the greater wealth that Macedonia could call upon after its gaining control of the gold and silver mines in the area of Mount Pangaeum and the lower Strymon, Philip had the resources to employ them on a much larger scale than other powers. Some of the sources give the impression that Philip used them frequently, but his operations are so ill-documented that it is hard to assess their importance. Apparently he increased their numbers after the mid-340s when he began to have access to Greek sources.

They were used for three types of duty. Firstly, they manned expeditions designed for limited and definite objectives such as the Euboean expedition of 342/341 or in the formation of a bridgehead in northwestern Asia Minor against the Persians in 336; they usually served in detachments of two to three thousand, though on one occasion a force of ten thousand is mentioned. Secondly, mercenaries were used as permanent garrisons at important points, as at Thermopylae. Thirdly, they were hired for special skills such as the Cretans who were hired for their expertise in archery. Their role was to be more important under Alexander. In the initial invasion of Persia approximately five thousand mercenary infantry were employed.

251. Diodorus Siculus, 16.8.7
The acquisition of Crenides in the Mount Pangaeum area in 356 generated income for Philip from its gold mines on a much more generous scale. Macedonian coinage from his reign has an unusually wide distribution. There is no doubt that such abundant resources allowed him to hire mercenaries and develop other aspects of his military strength on a scale far beyond that possible for the southern Greek powers.

After this Philip came to the city of Crenides and greatly adding to the number of its inhabitants he changed its name to Philippi, calling it after himself. The gold mines in its vicinity had low productivity and were of little significance. He so improved them so that they yielded a revenue of more than a thousand talents. From this source he quickly piled up wealth and because of his riches he brought the Macedonian kingdom to the highest eminence. He struck gold coins called Philippei and assembled a considerable force of mercenaries, many of them Greeks who were led by money to become traitors to their homelands.

252. Demosthenes, *Philippics* 3.49
This passage from a speech delivered probably in the summer of 341 is clearly polemical and exaggerates the importance of Philip's mercenaries but nonetheless must echo popularly held notions of Philip's military methods in Athens (see pp. 165–6).

But you hear he goes where he wants to, not at the head of a hoplite phalanx but because he is furnished with a force of light-armed troops, cavalry, archers and mercenaries.

Philip and his forces in action: the battle of Chaeronea

The military actions of Philip's reign are singularly ill-documented. Our major source, Diodorus Siculus, is rhetorical and inaccurate in his battle descriptions and ignores topography altogether. The best documented of Philip's battles is Chaeronea, fought in August 338. But our knowledge of the course of action is sketchy and the subject of much scholarly controversy.

The political developments that led to the battle are also poorly documented in the sources, primarily the Athenian political speeches of Aeschines and Demosthenes. In the second half of the 340s the Athenians appear to have moved towards a view that Macedonia's preponderance was now intolerable. A series of Athenian setbacks added an irrational element that hindered the appraisal of the lack of proportion between the means available to the Athenians and the ends they desired. The final impetus that drove Athens to war was Philip's Thracian campaign of 340/339 which threatened Athenian access to Black Sea grain.

Of crucial importance in such a conflict was the military power of Thebes which had the most effective hoplite force. After complicated maneuverings among the members of the Delphic Amphictiony (a league of states which controlled the shrine at Delphi), Thebes found itself on the opposite side from the Macedonian controlled majority. In the end Philip brought his army south in late autumn of 339 as the authorized military executive of the Amphictiony. Though Thermopylae was blocked by Thebes, other passes radiating south from Phocis were not. Philip bypassed Thermopylae by taking a more westerly route through Locris and seizing Elateia. This opened central Greece to him. At this juncture the attitude of the Boeotians who had still not committed themselves to Athens or Philip became the subject of negotiations during the winter of 339/338. In the end it appears to have been Thebes' desire to reassert its position in northern Greece and its fear of growing Macedonian power that led to its decision to ally with the Athenians against Philip. Once the decision was taken to resist Philip, Athenian citizens' levies were quickly sent to Thebes to form an allied army.

The winter of 339/338 was divided between skirmishing and diplomatic maneuvers by each side. Philip now faced a situation with the enemy holding narrow passes that precluded him from using his superior cavalry and the mobility of his phalanx. He turned the Greek position by a ruse. The allies pulled back to a position based on the Chaeronean plain and blocked the main route down the Cephisus but did not bar all access to the Boeotian plain. It was presumably chosen because it offered reasonable scope for hoplite warfare with natural obstacles on which such an army could rest its flanks and secure itself to some extent from the effect of the Macedonian cavalry. Philip occupied himself in western Greece, not moving against the Athenians, Boeotians and their allies until late summer 338.

The numbers and relative strength of both sides present something of a problem. The sources are not fully consistent, but it seems reasonable to conjecture that the Greeks possessed more infantry, perhaps 35,000 hoplites and 2000 cavalry. On the Macedonian side we are not told by Diodorus what proportion of the total of 30,000 infantry was actually Macedonian but 20,000 along with 2000 cavalry seem reasonable estimates.

Probably on the morning of 2 August the two armies deployed on the plain. The location of their lines is somewhat of a mystery. But the most reasonable disposition for the Greek army, given our sources and the topography, was that the Thebans occupied the right of the Greek line with the Sacred Band (see p. 40) at the extreme right anchoring its flank on the Cephisus, while the Athenians on the left were protected on their flanks by the foothills of Mount Petrachus so that the allies could fall back through a nearby pass if things turned against them. The other allies formed the center of the line.

The tradition appears to be firm that Philip held the right part of the Macedonian line opposite the Athenians while the left was commanded by his son Alexander. Many other details in Diodorus seem to be unacceptable. But the most likely development was some sort of maneuver by which the allied line could be breached or extended so that the Macedonian cavalry could roll them up. The exact way in which this was done remains unclear. The Greek casualties were heavy, as Diodorus reports. The result was a decisive victory for Philip that established his hegemony in Greece.

253. Diodorus Siculus, 16.85.2–86

Now that they had doubled their power by contracting the alliance with the Boeotians the Athenians took heart once again. Straight away they named as generals Chares and Lysicles and sent out their entire levy under arms to Boeotia. All of the Athenian youth turned out eagerly for the struggle and the army made its way quickly to Chaeronea in Boeotia. The Boeotians were amazed at the speed of the Athenians' arrival and themselves not less eagerly joined them under arms. The allies camped together and awaited the enemy's attack.

Though Philip had failed in his attempt to obtain the Boeotian League as an ally he nevertheless decided to go to war against the Athenians and Boeotians. He waited for all of his allies to appear and advanced into Boeotia with more than thirty thousand foot and not less than two thousand cavalry. Both sides were prepared for battle in their minds and hearts; both sides were also a match in courage. But the king surpassed his opponents in numbers and in generalship. He had fought many battles of various kinds and in the majority of them he had emerged victorious and so had a great fund of experience in such matters. As far as the Athenians were concerned the best of their generals had died . . . and of those who were left Chares was mediocre in the energy and planning that are required of a general.

At dawn the armies deployed. The king placed his son Alexander, who was still a boy though distinguished for his courage and speed of action, in command of one wing and near him the most distinguished of his commanders. Philip with picked troops commanded the other wing and arrayed the other units successively in accordance with the demands of the situation. The battle that ensued was a prolonged affair with many falling on both sides and for a time each side had hopes for a victory. Alexander, wanting to show his ability in competition with his father and not wanting to be outdone in the quest for glory or aided by good companions, was the first to break the enemy line. Striking down many he exerted strong pressure on the troops arrayed against him. The same thing happened in the case of those by his side and so the integrity of the enemy line was ruptured. As the bodies of the slain were piling up, the troops with Alexander forced their way in and put the enemy to flight. Then Philip himself, also in front of his forces, not wishing to yield the credit for the victory to Alexander, first forced back the troops opposite him and then by causing their flight became the source of victory. The Athenians lost more than a thousand dead in the battle and not less than two thousand were captured. Similarly the Boeotians had many killed and not a few taken prisoner. After the battle Philip erected a trophy and gave back the dead for burial. He made sacrifices for his victory to the gods and rewarded those who had distinguished themselves according to their actions.

254. Polyaenus, *Stratagems* 4.2.2

Some scholars have accepted this as a plausible maneuver designed to create a gap in the enemy line to allow the Macedonian cavalry to carry the day. It would fit with the tradition that Alexander advanced first with the cavalry as Philip could not reverse his men until after the Athenians had opened a sufficient gap to allow his son's charge to be successful. There are topographical problems with such a scenario and it has a disturbing parallel in the same author's description of the stratagem by which the Phocian general Onomarchus defeated Philip in 352. Still, it must remain within the realm of possibility.

At Chaeronea Philip's forces were deployed opposite to the Athenians and his men had given way and were bending back. The Athenian general Stratocles cried out to his men not to stop their pressure on the Macedonians until they had shut them up in Macedonia. He kept up his pursuit. Philip, saying that the Athenians did not know how to win, retreated step by step with his phalanx in close order and within the formation he was protected by his troops' weapons. After a short time occupying higher ground, he encouraged his men and reversing his phalanx he forcefully fell on the Athenians. His magnificent fight ended in his victory.

ALEXANDER THE GREAT

In the summer of 336 Philip was struck down by an assassin motivated by private resentments. His twenty-year-old son Alexander III came to an uncertain throne. Macedonia's expansion had been due to Philip and many thought it could be reversed. Alexander was an unknown quantity. But despite recent disputes with his father Alexander had already shown his abilities in 340 when he acted as regent. The Thracian Maidoi had rebelled and Alexander in a lightning campaign had crushed them. His military ability and his drive for domination were displayed with equal clarity.

He had inherited an unmatched army. No other force could rival its combination of heavy infantry and superb heavy cavalry. Outside the Balkans the Persians stood the best chance against it if they could combine effectively their vast resources in cavalry with their Greek mercenaries. But Persia was slow to mobilize and its forces did not possess the discipline and mobility that come from long experience operating in the field, as did the Macedonians. More importantly, the Persians possessed competent commanders but none of the caliber of the new Macedonian king.

The last part of Philip's bequest was the expedition against Persia. In the spring of 336 Philip had sent across a force of ten thousand cavalry and infantry to prepare a bridgehead for the expedition he would lead against the Persians in the name of Greek revenge and his own self-aggrandizement. Alexander stabilized his position in the Balkans and in Greece in 336 and 335. In the spring of 334 he began to march with his army eastward along the route that the Persians had followed in the opposite direction a century and a half before. Conquest played a stronger role in the young king's mind than revenge.

At Alexander's accession Persia must have seemed a tempting target for a king in financial straits. Moreover, its military weakness had grown increasingly obvious from the end of the fifth century. Macedonia had now neutralized the Greeks and possessed a decisive factor in a cavalry force that could match any the Persians could muster. Moreover, it was joined by a force of heavy infantry that the Persians could not match even with the use of mercenaries. In addition, advances in siege warfare (see pp. 157ff) had meant that fortified positions could not impede the Macedonians. This force was superior to anything the Persians could throw against it. Alexander could anticipate no really desperate resistance until he reached the eastern satrapies, and even if serious opposition should develop he could cope with it. There seemed to be no reason for him to limit his dreams of conquest and empire.

255. Diodorus Siculus, 17.17.3–5

Diodorus is the only extant source to give totals for various contingents of Alexander's expeditionary force against the Persians in the spring of 334. The twelve thousand heavy infantry were divided into an élite body of three thousand hypaspists (see no. 256) and six regular infantry battalions. If the regiments left behind in Macedonia are added to the total the full strength of the Macedonian phalanx would have been about 24,000. The 7000 allied troops were Greeks supplied in accordance with the terms of a league created by Philip. They play an almost non-existent role in the course of Alexander's campaigns. The other large infantry contingent was the 7000 drawn from various Balkan peoples.

The total given by Diodorus for the cavalry forces is incorrect. The sum of the numbers is in fact 5100. There are discrepancies over other totals for Alexander's forces in 334. Part of these can be accounted for by adding in the 10,000 troops sent out to prepare a bridgehead by Philip in 336. So the total muster was something over 40,000 infantry and 6000 horse. Though much smaller than the Persian forces it opposed, it is immense if compared with the numbers of troops contemporary Greek states were capable of raising.

Parmenion occupied a leading role down to his execution in 330. He had been one of Philip's most important commanders and aides. His sons Philotas and Nicanor occupied crucial posts in Alexander's army. During the Persian campaign he occupied a position equivalent to a second command, either leading the left of the battle line in major encounters or operating with independent forces. Antipater had also served Philip as a trusted advisor and commander. The passage opens at Troy where Alexander suitably inaugurated the campaign by ostentatiously linking it to the Trojan War.

Alexander paid honor to the tombs of the heroes, Achilles, Ajax and the rest, with offerings to the dead and other suitable marks of respect; he then began an accurate tabulation of his forces.

There were 12,000 Macedonian infantry, 7000 allied foot soldiers and 5000 mercenaries. All of these were under the command of Parmenion. The Odrysians, Triballians and Illyrians were also 7000 in total. In addition there were 1000 archers and Agrianians. This brought the total of all infantry to 32,000. He had 1800 Macedonian cavalry led by Parmenio's son Philotas. The Thessalian cavalry amounted to 1800 under Callas the son of Harpalus. The rest of the Greeks provided 600 cavalry commanded by Erigyius. The sum of the Scouts, Thracians and Paeonians was 900. They had as their commander Cassander. The total of all cavalry forces was 4500. The army left behind in Europe under Antipater consisted of 12,000 foot and 2000 cavalry.

Organizational changes

Infantry: the hypaspists

Though some have held that the hypaspists were an already existing unit of the Macedonian infantry there is no evidence for it before Alexander's reign. The title appears for the first time in an inscription from Alexander's first year. It appears to be an élite guard unit that formed the counterpart to the Companion cavalry. It contained a royal regiment, the agema, that corresponded to the Royal Squadron in the Companion cavalry. Their name "shield-bearers" is something of a puzzle, but it may have something to do with the apparently honorable post of carrying the king's shield for him in battle. As an élite unit they were the king's shield in a metaphorical and literal sense.

Though it is not directly stated in our sources they appear to have numbered three thousand or the equivalent of two phalanx battalions. They seem to have been organized in three battalions, two commanded by chiliarchs with the third, the royal Agema, perhaps under the direct command of the king. At the end of 331 a new form of organization was introduced (see no. 257).

In the major battles they were posted as a link between the Companion cavalry to their right and the rest of the phalanx. They were often used by Alexander in difficult operations and in combination with cavalry and light-armed troops. This has led some scholars to argue that they used lighter equipment than the remainder of the phalanx, but this seems precluded by their role as part of the heavy infantry. Their use in expeditions requiring movement and speed appears to be a result of their superior training and is not due to any difference in equipment.

256. Arrian, *Anabasis of Alexander* 2.4.3

Arrian is here narrating the arrival of Alexander in spring 333 at the main pass from central to the southeast coast of Asia Minor. The Cyrus referred to is probably the younger who camped here in the plain before the Gates on his ill-fated expedition of 401 (see no. 96). This pass could be turned in a number of ways and there may be some exaggeration about the opposition Alexander encountered and his measures to deal with the problem of crossing the Gates. This passage is a good illustration of the operational groups that often include hypaspists. It says nothing definite about their equipment and does not necessarily imply they are light-armed.

When he arrived at the camp of Cyrus, the one who campaigned with Xenophon, he saw that the Gates were guarded by a strong force. He left Parmenion there with the battalions of heavy infantry, but at the first watch Alexander took with him the hypaspists, the archers and Agrianians and led them during the night against the Gates.

Cavalry

257. Arrian, *Anabasis of Alexander* 3.16.11

This passage describes the arrival of the most substantial body of reinforcements that Alexander received, which arrived in the summer of 331, a levy of 15,000 foot and 500 cavalry. It included 6000 Macedonian infantry and 500 cavalry. These were the last Macedonian reinforcements that Alexander was to receive. At the same time and perhaps to institute a more ethnically varied cavalry force he multiplied the number of units by instituting two *lochoi* in every squadron. He also changed the previous practice of assigning officers of the same ethnic group, and in theory now made the selection of these upper echelon officers a matter of merit alone. Both nos 257 and 258 reflect the same changes, though Curtius, a Roman writer of the mid-first century AD, appears to have garbled his account.

Alexander assigned the cavalry reinforcements to the Companion cavalry and the infantry to their battalions according to their ethnic affiliation. He formed two *lochoi* in each *ila* of the Companion cavalry. These units had not previously existed in the cavalry and he appointed officers to command the *lochoi* from the body of his Companions on the basis of merit.

258. Quintus Curtius Rufus, *History of Alexander the Great* 5.2.6

At this time Alexander also made very useful changes in the military organization he had inherited from his predecessors. Previously cavalry had been assigned to their units on an ethnic basis; he now made an end of these distinctions and assigned these units to commanders on the basis of merit.

259. Arrian, *Anabasis of Alexander* 3.27.4

In addition to the changes in the selection of officers for the cavalry and the creation of new units in the wake of the execution of Philotas, the son of Parmenion, for conspiracy in autumn 330, Alexander divided the command of the Companion cavalry into two separate positions, as Arrian says, to avoid the concentration of too much power in the hands of a single individual.

Alexander now put two hipparchs in charge of the Companion cavalry, Hephaestion the son of Amyntor and Cleitus the son of Dropis, and so divided the Companions into two units. He had several reasons for doing so: first he did not want anyone, not even his most intimate friend, to be the center of their affections (besides himself) and also he wanted to put those who were most appropriate on account of their personal worth and courage in charge of his most formidable cavalry.

260. Arrian, *Anabasis of Alexander* 3.29.7

This is the first attestation of new cavalry units named hipparchies. These are larger units than the *ilai* since each hipparchy included at least two squadrons. Perhaps as early as 329 there were eight of them. How they relate to the two hipparchs mentioned above is not clear. But it may be that they are an answer to the same problem that Alexander saw with the infantry, the persistence of old loyalties. Another reason for their creation may have been a desire to enlarge the number of units to better deal with a greater range of missions, particularly the guerrilla and light cavalry fighting that occurred in Bactria and Sogdiana. Military reasons may thus lie behind this reorganization as well as political ones. Spitamenes and Dataphernes, both Bactrians, were the leaders of the Persian resistance in the northeastern satrapies. They were later defeated and executed.

After he heard this Alexander rested his army and led it forward at a slower pace than before. He sent Ptolemy, the son of Lagus, with three hipparchies of the Companion cavalry and all of the mounted javelin-men . . . and ordered him to make all haste to reach Spitamenes and Dataphernes.

The Greek allies

The Greek allies except for the Thessalian cavalry are rarely mentioned in action and appear for the most part as reserves and service troops. The dismissal of these troops at Ecbatana in Media in 330 marked an end to the façade of Alexander's campaign as a mission of revenge for Xerxes' invasion.

261. Diodorus Siculus, 17.74.3–4

Alexander, seeing that the Macedonians regarded the death of Darius as the end of the expedition, . . . assembled his allied Greek forces and, after praising their achievements, released them from service. He gave each cavalry trooper a bonus of a talent and also ten minas to each foot soldier. In addition, he gave them their agreed pay and added expenses for the journey home. Those who elected to remain in his service were given three talents apiece as a bonus.

The use of Orientals in the army

The year 331 marked the last year that Alexander received substantial reinforcements from Macedonia and its Balkan dependencies. Casualties had been heavy and the drain of the campaign must have taken their toll. The army would have to be adjusted to the reality that fewer Macedonians were available. At the same time the type of warfare that Alexander was involved with in eastern Iran and the steppes called for lighter armed foot and cavalry. These were the very types of troops that native levies could provide. The first clear indication of the use of native cavalry units is provided by employment of Bactrian and Sogdian cavalry formations in the winter of 328/327. Oriental units, including mercenaries, accompanied Alexander to India. With the conquest of India, Indian units were added as well. The Orientals were brigaded separately from the European troops and served as hostages as well. Orientals were kept out of positions of command until very late in the reign and then held these positions only under very special circumstances. By the end Alexander was clearly trying to construct an imperial army in place of a Macedonian one.

262. Quintus Curtius Rufus, *History of Alexander the Great* 8.5.1
The evidence for the incorporation of Orientals in the infantry is explicit. Orders were given to governors in 327 on Alexander's move south towards India for a force of thirty thousand Iranian youths to be trained to fight as Macedonian phalangites. The Iranians were to remain an independent unit.

However, when he was about to continue his campaign through India and as far as the Ocean, to avoid a threat to his plans by removing a danger to his rear he ordered thirty thousand young men to be selected, armed and led to him to serve as soldiers and hostages at the same time.

263. Diodorus Siculus, 17.108.1–3

At this time [324] thirty thousand Persian youths, selected for their appearance and physical strength, arrived at Susa. After they had been assembled at the king's orders, they were placed under the tutelage of supervisors and instructors in the military arts and were well equipped in the Macedonian fashion. They formed up in front of the city and displayed their military skills and discipline to the king who praised them highly. . . . Alexander had established this formation from a single age-class of Persians to serve as a counterweight to the Macedonian phalanx.

264. Arrian, *Anabasis of Alexander* 7.23.1–4
How practical this arrangement was is not clear. It seems unwieldy and was never tested. It implies that the normal file was sixteen men deep, though other depths were used by Alexander as well. It is one of the few passages that give us some idea of lower level officers and pay scales. Nothing comparable exists for the cavalry in our sources. The exact relation between pay and rank is not clear. The wages refer to monthly rates which are thirty drachmas for a trooper, forty

for the ten-stater man and sixty for the man on double pay. These are better rates than those paid to most fourth-century mercenaries. To these sums must be added the considerable bounties that Alexander dispersed in the course of his expedition. Peucastes was appointed governor of the Persian homeland in 325.

On Alexander's return to Babylon he found that Peucastes had arrived with an army of twenty thousand Persians. . . . Then he praised the Persians for their enthusiasm in being completely obedient to Peucastes and he also praised Peucastes for his well-organized government of them. He enrolled them in the Macedonian infantry battalions. He created a decad in which a Macedonian was decad commander and behind him in line was a double-pay Macedonian and then a ten-stater man who is so called from his rate of pay. His wages are less than the double pay men, but more than the common soldiers. Behind these men he placed twelve Persians and then closed the decad with a Macedonian. So a decad was now composed of four Macedonians – its commander and the others who were serving at higher pay rates – with twelve Persians. The Macedonians served with their usual equipment. The Persians included archers and men equipped with thonged javelins.

265. Arrian, *Anabasis of Alexander* 7.6.3–5
This narrative forms part of the background to Arrian's narration of the mutiny at Opis in Mesopotamia in late summer 324. It appears that the Oriental cavalry was brigaded separately from the Macedonian cavalry until this point. The exact arrangements under which the Orientals served are not known. It appears that four hipparchies were composed of Oriental troops with a fifth that mixed them with European cavalry in some fashion. This was another step in the trans-formation we have noted toward making the army an imperial institution. The numbers were small and restricted to an élite.

The Macedonians were also upset at . . . the fact that Alexander had enrolled in the Companion cavalry horsemen from Bactria and Sogdiana as well as Arachosians, Zaragians, Areians and Parthyaeoi. Also he had enrolled the so-called Persian Euacae. As many were enrolled as were distinguished by the rank or the beauty of their physique or excelled in some other suitable requirement. Further a fifth hipparchy was added, although it was not entirely composed of barbarian troopers, but when the whole of the cavalry force had been increased barbarians had been enrolled for this purpose. . . . Also they had been given Macedonian lances to use in place of their barbarian thonged javelins.

Alexander as a commander

Whatever the judgment of the ancient sources on Alexander's character there was no doubt of his military abilities. The Roman historian Livy, writing three centuries after Alexander's death, felt compelled to argue Rome's military superiority to him. He remained a symbol of military greatness throughout late antiquity and into the Middle Ages. The truth of the judgment is obvious. The qualities that he possessed that were crucial to his success were technical expertise – in the sense of a magnificent grasp of topography and the importance of reconnaissance and logistics – as well as intangible and personal qualities. One of his most remarkable assets was his ability to control and dominate his troops through the fatigue and difficulties induced by the prolonged, hard campaigning as well as in the stress of battle. The ethnic diversity of his force made this difficult, but its most important element, the Macedonian cavalry and infantry, were already linked to him by the personal bonds inherent in his kingship. His Balkan subjects were no doubt cowed by his earlier campaigns in Europe and attracted by the possibilities for booty and adventure in what must have seemed to be a campaign offering reasonable prospects of success. His Greek allies would at least have had the same possibilities before them and, at any rate, had little choice.

A central element in the moral dominance of the king over his men was provided by his sense of himself and his feel for the theatrical. From the beginning he stressed his ties by blood and temperament to the heroes of the Trojan War. It not only linked him to and provided a framework for a supposed Hellenic crusade to avenge the Persian invasion of Greece, but also closely associated him with the heroic mode of warfare that was emotionally attractive to his Macedonian and Greek troops. His sacrifices to heroes of the Trojan War, his visit to Troy, his games there and his exchange of his own arms for the heroic relics kept at the site were probably calculated acts, though at the same time apparently filled with genuine emotion. Feeling and calculation impelled Alexander to act the hero and in doing so he maintained his moral ascendancy. He acted as well in a continuing tradition of Greek and Macedonian command that had for the most part favored the leader's direct participation in battle. His father bore wounds that were witnesses to this tradition.

The genuineness of this heroic stance is visible in what might be termed the rash exposure of himself in the van of the battle and in his risking of death in action at the Granicus. Its sincerity is attested by the excess to which it could go. In his assault on the capital of the Indian Malli he senselessly risked his life to galvanize his troops whom he felt were losing their élan. But it worked. His refusal of the water for himself when his troops were suffering horribly from thirst in the Gedrosian desert is a more obvious and calculated example of the same style.

He failed to maintain this ascendancy and control on two occasions. The first time was at the Hyphasis River (Beas) in northwestern India in the summer of 326 when despite the suffering and the demoralization of his troops he was intent on crossing the river and proceeding with a plan of unlimited conquest. Even three days spent sulking in his tent could not produce the desired result. He resorted to face-saving gestures that allowed him to change his mind grace-fully. The second time was the mutiny at Opis in late summer 324 when his Macedonian troops felt they were being displaced, as in fact they were, by Orientals and were losing their privileged status. But he mastered the situation and laid the necessary foundation for his transition to being Great King. There was ostentatious attention to the welfare of his troops whether expressed by paying their debts or in paying allowances for their survivors.

In the course of battle his superb control over his men at Gaugamela indicates his ability to instill sufficient discipline to control his entire force and his cavalry units in particular. His successors were less skilled at it. Alexander's weaknesses in this area stemmed from too strong an egotism. He was sometimes blinded by the imperatives of his own desires to the needs of others, as at the Beas, and then he failed. But the failures were rare and his continued successes testify to his remarkable achievements.

In tactical matters he displayed the same remarkable psychological insight as in anticipating his opponents' strategy. At the Granicus he saw that the Persian force was really not capable of meeting his troops because of their equipment, numbers and position. He used his superior mobility to capitalize on Persian anxiety and draw them down into the river bed where they would be vulnerable to the superiority of the Macedonians. The same ability in also manifested at Issus. Though outmaneuvered by the Persian king, he anticipated Darius' tactics in the course of the battle, especially that his cavalry would be the decisive arm and that it would be deployed on his right. He created mobile flank guards and lured on the Persian center and right till a gap appeared.

The ability to anticipate was combined with an almost infinite inventiveness in devising expedients to meet new situations. The basic tactics he had inherited from Philip were to use his phalanx to pin and create gaps into which his main offensive weapon, the Companion cavalry, could drive and roll up the enemy to the left. Gaugamela is a perfect illustration of the genius of Alexander in creating such an opportunity in a situation where his exposed flanks might have given a lesser commander extreme anxiety. One is struck in this case, as in another set-piece battle against the Indian king Porus, by his almost infinite ability to adapt and tailor his depositions to his needs and to maximize his enemy's weaknesses.

This skill is evident not only in the four major set-piece battles that the king fought. From 330 until 327 Alexander was engaged in a very different type of warfare against rebels in Sogdiana and Bactria. This hit and run warfare put a premium on mobility and gave an advantage to his enemy that ended in the most disastrous Macedonian defeat that cost two thousand men. As a counter, Alexander devised flying columns composed of different arms to hunt down the rebels while garrisoning strategic points in order to deny them supplies and a safe retreat. Though often tried, such hit and run attempts now rarely met with great success and it is striking that Alexander could respond to this very different challenge successfully.

His weaknesses in this area were again the product of willfullness. The siege of Tyre and the campaign after the Brahmin rebellion down the lower Indus valley were undertaken in a spirit of frustration and anger. Though successful their price was out of all proportion and less costly means might have achieved the same goals.

It is this desire for conquest that was his greatest weakness as a soldier and affected his strategy. He formulated no overall plan as to how to protect and integrate what had been conquered. Politically and militarily it would have made far more sense to face the immense problem of creating a stable imperial state. If the so-called plans for future conquests disclosed after his death were true, then in this respect he falls short of his father who knew how to subordinate military means to political ends.

266. Plutarch, *Alexander* 15.7–8

In the spring of 334, while his army was crossing the Hellespont, Alexander went through a series of acts: a sacrifice before disembarking to the hero Protesilaus, followed by other sacrifices, jumping into the sea and casting a spear at the beach. These acts were followed by the visit to Troy mentioned here. This behavior was a deliberate attempt to emphasize and link Alexander to the heroes of the Trojan War and to portray his expedition as a continuation of it. It also emphasized the role of the expedition as an act of revenge for Xerxes' invasion a century and half before. Its effect would not be lost on Alexander's Greek allies.

Going up to Troy Alexander sacrificed to Athena and poured a libation to the [Greek] heroes. He anointed himself with oil and ran naked around the stele of Achilles with his Companions, as is the custom. He then crowned the stone with garlands, saying that Achilles was fortunate because while he lived he had a faithful friend and after his death a great herald [of his deeds].

267. Arrian, *Anabasis of Alexander* 6.26.1–3

The march to Gedrosia (the Makran) in the winter of 325/324 on the way back from India occasioned substantial losses. It was a miscalculation by Alexander based on poor reconnaissance and on the ambition to outdo mythical rivals. This story may or may not be true. There are at least three versions of it and Arrian does not fully vouch for it. But it is totally in character and a good illustration of Alexander's actual techniques and sense of the dramatic.

The story is that while the army was marching through sand and blistering heat because they had to reach the water that was the goal of their march, and had already gone some distance, Alexander himself was badly suffering from thirst and yet led the army. This was his way of doing such things to make the soldiers bear their distress more equitably. At this point some of the light-armed troops who had turned from the line of march to look for water discovered some in a shallow gully. The spring was small and weak. They collected the water easily and enthusiastically returned to Alexander as if they were carrying a rare treasure. As they were approaching, they poured the water into a helmet and carried it to the king. He received it and praised them for bringing it. He took it and in the sight of all poured it out on the ground. At the sight of this act the whole army was so heartened that you might think that they had had a drink of the water that Alexander had poured out. I find this act as evidence for his endurance and I praise it as proof of his qualities as a general.

Military actions

Tactical resourcefulness

268. Polyaenus, *Stratagems* 4.3.23

This event occurred in the winter of 336 when the Greeks, already restive, rebelled at the news of Philip's death. It was necessary to act to establish his authority.

Because the Thessalians held the pass at Tempe under guard, Alexander excavated the sheer rocks of Ossa and constructed small steps across these rocks. He and his army used them to climb up the mountain and reach the peak. So he crossed Ossa and gained Thessaly while the Thessalians guarded the narrows of the pass. Even today [late second century AD] travelers passing through Tempe can see the rocks on Ossa that had been shaped into stairs. The locals call them Alexander's Ladder.

269. Arrian, *Anabasis of Alexander* 4.4.4–5

This incident took place as part of his reconquest of Sogdiana and Bactria which he had first subdued in the spring and summer of 329. It was a particularly bloody action for the Macedonians. At its end a band of Scythians who had troubled the area previously appeared on the northern banks of the Jaxartes. Alexander successfully repeated the use of catapults as field artillery that he had practiced against tribes on the Danube. He then went on to successfully foil their circling tactics.

As soon as the hides had been prepared for crossing the river and his army was posted on the river bank in full equipment, the catapults on order bombarded the Scythians riding along the bank and some were wounded by the darts. One of them was pierced through his ox-hide shield and corselet and fell from his horse. The Scythians were terrified by the darts on account of their long range and because of the loss of a brave man and so they retreated a little from the bank. When Alexander saw that they had fallen into disorder from the darts he had the bugles sounded and began to cross the river at the head of his men. Then the rest of the army followed.

The battle of Gaugamela

This was in many ways Alexander's tactical masterpiece. Unfortunately, the course of the battle is obscure at many points. Arrian's account given here is the best of the extant narratives, although useful details can be found in several of the other sources. Arrian's account is rather episodic: it concentrates too much on Alexander on the right wing and neglects the left wing's fate. It also is not fully clear about the decisive events on the right. There seems to be a deliberate tendency in Arrian's account (it can be found at several points) to obscure and belittle Parmenio's contribution to the victory. Some of these difficulties may have been the result of contemporary confusion caused by the dust of the battlefield.

The exact location of the battlefield has been disputed. It is now generally accepted that it was the flat level plain today called the plain of Naqûr near the hill of Tel Gomel, the site of ancient Gaugamela, between the Kazir (Boumelus) and the Greater Zab. This was ideal for Darius' army. His army was now composed mostly of the superb cavalry of the eastern and northeastern satrapies, after the loss of the western provinces and the opportunity to recruit Greek mercenaries. Flat open land was exactly the type of battlefield suited to them and to the two hundred scythed chariots he had prepared to break the force of the Macedonian phalanx. Though he had infantry they were negligible and the phalanx was a critical problem for him. He even prepared fairways for the chariots. As long as he could assure his supplies he could comfortably await Alexander who had to seek him out.

Arrian claims to have access to a captured Persian order of battle; though his numbers are ridiculous, the dispositions make sense. Expecting Alexander to be on the right of his battle line with the Companion cavalry, Darius had his best cavalry on his left with a hundred scythed chariots to break up the hypaspists there and to allow the cavalry to charge through them. He must also have planned to contain Alexander on this wing – hence the heavy concentration of troops – and then to encircle him on both wings and destroy him. This explains the smaller number of scythed chariots in the center and on the right. The right of the Persian line was commanded by Mazaeus, the satrap of Babylonia, while Bessus, the satrap of Bactria, was commander on the left.

The Macedonian order of battle was the standard line: the main offensive weight was on the right wing with Alexander, and the line was probably set up in oblique fashion. Alexander realized the danger of encirclement while he sought to open up the gap for his cavalry charge, and it is in the construction of this defensive formation that his genius lay. By establishing a second phalanx line and setting up his flank guards, probably inclined at a forty-five degree angle back from his front, he created a formation that could be turned into a defensive square if necessary but could also function offensively by engaging the Persians in any attempt to surround the Macedonians, so giving an opportunity for the gap in the Persian line to develop.

None of the sources presents reasonable estimates for either army. It may be that Alexander had forty thousand infantry and about seven thousand cavalry. Given the course of the battle it is clear that the number of Persian infantry was of no importance as they played no role in the battle. The tactics of both sides indicate that the Persians enjoyed a large advantage in cavalry.

The course of the battle, fought on 1 October 331, was determined by Alexander's march to the right. Though it exposed his held back left wing to envelopment it threatened to put the Macedonians in a position to attack the Persians outside of the areas prepared for the scythed chariots. It was Darius' desire to contain this movement that led to his attempt to encircle Alexander's right and to try and keep him within the prepared area. The chariots in the end were easily disposed of by the flank guard or allowed to pass harmlessly through gaps in the Macedonian line. But fatally for Darius the movement to the left of his cavalry opened up a gap or at least a thinning of his force. Alexander saw this and immediately drove into it with part of the phalanx and the Companion cavalry. He then turned left towards Darius, and began to roll up the Persian line.

The Macedonian left was massively outflanked and unable to move forward in step with the right. A gap then opened in the left of the phalanx. The Persians were only able to get through some Indian and Persian units who plundered Alexander's camp but otherwise were easily disposed of. But this action was accompanied by an outflanking movement by Mazaeus. It was somehow checked by the charge of the Thessalian cavalry. The sources are very hazy on the course of events at this point.

The figures for losses that we have are as unreliable as the number of Persians engaged, and in fact they greatly exaggerate Persian losses while underestimating Macedonian ones. Persian losses were probably smaller than in earlier encounters as the majority were cavalry fighting in open territory to which they could easily escape. This would have been especially true of the Persian right.

270. Arrian, *Anabasis of Alexander* 3.11.3–15.6

Darius' army was drawn up in the following manner (Aristobulus informs us that a written copy of Darius' order of battle was captured later). The left wing was held by the Bactrian cavalry along with the horse of the Dahae and the Arachotians. Next to them were placed the Persians, horse and infantry mixed together, and then the Susians and the Cadusians. This was the arrangement of the left wing as far as the middle of the entire formation. On the right wing there were the troops from Coéle Syria and Mesopotamia, and farther to the right were the Medes, then the Parthyaeans and the Sacae, followed by the Topeirians and Hyrcanians. After these came the Albanians and the Sacesinians. This again was the line as far as the middle of the phalanx. In the center where the king was were his kinsmen and the Persians with golden apples fixed to their spear-butts, and then the Indians, the so-called resettled Carians and the Mardian bowmen. Next to them came the Uxians, the Babylonians, those along the coast of the Red Sea and the men of Sittacene who had been marshaled behind in deep formation. On his left Darius had placed as an advanced formation Scythian cavalry, one thousand Bactrians and a hundred scythed chariots. The elephants were stationed to the front of the royal squadron in the center along with fifty scythed chariots. In front of the Persian right were the Armenian and Cappadocian horse with fifty scythed chariots. The Greek mercenary infantry flanked the king on either side and were opposite the Macedonian phalanx as being the only unit capable of standing up to it.

Alexander's army was arrayed as follows: the Companion cavalry with the Royal Squadron which was commanded by Cleitus son of Dropis was on the right, then came the squadron of Glaucias. Next to it were the squadrons of Ariston, Sopolis son of Hermodorus, Heracleides son of Antiochus, Demetrius son of Althaemenes, Meleager and finally the troops commanded by Hegelochus son of Hippostratus. The entire Companion cavalry was under the command of Philotas son of Parmenion. The Macedonian infantry phalanx was joined to the Companion cavalry by the hypaspists whose royal company stood right next to the cavalry. They were led by Nicanor son of Parmenion. Then came five regiments of phalangite infantry. The left of the Macedonian phalanx was formed by the battalion of Craterus son of Alexander who also commanded the left wing of the infantry line. Then came the allied infantry under Erigyius son of Larichus and after them the Thessalian cavalry commanded by Philip son of Menelaus. The commander of the entire left wing was Parmenion son of Philotas. He was ringed by the Pharsalian cavalry who were the best and most numerous of the Thessalian horse.

The front of Alexander's line was arranged as I have described it. He set up in addition a second line to make his phalanx double-fronted. He ordered the commanders of this second line that if they saw that the army was surrounded by the Persian forces, they were to face about to the rear and receive the Persian attack.

To allow the phalanx to extend or to close up on the right wing, but at an angle, half of the Agrianians under Attalus and the Macedonian archers commanded by Brison were placed next to the Royal Squadron, and then next to them were posted the so-called old mercenaries under Cleander. To the front of the Agrianians and archers were the Cavalry scouts and the Paeonians led by Aretas and Ariston. In front of all of these were the mercenary horse under Menidas. The other half of the Agrianians, the archers and the javelin-men of Balacrus, were posted to the front of the Companion cavalry including the Royal Squadron. They were placed there to deal with the scythed chariots. Menidas and his men were instructed to turn at an angle and to attack the enemy in their flank as he was riding around their wing. This was the arrangement on Alexander's right. On his left, at an angle, were the Thracians under Sitalces and then the allied cavalry under Coeranus and then the Odrysian horse led by Agathon son of Tyrimmas. The mercenary cavalry, posted farthest forward, were commanded by Andromachus son of Hiero. The Thracian infantry had been detailed to protect the baggage. The total of Alexander's forces was seven thousand horse and forty thousand foot.

As the armies approached Darius and the troops around him were easily visible; they were arrayed opposite Alexander and the Royal Squadron. . . . But Alexander kept on leading his men to his right and the Persians extended in that direction. Their left far out-flanked the Macedonians. At this point the Scythian horse riding along the front of Alexander's line were in contact with his forward units, but Alexander still kept on to the right and was near to moving clear of the Persians' prepared ground. Then in fear that the Macedonians would reach unprepared ground that would be useless for his chariots Darius ordered the forward units of his left wing to encircle Alexander's right (where Alexander himself was in command) to prevent a further extension of that wing. When this happened Alexander gave the command for Menidas' mercenary cavalry to attack. The Scythian and Bactrian cavalry rode out to counter this and turned Menidas' horse as they outnumbered them. Then Alexander ordered Ariston's men, the Paeonians and the mercenaries to charge the Scythians and the barbarians gave way. The remaining Bactrians came up to the Paeonians and mercenary horse and rallied those on their side who had taken flight and made the cavalry battle a close contest. Many of Alexander's men fell, borne down by the numerical superiority of the barbarians and because the Scythians and their horses had better protection. But even as the Macedonians received their charges they countered them forcefully and drove them out of their formation.

At this point the Persians sent forward the scythed chariots straight at Alexander's portion of the battle line to disrupt the formation of his line. They were disappointed in this expectation. Some of the chariots were bombarded as they approached by the

Agrianians and the javelin-men of Balacrus who had been stationed in front of the Companion cavalry; seizing the reins from the drivers and crowding around the horses, they cut the traces. Some of the chariots did pass through the ranks which parted as they had been instructed. Through this maneuver the men were unharmed and the chariots passed through untouched. Then the Macedonian grooms and the royal hypaspists overwhelmed them.

When Darius led forward his whole line Alexander ordered Aretas to charge the enemy who were riding around the right of the Macedonian army to encircle it. The king himself led forward his section of the line, but when the enemy cavalry that been sent to aid those who were being encircled on the right wing had created a gap in front of the Persian formation, he turned his forces towards the gap after forming the Companion cavalry and phalanx arrayed with it. He led them forward at full speed and with a loud shout went straight at Darius himself. For a little while the battle remained a hand-to-hand encounter. But then Alexander and his cavalry forcefully attacked the Persians, shoving them and thrusting at their faces with their spears, and the Macedonian phalanx drawn up in dense order with its projecting sarissa points were now closely attacking them. All of this appeared equally terrible to Darius who was already in a panic. He was the first to turn and flee. The Persians who were riding around the right wing were also panicked by the charge of Aretas' men.

So on the right there was a tremendous rout of the Persians and the Macedonians kept on cutting them down during their pursuit. But the battalion of Simmias was no longer able to keep pace with Alexander in the pursuit. They halted and fought where they were when it was announced to them that the left wing was in trouble. The Macedonian formation had broken there and some Indian and Persian cavalry were driving through the gap to attack the baggage animals. At that point the struggle became intense. For the Persians confidently attacked men who were for the most part unarmed and who did not expect that anyone would cut their way through the double-phalanx and fall upon them. When the Persians made their attack, the barbarian prisoners joined with them. The officers of the troops acting as a reserve to the first phalanx speedily learned of the attack and turned their troops about, as they had been ordered, and appearing in the Persian rear cut down many of them as they were bunched together around the baggage animals. The survivors gave way and fled.

The Persian right which was as yet still unaware of Darius' flight rode around Alexander's left wing and fell on Parmenion's troops. While the Macedonians were caught between two fires at this point Parmenion sent a messenger to Alexander to announce as fast as possible that the left wing was in trouble and needed help. When Alexander learned of this he broke off his pursuit and turned with the Companion cavalry and charged the Persian right. He first attacked the fleeing Parthyaeans, some Indians and the Persian cavalry. These were the best and largest enemy formations. This was the most intense cavalry engagement of the entire battle. The barbarians, arrayed in depth since they were arranged in squadrons, turned about and fell on the Macedonians face to face. There was no casting of javelins or the counterwheeling that are normal in cavalry battles; rather each trooper tried to cut his way through the men directly opposite him as the only path to safety. In their struggle they killed and were killed without quarter since they were fighting not for another's victory but for their own survival. In this action about sixty of the Companions who were with Alexander fell and Hephaestion himself as well as Coenus and Menidas were wounded. But Alexander still emerged victorious.

Those who did succeed in breaking through fled as quickly as they could, so Alexander was on the point of attacking the enemy's right. But while Alexander had been engaged the Thessalian cavalry, fighting brilliantly, came off as well as the king. Now the right wing of the enemy was also in flight when Alexander met them; so he turned away from them and resumed his pursuit of Darius again. It was continued as long as there was light. Parmenion's men, pursuing those opposite them, followed on. But when Alexander crossed the Lycus River he encamped to give a little rest to his men and horses. Parmenion took the enemy's camp, including the baggage, elephants, and camels. . . .

Approximately one hundred of Alexander's cavalry died and over a thousand animals were lost due to wounds or the rigors of the pursuit. About half of these belonged to the Companions. It is said that there were thirty thousand barbarian dead and that far more were captured alive along with the elephants and the chariots that had not been destroyed in the battle.

5

HELLENISTIC WARFARE

The early and unexpected death of Alexander the Great in 323 BC left a huge empire with territory in Greece and the East. Its administrative structure was a ramshackle affair that required years of administrative and bureaucratic effort to develop into a stable state. Crucial for the future was the absence of any regularized system of succession and the lack of any suitable candidates from Alexander's family to replace him. The solution to these problems were to consume the next forty years. A struggle broke out among Alexander's major commanders over succession that was to fall into two phases. The first ended at the battle of Ipsus in 301 and ended the possibility that the empire would survive as a single unit. The next phase divided Alexander's inheritance among dynasties founded by his generals: the Lagids in Egypt, the Antigonids in Macedonia and the Seleucids who possessed the largest of the new states stretching from the Aegean to northwestern India. The process was not totally completed at this point and other smaller states fragmented off or established themselves, but by the end of the first quarter of the third century an unstable balance had been reached among these three greater successor states as well as lesser but still important powers such as Rhodes, the Attalid kingdom in western Asia Minor and various leagues in Greece. The older city-states were sometimes important for various political, economic or even cultural reasons, but their day as great powers had passed.

Most inhabitants of the East, which had a long tradition of monarchical rule, lived under some form of kingship patterned on various combinations of Macedonian, Greek and native traditions. Though each of these monarchies worked out particular solutions to their special problems a general pattern of kingship emerged. It was a personal régime based on the mutual ties between the king, his "Friends", that is his closest advisors, chief administrators and his army. Almost all were of Macedonian or Greek extraction. These monarchies relied on a much more elaborate and bureaucratically structured administrative arm necessary for the infinitely larger and politically, socially and ethnically more complex territories than those of the older city-states.

The army remained the key element and warfare remained endemic in the Hellenistic world. Its importance was conditioned by its centrality to the idea of kingship. It was a monarchy created and legitimized by war, and success in war

197

was the monarch's most important characteristic. It was no coincidence that the first assumption of the title of king by various generals struggling over the succession came in the wake of military victories. Success not only guaranteed the continued survival of these states, but also pillage, booty and the acquisition of profitable agricultural land assured the revenues that they required. The wealth needed was on a far vaster scale than earlier, and not the least cost weighing on the new monarchies was that of maintaining military establishments that were immense by earlier standards.

During this time armies increased in size. At the beginning of the period the major battles appear to have been fought by forces about the size of Alexander's, that is about 40,000 foot and 5000 to 6000 cavalry. By the middle of the third century the armies of the Asian powers such as the Seleucids and the Ptolemies in Egypt had grown enormously. For major campaigns by the late third century both sides could put roughly between 70,000 and 80,000 men in the field. At the battle of Raphia the armies of both sides totaled over 140,000 troops. European armies remained smaller, with the Macedonian kingdom typically fielding between 25,000 and 35,000 men. These armies made much greater demands on manpower. The situation was complicated by the fact that almost all of the major successor states except the Seleucids – and they form only a partial exception – used Greek and Macedonian soldiers as the core of their field armies. The preference for such nationalities encouraged immigration and then settlement from those lands. Often troops arrived as mercenaries and then were settled under various schemes by governments anxious to secure a permanent and easily accessible pool of military manpower.

Each major state developed a system of contracts, land grants and other incentives to attract Greek and Macedonian mercenaries (see p. 221). Methods of recruitment varied from the use of recruiters to the contracting of alliances which guaranteed that one of the contracting parties would, in effect, supply mercenaries. Macedonia was a partial exception to these trends and will be discussed below.

In the third century the dominant areas for mercenary recruitment and the largest element in Hellenistic armies was formed by immigrants, especially from northern and central Greece and Crete. By 200 the supply of Greek mercenaries and the proportion in service decreased rapidly, with the hiring of Greek mercenaries from the homeland virtually ceasing. Macedonians also formed an important element at first among colonists. Immigration appears to have dried up because of Macedonia's own military demands; however Macedonian colonists already settled overseas appear to have maintained a steady Macedonian presence and unlike Greek colonists they seem to have sustained a steady reproductive rate.

Other areas filled the gap left. In the early third century Thrace was of importance, providing light-armed or cavalry units. From their entry into the Greek world, beginning with the invasions of 279, the Gauls were recruited into the Macedonian military and into Attalid service in Asia Minor. By the end of the period, at least in the Egypt of the late second and first centuries, Semitic speakers and Iranians seem to have formed an increasing proportion of those in military service. After 217 Egypt had begun to make extensive use of natives who had earlier been excluded from anything beyond police service. The Seleucids also employed native troops. But they were never to become a dominant element in Hellenistic warfare. Macedonia was an exception. The majority of its forces, about two-thirds, were recruited as a national army. The same was true of the Greek leagues like the Achaean and Aetolian.

In their formations and tactics the armies of the Hellenistic period were direct descendants of the army of Philip and Alexander. The order of battle remained the same, with cavalry massed on the wings and linked on the right side of the battle line to the infantry phalanx by élite infantry units bearing titles that differed from kingdom to kingdom. Important roles were also still reserved for light-armed troops on the flanks and in pursuit. These forces kept the complex combinations of different arms that had characterized Alexander's army. For the first three-quarters of a century after Alexander, cavalry often acted as the decisive arm, but because of financial reasons the infantry phalanx came to dominate. The major problem was that the attempt to strengthen the phalanx led to it become increasingly rigid. Its loss of flexibility led to a fossilization that inhibited its ability to meet new adversaries like the Parthians and the Romans successfully.

One clear sign of the increasing complexity of military technique is a change in the position of the commander in battle. Though he continued to participate personally in the battle, his position on the extreme end of the line appears to have allowed the Hellenistic commander to maintain control of his troops after the beginning of an engagement and to continue to direct them during the battle. This was a distinct departure from previous practice. This increasing emphasis on the general's command function is connected with the appearance of the first true reserve formations in the late fourth century. These formations made sense only if a commander could maintain enough disengagement from the actual battle to use them effectively.

In the area of siege warfare technical advances in offense and defense were made, as is evident from the various contemporary manuals. The most notable was the spread of the use of catapults; new styles of fortification were also designed to counter the use of torsion artillery and other technical developments.

The period as a whole was one of warfare on an increased scale and of developing sophistication within the boundaries set by the Macedonian armies of Philip and Alexander. But these trends were accompanied by an increasing rigidity and fossilization that would prove dangerous when enemies with sophisticated and more flexible military systems emerged.

SOME COMMON CAUSES OF WAR

War and kingly virtue

271. The *Suda* s.v. Kingship

This is a summary from an unknown source that emphasizes the practical side of the bases of royal authority and, as the passage illustrates, seems to be grounded in the political situation after Alexander's death. Political thought emphasized the importance of inherited talent and linked it to an élite aristocracy, as was traditional. In the absence of inherited claims after Alexander's death his generals had to rely on titles conferred by military success.

Neither has nature produced the institution of kingship among men, but it is the creation of those who can command armies and administer affairs with expertise. Philip [II] and the successors of Alexander are examples of such men. Kinship in kingship confers no advantage on a natural son, if he has a natural lack of ability, but those who are in no way related have become kings of almost the entire inhabited world.

272. A Decree of Troy in Honor of the Accession of Antiochus I, OGIS 219, Frisch 32

This decree by the Trojan assembly was voted probably in 278 or 277. After the assassination of his father Seleucus I, Antiochus I (281–261) found himself in a very difficult political situation in Syria and Asia Minor. Antiochus tried to solidify his authority by a lightening of burdens which the decree reflects, so that he could turn his attention to the more serious situation in Syria. Military victory created charisma and let the king appear as preserver and benefactor to his Greek subjects. These are the two most common royal titles in this period.

Seleucis was a Seleucid province in northern Syria among whose major cities were the important military centers of Apamea and Laodicaea. The peace referred to is probably that between Antiochus and Antigonus Gonatus in 279 or 278.

When Nymphius son of Diotrephes was *epimenios* and Dionysius son of Hippomedon was *epistrategos*, Demetrius son of Dies proposed the following motion: Since King Antiochus son of King Seleucus, at the beginning of his reign, pursued a wise and glorious policy in re-establishing the peace and old-fashioned prosperity of the cities of Seleucis which were suffering misfortune due to rebels against the king's cause, and in addition he launched expeditions against those who were harming his affairs and regained his ancestral kingdom, so, engaging in a glorious and just undertaking, with his "Friends" and his army, he was avid to come to battle; with divine favor and aid he has restored the ancestral arrangements. Now arriving at those places on this side of the Taurus Mountains, he has with all enthusiasm and zeal restored peace to the cities and has gloriously enhanced his affairs and kingdom, most especially through his personal excellence and with the support of his "Friends" and army.

273. Theocritus, *Idylls* 17.91–105

This was composed in Alexandria, perhaps after 273 in honor of Ptolemy II, and contemporary with the First Syrian War of 274–271. The encomium, praising ancestry, liberality, piety and conjugal harmony, also throws in relief the major virtues of a Hellenistic king. It emphasizes two crucial military duties of the successful king, to protect what he has and to add to his revenues by his military victories.

All of the sea, the earth and the rushing rivers acknowledge Ptolemy;
   Around flows a crowd of cavalry and a crowd of infantry equipped with flashing bronze.
   In wealth he outweighs all other kings; so much wealth flows into his household each day from everywhere. His people go about their tasks in security;
   For no one dares to cross the Nile fertile in monsters,
   No one who comes by land raises the cry of war in foreign villages;
   Nor has any swift ship from the sea, girded for war, surged forward to pillage Egypt's cattle.
   So powerful is the man established on these broad plains, blond Ptolemy who knows how to shake the spear of war and who as a good king guards what he has inherited and himself adds to it.

Kings, ambition and war

274. Plutarch, *Pyrrhus* 12.2–5
The passage refers to the treaty struck by Pyrrhus and the Macedonian general Lysimachus to dismember the Macedonian kingdom of Demetrius Poliorcetes after his loss of control due to his unpopular policies in 288 or 287.

This treaty was advantageous to them for the moment and stopped their war. Soon they recognized that it was not an end of their enmity, but the division of territory was a cause for recrimination and dispute. Their grasping for more could not be limited by sea, mountain or uninhabited wilderness, and the boundaries that separated Europe and Asia did not set limits to their desire. How, if their possessions touched upon and bordered each other's, could they not commit wrongs while remaining in their present territorial limits? They fought constantly and they were naturally disposed to plots and jealousy. For them the designations of war and peace were names that they used like money for their own advantage in a given set of circumstances and had nothing to do with justice. They were better men when they openly confessed that they were at war than when they called their inactivity and laziness in committing wrongful acts as justice and friendship.

The ideal king

275. Ptolemy III Euergetes' Exploits in the Third Syrian War, OGIS 54
Compare this selection with the description of this king's exploits above (no. 273). Ptolemy III's dates are 247–221. The grandiloquent language recalls typical Eastern conquerors. This may in part stem from the inscription's origin as a decree of a corporation of native priests. Arsinoe was both Polemy's sister and consort. The war referred to is the Third Syrian war of 246–241 and

resulted from a personal quarrel with the Seleucid king, Seleucus II. Whatever the extent of Ptolemy's initial conquests, almost all of it was retaken by the Seleucids. The inscription celebrates not only the martial exploits of the king but also his fulfillment of his religious duties. His father was Ptolemy II Philadelphus.

The Great King Ptolemy son of Ptolemy and Queen Arsinoe, Brother and Sister Gods . . . descended from his ancestor Heracles son of Zeus on his father's side and from Dionysus son of Zeus on his maternal side. He succeeded his father as king of Egypt, Libya, Syria, Phoenicia, Cyprus, Lycia, Caria and the Cyclades Islands. He made an expedition against Asia with infantry, cavalry, ships and elephants from the Troglodytes and Ethiopia (which his father and he himself were the first to hunt in these places) and they brought them to Egypt and readied them for use in war. He conquered all of the land on this side of the Euphrates, Cilicia, Pamphylia, Ionia, the Hellespont and Thrace. He brought under his dominion all of the troops in these places and the Indian elephants. Establishing his dominion over all of the rulers in these lands, he crossed the Euphrates and subdued Mesopotamia, Babylonia, Susiana, Persia, Media and the rest of Asia as far as Bactria. He sought out those sacred objects that had been carried away by the Persians from Egypt and brought them back with other treasures to those places in Egypt.

Economic motives for warfare

276. Polybius, *Histories* 4.47.3–6
Rhodes was at this time the preeminent naval state and heavily dependent on overseas trade especially with the Black Sea and in particular with Bithynia. The war soon ended, with a peace concluded by the autumn of the same year that abolished the Byzantine toll at the straits in return for an end of hostilities with Rhodes. The Rhodian chief magistrates were probably generals.

The Rhodians were aroused to anger both because of their own losses and those suffered by their neighbors. At first they sent an embassy along with their allies to the Byzantines to demand that the Byzantines abolish the tolls they levied on shipping. The Byzantines were not disposed to give in on anything, and were persuaded in opposing this demand. They thought that their chief magistrates Hecatodoron and Olympiodorus had spoken correctly to the Rhodian envoys. At that point the Rhodians had left accomplishing nothing. On their return they voted for war against the Byzantines on account of the reasons I just mentioned.

277. Polybius, *Histories* 4.3.1–4
This passage forms part of Polybius' discussion of the origins of the Social War which lasted from 221 to 217 and pitted Macedon and the Achaean League against the Aetolians and their allies. He assigns the responsibility for it to the Aetolian love of plunder. His hostility to the Aetolians is consistent throughout his work and stems from his own Achaean origins – the two leagues were perpetually at loggerheads. It is probably true that pillage played an important

role in the Aetolian economy, as it did in that of various Hellenistic kingdoms, and that its importance was often greater than that of peaceful trade. The Antigonus referred to is Antigonus Doson (227–221) who was followed by his son Philip V.

The Aetolians had long been unhappy with the peace because they had been required by it to live from their own resources when their normal custom had been to live off their neighbors. Further, they required large resources because of their natural covetousness which enslaved them, and they lived a grasping and savage life, considering everyone their enemy and no one their friend. While Antigonus lived they kept the peace in fear of the Macedonians. When he died and left his son Philip who was still a child, they changed their attitude and despising Macedon they sought incitements to and pretexts for throwing the Peloponnese into confusion, led on in their depredations by their ingrained habit of pillaging that territory and considering themselves to be a match for the Achaeans in war.

HELLENISTIC ARMIES

All Hellenistic armies maintained the basic order bequeathed to them by Alexander. Their core was formed by the ordinary troops of the infantry phalanx linked to other formations. On the right they were linked to a unit of élite phalanx infantry equivalent to guards units called by various titles connected with the characteristics of their shields. At various times they are known as either the hypaspists, silver shields or bronze shields. One subunit consisted of the royal bodyguard, the Agema, a title also used in Alexander's army late in his reign. That élite formation linked the infantry to the élite Companion cavalry units, including the royal horse guard, on the right where the king was often stationed. The other wing was also formed of cavalry, with light-armed infantry and horse also posted on the flanks or to the front as flank guards and to provide for an elastic offensive and defense. The close imitation of Alexander's model is clear. The increasing use of foreign mercenaries must have made the appearance of these armies far more diverse than earlier formations. One new development was the use of true reserve troops behind the lines.

There was little change in tactics in the three centuries after Alexander. For about a century the basic goal of the commander was to create a gap in the enemy army, as at Paraetacene, or to strip the infantry of its cavalry support by driving it off. The cost of training and maintaining cavalry gradually led to the growing importance of the infantry phalanx. Later battles were often slogging matches between phalanxes, as at Sellasia in 222 or Raphia in 217 (see no. 297). A feature retained from the Classical period and transmitted through Alexander was the notion of an offensive and defensive wing. The destruction of Demetrius' offensive cavalry wing at the battle of Gaza in 312, despite a shield of light-armed troops, ended his chances of success.

The general characteristics of large set-piece battles in the Hellenistic period are remarkably stable. The armies were homogeneous in equipment and training if not in ethnic composition. As in siege warfare, there was some technological experiment, especially with the use of elephants, but the older arms remain decisive.

The infantry phalanx

Under Alexander the phalanx had remained relatively flexible, but with the decrease in the importance of other arms its frontal shock became the decisive factor by the third century on Hellenistic battlefields. There were attempts to counter this excessive rigidity and inability of the phalanx by interposing different types of troops, as Pyrrhus did in Italy (see below), but the trend was to tighten formations and to lengthen the sarissa. Its size had stabilized at twenty-one feet by the late third century. Remarkably little is known about the elements of the phalanx. There is some inscriptional and literary evidence but the majority of information comes from later technical manuals which betray a fascination with geometric regularity that casts doubt on their accuracy. Tactical maneuvers are obscure except for certain basic evolutions such as the *synaspismos* or closing up to increase the phalanx's density of spear points. The usual depth of sixteen men remained normal.

278. Polybius, *Histories* 18.28.1–32.5
This passage occurs in the context of the great Macedonian defeat by the Romans at Cynoscephalae in 198. There is no evidence, as was once thought, for various ranks having sarissas of different lengths. The three feet between the men was measured from the right shoulder of one infantryman to the right shoulder of the soldier to his right. The battle of Magnesia (no. 283) offers an excellent illustration of the phalanx's inability to maneuver effectively.

In my sixth book I made a promise that on a suitable occasion I would compare Roman and Macedonian equipment and the formation of each and the advantages and disadvantages that each style entails. . . . I shall now make an attempt to fulfill that promise. It is easy to see that when the phalanx is able to manifest its particular characteristics nothing can withstand its frontal attack or charge. When it is closed up in battle formation each man occupies a space of three feet wide and the length of a sarissa is according to its earlier design sixteen feet long, but in current use it is twenty-one feet. Since one must subtract the distance between the wielder's hands and the length of the counterweight behind to the projecting part, it is evident that the sarissa must project fifteen feet in front of the body of each hoplite when he holds it in both hands as he charges the enemy. The result of this is that the sarissas of the second, third, and fourth rank extend farther than those of the fifth rank. The sarissas of the latter extend three feet in front of the men in the front rank whenever the phalanx is properly closed up. . . . [Then] it is clear that five sarissas extend in front of each man in the front rank, each separated by a distance of three feet from the other.

From this information one can easily conjecture the form of the assault of the whole phalanx with its projecting weapons, both as to its appearance and its force when it is sixteen men deep. Those troops behind the fifth row are unable to bring their weapons to bear in the attack. Given this, each does not level his sarissa man against man, but holds it slantwise over the shoulders of the men in front of him and provides shelter for the formation by keeping off, through the density of their sarissas, missiles that pass over the front ranks and might fall on those in the rear. Also by the weight of their bodies they exert pressure on the men to their front and add force to the assault, further because of the denseness of the formation those in front cannot turn about.

What is the reason then for the success of the Romans and the defeat of those armies that use the phalanx formation? In war both the times and places for action are unlimited, but the phalanx is suitable as far as time and place are concerned in only one way. . . . It is generally acknowledged that the phalanx needs level and bare ground without obstacles such as ditches, ravines, depressions, embankments and river beds. All of these obstacles can hamper and break up the phalanx. Given this, one can hardly find within an area of twenty stades or even more places without such hindrances, as all would admit. And if our enemies refuse to encounter us, but go around and sack the land and cities of our allies, how can such a formation help us? Remaining in a place where it can be effective, it cannot help its allies or even preserve itself, since the flow of supplies is easily hindered by the enemy while they control the open country. But if the phalanx leaves favorable ground to better the situation, it will be easily defeated by the enemy. Even in those cases where the phalanx descends to favorable ground, if the whole of it is not used when it can be and the favorable moment is not seized, it is easy to see from what the Romans do what will happen if even a small portion of the phalanx is held back at the decisive moment from the charge. This is not a matter for argument but can easily be proved by past events. The Romans do not extend their line equally to face the attacking phalanx frontally, but retain some men in reserve while the rest are thrown into battle. If the phalangites should drive back those troops that they are attacking, they are in turn repulsed by the reserve and their formation broken up. In attack or defense the phalanx leaves behind parts of its own army and when this happens the spaces provide an opportunity for the enemy's reserve, to not move against the front of the phalanx but to outflank it and attack its sides and back.

279. Plutarch, *Flamininus* 8.2–4

This passage from Plutarch vividly illustrates that generalized picture of the phalanx's strengths and weaknesses given in the previous selection. The battle took place on the hills of Cynoscephalae in Thessaly in the spring of 197 against the Romans under the proconsul Titus Flamininus. The engagement initially developed piecemeal and, as Polybius makes clear, in an area especially unfavorable to the maneuvers of the phalanx and not in accordance with Philip V's plans.

Philip prevailed on his right wing; descending from high ground, he threw his entire phalanx at the Romans who were unable to withstand the weight of the locked shields and the sharpness of the projecting sarissa points. But the king's left was dispersed among the hills and was out of alignment. Titus, despairing of his defeated wing, quickly rode to his other and attacked the Macedonians who were prevented by irregularity and roughness of the ground from forming up their phalanx and maintaining its proper depth, which is the strength of their formation. In addition, they suffered in individual combat because of the weight of their arms and their difficulty in handling them. For the phalanx is like an invincible animal in its strength as long as it maintains it unity and sustains its single locked-shield formation. But once this unity is lost, each phalangite loses his individual strength both because of the way he is armed and on account of the fact that he derives his strength from the mutual support of the parts of his formation in an effective whole and not because of individual ability. The right wing of the Macedonians was routed and some of the Roman forces pursued the fugitives while others moved around the flanks of those who were still fighting and fell upon them, cutting them down. This action quickly resulted in the victorious Macedonian wing facing about, dropping its arms and turning to flight.

280. Polybius, *Histories* 18.28.10

This variation in the phalanx formation was used against the Romans at the battle of Ausculum in 279. Other similar expedients are attested, though none gained wide currency.

Indeed Pyrrhus used not only Italian arms but also Italian units. He placed alternately maniples and the units of the phalanx in his battles with the Romans.

Cavalry

Given the expense and difficulty of maintaining a cavalry force, the ratio between cavalry and infantry constantly decreased in the course of the period in the major Hellenistic armies. It fell from about one to five after Alexander to about one to eight by the end of the third century. The highest figure we possess is a combined force of about 21,000 cavalry out of a total of all armed forces of 155,000 at Ipsus in 301.

Heavy cavalry gradually changed its role from that of deciding the battle to one in which its main task by the later Hellenistic period, as at Raphia, was to defeat the opposing cavalry and ensure that the infantry could advance unmolested.

Cavalry still had the same uses as it had in the Classical period. It still was unable to face unbroken heavy infantry and would only be able to do so after the technological advances that resulted in the stirrup and an appropriate saddle as well as larger horses. Light cavalry was also used in this period as a flank guard or screen and to provide an elastic defense, an advance owed to Alexander and visible already at Gaugamela (see no. 270).

281. Polybius, *Histories* 12.18.2–3 = Callisthenes FGrH 124 F35

We know very little about Hellenistic cavalry formations. The largest unit seems typically to have been the hipparchy, as it was in the later army of Alexander, and below that came the *ila*. The smallest unit was the *oulamos*. If we accept Polybius' figures it may be that an *ila* contained 128 men. These calculations are part of Polybius' criticism of an earlier historian's account of the battle of the Issus.

There were thirty thousand cavalry, as Callisthenes himself says, and thirty thousand mercenaries. It is easy to figure out how much space is required to contain them; for the majority of cavalry are arrayed eight deep for real effectiveness and between each *ila* there needs to be a space equal to the frontage of the troop to allow them to wheel and to easily face about.

282. Polybius *Histories* 3.117.4–5

Polybius is referring to the cavalry flank and rear attacks on the Roman force that completed the encirclement of that force and assured its defeat. It is the vulnerability of isolated heavy infantry that is uppermost in the historian's mind (see no. 278).

All the rest [of the Romans], about seventy thousand, died bravely. At this battle [Cannae] and in earlier actions their cavalry was crucial to the Carthaginians. This made it clear to posterity that it is better to give battle with half as many infantry as the enemy but to have an overwhelming superiority in cavalry, than to go into battle evenly matched in all respects.

Light-armed troops

The role of the light-armed infantry remained unchanged. They could be especially effective in reconnaissance and patrol. In major battles they were rarely the decisive force, but were effective in conjunction with heavy infantry and cavalry.

Among the Greeks the Aetolians had a reputation as effective light-armed javelin troops. Cretans and Rhodians maintained their near monopoly in specialist units of archers and slingers. But the majority of these troops were provided in most of the major Hellenistic armies by non-Greek peoples. The Thracians remained important as peltasts and cavalry, as they had in the Classical period. Their Illyrian neighbors also had a central role in this branch of warfare. Mysians from Asia Minor provided light troops as well as cavalry. For the most part the non-Greek, ethnic composition of an army varied depending on the manpower resources that the major powers had available.

283. Livy, 35.29.1–30.8

In 206 Nabis became regent at Sparta. Sparta and Achaea were separated by traditional hatreds that stemmed from continued attempts by the Achaean League to incorporate Sparta. Nabis resisted successfully until politics forced him to obstruct the Romans to some extent. The Aetolian League was displeased with the Romans and, in anticipation of Antiochus III's invasion, canvassed Nabis among others to join in a revolt against Rome. The Spartan leader, who had lost territory because of Rome, took up the opportunity and began by starting rebellions in various seaboard towns in Laconia. He settled down to besiege Gytheum in which an Achaean garrison was trapped. Under Philopoemen the Achaeans defeated Nabis near Mt Barbosthenes and retook Gytheum and other coastal towns. Tarentine cavalry were light cavalry who fought with javelins and had two horses. Presumably they originated at the Greek colony of Tarentum in southern Italy. This passage is an excellent illustration of the continued use of light-armed troops in pursuit after the defeat of the enemy in battle, especially over broken ground.

At dawn the light-armed Cretans and the Tarentine horse began the battle on the river banks. The Cretan Telemnestus commanded his countrymen and Lycortas from Megalopolis led the cavalry. The enemy also used Cretan and Tarentine auxiliaries as protection for their water carriers. For a considerable time the battle was in doubt since both sides were equipped in the same way and had the same type of troops, but as the fight progressed Nabis' auxiliaries began to prevail by reason of their superiority in numbers. Philopoemen had instructed his auxiliary commanders to put up a reasonably strong resistance and then flee and draw the enemy on into ambush. The Spartans pursued in a dispersed fashion through the defile and many were wounded or killed before they saw their enemy hidden in ambush. The heavy-armed infantry had been resting in a formation that extended the width of the valley and easily received their men in the gaps in their formation. They then rose up fresh, untouched and in order and fell upon an enemy disordered, dispersed and also worn out by their exertions and wounds. The victory was not in doubt. . . . Philopoemen ordered the auxiliaries to press and pursue the enemy as much as they could, moreover flight would not be easy even for their cavalry. He himself led his heavy infantry by a more open route to the Eurotas River. He encamped there at sunset and awaited the light-armed troops whom he had left to pursue the enemy.

Elephants

From the death of Alexander until *c.* 160, elephants played a subsidiary but important role in Western warfare. Both Indian and African elephants were employed and the ancients regularly state that African elephants were smaller than their Indian counterparts and that they were afraid to face them. In fact the Ptolemies, the chief source of African elephants, used the forest elephant, the smaller of the two African species (the other is the bush), which are smaller than the Indian.

The Ptolemies monopolized the supply of African elephants for warfare as the Seleucids did the supply of Indian elephants. The number of elephants present at various major battles declined markedly in the course of the third century. Elephants are difficult to breed in captivity and over-hunting was certainly a factor in the extinction of the African elephants. The numbers of Indian elephants also declined severely but that must, in part, be due to the loss of large areas like Bactria from which the Seleucids had drawn their supply.

In war the elephant's major function was to terrify the enemy and to wreak as much destruction as was possible. They were used in three basic ways in battle: as a screen against cavalry (see no. 285 below), to attack infantry and to break into towns or fortifications under siege. After 300 many of the larger elephants carried towers with two to four men armed with missile weapons. They were armored and on occasion even the tips of their trunks were protected.

We know little of their organization, but if Asclepiodotus is accurate they were organized in *ilai* of perhaps eight animals with other units forming multiples of two under a single overall commander of the elephant corps. Each animal had a mahout and it may have been Indian practice that lay behind the methods followed in the West.

In most of these roles the elephant was not conspicuously successful. It was too vulnerable to missile weapons and traps to be of great use in siege warfare. Well-trained infantry could successfully deal with them and their tendency to stampede when panicked could wreak as much havoc among their friends as among their foes. They were in the end reduced to a ceremonial role that was retained under the Romans.

284. Asclepiodotus, *Tactics* 7.9

This is the only extant passage that deals with the organization of elephant units. It is difficult to know how strongly mathematical symmetry has effected accuracy. We do know the names of several elephant commanders, such as Philip who was in charge of Antiochus III's elephants at Raphia and Magnesia.

Although we rarely find use for chariots and elephants . . . As far as elephants are concerned, the commander of a single animal is an animal-commander, the commander of a unit of two is called a two-animal commander and his command an animal unit. A commander of a four-animal unit is a senior animal commander and his unit is like named. A leader of a formation of eight is an *ilarch* and of sixteen an elephant leader. A thirty-two animal unit is commanded by a wing commander and a sixty-four animal formation by a phalanx leader.

Elephants and cavalry: the battle of Ipsus

This battle, fought in the summer of 301 in Phrygia, ended the possibility that Alexander's empire would be united once again under a single dynasty, the Antigonids. The details of the battle are sketchy at best, but elephants seem to have played a decisive role. The sources claim the presence of perhaps a total on both sides of five hundred elephants, with the opponents of Demetrius and his father Antigonus enjoying a vast advantage in numbers. The crucial turning-point in the battle was the use by Seleucus of his elephants to cut off the victorious cavalry of Demetrius and so expose the vulnerable flank of the phalanx. But horses, like men, could be trained to face them.

285. Plutarch, *Demetrius* 29.4–5

When battle had been joined, Demetrius with the largest and best part of the cavalry swooped down on Antiochus, the son of Seleucus, and fought brilliantly until he routed the enemy, but he was violent in pursuit and acted with an enthusiasm out of keeping with the situation and so spoiled his victory. He was unable to turn round again and rejoin the infantry, since the enemy's elephants stood between. Then Seleucus and his staff, although they saw that the other side's infantry was denuded of its cavalry, did not attack but routed them by creating the fear of a direct attack and encircled them, allowing the infantry to change sides.

Attacking walls and camps: Polyperchon at Megalopolis

286. Diodorus Siculus, 18.71.2–6

Most of the attempts by Greek commanders to use elephants this way ended in failure, as did the effort by the Carthaginians to force the Roman trenches at Panormus in Sicily in 262 during the First Punic War. Polyperchon was one of the older generation of Alexander's commanders who was designated as royal regent in 319 on the death of the former regent Antipater. This immediately ignited a coalition of other would-be successors in Asia and Europe. In Europe his most important opponent was Antipater's son Cassander, who had driven him out of central Greece by 317. He then fell back upon his base in the Peloponnese where Megalopolis declared for his enemy.

Since the Megalopolitans alone preserved their friendship with Cassander Polyperchon decided to besiege their city. The account in Diodorus underlines the vulnerability of elephants and the failure to devise any effective armor for them. It makes clear why consistent failure attended their use in siege warfare.

The next day Polyperchon cleared the breach and made it passable for the elephants with the plan to use their strength to capture the city. The Megalopolitans under Damis, who had served with Alexander in Asia and was experienced in the nature and ways of elephants, achieved complete success against them. Damis countered the strength of the animals with his native intelligence and rendered their immense bodies useless. First he studded a great many large doors with sharp nails and laid these in shallow trenches, and he covered over the points of these devices while leaving an open path through them to the city. He stationed no troops in front of them but on the wings he placed a mass of javelin-men, archers and catapults.

After Polyperchon had cleared the whole of the breach and was in the process of making an attack with countless elephants, a unexpected thing happened to the elephants. Since there was no resistance to their front, the Indian mahouts forced the elephants to attack straight into the city. Charging forward with their usual force they fell upon the studded doors; their feet wounded by the nails and pierced by their own weight, they could not go forward or turn round and retreat because of their pain when they moved. While this was going on their mahouts were killed or lost what control they had amid the shower of missiles raining on them from both flanks. The elephants as a result of the hail of missiles and the special nature of the pain caused by the wounds inflicted by the nails turned back through the troops of their own side and trampled many of them. Finally, the elephant with the greatest courage and which was most formidable collapsed. Of those left the majority were rendered useless, while others brought death to their own side.

Weapons

During the Hellenistic period there were few major developments in armor or offensive weapons. The major innovations in infantry weaponry and armor had been made under Philip and Alexander (see pp. 169ff.). The stability of heavy infantry tactics more or less dictated that its equipment remain unchanged. Both élite and regular units of the phalanx retained the sarissa as their principal offensive weapon. It is with this weapon that some experimentation is visible (see p. 170).

Fourth-century trends remained in force; body armor, except for officers and front-rank troops, had been abandoned, though a metallic helmet was retained. The principal protection for the phalangite besides his sarissa remained the small two-foot shield suspended by a thong from the shoulder. Despite the limitations of the equipment its success is attested by the spread of this style of fighting and its accompanying weaponry within Greece itself. One noticeable difference, though not of striking importance, was the introduction of a long oval shield, the *thureos*. It was used by Greeks in the northern Peloponnese, Gauls and various types of light infantry. It may have been of Italian origin and was employed by mercenaries in the East. Light-armed troops fought with the same variety of equipment as they had earlier.

Cavalry equipment developed more extensively. Regular heavy cavalry adopted a shield in the course of the third century that appears to have been oval (cf. p. 173 above), along with metal helmets and breastplates. The main offensive weapon remained the shorter cavalry sarissa. Lighter armed cavalry often used the oval shield and a variety of lances and javelins.

One innovation was the cataphract. His equipment was of central Asian origin mediated through Iran. He was protected by a heavy coat of mail that reached to the thigh, and by the first century he carried a shield. His horse was often armored with a metal breastplate and might be clothed in mail. The main offensive weapon was a long lance but the bow and arrow were often carried as well. Mobility would seem to have been a problem and we have evidence that it was (see no. 278). The Seleucids, who had direct experience of them, employed many of these troops.

There was also development in siege warfare. It is visible in the greater size of existing weapons and designs for repeating catapults and other novelties, though it is unclear if any of these weapons were actually used in combat.

The spread of the Macedonian phalanx

The major Greek states that had retained hoplite equipment abandoned it for weaponry on the Macedonian pattern, though some of the more backward areas were slow to do so.

287. Plutarch, *Philopoemen* 9.1–5

This reform was carried after Philopoemen was elected general of the Achaean League in 209/208, and appears to have been part of an attempt to make Achaea an independent military power able to stand up to Sparta, which had carried out the same reform earlier.

Philopoemen started by changing the tactical formations and equipment of the Achaean troops which were deficient. . . . Their formation and disposition in battle was not the customary one and they formed a phalanx that did not have great force in attack nor a method for forming in close order like the Macedonians, and so they were easily over-whelmed in battle and dispersed. Philopoemen made this clear to them and persuaded them take up the Macedonian shield and sarissa instead of the rectangular shield and the spear, also to arm themselves with helmet, breastplate and greaves and to fight firmly from a fixed position instead of on the run like peltasts.

The cataphract

288. Justin, *Epitome* 41.2.7–10

Seleucid control in the eastern portion of its empire had never been strong and large sections of it had been lost by the last third of the third century. By mid-century the nomadic Parthians invaded and conquered the provinces of Hyrcania and Parthia. By the early 230s they had established a feudal kingdom that was to become one of the great powers of the East for the next five hundred years. The Eastern origin of this form of cavalry is clear. The reference to the fight in flight is to the famous "Parthian shot" back over the rear of the horse.

[The Parthians] are ignorant of close fighting or sieges. They fight on horseback and either charge the enemy or, while in flight, they fight from behind. Indeed they often pretend to flee to expose their enemy to attack because of his incautious pursuit. They use the drum and not the horn to send signals on the battlefield. They cannot fight for long periods, indeed, if their endurance matched the violence of their onslaught, they would be irresistible. Often in the heat of battle they retreat and return from their flight soon after the battle's end, so that at the point when you think yourself certainly victorious then you must undergo the real contest. Their armor consists of metal scales for their horses and for themselves and they cover the entire body of the rider and his horse.

Horse archers: Carrhae

Though popular in the East as the main weapon of offense, the horse archer had never been a central weapon in the West. He did appear occasionally, however, and in the fifth and fourth centuries the Athenians maintained a small force of horse archers (see no. 81). It may have been influences from the steppes that led the Parthians to concentrate on horse archers and light cavalry. The problem with horse archers was assuring a supply of arrows. At the battle of Carrhae, Crassus faced an enemy commander who was commanding his own private army of retainers. The total Parthian force was perhaps ten thousand. Their army consisted of a mixture of heavy lancers and horse archers. It was the horse archers who were the most effective, as the following account makes clear. The Parthian bow far outranged that of the Romans. The Roman general had about 32,000 troops including 28,000 legionaries and 4000 cavalry. On approaching the Parthians Crassus formed his men into a hollow square. Unable to catch the Parthians, and densely packed, the Romans suffered without being able to strike back effectively. The decisive element in the Parthian victory was an innovation by the Parthian general, which is not heard of again, of increasing the supply of arrows by having reserve supplies carried along by a corps of a thousand camels.

The Romans, after a few days of being exposed to constant pressure and the treacherous capture of their commander, finally disintegrated and the survivors were taken into captivity.

289. Plutarch, *Crassus* 24.4

The Parthians stood off from the Romans and began to discharge their arrows at them from every direction, but they did not aim for accuracy since the Roman formation was so continuous and dense that it was impossible to miss. The impact of the arrows was tremendous since their bows were large and powerful and the stiffness of the bow in drawing sent the missiles with great force. At that point the Roman situation became grave, for if they remained in formation they suffered wounds, and if they attempted to advance they still were unable to accomplish anything, although they continued to suffer. For the Parthians would flee while continuing to shoot at them and they are second in this style of fighting only to the Scythians. It is the wisest of practices for it allows you to defend yourself by fighting and removes the disgrace of flight.

For a while the Romans expected the Parthians to break off the battle after they expended their arrows, or to come to close quarters, and they gained confidence from these thoughts. But then they realized that there were many camels arrayed beside the enemy, carrying full loads of arrows from which those who had shot replenished their supply.

Major battles

Paraetacene

This battle is one of the most interesting and accurately described of all Hellenistic battles. The extant accounts ultimately derive from a good contemporary source. Of further importance is that the battle presents two of the best of the generals among Alexander's successors, each of them talented and having at his disposal the various weapons and techniques that Alexander had bequeathed before such techniques had become stereotyped and fossilized.

The battle was the result of the complicated maneuverings among Alexander's successors after his death as they jockeyed for power. Antigonus and Eumenes, both holding the overall commands for their respective sides as "general of Asia," had been locked in intermittent struggle in which Antigonus had twice defeated Eumenes and which finally ended in Eumenes' capture and death in 316. In 317 Antigonus advanced on Eumenes who withdrew behind the barrier of the Tigris to collect troops and elephants to meet him. This encounter took place in the autumn of 317 at Paraetacene in Susiana in southwestern Iran near modern Isfahan. Though it ended in a draw the battle is an excellent illustration of large-scale Hellenistic encounters on the field.

The battle orders on both sides were essentially those of Alexander, and the cavalry was still perceived as the decisive arm. One discernible difference from Alexander's time is the presence among Eumenes' troops of the first real reserve which in this case consisted of three hundred élite horse. Elephants were used in the battle, arrayed in front of the infantry with light-armed troops in the gaps between them. The battle was fought out as separate actions on the wings. Elite units decided the result. Flank guards stationed at an angle were in evidence. The draw resulted from the last recorded Hellenistic cavalry charge into a gap in a major action. Antigonus and his cavalry fighting against the enemy cavalry on the phalanx's left drove it off and exposed the phalanx's left wing. It was this encounter that led to the eventual withdrawal of Eumenes' army. It was Hellenistic generalship at its best.

290. Diodorus Siculus, 19.27.1–31.5

Antiochus had (including the reinforcements brought by Pithon and Seleucus) more than 28,000 infantry, 8500 cavalry and 65 elephants. The commanders on either side used different formations; they were also competing in displaying their superiority in tactical skill to each other. On his left Eumenes placed Eudaemon who had brought the elephants back from India and led a squadron of 150 horse. Eumenes placed as an advance guard for them two *ilai* of lancers totaling fifty men. He stationed them next to the rise in the hill. Right beside them he stationed the general Stasander with his own cavalry force of 950. Then he placed Amphimachus the satrap of Mesopotamia with 600 horse and then 600 more from Arachosia who had been under Sibyrtius, but now after his flight were commanded by Cephalon. Right after them, he stationed the 500 from Paropanisadae and an equal number of Thracians from the colonies in the upper satrapies. In front were the forty-five elephants placed at an angle, and in the gaps between them Eumenes stationed a sufficient number of archers and slingers. Having strengthened his left wing he placed the phalanx next to it. The mercenaries occupied the extreme left of phalanx, more than 6000 in total, then came 5000 men of all ethnic groups armed in the Macedonian fashion. Then he stationed his Macedonian Silver Shields, who numbered more than 3000 and who had never lost a battle and were much feared by the enemy for their prowess. Finally he arrayed his hypaspists, who numbered more than 3000. Both of these units were under the command of Antigenes and Teutamus. In front of the phalanx he positioned forty elephants and filled up the intervals between them with light-armed men. On the right wing he located his cavalry. Bordering the phalanx were 800 Carmanians under their satrap Tlepolemus, then came the 900 so-called Companions and the Agema of Peucestes and Antigenes, 300 horse in a single *ila*. On the extreme right came his own guards squadron, also with 300 troopers and an advance guard for them of two *ilai* of Eumenes' slaves, each unit with fifty horse and as a flank guard four *ilai* with 200 select cavalry. As a separate formation he stationed 300 cavalry picked from all the units for their speed and strength behind his guards. In front of the whole of his right he placed forty elephants. His entire force totaled 35,000 foot, 6000 cavalry and 114 elephants.

After Antigonus had looked down upon the battle dispositions of the enemy, he formed up his own army in a manner suitable to countering the enemy's arrangements. He saw that the enemy's right wing had been strengthened by elephants and the most effective cavalry and so he arrayed against them his light horse who were arranged in open order and were to avoid close combat. Rather, they were to fight by wheeling and in this way render that part of the enemy force in which Eumenes placed his greatest faith useless. Antigonus also placed on this wing horse archers and lancers from Media and Parthia. These totaled 1000 and were well adapted to encounters of maneuver. Right after them he placed 2200 Tarentines, selected for their skill in ambush and their loyalty to him. Then 1000 cavalry from Phrygia and Lydia, 1500 under Pithon and 400 lancers with Lysander. On his extreme left he placed the so-called two-horse men and the 800 cavalry from the upper colonies. This completed the troops on the left, who were all under the command of Pithon.

The first of the infantry were the mercenaries, more than 6000 in number. Then came the 3000 Lycians and Pamphylians. After these more than 8000 troops of all nationalities, armed like Macedonians, and on the extreme right of his phalanx he placed approximately 8000 Macedonians who had been given to him by Antipater when he had been appointed as regent for the kingdom. On the right wing, the first of the cavalry was a mixed group of 500 mercenaries, then there were 1000 Thracians. After them came 500 allies, then the so-called Companions, about 1000 in total, with his son Demetrius in command, who then was for the first time about to go into battle along with his father. On the extreme right of this wing was the Agema of 300 cavalry, commanded by Antigonus himself, with whom he would share the impending danger. As an advance guard Antigonus placed three *ilai* of his own slaves and parallel to them an equal number of units reinforced by a hundred Tarentines. In front of the whole line he placed the thirty strongest of his elephants at an angle and filled up the gaps between them with élite light-armed units. The majority of the remainder of the animals were placed in front of the phalanx and a few were stationed with the horse on his left. With his army arrayed this way he came down against his enemy, advancing at the oblique with his right, the wing he most trusted, thrown forward. The left was held back since he had decided to avoid battle with one and seek it out with the other.

When the armies were close to each other and the battle signals had been given, each side sounded its battle cry alternately with the other many times and the trumpeters blew the signal for battle. First came the cavalry of Pithon, which lacked firmness and had no advance guard worthy of name but were superior to those arrayed against them in numbers and maneuverability, and they attempted to use their advantages. They thought it unsafe to confront the enemy's elephants directly, but rode around their flanks and bombarded their sides with a thick rain of missiles and so began to wound them. They were untouched on account of their speed but severely injured the animals who because of their massiveness were not able to pursue or retreat when there was an opportunity. Eumenes, observing the sufferings of the wing, summoned Eudemus who commanded the light horse on the left of his cavalry; leading out his whole formation on that wing he attacked his opponents with his light-armed infantry and light cavalry. The elephants followed in his wake and Eumenes easily routed Pithon's men and pursued them up to the high ground. While this was happening the infantry on both sides had been engaged and finally, after many on both sides had fallen, Eumenes' men prevailed because of the excellence of the Silver Shields. Though this formation was composed of men now advanced in age, because of their experience they were superior in daring and skill so that no one could stand up to them face-to-face. Though there were only three thousand, they were the offensive edge of the army.

Although Antigonus saw that his left had been routed and his whole phalanx had been thrown into confusion, he paid no attention to those who counseled flight to the hills to collect survivors of the flight and to preserve the wing he was stationed on. Rather he cleverly took advantage of an opportunity unexpectedly offered to him and in this way saved his fleeing men and gained the victory. The Silver Shields of Eumenes and his other infantry, as soon as they had put to flight the troops opposed to them, had pursued them as far as the near high ground. However, a gap had opened in their formation and Antigonus rode through the gap with a detachment of his cavalry and fell upon the flank of the troops with Eumenes on his left. He routed his opponents quickly because of their surprise and killed many of them. He then sent out his lightest horse to gather his routed forces and formed them up into a battle line again along the high ground. The reason for this was that when Eumenes and his officers learned of the rout of their forces they called back by trumpet those of their troops engaged in pursuit with the intention of coming to the aid of those with Eudamus.

Although darkness was coming on both sides rallied their fleeing troops and put them in battle order again, such was the desire for victory not only of the commanders but also of the common soldiers. The night was clear and there was a full moon and since the armies were forming up parallel to each other and were separated by only about a quarter mile, the noise of their weapons and the snorting of the horses seemed to be close to everyone. When they were about thirty stades from the fallen and forming from column into line the midnight hour overtook them. Both sides were suffering from the difficulty of the march and the effects of the battle and also from hunger. All of this compelled them to break off battle and to encamp. Eumenes wanted to undertake a march back to the dead and by gaining control of them to make his claim to victory indisputable. His soldiers did not agree, and shouting that they wanted to return to their baggage, which was far off, they compelled him to yield since he was incapable of harshly punishing the soldiers – many were in contention with him for command and he did not see this as an opportune time to punish disobedience. Antigonus had the opposite situation: his control of his men was firm and without the need to pander to them. He made his men encamp by the bodies and so by becoming master of the disposal of the bodies he claimed the victory, making it clear that he who gains control of the bodies of the fallen is the master of the field. In the battle the casualties were for Antigonus 3700 and 54 horse killed: the wounded numbered more than 4000. Eumenes suffered the death of 5400 foot and a very few cavalry with more than 900 wounded.

The battle of Magnesia

By the fall of 190 the Roman army had crossed over into Asia Minor to confront Antiochus III, the Seleucid king who had assembled an army of about seventy thousand men. After the failure of further negotiations and in the face of an unacceptable Roman ultimatum he was forced to fight. The crucial battle took place at Magnesia, near Mount Sipylus in central western Asia Minor, in mid-December. The Romans had about 30,000 troops including 2,800 cavalry. Among their most important allies was Eumenes II of Pergamum who stood to benefit greatly from Antiochus' defeat. His troops were stationed on the right of the Roman line where the Romans feared they would be outflanked. It was his attack that exposed the left flank of the left wing of the phalanx while it was broken frontally by the Romans. While this was happening the Roman left was being forced back by Antiochus and his cavalry. It is a perfect illustration of the difficulties of the phalanx once its flanks were exposed, as outlined by Polybius above (see no. 278). For the mail-clad horsemen or cataphracts, see no. 288.

291. Appian, *The Syrian Wars* 33–35

The day [of the battle] was hazy and gloomy, so that visibility was obscured and the fall of their missiles were rather ineffective, as is usual in humid and gloomy air. When Eumenes saw this, he disregarded the other forces posted opposite to him, but was especially fearful of the onrush of the chariots arrayed opposite. He collected all of his slingers, javelin-men and other light-armed troops and ordered them to run around the chariot horses and to bombard the horses rather than the drivers. Since if a horse pulling a chariot is wounded, the chariot is put out of action and the majority of the rest of the line is thrown into disorder since they fear the scythes of their own chariots. That is exactly what happened. The horses were wounded and charged their own side. The camels were the first to sense the disorder since they were arrayed next to the chariots, and after them the mail-clad cavalry who because of the weight of the armor could not easily avoid the scythed chariots. There was tremendous noise and confusion of every description starting from these troops and then proceeding to the whole of the battle-field. It was fed by suspicion more than fact. . . .

When Eumenes saw that his first maneuver had been successful and that the battle area had been cleared of the camels and the chariots, he sent his own cavalry together with the Italian and Roman horse in line next to them against the Galatians, Cappadocians and the other mercenaries opposite him, cheering loudly and calling out that they were charging men without experience of battle and deprived of their advance supports. His men believed him and the weight of their charge routed the enemy and also those cavalry next to them and the mailed cavalry who had already been thrown into confusion by the chariots. The weight of their equipment was such that they could not flee or wheel quickly and they were caught and cut down. This was the course of events on the left of the Macedonian phalanx.

The Macedonian phalanx, as it was flanked by horse on both wings, was drawn up in close order in a rectangular formation. But when it was denuded of its cavalry on both wings it opened and received inside itself its light-armed troops and then closed up again. Domitius easily encircled the dense rectangle with his cavalry and light-armed troops and since the phalanx was not able to charge nor deploy its very dense formation it suffered terribly.

Mercenaries

All of the major and many of the minor Hellenistic states, except for some of the Greek leagues, depended heavily – at least, initially – on mercenary troops. Until quite late in the period most troops were not drawn from the native populations. Natives, if used at all, were relegated to police functions. This was especially true at the upper reaches of the officer corps, which remained Greek or Macedonian.

Mercenary pay varied greatly. Generally it included food plus money in wages, the proportion varying by time and place. It appears that real wages declined in this period and that the life of a mercenary became less attractive. They were well paid in the third century, but less so in the second. Contracts usually were for nine or ten months and arrears were frequent. Their pay and supplies were a heavy drain on the treasuries of Hellenistic states.

The mercenary tended to retain his group identification and develop institutions that were congenial to his occupational and social group. Occasional attempts were made to integrate him into the life of Greek cities with which he was involved. Smyrna about 230 granted citizenship to soldiers at nearby Magnesia near Mt Sipylus. But in general mercenaries developed their own social and religious groups, with the local gymnasium association serving as an especially important center in Egypt.

At best mercenaries remained an uncertain quantity. Their availability might be insufficient or their loyalty might be undermined by more lucrative offers. Integrating them into one's forces without prior training might be a problem. This problem may have become worse as the supply of Greeks and Macedonians dried up and other groups replaced them. Ethnic prejudice may also have played its part. It may be that the increasing number of non-Greek mercenaries and the need to acculturate and train them may have accelerated the trend to replace mercenary forces with troops permanently domiciled within a state and dependent on grants of land for financial security. It was a way of securing a supply of troops and of linking them to their employers.

Two types of recruiting were common in this period. It was either carried out by recruiting agents or through diplomatic channels and interstate treaties that included clauses allowing citizens to serve as troops for the the contracting parties. These methods had been used earlier. Crete, politically unstable and beset by economic and social misery, was a fertile ground for the second type of mercenary recruitment and much of our extant evidence is from it.

292. Diodorus Siculus, 18.61.4–5
The reference is to the recruiting carried out by Eumenes of Cardia in 318 in response to the advance of his enemy Antigonus against his position in Cappadocia (see no. 291).

[Eumenes] chose the most capable of his friends and, providing them with ample funds for the recruiting of mercenaries, he dispatched them, after establishing a high rate of pay. Some went straight to Pisidia and Lycia and the neighboring areas, and traveling around they zealously enrolled mercenaries. Others made their way to Cilicia and still others to Coele Syria and Phoenicia. Some also went to the cities in Cyprus. Given the publicity accorded to the recruiting and that the high rate of pay was attractive, many came voluntarily from the cities of Greece and enrolled themselves for the expedition. In a short time they assembled more than ten thousand infantry and two thousand cavalry in addition to the Silver Shields and those who had come with Eumenes.

293. An Agreement Between Eumenes I and his Mercenaries, OGIS 266
This agreement probably dates from soon after the accession of Eumenes I as ruler of what was to become the new Attalid kingdom of Pergamum on the northwestern coast of Asia Minor, perhaps between 263 and 261, and was concluded after a four-month revolt by the mercenaries in protest against their conditions of service. These outposts may have been established in anticipation

of a Seleucid attack. The first mercenary post at Attaleia lay 35 km east of the capital at Pergamum, while Philetaireia lay to the north somewhere in the south-eastern Troad. The retention of these mercenaries and their being placed under contract is evidently part of Eumenes' attempt to further emancipate himself from Seleucid control and to establish his own independent kingdom.

The *medimnos* is equal to about 48 liters of grain or about 190 days ration for a man. The *metretes* equals about 48 liters of wine. One should note the ten-month working year and the practice of commuting rations in kind for money. The dating reference is to the forty-fourth year of the Seleucid era, which is equivalent to 269/268 BC. The poplar-crowned soldiers presumably are those who are receiving special bonuses.

The requests which Eumenes, son of Philetaerus, granted to soldiers in Philetarea and Attalea. Eumenes will pay as the price of grain four drachmas per *medimnos* and for wine four drachmas per *metretes*. Eumenes will retain a ten-month service year and not allow an intercalary month.

Those who have fulfilled the requisite years of service and no longer are employed shall receive their allowances for the previous time served.

Allowances for orphans shall be received by next of kin or by whomever the soldier grants these right to [by testament].

In the matter of taxes, the freedom from them [allowed] in the forty-fourth year shall be valid. If someone becomes unemployed or so requests it, he shall be released from service and will be able to remove his goods free of taxes.

Concerning the pay which Eumenes agreed to give for the four-month period: it shall be given as agreed and not as a part of standard pay. Soldiers who have been crowned with poplar crowns are to take the grain ration for the time that they are crowned.

Let this agreement and its accompanying oath be engraved on four stone pillars and let these pillars be set up in the temple of Athena in Pergamum, one at Gryneum, one on Delos and one in the Aesclepianum on Mytilene.

Paramonius and the commanders as well as the soldiers under them at Philetaerea and Attalea and Atinas the cavalry commander and his cavalry command and Oliochus and the Trallians commanded by him have sworn the following oath:

I swear by Zeus . . . I am totally reconciled with Eumenes the son of Philetaerus and well disposed towards him and his people. I will not plot against him nor take up arms against him; I will not desert him but I will fight on his behalf personally and for the sake of his interests even to the point of death. I will provide other necessary service happily and without hesitation and with all enthusiasm as far as it is in my power. If I discover someone plotting against Eumenes son of Philetaerus or against his interests, I will not allow it to the best of my power, but I will inform as quickly as I can or as soon as I can on the person involved to Eumenes or to someone who will reveal the matter to him as speedily as possible. I will guard anything I receive from him whether a city, fort, ship, money or anything else and I will return it correctly and rightly to Eumenes son of Philetaerus or to his deputy as long as his agreement with me remains in force. I will receive no communications from the enemy nor envoys nor will I send any myself. . . .

Oath of Eumenes:

I swear by Zeus . . . that I will be well disposed to Paramonius and the commanders and the other mercenaries in the unit at Philetaerus under Mount Ida commanded by

Paramonius and to Arcides and the garrison under him and Philonnides and those
volunteers bound by oath . . . as long as they serve with me I will not plot against them
nor will any agent of mine do so and I will not give up to an opponent either their
persons or anything belonging to them nor will I surrender their commanders or those
chosen by them in their assembly, in any way or on any pretext; and I will not bear arms
against [them].

THE ARMIES OF THE GREAT POWERS

Egypt

The composition of the Egyptian army was similar to those of the other great
monarchies for most of its existence. It comprised three categories of troops:
mercenaries, regular troops, and natives. This latter category only becomes truly
significant under Philopater before the battle of Raphia in 217.

The regular troops were the *Macedones*. They were settlers and cleruchs,
mostly of Greek ethnic background, that supplemented Alexander's original
Macedonian army of occupation. The category of mercenaries is self-explanatory.
Their main uses will have been to staff the provinces and garrisons of the
Ptolemaic empire and in times of crisis were used to increase available manpower.
Native Egyptians were few before Raphia and limited to the descendants of the
native Egyptian military class, the *machimoi*. After Raphia all natives were now
possible candidates for military service.

The soldiers of the regular army continued to be known as *Macedones*, but it
is clear that this is a pseudo-ethnic term. Macedonian immigration after the first
few years following the death of Alexander was negligible. These troops are both
cavalry and infantry. The cavalry was organized in hipparchies (see no. 265), of
which nine are known. Four of these units bore ethnic terms that refer to non-
Macedonians: Persians, Thessalians, Thracians and Mysians. These hipparchies
were, as normal, subdivided into *ilae* and smaller units.

In addition to the regular cavalry there were also regular infantry units. These
were the troops that formed the phalanx and seem to have numbered about
twenty-five thousand men at full strength. It is not clear if there were any light
formations among these troops. There is no certainty, but the light-armed
mercenaries present at Raphia would indicate that such troops were hired as
necessary.

The élite of the kingdom's regular army was formed by guards units comprised
of cavalry and infantry. At Raphia a royal Agema of three thousand infantry and
seven hundred horse was present. From at least 218 Egyptian troops were
enrolled and mercenaries served, and in late Ptolemaic Egypt they may have
formed the majority of these units. There were also smaller scattered garrisons of
mercenaries.

The mercenaries in Egyptian service either fought in separate specialist units
or were recruited as hoplites. Mercenary cavalry also formed an important element

in the Ptolemaic army. The Ptolemies attempted to limit their dependence on foreign mercenaries by establishing a system of land grants, thereby making their troops landholders (cleruchs). The grant was initially in return for military service. But the system never eliminated the need for mercenaries and even then need outstripped supply so that by Raphia large numbers of Egyptians had to be used. Gradually the emphasis shifted back to mercenaries, as cleruchs converted their grants into hereditary holdings and detached themselves from military service. But the state failed to recruit enough mercenaries or to control them sufficiently and the late Ptolemaic army was generally ineffectual and more active in civil war than against foreign enemies.

294. Callixenus of Rhodes, FGrH 627, F35

This account is from a work on Alexandria by a Callixenus who wrote about the middle of the second century. This scene may have been part of a festival in honor of the Lagid house held in 270. Ptolemy II's dates are 282–246. According to references to his royal records in later sources his total forces consisted of 40,000 cavalry and 200,000 infantry, which are far too high to be credible.

Finally Ptolemy's military forces, both cavalry and infantry, all armored splendidly, marched in the procession. There were 57,600 infantry and 23,200 horse. All of them marched, each dressed in the proper equipment and with a full kit of the appropriate armor and weaponry. Besides those who possessed all the necessary equipment there were many other kits laid up in storage and their number is not easily countable.

The cleruchy

The cleruchy was an institution designed to stabilize the numbers and pay of the armed forces. Its aim was to convert mercenaries into resident regular troops. The instrument was a grant of the use of a *cleros* or lot from royal land in return for the fulfillment of a number of stipulations, the most important of which was military service. At the death of the holder the lot reverted to the king who could then redistribute it to another individual in return for the same services. The grant also appears to have contained some sort of lodging for the cleruch. Such an allotment of land did not necessarily imply actual farming, for some cleruchs leased their land and lived off the rent in the cities.

At first the cleruchs appear to be Greeks or Macedonians, but later natives were given grants which continued a tradition going back to Pharaonic times. The size of the lots varied tremendously, with some high officers receiving grants two thousand times the size of the smallest grants made to native soldiers.

295. A Letter by Asclepiades, an Official in the Arsinoite Nome, in 238/237, P. Hibeh 81

This region in middle Egypt has provided us with our richest source of information on cleruchs. It shows that the government still retained the ultimate ownership of cleruchic land in the last third of the third century. The end of the letter makes it clear that the lots of soldiers of the same unit were distributed in adjacent areas.

Artemidorus. I have written below a copy for your information of the letter to Nicanor. Ninth year, Phaophi 29.
To Nicanor: The cavalrymen listed below have died. Repossess their allotments for the royal treasury.
  At Boubastis, in the *lochos* of Epimenes, Sitalces the leader, son of . . .
  At Theogeneis, *lochos* of Lacon . . . machus son of Sca . . . , captain. . . .

296. A Petition of Cavalry Settlers of the Arsinoite Nome to Ptolemy Euergetes II and Cleopatra II, April 4, 144 BC, Meyer, *Griech. Texte aus Ägypten* no. 1

A crucial development in the severe military decline of the Ptolemaic monarchy was the conversion of cleruch lots into hereditary tenures, which resulted in the loss of the king's ability to enforce the attached military duties. At first only male descendants capable of carrying out the duties involved were allowed. By the second century the emphasis had shifted away from military service to the cultivation of the land and the payment of monetary taxes. In the first century women could succeed, and if the cleruch died intestate his lot passed to his nearest male relative. It had become private property and its connection with military service had been severed. The Great Gods referred to are Ptolemy and his sister and wife Cleopatra. The title of First Friend is an administrative and bureaucratic title of a functionary in the bureaucracy. It was essentially honorific. An *epistates* was an official in charge of local administration.

We petition you, O Great Gods, not to overlook us who live on little and whose property has been diminished, but if our case appears valid in your eyes to instruct Apollodorus who is a member of the class of First Friends, *epistates* and secretary of the Settler-Cavalry and Dionysius the chief bodyguard . . . to allow us and our descendants to retain the lots of land that we have measured out without denunciations, complaints, accusations and threats growing out of any cause whatsoever. . . . We ask that the clemency decrees remain in force by which we have obtained the right not to be held liable to charges not in accordance with our rank as Cavalry-Settlers, but to pay the dues that fall on such a rating which those enrolled in this rank have paid before us. If this petition is granted we will have received life-long help from you.
Good Fortune.
To Apollodorus. Grant it. Year twenty-six on Phamneoth.

The arming of the native Egyptians for Raphia and its consequences

297. Polybius, *Histories* 5.107.1–3

Polybius is exaggerating the direct connection between Raphia and the problems that followed. Egypt entered a period of increasing impotency abroad and financial weakness at home. The weakness was exacerbated for the local population by increased exactions to compensate for other revenue.

A war broke out right after this between Ptolemy [IV] and the native Egyptians. The king's measure of arming the natives was very well thought out in relation to his current needs, but he failed badly in planning for the future. For the Egyptians became arrogant because of their victory at Raphia and were no longer content to comply with orders; they began to look for a figurehead and leader, thinking they were competent to look after themselves. The affair ended but not for quite some time.

The Seleucid army

The core of the Seleucid army, like that of the other Hellenistic states, was its phalanx armed in the Macedonian fashion. The Seleucid phalanx was composed of two basic elements. The generalized mass of the phalanx was formed for the most part from Greco-Macedonian colonists or their descendants and organized in military settlements. The other element was the élite unit of the Silver Shields formed from the pool of military colonists. Unlike the rest of the phalanx it was retained as a standing army and stationed at the capital Antioch.

The cavalry was more ethnically diverse, and we know that certain select units, in particular the Agema, were provided by Iranians. Light-armed troops came from the varied population of the kingdom. The Seleucid monarchs appear more willing to utilize native levies than the Ptolemies. The only conspicuously absent groups were Syrians and Mesopotamians from the political and economic heartland of the empire, and one may suspect a reluctance to arm natives who might prove a political danger.

The core of the army was drawn from a series of military settlements spread in strategic locations throughout the empire. The kings seem to. have been remarkably successful in maintaining the supply of required manpower and the Seleucids never had to resort to a massive arming of the native population in the style of Ptolemy IV. The same success is visible in the fact that the Seleucids did not employ mercenaries except in times of crisis. The empire as a whole was able to muster a phalanx of about 45,000 and about 8000–8500 cavalry in addition to light-armed troops. Elephants and scythed chariots were also used.

A military headquarters was maintained at Apamea in northern Syria. It included facilities for military administration and training, provided stables for the royal war elephants and served as an arsenal. There were also troops stationed at strategic points throughout the empire.

298. Polybius, *Histories* 30.25.1–11

This account of the military procession staged by Antiochus IV at Daphne, a fashionable suburb of Antioch, in 166 or 165 is one of the most valuable passages we have on the strength and composition of the Seleucid army in this period. The troops in the parade seem to represent the full strength of the western forces available to the Seleucid monarch, totaling 41,000 foot and 4500 cavalry. Several features ought to be noticed. The 5000 men who had probably been phalangites were now equipped in Roman fashion. The silver shield bearers are the members of the royal guard. The citizen cavalry are the cavalry drawn from the military settlements. The text is uncertain as far as the phalanx numbers are concerned. For cataphracts see no. 289. Notice the presence of native light-armed troops.

This same king, when he heard of the games that had been given by Aemilius Paulus the Roman general, wanted to top Paulus by his munificence and sent out ambassadors and sacred envoys to the cities to announce the games he was going to present at Daphne. The result was that many of the Greeks were anxious to attend. The festival opened with a procession carried out in the following manner. It was led by 5000 men in the prime of life equipped in Roman fashion with cuirasses of chain mail and after them the same number of Mysians. Right after them were 3000 Cilicians armed as light infantry, wearing gold crowns. . . . Then there marched 3000 Thracians and 5000 Galatians. Next came 20,000 Macedonians of whom 5000 carried bronze shields and the remainder silver shields. Then there followed 240 pairs of gladiators. Behind them rode 1000 Nisaean cavalry and 3000 citizen cavalry of whom the majority had gold trappings and crowns, while the others had silver trappings. Then came the so-called Companion cavalry, 1000 in number and with gold trappings. Right behind was the unit of Friends, equal to the Companions in number and adornment. Then 1000 select cavalry followed by the so-called Agema of about 1000 men which had the best reputation as a fighting unit of the cavalry. Finally there came the formation of the cataphracts whose appellation fitted both men and horses who were both encased in mail. They totaled 1500. All of the units mentioned had purple surcoats, many of which were embroidered with golden animal designs. Then came 100 six-horse chariots, 40 four-horse and a chariot drawn by a pair of elephants. Last there came thirty-six elephants fitted-out in single file.

The military settlements

The Seleucid kings, like the Ptolemies, assigned lots to their soldiers from which those troops maintained themselves and which tied them to the monarchy.

The population of these settlements (*katoikiai*) was primarily drawn from the immigrant Greco-Macedonian population. Even in the second century the majority were of Macedonian descent. The settlements ranged in size and status from villages to city foundations. After 188 many of the smaller village settlements were joined together to form cities. These military foundations were concentrated in central and western Asia Minor and in northern Syria. The same system was used for cavalry and infantry. There is no doubt the Seleucids developed a more successful solution and that their military colonies managed to maintain themselves while the Egyptian cleruch failed to keep his military character.

299. Josephus, *Jewish Antiquities* 12.148–151

This letter from Antiochius III to his general Zeuxis, who was probably governor of Mesopotamia, was probably written between *c.* 213 and 204. The Jews had early been incorporated by the Seleucids and Jewish colonies are attested in Asia Minor and in Mesopotamia. By the second century Jewish mercenaries are widely attested. The letter is important for revealing what must have been the typical procedure followed in founding such colonies. The colonist receives not only an allotment of land but a ten years' tax remission. "His father" in the initial greeting is an honorary title.

King Antiochus to Zeuxis his father, greetings. If you are healthy, it is well, I am well. Learning of the rebellions in Lydia and Phrygia I have considered it a matter warranting great attention, and after taking counsel with my Friends about what ought to be done, I have decided to transfer two thousand Jewish households with their baggage from Mesopotamia and Babylonia to the appropriate forts and strategic places. I am persuaded that these people will be well-disposed guardians of our interests because of their piety towards the Divine. . . . When you lead them to the aforesaid places, give each of them a plot of land for the erection of a residence and land for farming and for viticulture. They shall be tax exempt on farm produce for the space of ten years.

300. An Agreement for Sharing of Citizenship between Smyrna and Magnesia Ad Sipylum soon after 243, SV no. 492

The inscription dates from soon after the succession of Seleucus II (246–226/ 225). It records a decree by the assembly of Smyrna to conclude a pact of friendship, involving the grant of citizenship in Smyrna, with the citizens of Magnesia near Mt Sipylus and the settlers (*katoikoi*) who have received lots at Magnesia, including its garrison as well as cavalry and infantry at the camp that must have been near the city. The motivation behind the decree was the assurance of the loyalty of these troops to Seleucus II. The status of the settlers is not totally clear but they are most likely to have been military settlers. The inscription shows something of the organization and the complex interweaving between the Greek cities and military settlements and garrisons. It also makes a clear connection between the possession of Greek identity and the conferment of citizenship, as well as showing the bond between the Greek city and the Seleucid military colony.

Resolved by the people, on a proposal of the generals, that: when previously at the time King Seleucus crossed over into Seleucis, at a time when our city and land were beset by many dangers, the people had maintained its goodwill and friendship towards the king, not overawed by the attack of the enemy nor concerned about the destruction of its property, but placing everything second to sustaining its decision and participating in affairs in the king's best interests as it had done from the beginning. As a result King Seleucus, pious towards the gods and loving to his parents, a man of great spirit and knowing how to return gratitude to his benefactors, honored our city because of its goodwill and the zeal it showed for his affairs and also for the sake of the cult of his father, the god Antiochus, and of his mother, the goddess Stratonice. . . .

Now after the king has crossed into Seleucis, the generals, anxious too that the affairs of the king remain in an advantageous state, have sent a delegation to the settlers [*katoikoi*] in Magnesia and the infantry and cavalry in the camp and they have sent one of themselves to urge them to permanently maintain their friendship for the king, alliance with him and to watch over his affairs. The settlers and soldiers in the camp have enthusiastically received the proposals of the generals and have announced that they will have the same attitude as our people in what concerns everything that benefits King

Seleucus. They have sent ambassadors to us from the settlers Potamon and Hierocles, and from the soldiers in the camp Damon and Apolloniceres. . . .

Friendship has been concluded upon the following terms between the Smyrneans and the settlers in Magnesia, the cavalry and infantry in the city, and those in the camp and their remaining inhabitants: the Smyrnaeans have given citizenship to the Magnesian settlers in the city and in the camp and the others, on which condition they will maintain their alliance and goodwill towards the affairs of King Seleucus with all enthusiasm for all time, and preserving and guarding what they receive from King Seleucus, they will return it to him. They will be fellow citizens of the Smyrnaeans according to the laws of the city and will without dispute have the same friends and enemies as the Smyrnaeans.

Citizenship will be given to the settlers in Magnesia, the infantry and cavalry in the city, and those units in the camp on an equal basis with the other citizens. Also citizenship will be granted to all others in Magnesia as long as they are Greeks and free.

Macedonia

With the establishment of the Antigonid house in Macedonia, quiet finally settled over a state that had been under almost constant military pressure since Alexander. Perhaps half of those eligible for military service had been swept away in the fifty years since Alexander's death in war or through emigration.

The Macedonian kings were conscious of the need to husband their manpower and hired mercenaries not only for long-term garrison duties but also as expendable substitutes for their own forces. A number of treaties are extant between Cretan cities and the Macedonian kings arranging for mercenary service. The use of mercenaries was limited by the slender resources of the Antigonids in comparison to their rivals. The national army had a fairly constant number of effectives of around twenty-five thousand. The officer core was still composed of Macedonian nobles. Like the Aetolian and Achaean Leagues, its major rivals, it possessed a citizen army as its core. The destruction of the Macedonian monarchy by the Romans in 167 was more the result of superior Roman manpower and than of any decrease in the effectiveness of Macedonia's army.

301. Diodorus Siculus, 18.12.2

The movement referred to in this passage is a rising of many of the Greek states under Athenian leadership in the wake of Alexander's death, the Lamian War. It is crucial to note that the League's early successes appear to have been due to the lack of manpower experienced by the Macedonian regent Antipater. It was the return of time-expired Macedonian veterans that made the eventual Macedonian victory in the next year possible.

When [Antipater] learned of the concerted movement of the Greeks that had taken place against him, he left Sippias as general of Macedonia, gave him enough troops and ordered him to conduct a levy of as many as possible. He assembled his army of thirteen thousand Macedonians and six thousand cavalry. (At this time Macedonia lacked citizen-soldiers because of the great number that had been sent off to Asia as replacements for the army.)

302. Diodorus Siculus, 20.110.3–4

The reference is to Demetrius' Macedonian campaign against his rival Cassander in 302. It ended in a compromise because of his need to come to his father's aid in Asia. The passage illustrates what appears to have been a fairly typical Macedonian force in the years after Alexander death.

As Cassander saw that Demetrius' affairs were going forward according to the latter's plans, he more strongly garrisoned in advance Thebes and Pherae and gathered all of his forces and encamped opposite Demetrius' army. Cassander had a total of 29,000 foot and 2000 horsemen. Demetrius had 1500 cavalry and not less than 8000 Macedonian infantry; his mercenary forces was 10,500, there were also light-armed formations and all types of adventurers who had assembled for war and pillage and who numbered more than 18,000; the resulting grand total was about 56,000 foot.

SUGGESTED READINGS

1 EARLY GREEK WARFARE: HOMER AND THE DARK AGES

The Bronze Age and the Homeric background

Cambridge Ancient History, 3rd edn, vol. 2, pts 1–2 (Cambridge, 1973–1975).
Chadwick, J., *The Mycenaean World* (Cambridge, 1976).
Desborough, V. R. d'A., *The Last Mycenaeans and their Successors* (Oxford, 1964).
Dickinson, O. P. T. K., *The Aegean Bronze Age* (Cambridge, 1994).
Drews, R., *The End of the Bronze Age: Changes in Warfare and the Catastrophe ca. 1200* (Princeton, 1993).
Finley, M. I., *The World of Odysseus²* (Harmondsworth, 1978).
Harding, A. F., *The Mycenaeans and Europe* (London and Orlando, Fla., 1984).
Hooker, J. T., *Mycenaean Greece* (London, Henley and Boston, 1976).
Murray, O., *Early Greece²* (Cambridge, 1993).
Taylour, Lord William, *The Mycenaeans* (rev. edn, London, 1983).
Vermule, E., *Greece in the Bronze Age* (Chicago, 1964).
Wace, A. J. B. and Stubbings, F. H., edd., *A Companion to Homer* (New York, 1962).
Wood, M., *In Search of the Trojan War* (London, 1985).

The Homeric poems

Fenik, B. C., *Homer: Tradition and Invention* (Leiden, 1978).
Griffin, J., *Homer on Life and Death* (Oxford, 1980).
Griffin, J., *Homer: The Odyssey* (Cambridge, 1987).
Heubeck, A., West, S. and Hainsworth, J. B., *A Commentary on Homer's Odyssey* (Oxford, 1988–1992).
Kirk, G. S., *The Songs of Homer* (Cambridge, 1962).
Kirk, G. S., *Homer and the Oral Tradition* (Cambridge, 1976).
Kirk, G. S., ed., *The Iliad: A Commentary*, 6 vols (Cambridge, 1985–1993).
Silk, M. S., *Homer: The Iliad* (Cambridge, 1987).

Warfare in the poems

Crouwel, J. H., *Chariots and other Wheeled Vehicles in Bronze Age Greece* (Amsterdam, 1981).
Fenik, B. C., *Typical Battle Scenes in the Iliad* (Wiesbaden, 1968).

Greenhalgh, P. A. L., *Early Greek Warfare* (Cambridge, 1973)

Kirk, G. S., "The Homeric Poems as History," Cambridge Ancient History, vol. 2, ch. 39b (Cambridge, 1964).

Lorimer, H. L., *Homer and the Monuments* (London, 1950).

Nagy, G., *The Best of the Achaeans: Concepts of the Hero in Archaic Greek Poetry* (Baltimore, 1980).

Wees, H. van, *Status Warriors: War, Violence and Society in Homer and History* (Amsterdam, 1992).

2 THE AGE OF HOPLITE WARFARE

General histories of Greece

Andrewes, A., *The Greeks* (London, 1967).

Bengtson, H., *History of Greece*, translated and updated by E. F. Bloedow (Ottawa, 1988).

Boardman, J., Griffin, J. and Murray, O., *The Oxford History of Greece and the Hellenistic World* (Oxford, 1991).

Bury, J. B. and Meiggs, R., *A History of Greece to the Death of Alexander the Great* (4th edn, London, 1975).

Cambridge Ancient History, 2nd edn, vol. 4: *Persia, Greece and the Western Mediterranean c. 525–479 BC* (Cambridge, 1988).

Fine, J. V. A., *The Ancient Greeks: A Critical History* (Cambridge, Mass., 1983).

Finley, M. I., *Politics in the Ancient World* (Cambridge, 1983).

Hammond, N. G. L., *A History of Greece to 322 BC* (3rd edn, Oxford, 1986).

Hurwitt, J., *The Art and Culture of Early Greece, 1100–480 BC* (Ithaca, N.Y., 1985).

Sealey, R., *A History of the Greek City-states ca. 700–338 BC* (Berkeley, 1976).

General works on Greek warfare

Adcock, F. E., *The Greek and Macedonian Art of War* (Berkeley, 1957).

Connolly, P., *Greece and Rome at War* (London, 1981).

Ducrey, P., *Warfare in Ancient Greece* (New York, 1986).

Ferrill, A., *The Origins of War* (London, 1985).

Garlan, Y., *Warfare in the Ancient World: A Social History* (New York, 1975).

Pritchett, W. K., *The Greek State at War I–V* (Berkeley, 1971–1991).

Rich, J. and Shipley, G., *War and Society in the Greek World* (London, 1993).

Spiegel, N., *War and Peace in Classical Greek Literature* (Jerusalem, 1990).

Warry, J., *Warfare in the Classical World* (New York, 1980).

The Archaic period and the introduction and development of hoplite warfare

Anderson, J. K., "Hoplites and Heresies: A Note," *JHS* 104 (1984) 152.

Andrewes, A., *The Greek Tyrants* (London, 1956).

Burn, A. R., *The Lyric Age of Greece* (London, 1960).

Cambridge Ancient History, vol. 3, pt 3 (Cambridge, 1982).

Cartledge, P., "Hoplites and Heroes: Sparta's Contribution to the Technique of Ancient Warfare," *JHS* 97 (1977) 11–27.

Cartledge, P., *Sparta and Lakonia: A Regional History 1300–362 BC* (London, 1979).

Connor, W. R., "Early Greek Land Warfare as a Symbolic Expression," *P&P* 119 (1988) 3–29.

Frost, F. J., "The Athenian Military before Cleisthenes," *Historia* 33 (1984) 283–294.

Hanson, V. D., *The Western Way of War: Infantry Battle in Classical Greece* (New York, 1989).

Lazenby, J. F., *The Spartan Army* (Warminster, 1985).

Lorimer, H. L., "The Hoplite Phalanx," *ABSA* 42 (1947) 76–138.

Lorimer, H. L., "The Hoplite Phalanx with Special Reference to the poems of Archilochus and Tyrtaeus," *ABSA* 42 (1947) 167–187.

Morris, I., *Burial and Ancient Society: The Rise of the Greek City-state* (Cambridge, 1987).

Murray, O., *Early Greece* (2nd edn, Cambridge, Mass., 1993).

Salmon, J., "Political Hoplites," *JHS* 97 (1977) 84–101.

Snodgrass, A. M., *Archaic Greece: The Age of Experiment* (Berkeley and Los Angeles, 1980).

Snodgrass, A. M., "Hoplite Reform and History," *JHS* 85 (1965) 110–122.

Greek weapons and armor

Chase, C. H., "Shield Devices of the Greeks," *HSCP* 13 (1902) 61–127.

Snodgrass, A. M., *Early Greek Armour and Weapons* (Edinburgh, 1964).

Snodgrass, A. M., *Arms and Armour of the Greeks* (Ithaca, N.Y., 1967).

The role of sports in warfare

Anderson, J. K., *Hunting in the Ancient World* (Berkeley and Los Angeles, 1985).

Bothwick, "P. Oxy. 2738: Athena and the Pyrrhic Dance," *Hermes* 98 (1970) 318–331.

Harris, H. A., *Greek Athletes and Athletics* (London, 1964).

Poliakoff, M., *Combat Sports in the Ancient World* (London, 1987).

Wheeler, E. L., "The Hoplomachia and Greek Dances in Arms," *GRBS* 23 (1982) 223–233.

Light-armed troops

Best, J. G. P., *The Thracian Peltasts and their Influence on Greek Warfare* (Groningen, 1969).

Cavalry

Anderson, J. K., *Ancient Greek Horsemanship* (Berkeley and Los Angeles, 1961).

Bugh, G. R., *The Horsemen of Athens* (Princeton, 1985).

Military command

Connor, W. R., *The New Politicians of Fifth Century Athens* (Princeton, 1971).

Fornara, C., *The Athenian Board of Generals from 501 to 404*, Historia Einzelschrift 16 (1971).

Lengauer, W., *Greek Commanders in the Fifth and Fourth Centuries BC: Politics and Ideology: A Study in Militarism* (Warsaw, 1976).

Diplomacy and treaties

Adcock, F. E., and Mosley, D. J., *Diplomacy in Ancient Greece* (New York, 1975).

Bauslaugh, R. A., *The Concept of Neutrality in Classical Greece* (Berkeley and Los Angeles, 1991).

Karavites, P., "Greek Interstate Relations and Moral Principles in the Fifth Century BC," *PP* 39 (1984) 161–192.

Lateiner, D., "Heralds and Corpses in Thucydides," *CW* 71 (1977) 97–106.

Meiggs, R., *The Athenian Empire* (Oxford, 1972).

Mosley, D. J., "Diplomacy in Classical Greece," *AncSoc* 3 (1972) 1–16.

Phillipson, C., *The International Law and Custom of Ancient Greece and Rome* (London, 1911).

Rhodes, P. J., *The Athenian Empire*, Greece and Rome New Surveys in the Classics 17 (Oxford, 1985).

Starr, C. G., *Political Intelligence in Classical Greece* (Leiden, 1974).

Ste Croix, G. de, *The Origins of the Peloponnesian War* (London, 1972).

Hoplite battles

Buckler, J., "Epameinondas and the EMBOΛON," *Phoenix* 39 (1985) 134–143.

Cawkwell, G., "Orthodoxy and Hoplites," *CQ* 39 (1989) 375–389.

Devine, A. M., "EMBOΛON: A Study in Tactical Terminology," *Phoenix* 37 (1983) 201–217.

Fraser, A. D., "The Myth of the Phalanx Scrimmage," *CW* 36 (1942) 15–16.

Grundy, G. B., *Thucydides and the History of his Age* (2nd edn, London, 1948).

Halladay, A. J., "Hoplites and Heresies," *JHS* 102 (1982) 94–103.

Hamilton, C. D., *Agesilaos and the Failure of Spartan Hegemony* (Ithaca, N.Y. and London, 1991).

Hamilton, C. D., *Sparta's Bitter Victories* (Ithaca, N.Y., 1979).

Hansen, M. H., "The Number of Athenian Hoplites in 431 B.C.", *SO* 56 (1981) 19–32.

Hanson, V. D., *Hoplites: The Classical Greek Battle Experience* (London and New York, 1991).

Henderson, B. W., *The Great War between Athens and Sparta* (London, 1927).

Kagan, D., *The Archidamian War* (Ithaca, N.Y., 1974).

Kagan, D., *The Peace of Nicias and the Sicilian Expedition* (Ithaca, N.Y., 1981).

Krentz, P., "The Nature of Hoplite Battle," *ClasAnt* 4 (1985) 13–20.

Pritchett, W. K., *Studies in Greek Topography*, vol. 1 (Berkeley, 1971).

Ridley, R. T., "The Hoplite as Citizen: Athenian Military Institutions in their Social Context," *AC* 48 (1979) 508–548.

Watley, N., "On the Possibility of Reconstructing Marathon and other Ancient Battles," *JHS* 84 (1964) 119–139.

Woodhouse, W. J., *King Agis of Sparta and his Campaign in Arkadia in 418 B.C.* (Oxford, 1933).

The Persian Wars

Balcer, J., "The Persian Wars Against Greece: A Reassessment," *Historia* 38 (1989) 127–143.

Burn, A. R., *Persia and the Greeks* (London, 1962).

Cambridge Ancient History, vol. 4, *Persia, Greece and the Western Mediterranean c. 525–479 BC* (Cambridge, 1988).

Cook, J. M., *The Persian Empire* (New York, 1983).

Grundy, G. B., *The Great Persian War and its Preliminaries* (London, 1901).

Hammond, N. G. L., *Studies in Greek History* (Oxford, 1973).
Hignett, C., *Xerxes' Invasion of Greece* (Oxford, 1963).
Maurice, F., "The Size of the Army of Xerxes in the Invasion of Greece, 480 B.C.," *JHS* 50 (1930) 210–235.
Shrimpton, G., "The Persian Cavalry at Marathon," *Phoenix* 34 (1980) 20–37.
Starr, C. G., "Why did the Greeks Defeat the Persians?," *PP* 17 (1962) 321–332.
Wardman, A. E., "Tactics and Tradition of the Persian Wars," *Historia* 8 (1959) 49–60.

The aftermath of battle

Bradeen, D., "The Athenian Casualty Lists," *CQ* 63 (1969) 145–159.
Clairmont, C. W., *Patrios Nomos: Public Burial in Athens During the Fifth and Fourth Centuries B.C., the Archaeological, Epigraphic-literary and Historical Evidence*, BAR International Series 161 (1983).
Hammond, N. G. L., "Casualties and Reinforcements of Citizen Soldiers in Greece and Macedonia," *JHS* 109 (1989) 56–68.
Hanson, V. D., *Warfare and Agriculture in Classical Greece* (Pisa, 1982).
Jackson, A. H., "Some Recent Work on the Treatment of Prisoners of War," *Talanta* 2 (1970) 37–53.
Krentz, P., "Casualties in Hoplite Battles," *GRBS* 26 (1985) 13–20.
Kurtz, D. C., and Boardman, J., *Greek Burial Customs* (Ithaca, N.Y., 1971).
Loraux, N., *The Invention of Athens: The Funeral Oration in the Classical City* (Cambridge, Mass., 1986).
Panagopoulos, A., *Captives and Hostages in the Peloponnesian War. Fugitives and Hostages in the Peloponnesian War* (Amsterdam, 1989).
Rouse, W. D., *Greek Votive Offerings* (Cambridge, 1902).
Thompson, D. B., "The Persian Spoils in Athens," in Weinberg, S., ed., *The Aegean and the Near East: Studies Presented to Hetty Goldman* (New York, 1956) 281–291.
Vanderpool, E., "A Monument to the Battle of Marathon," *Hesperia* 35 (1966) 93–106.
Vermeule, E., *Aspects of Death in Early Greek Art and Poetry* (Berkeley, 1979).
West III, W. C., "The Trophies of the Persian Wars," *CPh* 64 (1969) 7–19.

Siege warfare

Landels, J. G., *Ancient Engineering* (London, 1978).
Lawrence, A. W., *Greek Aims in Fortification* (Oxford, 1979).
Marsden, F. W., *Greek and Roman Artillery* (Oxford, 1969).
Ober, J., "Early Artillery Towers: Messenia, Boiotia, Attica, Megarid," *AJA* 91 (1987) 569–604.
Winter, F. E., *Greek Fortifications* (Toronto, 1971).

Truces and peace treaties

Lewis, D. M., "The Treaties with Leontini and Rhegion (Meiggs-Lewis 63–64)," *ZPE* 22 (1976) 223–225.
Westlake, H. D., "Thucydides and the Uneasy Peace," *CQ* 21 (1971) 315–325.
Wick, T. E., "Athens' Alliance with Rhegium and Leontini," *Historia* 25 (1976) 288–304.

3 THE FOURTH CENTURY

General works

Cambridge Ancient History, vol. 6, *The Fourth Century* (Cambridge, 1994).
Hornblower, S., *The Greek World 479–323 BC* (London, 1983).
Sealey, R., *A History of the Greek City-States ca. 700–338 BC* (Berkeley and Los Angeles, 1976).

Aspects of the history of the fourth century

Buckler, J., *The Theban Hegemony 371–362 BC* (Cambridge, Mass., 1980).
Cargill, J., *The Second Athenian League: Empire or Free Alliance?* (California, 1981).
Cartledge, P., *Agesilaus and the Crisis of Sparta* (London, 1987).
Hamilton, C. D., *Agesilaus and the Failure of Spartan Hegemony* (Ithaca and London, 1991).
Hornblower, S., *Mausolus* (Oxford, 1982).
Parke, H. W., "The Development of the Second Spartan Empire," *JHS* 50 (1930) 37–79.
Perleman, S., "The Causes and Outbreak of the Corinthian War," *CQ* 14 (1964) 64–81.
Ryder, T. T. B., *Koine Eirene* (Oxford, 1965).
Sanders, L. J., *Dionysius I of Syracuse and Greek Tyranny* (London, 1988).
Westlake, H. D., "The Spartan Intervention in Asia 400–397 BC," *Historia* 35 (1986) 405–426.
Westlake, H. D., *Thessaly in the Fourth Century BC* (London, 1935).

Tactical innovation in hoplite warfare

Anderson, J. K., *Military Theory and Practice in the Age of Xenophon* (Berkeley and Los Angeles, 1970).
Buckler, J., Epaminondas and the EMBOΛON," *Phoenix* 39 (1985) 134–143.
Buckler, J., "Plutarch on Leuktra," *SO* 55 (1980) 75–93.
Devine, A. M., "EMBOΛON: A Study in Tactical Terminology," *Phoenix* 37 (1983) 201–217.
Gray, V. J., "Two Different Approaches to the Battle of Sardes in 395 BC: Xenophon *Hellenica* 3.4.20–24 and *Hellenica Oxyrhynchea* III (6). 4–6," *CSCA* 12 (1979) 183–200.
Hamilton, C. J., "The Generalship of King Agesilaus of Sparta," *AncW* 8 (1983) 119–127.
Hanson, V. D., "Epameinondas, the Battle of Leuktra (371 B. C.) and the "Revolution" in Greek Battle Tactics," *ClasAnt* 7 (1988) 190–207.
Snodgrass, A. M., *Arms and Armor of the Greeks* (Ithaca, N.Y., 1967).
Tuplin, C. J., "The Leuctra Campaign: Some Outstanding Problems," *Klio* 69 (1987) 72–107.
Wylie, G., "Agesilaus and the Battle of Sardis," *Klio* 74 (1992) 118–130.

Developments in the use of light-armed troops

Anderson, J. K., *Military Theory and Practice in the Age of Xenophon* (Berkeley and Los Angeles, 1970).
Best, J. P. G., *Thracian Peltasts and their Influence on Greek Warfare* (Groningen, 1969).
Pritchett, W. K., *The Greek State at War* (Berkeley, 1974).

Eastern influences

Anderson, J. K., *Military Theory and Practice in the Age of Xenophon* (Berkeley and Los Angeles, 1970).

Rahe, P. A., "The Military Situation in Western Asia on the Eve of Cunaxa," *AJP* 101 (1980) 79–98.

Mercenaries

Cook, M. L., "Timokrates' 50 Talents and the Cost of Ancient Warfare," *Eranos* 88 (1990) 69–97.

Lengauer, W., *Greek Commanders in the 5th and 4th Centuries BC: Politics and Ideology, A Study in Militarism* (Varsovie, 1979).

Miller, H. F., "The Practical and Economic Background to the Greek Mercenary Explosion," *G&R* 31 (1984) 153–160.

Parke, H. W., *Greek Mercenary Soldiers* (Oxford, 1933).

Sinclair, R. K., "The King's Peace and the Employment of Military and Naval Forces 387–378," *Chiron* 8 (1978) 29–54.

Whitehead, D., "Who Equipped Mercenary Troops?," *Historia* 40 (1991) 105–112.

Siege warfare

Harding, P., "Athenian Defensive Strategy in the Fourth Century," *Phoenix* 42 (1988) 61–71.

Ober, J., *Fortress Attica: Defense of the Athenian Land Frontier, 404–322 BC* (Leiden, 1985).

4 THE RISE OF MACEDONIA: PHILIP AND ALEXANDER

Macedonia before Philip

Adams, W. L., and Borza, E. N., edd., *Philip II, Alexander the Great and the Macedonian Heritage* (Washington, 1982).

Barr-Sharrar, B., ed., *Macedonia and Greece in Late Classical and Early Hellenistic Times* (Washington, 1982).

Borza, E. N., *In the Shadow of Olympus: The Emergence of Macedon* (Princeton, 1990).

Dell, H. J., ed., *Ancient Macedonian Studies in Honor of Charles F. Edson* (Thessaloniki, 1981).

Edson, C. F., "Early Macedonia," *Archaia Makedonika* 1 (1970) 17–44.

Errington, R. M., *A History of Macedonia* (Berkeley and Los Angeles, 1990).

Hammond, N. G. L., *A History of Macedonia*, vols 1 and 2 (Oxford, 1972–9).

Hammond, N. G. L., "The King and the Land in the Macedonian Kingdom," *CQ* 38 (1988) 382–391.

Hammond, N. G. L., *The Macedonian State: Origins, Institutions, and History* (Oxford, 1989).

Hornblower, S., *The Greek World 479–323 BC* (New York, 1983).

The age of Philip II

Bosworth, B. A., "Philip II and Upper Macedonia," *CQ* 21 (1971) 93–105.

Cawkwell, G. L., *Philip of Macedon* (London, 1978).

Ellis, J. R., *Philip II and Macedonian Imperialism* (London, 1976).

Ellis, J. R., "The Dynamics of Fourth Century Imperialism," *Ancient Macedonia* 2 (1974) 103–114.

Errington, R. M., "Review-discussion: Four Interpretations of Philip II," *AJAH* 6 (1981) 69–89.

Fredericksmeyer, E. A., "On the Final Aims of Philip II," in Adams, W. L., and Borza, E. N., edd., *Philip II, Alexander the Great and the Macedonian Heritage* (Washington, 1982) 85–98.

Hammond, N. G. L., *Philip of Macedon* (London, 1994).

Hatzopoulos, M. B., "Succession and Regency in Classical Macedonia," *Archaia Makedonika* 4 (1986) 279–292.

Alexander the Great

Badian, E., "Alexander the Great and the Loneliness of Power," in *Studies in Greek and Roman History* (Oxford, 1964). 192–205.

Badian, E. "Alexander the Great and the Unity of Mankind," *Historia* 7 (1958) 425–444.

Bosworth, A. B., *A Historical Commentary on Arrian's History of Alexander I* (Oxford, 1980).

Bosworth A. B., *Conquest and Empire: The Reign of Alexander the Great* (Cambridge, 1988).

Errington, R. M., "Alexander the Philhellene and Persia," in Dell, H. J., ed., *Ancient Macedonian Studies in Honor of Charles F. Edson* (Thessaloniki, 1981) 139–143.

Green, P., *Alexander of Macedon* (London, 1974).

Griffith, G. T., ed., *Alexander the Great: The Main Problems* (Cambridge, 1966).

Hamilton, J. R., *Alexander the Great* (London, 1973).

Hammond, N. G. L., *Alexander the Great: King, Commander, and Statesman* (Park Ridge, New Jersey, 1981).

Heisserer, A. J., *Alexander and the Greeks* (Norman, Okla., 1980).

Hekel, W., "Factions and Macedonian Politics in the Reign of Alexander the Great," *Archaia Makedonika* 4 (1986) 293–305.

Higgins, W. E., "Aspects of Alexander's Imperial Administration: Some Modern Methods and Views Reviewed," *Athenaeum* 58 (1980) 129–152.

Hornblower, S., *Hieronymus of Cardia* (Oxford, 1981).

Lane-Fox, R., *Alexander the Great* (London, 1973).

Milns, R. D., *Alexander the Great* (London, 1968).

Tarn, W. W., *Alexander the Great*, 2 vols (Cambridge, 1948).

Wilcken, U., *Alexander the Great* (New York, 1967).

The armies of Philip and Alexander

Anson, E. M., "Alexander's Hypaspists and the Argyraspists," *Historia* 30 (1981) 117–120.

Anson, E. M., "Hypaspists and Argyraspists after 323 BC," *AHB* 2 (1988) 131–133.

Anson, E. M., "The Hypaspists: Macedonia's Professional Citizen-soldiers," *Historia* 34 (1985) 246–248.

Badian, E., "Orientals in Alexander's Army," *JHS* 85 (1965) 160–161.

Bosworth, A. B., "Macedonian Manpower under Alexander the Great," *Archaia Makedonika* 4 (1986) 115–122.

Brunt, P. A., "Alexander's Macedonian Cavalry," *JHS* 83 (1963) 27–46.

Ellis, J. R., "Alexander's Hypaspists Again," *Historia* 24 (1975) 617–618.

Engels, D., "Alexander's Intelligence System," *CQ* 30 (1980) 327–340.

Engels, D., *Alexander the Great and the Logistics of the Macedonian Army* (Berkeley, 1978).

Griffith, G. T., "Peltasts and the Origins of the Macedonian Phalanx," in Dell, H. J., ed., *Ancient Macedonian Studies in Honor of Charles F. Edson* (Thessaloniki, 1981) 161–167.

Hammond, N. G. L., "The Various Guards of Philip II and Alexander III," *Historia* 40 (1991) 396–418.

Heckel, W., *The Marshals of Alexander's Empire* (London, 1992).

Milns, R. D., "Army Pay and the Military Budget of Alexander the Great," in *Zu Alexander der Grosse: Festschrift G. Wirth* (Amsterdam, 1987) 233–256.

Milns, R. D., "The Army of Alexander the Great," in Bosworth, A. B., ed., *Alexandre le grand: image et réalité* (Geneva, 1976) 87–129.

Milns, R. D., "The Hypaspists of Alexander III: Some Problems," *Historia* 20 (1971) 186–196.

Macedonian military equipment

Andronikos, M., "Sarissa," *BCH* 94 (1970) 91–107.

Andronikos, M., "The Finds from the Royal Tombs at Vergina," *PBA* 65 (1979) 355–367.

Andronikos, M., *Verghina* (Athens, 1984).

Manti, P. A., "The Cavalry Sarissa," *AncWorld* 8 (1983) 73–80.

Markle III, M. M., "Macedonian Arms and Tactics under Alexander the Great," in Barr-Sharrar, B., ed., *Macedonia and Greece in Late Classical and Early Hellenistic Times* (Washington, 1982) 87–111.

Markle III, M. M., " The Macedonian Sarissa, Spear, and Related Armor," *AJA* 81 (1977) 323–339.

Markle III, M. M., "Use of the Sarissa by Philip and Alexander of Macedon," *AJA* 82 (1978) 483–497.

Marsden, E. W., "Macedonian Military Machinery and its Designers under Philip and Alexander," *Archaia Makedonika* 2 (1977) 211–223.

Campaigns and battles

Badian, E., "The Battle of the Granicus: A New Look," *Ancient Macedonia* 2 (1981) 271–293.

Bosworth, A. B., "The Location of Alexander's Campaign against the Illyrians in 335 BC," in Barr-Sharrar, B., ed., *Macedonia and Greece in Late Classical and Early Hellenistic Times* (Washington, 1982) 75–84.

Buckler, J., *Philip II and the Sacred War* (Leiden and New York, 1989).

Burn, A. R., "Notes on Alexander's Campaigns 332–330 BC," *JHS* 72 (1952) 81–91.

Davis, E. W., "The Persian Battle Plan at the Granicus," *James Sprunt Studies in History and Political Sciences* 46 (1964) 33–44.

Devine, A. M., "Grand Tactics at Gaugamela," *Phoenix* 29 (1975) 374–385.

Devine, A. M., "The Battle of Gaugamela: A Tactical and Source-critical Study," *AncWorld* 13 (1986) 87–116.

Devine, A. M., "The Macedonian Army at Gaugamela: Its Strength and the Length of its Battle-line," *AncWorld* 19 (1989) 77–79.

Devine, A. M., "The Strategies of Alexander the Great and Darius III in the Issus Campaign, 333 BC," *AncWorld* 12 (1985) 25–37.

Eggermont, P. H. L., *Alexander's Campaigns in Sind and Baluchistan,* Orientalia Lovaniensia 3 (Leuven, 1975).

Foss, C., "The Battle of the Granicus: A New Look," *Ancient Macedonia* 2 (1977) 495–502.

Griffith, G. T., "Alexander's Generalship at Gaugamela," *JHS* 67 (1947) 77–89.

Hamilton, J. R., "The Cavalry Battle at the Hydaspes," *JHS* 76 (1956) 26–31.

Hammond, N. G. L., "Alexander's Charge at the Battle of Issus in 333 BC," *Historia* 41 (1992) 395–406.

Hammond, N. G. L., "The Battle of the Granicus River," *JHS* 100 (1980) 73–88.

Hammond, N. G. L., "The Two Battles of Chaeronea (338 BC and 86 BC)," *Klio* 31 (1938) 186–218 = *Studies in Greek History* (Oxford, 1973) 534–557.

Marsden E. W., *The Campaign of Gaugamela* (Liverpool, 1964).

Rahe, P. A., "The Annihilation of the Sacred Band at Chaeronea," *AJA* 85 (1981) 84–87.

5 HELLENISTIC WARFARE

General works on Hellenistic history

Allen, R. E., *The Attalid Kingdom: A Constitutional History* (Oxford, 1983).

Austin, M. M., "Hellenistic Kings, War, and the Economy," *CQ* 36 (1986) 450–466.

Avi-Yonah, M., *Hellenism and the East: Contacts and Interrelations from Alexander to the Roman Conquest* (Jerusalem, 1978).

Bell, H. I., *Egypt from Alexander to the Arab Conquest* (Oxford, 1948).

Bevan, E. R., *The House of Ptolemy: A History of Egypt under the Ptolemaic Dynasty* (London, 1927).

Billows, R. A., *Antigonos the One-eyed and the Creation of the Hellenistic State* (Berkeley, 1990).

Bowman, A., *Egypt after the Pharaohs, 332 BC–AD 642* (Berkeley and Los Angeles, 1986).

Burstein, S. M., *The Hellenistic Age from the Battle of Ipsos to the Death of Kleopatra VII* (Cambridge, 1985).

Cambridge Ancient History, vol. 7, pts 1–2, *The Hellenistic World* (Cambridge, 1984–1989).

Cambridge Ancient History, vol. 8, *The Rise of Rome to 220 BC* (Cambridge, 1989).

Cary, M., *A History of the Greek World from 323 to 146 BC* (London, 1932, rev. 1968).

Davis, C. M. and Kraay, N., *The Hellenistic Kingdoms: Portrait Coins and History* (London, 1973).

Edson, C., "Imperium Macedonicum: The Seleucid Empire and the Literary Evidence," *CPh* 53(1958) 153–170.

Errington, R. M., *Philopoemen* (Oxford, 1969).

Grainger, J. D., *Seleucus Nikator: Constructing a Hellenistic Kingdom* (London and New York, 1990).

Green, P., *Alexander to Actium* (Berkeley and Los Angeles, 1990).

Grimal, P., *Hellenism and the Rise of Rome* (London, 1968).

Gruen, E. S., "Aratus and the Achaean Alliance with Macedon," *Historia* 21 (1972) 609–625.

Gruen, E., "The Coronation of the Diadochoi," in Eadie, J., and Ober, J., edd., *The Craft of the Ancient Historian: Essays in Honor of Chester G. Starr* (Lanham, MD and London, 1985) 253–271.

Gruen, E., *The Hellenistic World and the Coming of Rome* (Berkeley and Los Angeles, 1984).

Hammond, N. G. L. and Walbank, F. W., *A History of Macedonia,* vol. 3: *336–167 BC* (Oxford, 1988).

Hansen, E. V., *The Attalids of Pergamum* (2nd edn, Ithaca, New York, 1971).

Hornblower, S., *Hieronymus of Cardia* (Oxford, 1981).

Kuhrt, A. and Sherwin-White, S., *Hellenism in the East: The Interaction of Greek and Non-Greek Civilizations from Syria to Central Asia after Alexander* (London, 1987).

Larsen, J. A. O., "Phocis in the Social War of 220–217 BC," *Phoenix* 19 (1965) 116–128.

Larsen, J. A. O., *Greek Federal States* (Oxford, 1968).

Lund, H. S., *Lysimachus: A Study in Early Hellenistic Kingship* (New York, 1992).

Mooren, L., "The Nature of the Hellenistic Monarchy," in *Egypt and the Hellenistic World*, Studia Hellenistica 27 (Louvain, 1983) 205–240.

Rostovtzeff, M., *The Social and Economic History of the Hellenistic World* (Oxford, 1941).

Simpson, R. H., "Antigonus the One-Eyed and the Greeks," *Historia* 8 (1959) 385–409.

Tarn, W. W., *Antigonus Gonatus* (London, 1913).

Tarn, W. W. and Griffith, G. T., *Hellenistc Civilization* (3rd edn, London, 1952).

Walbank, F. W., *Philip V of Macedon* (Cambridge, 1940).

Walbank, F. W., *The Hellenistic World* (rev. edn, London, 1991).

Walbank, F. W., "Were there Federal States?" in *F. W. Walbank: Selected Papers* (Cambridge, 1985) 20–37.

Welles, C. B., *Alexander and the Hellenistic World* (Toronto, 1970).

The major armies

Anson, E. M., "Hypaspists and Agyraspids after 323," *AHB* 2 (1988) 131–133.

Bar-Kochva, B., *The Seleucid Army: Organization and Tactics in the Great Campaigns* (Cambridge, 1976).

Cohen, G. M., *The Seleucid Colonies: Studies in Founding, Administration and Organization*, Historia Einzelschriften 30 (1978).

Developments in strategy, tactics and technology

Adams, W. L., "Antipater and Cassander: Generalship on Restricted Resources in the Fourth Century," *AncWorld* 10 (1984) 79–88.

Errington, R. M., "Philopoeman's Reform of the Achaean Army," *CPh* 62 (1967) 104–105.

Scullard, H. H., *The Elephant in the Greek and Roman World* (London, 1974).

Tarn, W. W., *Hellenistic Military and Naval Developments* (Cambridge, 1930).

Thompson, W. E., "PSI 1284: Eumenes of Cardia vs. the Phalanx," *CE* 59 (1984) 113–120.

Campaigns and battles

Devine, A. M., "Diodorus' Account of the Battle of Gaza," *ACD* 27 (1984) 31–40.

Devine, A. M., "Diodorus' Account of the Battle of Paraitacene (317 BC) and of the Battle of Gabiene," *AncWorld* 12 (1985) 75–96.

Devine, A. M., "The Generalship of Ptolemy I and Demetrius Poliorcetes at the Battle of Gaza (312 BC)," *AncWorld* 20 (1989) 29–36.

Gabbert, J. J., "The Grand Strategy of Antigonus II Gonatus and the Chremonidean War," *AncWorld* 8 (1983) 129–136.

Hammond, N. G. L., "The Battle of Pydna," *JHS* 104 (1984) 31–47.

Morgan, J. D., "Sellasia Revisited," *AJA* 85 (1981) 328–330.

Pritchett, W. K., "Philip's Campaign in the Peloponnesos in 219/8 BC," in Pritchett, W. K., *Studies in Ancient Greek Topography,* 6 (Berkeley, 1989) 1–78.

Pritchett, W. K., "Philip's Campaign in Northwest Greece in 219 BC," in Pritchett, W. K., *Studies in Ancient Greek Topography,* 7 (Amsterdam, 1991) 1–39.

Thompson, W. E., "Philip V's Peloponnesian Campaigns in the Social War," *RhM* 132 (1989) 141–148.

INDEX OF PASSAGES CITED

LITERARY SOURCES

240

Inscriptions and Papyri

Papyri

INDEX